CONGRESS *of* STATES

CONGRESS *of* STATES

PROCEEDINGS *of the* PROVISIONAL CONGRESS *of the* CONFEDERATE STATES *of* AMERICA

Edited by R. David Carlson

THE UNIVERSITY OF ALABAMA PRESS
Tuscaloosa

The University of Alabama Press
Tuscaloosa, Alabama 35487–0380
uapress.ua.edu

Typeface: Garamond Premier Pro

Cover image: "The Southern Confederacy during open session at the Capitol in Montgomery, Alabama. Howell Cobb presiding"; *Frank Leslie's Illustrated Newpaper*, March 2, 1861
Cover design: Lori Lynch

Cataloging-in-Publication data is available from the Library of Congress.
ISBN: 978-0-8173-2165-9 (cloth)
ISBN: 978-0-8173-6091-7 (paper)
E-ISBN: 978-0-8173-9461-5

CONTENTS

ACKNOWLEDGMENTS

Congress of States, like the Confederate Congress it describes, owes itself to a national crisis. The Covid-19 pandemic that began over the winter of 2019–20, like the secession crisis of 1861–62, resulted in an extensive reconfiguration of American life. It separated friends and families and raised doubts about those outside one's inner circle. Ideological rifts drove wedges in old loyalties and led many people to question the legitimacy of governmental responses. Mitigation efforts demanded deep sacrifices, and Americans faced the challenge of restructuring how they interacted with the world around them. So it was that in March 2020, as universities transitioned to online learning and their faculty and students retreated into isolation, I found time to indulge a seemingly minor, yet nagging, question. What follows is the result, the by-product of idle curiosity and Covid-induced isolation.

Confederate congressional records were at the center of my graduate school research into Southern conscription policy, not only the official congressional journals but also the contemporary press reportage of congressional activity, some of which was republished by the *Southern Historical Society Papers* in the early twentieth century. In particular, I was drawn to the February 1862 speech of Thomas Bocock, the newly elected Speaker of the House, in which he asked his fellow congressmen whether their government, "without injury to its own integrity[, could] supply the machinery and afford the means requisite to conduct this war," a question foreshadowing the political conflict between decentralized government and centralized military authority accompanying proposals for conscription later that year.

Journalistic errors are to be expected, and the Confederate press was not immune from its fair share of faulty reporting. But one error, for whatever reason, proved consistently bothersome. Per the *Southern Historical Society Papers*, Bocock gave his opening day speech to the First Confederate Congress on February 18, *1861*, not the correct year of *1862*. It was obviously a typographical error. Indeed, a review of the original report in the February 19, 1862, edition of the Richmond *Examiner* showed the same typographical error, and editorial diligence on the part of the Southern Historical Society simply carried the error forward.

But that simple mistake gave rise to additional questions. Prior to the seating of the First Congress, a Provisional Congress legislated for the Confederate States, created the Southern nation, its government, its military, and its diplomatic corps.

Where was the reportage on that Congress's sessions? Why did the *Southern Historical Society Papers* include one Congress and not the other? The misprint of a single date served not as evidence of a simple typesetting error but the absence of an entire Congress's worth of press. That missing reportage, compiled and edited from newspapers published across the Confederacy, is gathered here for the first time.

Although researched in isolation, this project nonetheless could not have been completed without the help of several others, and so my thanks are extended to the faculty and staff of the Department of History and Philosophy at Troy University (especially Tim Buckner who read early versions of the introductory essay); Troy University Library; Claire Lewis Evans, Daniel Waterman, and Sara Hardy at the University of Alabama Press; the anonymous readers who offered valuable suggestions on revision and expansion of the project; the untold numbers of archivists, librarians, programmers, digitizers, and editors who work tirelessly to make the past accessible via the internet; and, most importantly, my family.

INTRODUCTION

In 1923, volume forty-four of the *Southern Historical Society Papers (SHSP)* marked a sea change in the direction of that publication. For almost fifty years, its sponsor organization, the Southern Historical Society (SHS), had expounded a history of the Civil War strictly in line with Lost Cause politics and sentimentality. Essayists had extolled the virtues of states' rights and woven rose-colored reminiscences of plantation life. Veterans had praised the memory of Robert E. Lee, recounted battlefield experiences, and shared letters and documents from their private collections. That began to change under the editorial guidance of Civil War historian Douglas Southall Freeman. The process was not quick or clean. Freeman's coeditor, Confederate veteran George L. Christian, continued to espouse Lost Cause sentiments, but Freeman, with the assistance of Virginia state librarian H. R. McIlwaine, began to transform the *SHSP* into a legitimate historical journal.

Between 1923 and 1959, the *SHSP* published nine volumes of the "Proceedings of the Confederate Congress," journalistic transcriptions of Confederate congressional activities, as an addendum to the Congress's legislative minutes.[1] The official seven-volume *Journal of the Congress of the Confederate States of America, 1861–1865* (JCCSC) had been an invaluable contribution to Civil War historiography when it was released by the US Congress in 1904–5, but it was limited. As Freeman explained, the official journals provided only rudimentary information on congressional events by listing the authors of bills, movers of resolutions, the results of votes, and lists of appointments and military commissions. But they omitted even passing references to larger debates and only in cases of presidential addresses did they include texts of speeches. As a result, the official journals "form[ed] but a skeleton" of Confederate congressional activity with "little historical importance and no human interest."[2] Freeman believed contemporary newspapers provided richer material. As the seceded Southern states embarked on the process of nation building, editors and reporters converged on Montgomery and later Richmond to record history in the making. From seats on the floor and in congressional galleries, they took stenographic notes and recorded debates in their entirety. They requested copies of speeches, bills, and resolutions and reprinted them in full. By tapping journalistic resources, Freeman believed "Proceedings" could rejuvenate the historical record, put "flesh on the dry bones" of the *Journal,* and breathe life into the cold formality of congressional minutes.[3] The resulting editorial series has proven arguably one of our most important resources for Confederate political history.

Still, nearly one hundred years later, some bones remain bare. On February 4, 1861, delegates from six seceded Southern states met in Montgomery, Alabama, to discuss the creation of a Southern national government.[4] Lacking the credentials to act in either a constitutive or legislative manner, they were authorized neither to create that government nor act as one. Yet most delegates understood that time was of the essence. Eight additional slaveholding states had yet to leave the Union, and their reluctance was slowing secession's momentum. Meanwhile, the inauguration of Abraham Lincoln as president of the United States was less than a month away. Might it be that Lincoln would use his newly gained presidential authority to check further border states secessionists and pressure isolated Deep South states to rejoin the Union? Immediate action on state creation by Southern delegates might not only encourage border state secession but provide the necessary resources for a defense against Northern aggressions.[5] Not everyone agreed. South Carolina delegates insisted that the gathering was a conference of independent states meeting solely for consultation. Most, however, accepted the argument of Georgian Alexander H. Stephens: the gathering must assume powers not expressly given it by state commissions. It must become a "Congress of States," a fully functioning government.[6] Almost immediately after convening, the conference recognized itself as a de facto constitutional convention and national legislature. Yet, as important as this governing body proved to the rise of the Confederate state, Freeman and the SHS omitted its minutes from "Proceedings of the Confederate Congress." An entire year of Confederate congressional records remains unfleshed.

Congress of States brings together, for the first time, journalistic reports of all five sessions of the Provisional Congress of the Confederate States to provide a more vibrant accounting of the congressional record than that contained in the official *Journal*.[7] In so doing, it fills gaps in the historical record and corrects methodological defects that have limited our understanding of congressional events in the early days of the Confederacy. Additionally, it reveals questions that weighed heavily both on the governing elite and the general population and suggests new areas of research into those questions.

The Provisional Confederate Congress has received scant attention from historians. Wilfred Buck Yearns, for example, admitted the Provisional Congress was composed of talented men, but claimed that, as a "creature of [state secession] conventions," it was a body largely inconsequential to Southerners who looked to Pres. Jefferson Davis for political leadership.[8] While Yearns went on to provide a much fuller (and more favorable) accounting of the Provisional Congress in his study *Confederate Congress*, most historians appear to be guided by his initial assessment. The Provisional Congress created a government and elected a president but little else.[9] In truth, the Provisional Congress was exceedingly important, single-handedly serving functions typically performed by three separate institutions—a constitutional convention, an electoral college, and a national legislature.[10] Unfortunately, historians have concentrated on the former two at the expense of the latter. In the middle of creating a government, electing a president, mobilizing a military, and negotiating with foreign governments, it responded with legislation addressing constituent concerns about how this exercise in independence would affect them. What did independence mean for personal and national identity, and what was the individual's role in that process? How would the real, personal, and intellectual property protections once offered by the US government translate to the Confederate government? Could Confederates continue to seek redress from a US government to whom they no longer owed allegiance? What effect did independence have on the business environment both at home and abroad? The challenge for historians is to incorporate these legislative questions into the larger constitutive story. Doing so will allow a better understanding not only of what the Provisional Congress provided its constituents but what those constituents wanted from their government.

While conceived as an expansion on "Proceedings," *Congress of States* should not be understood as condoning or endorsing the Lost Cause philosophy that spawned the early Southern Historical Society or its publications. Indeed, "Proceedings" was Freeman's attempt to shift the SHS's focus from dangerous neo-Confederatism and racist sentimentalism to legitimate historical research. He understood that Confederate source materials—handled properly—retained value despite or perhaps even *because* of the heavy historical burdens they carried, as it is hoped *Congress of States* continues to demonstrate. This was not necessarily the case in 1869 when Major General Dabney Maury and other high-ranking Confederate veterans gathered in New Orleans to create the SHS for decidedly different purposes. Maury was keenly aware that untold numbers of Confederate documents had been lost at the end of the war: destroyed with the burning of Richmond, lost in the evacuation of the government, kept by Union soldiers as souvenirs or Confederates as important records, or most troubling to Maury, seized by the United States Government. Even before the war ended, the Lincoln administration had begun the process of organizing and archiving records for a detailed history of the war. How could southerners be assured that their version of history was told and told correctly? Although the War Department's War Records Office (WRO) actively encouraged southerners to share or donate their collections, it proved unwilling to honor southern requests for reciprocal access. As a result, Maury and others feared the WRO might create a history of the war that gave short shrift to the southern perspective while denying southerners the ability to respond.[11]

Maury thus envisioned the SHS as both creator and defender of Confederate history with the goal of gathering and preserving Confederate records and reminiscences in a project paralleling the WRO's official government archival program. Achieving this would not be easy. Society membership was low, and the organization struggled to attract subscribers. Fewer than one hundred veterans joined the first year; by the next, only forty-two remained.[12] Membership grew when SHS headquarters moved to Richmond in 1873, peaking somewhere between two thousand and three thousand members but then falling by over one thousand members in 1876.[13] Several factors appear to have worked against SHS growth. The move to Richmond, a move the society's leadership thought might broaden its appeal through association with the former Confederate capital, actually gave the organization a heavy Virginia accent that rarely looked beyond the Old Dominion for donations and publishable submissions. Its founding members were elite former military officers who wished to refight battles, and the core membership never strayed far from that description. The group neither welcomed enlisted veterans nor had the same draw as other veterans' groups that did.[14] Ongoing efforts to redeem southern governments from federal control may have furthered subscription woes. Former Confederate officers may have been wary of joining an organization openly in conflict with the War Department, fearful that such membership might adversely affect political redemption. In addition, former Confederate general Robert E. Lee's support for national reconciliation may have discouraged many people from participating in what was an openly sectionalizing project. Few former Confederates, it seemed, were willing to break with their vaunted commanding officer.[15] Despite these early trials, the SHS began to gather what materials it could—original battle reports and postwar battle analyses, military correspondences and veterans' reminiscences, memorials to the fallen dead, and texts of important wartime and postwar speeches—all with the goal of creating a Confederate archive that rivaled the United States'.

In time, the War Department issued its documentary history. Published between 1881 and 1901, the massive 128-volume, 140,000-page *Official Records of the War of the Rebellion* (later renamed *War of the Rebellion: A Compilation of the Official Records of the Union and Confederate Armies* and usually referred to as the *OR*) has become the most widely referenced primary source on the Civil War. Combined with its companions—the 30-volume *Official Records of the Union and Confederate Navies* (1894–1922) and the *Atlas of the War of the Rebellion* (1892)—the *OR* is considered a relatively unbiased record of Northern and Southern wartime governmental, military, and diplomatic affairs.[16] Not so the SHS's *Southern Historical Society Papers*.[17] By the time the society began publishing its journal in 1876, Maury had stepped down and Lee had died. Confederate general Jubal Early, a quintessential unredeemed rebel, assumed the editorship and began to shape Confederate history in a Lost Cause counteroffensive to national reconciliation.[18] In the pages of the *SHSP*, Early reprinted selected battle accounts, veterans' testimonies, private letters, and reminiscences to reflect a Confederate history that made no apologies for the war. He deified Robert E. Lee as a faultless military commander and attacked former Confederates such as James Longstreet who promoted reunion and Republican Party rule. He provided reports comparing Northern and Southern logistics, supply, enlistments, troop retention, transportation, weaponry, tactics, and strategies to demonstrate that Union victory had come as a result of Confederate exhaustion rather than battlefield defeat. The war, Early argued, was a righteous cause lost for which no apologies were due.[19] The *SHSP* were, by design, a historical weapon in a political fight over the memory of the Civil War.

By the 1920s, the SHS was a dying institution. Continuing publication expenses saddled the organization with debts that dwindling membership rolls could not meet. The *SHSP*, which had begun as a semiannual publication, became an annual in 1879 and appeared only sporadically after 1910. As early as 1884, the society leadership considered dissolving the organization and donating its holdings to the Virginia Historical Society.[20] When Richmond *News Leader* editor Douglas Southall Freeman accepted a seat on the SHS Publications Committee in the late 1910s and later assumed the organization's presidency in 1926, the organization had a miniscule budget, no staff, and a disappearing membership base. The Southern Historical Society would not last much longer, but Freeman believed the organization might have time to complete one final project.[21]

Freeman was already a well-respected journalist and southern historian. He had published *A Calendar of Confederate Papers*, an edited volume of original documents held by the Richmond's Confederate Museum, in 1908, the same year he graduated from Johns Hopkins University.[22] Seven years later, he published *Lee's Dispatches to Jefferson Davis, 1862–1865*, another edited volume, this time of more than two hundred of Lee's field dispatches owned by Georgia bibliophile Wymberly Jones de Renne.[23] He was soon to begin research on his magnus opus, the Pulitzer Prize–winning biography *R. E. Lee* (1934–5). Freeman was a meticulous and exhaustive researcher who, while focusing his studies on a cornerstone of the Lost Cause—the heroic, almost mythical, character of Robert E. Lee—did his best to avoid that ideology's maudlin sentimentalism and racist nostalgia.[24] Although the *SHSP* had already drifted away from the aggressive editorial leadership of Early to become little more than a clipping service for previously published essays and memorials, it was Freeman who pushed the journal's rejection of the Lost Cause to become a vehicle for original research in Confederate history.[25]

Freeman suggested publishing the proceedings of the Confederate Congress as reported by journalists of the period, a project he believed would fill up to ten volumes of the *SHSP*. The official journal, published by Congress in 1904–5, was available in limited editions and difficult to find. At its best, it provided only itemized agendas with few details. Freeman believed that a collection of newspapers accounts, most of which contained detailed stenographic transcriptions of speeches and debates, might be "the only source from which the meagre entries of the Journal could be supplemented and illuminated."[26] Perhaps more importantly, the project required neither a large staff nor a substantial budget.[27] The Richmond papers *Examiner* and *Daily Dispatch* had locally available archives and provided access to the official voice of the Davis administration (*Examiner*). There would be no need to travel and no need to coordinate with distant private and public collections for access and copy privileges. Properly managed, the "Proceedings of the Confederate Congress" might serve a fitting and relatively inexpensive eulogy for the SHS.

Despite such good intentions, Freeman and the SHS never overcame the limitations imposed by financial insecurity. The first four volumes appeared between 1923 and 1930.[28] Although complete in their transcriptions, the works lacked the voluminous notations for which Freeman was known. Scattered footnotes referenced intersections between the "Proceedings," the official journals, and key wartime events but noted little else. Distracted by research for his Robert E. Lee biography, Freeman could not commit himself to the job personally, and lacking funds to hire proper transcriptionists and editors, he released the project in a form inconsistent with his usually high standards of research. The challenges only increased with the Great Depression. Although the SHS weathered the stock market crash in 1929, it lost most of its financial reserves when the bank holding its deposits and mortgage bond investments collapsed in the early 1930s. It would not be until 1941 that the sale of back issues of the *SHSP* and the financial wizardry of society treasurer Deane H. Maury brought in enough revenue to complete the fifth volume and another year before the society could claim to have enough money to finish the project.[29] Even then, the dearth of society members and the resultant lack of income rendered the issue of new volumes erratic. Volume six came out in 1943; another ten years passed before the seventh was released.

Freeman died in 1953, leaving J. Ambler Johnston the only member of the Southern Historical Society. Unable to complete the project his friend had begun thirty years earlier, Johnston transferred SHS holdings, including the manuscripts for three more volumes of proceedings, to the Virginia Historical Society (VHS). Freeman and Johnston had already decided these would close the run of the *SHSP*, and Freeman had asked Civil War historian Frank Vandiver of Washington University to write new introductions for them.[30] Under VHS supervision, the final three volumes of the "Proceedings of the Confederate Congress" and the final issues of the *Southern Historical Society Papers* were published in 1953, 1958, and 1959.[31]

As important as the "Proceedings of the Confederate Congress" remains, it is not without problems. The raison d'être of this book was one: the omission of the proceedings of the Provisional Congress. When the Provisional Congress first sat in Montgomery in February 1861, Virginia had not yet seceded. The Richmond press occasionally reported on the Montgomery Convention, but those events remained rather distant to a state still weighing the value of its membership in the United States. Both the Richmond *Enquirer* and the Richmond *Daily Dispatch* were more concerned with affairs in Virginia and Washington, DC, than they were to the actions of an inchoate southern government. By the time the Davis administration decided to relocate the provisional Confederate government to Richmond, when Virginia papers would have paid greater attention to congressional affairs, Congress had shut its doors to the press to safeguard military planning. It was not until the permanent government was operational that journalists once again entered the congressional chambers and published their reports.

If the omission of provisional congressional affairs from "Proceedings" is thus understandable, it nonetheless frustrates our understanding of Confederate nation building. The reports that follow exist at the intersection of government and society, and the editorial decisions surrounding their publication raise intriguing questions about government record keeping, the public consumption of information, and the role of the press as an information gatekeeper. In early 1861, the relationship between public knowledge and government secrecy was tense. Congressional delegates understood the need, indeed the desire, for open legislative sessions. Public displays of confederal unity, especially during the secession crisis, provided comfort for wary Southerners. Images of delegates engaged in a concerted, even redemptive, effort to regain the promise of American independence might also attract wavering border states and deter potential responses by the United States. Yet they understood the need for secrecy as well. Information was valuable and the less the United States knew about Southern organization and defense plans the better. So, while delegates to the Provisional Congress legislated as much as they could in open session to provide good press, they were quick to motion for secrecy once the image of unity had been created. This test of the boundaries of public knowledge and governmental secrecy is not reflected in the official journals. It is captured, even if slightly, within the journalistic proceedings.[32]

These records illuminate subjects that politicians, editors, and the public deemed important amid the transitions of secession and national birth. Not every congressional event was covered suggesting both editorial and congressional desires to present and a public desire to consume specific information. As mentioned above, the display of governmental effectiveness and unanimity served to demonstrate a successful separation from the United States and creation of the Confederate States. Secession,[33] the drafting of the provisional and permanent constitutions,[34] the admission of new states,[35] the creation of executive and judicial departments,[36] the establishment of diplomatic relationships,[37] and the development of national symbols[38] were key elements in the ratification of independence—constitutive functions that garnered the most press coverage. In fact, the submission of designs for a national flag and seal was the single most reported item, representative both of the public's desire to achieve an independent national identity and to participate in its creation. Thus, reportage did not simply serve idle curiosity; it reflected those areas in which government and society necessarily cooperated in creating the Confederacy, an act made all the more difficult by ongoing debates over secrecy.

These records also suggest additional areas of research. The confederacy of slaveholding states that began in 1861 was tenuous at best. Many Southerners questioned whether the seceded states then meeting in Montgomery would be joined by others in the coming months. Some worried how the Buchanan and Lincoln administrations would react, indeed how many Southerners might react should secession become war. Still others questioned if Southerners would accept a new central government when they had just declared independence from the old. What effect did the publication of these minutes have on public support? Did the publication of congressional debates demonstrate that disparate Southern states could work together to create a new and independent nation? Did the publication of speeches on free trade, patent protections, the adjudication of financial claims, and volunteer troops support the government's claim that it was both less intrusive and more protective of the people's interests? Did the publication of congressional prayers and eulogies for fallen comrades like Francis Bartow, John Tyler, and John Hemphill create a national religious community with a shared sense of loss, purpose, and destiny? Did resolutions and commendations for commanding generals at Fort Sumter, Manassas, and Belmont give civilians a sense of ownership to these early Confederate victories? Bound together in work, faith, loss, and celebration, even if through vicarious journalistic experiences, did minutes such as these serve not simply to record important political events but to unite the Southern population behind the Confederate experiment?

Alongside the constitutive functions of Congress, administrative activity garnered attention as Confederates sought assurances that their new government could protect Southern interests effectively. The creation and staffing of congressional committees and governmental departments,[39] the management of financial and economic affairs,[40] the administration of public lands, the designation of ports of entry, the registration of maritime vessels, the adjudication of cases from US federal courts and financial claims against the US government, and the enforcement of patent, copyright, and customs laws all served to demonstrate the early political viability of the Confederacy.[41] And should the Confederacy come under threat of Union attack, Congress sought to assure Southerners through discussion, though limited in public, of military organization;[42] the development of foundries and armories;[43] and the research, development, and procurement of supplies, munitions, and transportation.[44] The contents of the minutes as released to the public thus represent a confluence of several needs: the government's need to demonstrate organization and efficiency, the press's need to attract readership by highlighting specific aspects of congressional debate, and the public's need to have a sense of involvement in the process of national creation.

The corrective to the first defect—Freeman's omission of provisional congressional activity due to scant newspaper sources—suggests a remedy for a second problem. Freeman relied on newspaper reports from either the *Enquirer* or *Daily Dispatch* cross-referenced with the official *Journals* to cover congressional events. Such a strategy, while cost effective, leaves room for errors and omissions. As was evident from the collection of reports for this book, journalistic accounts could vary in content and detail. The location of reporters' seats in the congressional hall, the room's acoustics, as well as the ambient noises inherent in any gathering of this size, affected journalists' ability to record accurately what was said. Names were missed or misheard, phrases and sometimes entire sections of speeches omitted. Not all of the delegates to the Congress were known to the reporters, leading to the misidentification of speakers. Some reporters were guided as much by what their political patrons wanted as by their desire to report the news.[45] Thus, while the general outlines of journalists' reports might be similar, details could be missing, disorganized, biased, or incorrect. A single source reliance such as that used in "Proceedings" offers no check on these possible errors and suggests the possibility that a recompilation of the full congressional record in "Proceedings" is in order.

Congress of States offers a synthesis of daily press reports from newspapers in Richmond, Virginia; Montgomery, Alabama; Charleston, South Carolina; New Orleans, Louisiana; and Savannah and Augusta, Georgia, and in so doing provides checks on potential errors and omissions.[46] Research relied almost exclusively on visual searches of newspapers available in online databases. While the advent of online research has opened many avenues of investigation, it has also saddled them with inconsistent search results. Many newspaper databases suffer from poor image scans, faulty optical character recognition, and lack of proofreading for searchable texts. Research began with database search engines, but the brunt of the research involved visual searches of each issue for articles that database and scanning errors may have omitted. Thus, the inclusion of additional newspapers through internet databases mediated the problem of limited resources and source bias in Freeman's "Proceedings," while a distrust of those databases broadened the search further and allowed for more robust cross-referencing and fact checking. Press reports were then compared both with each other and with the official journal. The report containing what appeared to be the most complete coverage of the day's events was given primary status with the remaining reports providing confirmation of, correction to, and supplements to the primary. In cases where the order of events was in dispute, the order provided by the official journal was given preference; however, in no case was information from the journal merged with that from press reports. In cases where the correct order could not be determined or discrepancies between sources could not be resolved, explanations and sometimes alternative information are provided as endnotes. Supplementary documents and images not presented in open session and not contemporaneously available to the Confederate reading public are referenced in brackets as [*document xx*] or [*image xx*] and are available in appendix I and II. Documents that referred to closed sessions and bills passed by Congress have been included only if included in press reports and integral to open session debate or discussion. Otherwise, these documents may be found in official congressional publications.[47]

CHRONOLOGY OF EVENTS

1860

November 6	Abraham Lincoln is elected president of the United States.
December 20	South Carolina secedes.

1861

January 3	South Carolina commissioners propose a convention to meet in Montgomery, Alabama, for the creation of a provisional Confederate government.
January 9	Mississippi secedes.
January 10	Florida secedes.
January 11	Alabama secedes.
January 19	Georgia secedes.
January 26	Louisiana secedes.
February 1	Texas convention approves secession pending a popular vote.
February 4	First session of the Provisional Congress begins in Montgomery. Howell Cobb of Georgia is elected president of Congress.
February 6	North Carolina authorizes commissioners (unofficial delegates) to the Montgomery Convention.
February 9	Members of Congress sign the Provisional Confederate Constitution. Jefferson Davis of Mississippi and Alexander H. Stephens of Georgia are unanimously elected president and vice president, respectively.
February 11	Alexander H. Stephens is inaugurated vice president of the Confederate States of America.
February 12	Standing congressional committee appointments are announced.
February 15	Texas delegation is admitted to Congress.
February 18	Members of Congress sign Permanent Confederate Constitution. Jefferson Davis is inaugurated president of the Confederate States of America.
February 21	Congress passes legislation creating the Executive Department

	and the Departments of State, Treasury, War, Navy, and Post Office.
February 23	Texas voters approve secession.
February 28	The Confederate government assumes control of military operations in all Confederate states.
March 2	Texas is admitted to the Confederacy.
March 4	Abraham Lincoln is inaugurated.
March 6	Congress passes legislation creating the Confederate regular army and authorizes President Davis to accept an additional one hundred thousand state-raised twelve-month volunteer troops.
March 11	Permanent Constitution of the Confederate States is adopted.
March 15	Congress passes legislation creating the Confederate Bureau of Indian Affairs.
March 16	Congress passes legislation organizing the Confederate Navy and the Confederate judicial system.
	First session of the Provisional Congress ends.
	Territory of Arizona allies with the Confederacy.
April 9	Gustavus V. Fox leaves New York aboard the steamer *Baltic* to relieve Fort Sumter.
April 12	South Carolina opens fire on Fort Sumter.
April 14	Major Robert Anderson surrenders Fort Sumter to Confederate general Pierre G. T. Beauregard.
April 15	Lincoln calls for seventy-five thousand state militiamen to suppress the Southern rebellion.
April 17	Virginia secedes.
April 29	Second session of the Provisional Congress begins in Montgomery.
May 6	Arkansas secedes.
	Provisional Confederate Congress recognizes a state of war between the Confederacy and the United States.
May 7	Virginia is admitted to the Confederacy.
May 8	Congress broadens its March 6, 1861, troop authorization to accept volunteer troops regardless of place of enlistment.
May 11	Congress broadens its March 6, 1861, troop authorization to accept volunteer troops without formal requests to state governors.
May 16	Congress increases the size of the Confederate regular army.
May 17	Congress authorizes the admissions of North Carolina and Tennessee in anticipation of those states' secessions during congressional recess.
May 20	Arkansas is admitted to the Confederacy.
	North Carolina secedes.

	Congress votes to move the Confederate capitol to Richmond, Virginia.
May 21	Congress passes legislation creating the Confederate Patent Office.
	Congress calls for elections under the permanent Confederate Constitution to be held November 6, 1861.
	Second session of the Provisional Congress ends.
June 8	Tennessee secedes.
July 20	Third session of the Provisional Congress begins in Richmond.
July 21	First Battle of Manassas (Bull Run) begins.
	Congressman Francis S. Bartow of Georgia is killed in battle.
August 8	Congress authorizes President Davis to accept an additional four hundred thousand twelve-month state-raised volunteer troops.
August 21	Congress authorizes President Davis to accept local defense troops for certain exposed locations.
August 22	Congress passes legislation creating uniform naturalization laws for enlisted military personnel not already citizens of a Confederate state.
August 31	Third session of the Provisional Congress ends.
September 3	Fourth session of the Provisional Congress, a one-day session, meets in Richmond.
November 7	Battle of Belmont begins.
November 18	Fifth session of the Provisional Congress begins in Richmond.
November 28	North Carolina is admitted to the Confederacy.
December 10	Kentucky is admitted to the Confederacy.
December 11	Over five hundred acres of Charleston, South Carolina, burn.
December 16	Kentucky delegation is admitted to Congress.

1862

January 3 or 4	Congressman John Hemphill of Texas dies.
January 18	Former US President John Tyler of Virginia dies.
	Congress organizes the Territory of Arizona.
	Congress broadens its March 6, 1861, troop authorization to accept three-year troops.
February 17	Fifth session of the Provisional Congress ends.

CONGRESS *of* STATES

CONGRESSIONAL ORGANIZATION

CONGRESSIONAL LEADERSHIP

Temporary Officers

(Served only to oversee the selection of permanent officers, February 4, 1861)

Robert W. Barnwell, chair

Albert R. Lamar, secretary

Officers

Howell Cobb, president

Johnson J. Hooper, secretary

Robert E. Dixon, assistant secretary

Wiley N. Hutchins, journal clerk

Robert Wynn, doorkeeper

John Wadsworth, messenger

STANDING COMMITTEE MEMBERSHIP

Committee on Accounts

Created February 12, 1861

James B. Owens, chair
Alexandre DeClouet, chair (succeeded Owens, March 4, 1861; resigned committee seat, March 13, 1861)
Josiaah A. P. Campbell
Robert H. Smith
Martin J. Crawford
John Gregg (replaced Owens, March 4, 1861)

Reorganized July 29, 1861

Alexandre DeClouet
Josiah A. P. Campbell
Robert H. Smith
Martin J. Crawford
John Gregg
William M. Cooke, Sr. (added December 9, 1861)

Committee on Claims

Created May 8, 1861

John Gregg, chair
Benjamin H. Hill
Henry Marshall
Jehu A. Orr
George T. Ward
Henry C. Jones

Reorganized July 29, 1861

John Gregg, chair
Benjamin H. Hill
Henry Marshall
Jehu A. Orr
George T. Ward
Henry C. Jones

Committee on Commercial Affairs

Created February 12, 1861

Christopher G. Memminger, chair
Alexandre DeClouet, chair (succeeded Memminger, February 22, 1861; resigned committee membership March 13, 1861)
Martin J. Crawford
Jackson Morton
Jabez L. M. Curry
William P. Miles (replaced Memminger, February 22, 1861)

Thomas N. Waul (added March 6, 1861)
William W. Watkins (added May 18, 1861)

Reorganized July 29, 1861

Martin J. Crawford
Alexandre DeClouet
Jackson Morton
Jabez L. M. Curry
William P. Miles
Thomas N. Waul
William W. Watkins
George Davis
William H. MacFarland
David M. Currin (added December 9, 1861)
George G. Vest (added December 9, 1861)

Committee on Commercial and Financial Independence

Created August 10, 1861

Thomas S. Bocock
Augustus H. Garland
Richard W. Walker
George T. Ward
Benjamin H. Hill
John Perkins Jr.
Willy P. Harris
John M. Morehead
Robert B. Rhett, Sr.
John Hemphill

Committee on Engrossment

Created February 12, 1861

John Gill Shorter, chair
William S. Wilson
Augustus H. Kenan
Colin J. McRae
Francis S. Bartow
Jehu A. Orr (replaced Wilson, April 29, 1861)

Reorganized July 29, 1861

John Gill Shorter, chair
Augustus H. Kenan
Colin J. McRae
Jehu A. Orr

Committee on Finance

Created February 12, 1861

Robert Toombs, chair
Robert W. Barnwell
Duncan F. Kenner
William S. Barry
Colin J. McRae
Robert M. T. Hunter, chair (added May 10, 1861)

Reorganized July 29, 1861

Robert Toombs, chair
Robert W. Barnwell
Duncan F. Kenner
William S. Barry

Colin J. McRae
John Hemphill
Robert M. T. Hunter
John M. Morehead
James A. Seddon
John F. House (added December 9, 1861)
Aaron Conrow (added December 9, 1861)
Henry C. Burnett (added December 24, 1861)

Committee on Flag and Seal of the Confederacy

Created February 9, 1861

William P. Miles, chair
John Gill Shorter
Jackson Morton
Francis S. Bartow
Edward Sparrow
James T. Harrison

Reorganized July 29, 1861

William P. Miles, chair
John Gill Shorter
Jackson Morton
Edward Sparrow
James T. Harrison
Alexander Boteler (added January 29, 1862)
Jabez L. M. Curry (added January 29, 1862)
Henry C. Jones (added January 29, 1862)

Committee on Foreign Affairs

Created February 12, 1861

Robert B. Rhett Sr., chair
Eugenius A. Nisbet
John Perkins Jr.
Richard W. Walker
Laurence M. Keitt
William C. Rives (added May 13, 1861)

Reorganized July 29, 1861

Robert B. Rhett Sr., chair
Eugenius A. Nisbet
John Perkins Jr.
Richard W. Walker
Laurence M. Keitt
Louis T. Wigfall
William C. Rives
James Mason
Abraham W. Venable (to Naval Affairs, December 6, 1861)
James H. Thomas (added December 9, 1861)
John B. Clark, Sr. (added December 9, 1861)
Thomas B. Monroe (added December 24, 1861)

Committee on Indian Affairs

Created February 12, 1861

Jackson Morton, chair
Stephen F. Hale
David P. Lewis
Laurence M. Keitt
Edward Sparrow
Thomas N. Waul (added March 6, 1861)
Henry C. Jones (replaced Lewis, April 29, 1861)
Robert W. Johnson (added May 18, 1861)

Reorganized July 29, 1861

Jackson Morton, chair
Stephen F. Hale
Laurence M. Keitt
Edward Sparrow
Thomas N. Waul
Henry C. Jones
Robert W. Johnson
Allen T. Davidson
Alexander Boteler (added December 9, 1861)
John B. Clark Sr. (added December 9, 1861)

COMMITTEE ON MILITARY AFFAIRS

Created February 12, 1861

Francis S. Bartow, chair (died July 21, 1861)
W. Porcher Miles, chair (succeeded Bartow, July 21, 1861)
Edward Sparrow
Augustus H. Kenan
J. Patton Anderson
John Gregg (added March 6, 1861)
George T. Ward (replaced Anderson, May 2, 1861)
Waller R. Staples (added May 10, 1861)

Reorganized July 29, 1861

W. Porcher Miles, chair
Edward Sparrow
Augustus H. Kenan
John Gregg
George T. Ward
Waller R. Staples
William B. Preston
William W. Avery
Stephen F. Hale (added November 29, 1861)
Willy P. Harris (added November 29, 1861)
John D. C. Atkins (added November 29, 1861)
William B. Ochiltree (added November 29, 1861)
Thomas A. Harris (added December 9, 1861)
Thomas Johnson (added December 24, 1861)
Roger A. Pryor (added January 8, 1862)

COMMITTEE ON NAVAL AFFAIRS

Created February 12, 1861

James Chesnut Jr., chair
Charles M. Conrad
Robert H. Smith
Augustus R. Wright
James B. Owens
Williamson S. Oldham (added March 6, 1861)

Reorganized July 29, 1861

James Chesnut Jr., chair
Charles M. Conrad
Robert H. Smith
Augustus R. Wright
James B. Owens
Williamson S. Oldham
Thomas S. Bocock
Richard C. Puryear

Thomas H. Ruffin
Colin J. McRae (added December 6, 1861)
Abraham W. Venable (from Foreign Affairs, December 6, 1861)
Thomas M. Jones (added December 9, 1861)
William M. Cooke Sr. (added December 9, 1861)
David M. Currin (added December 10, 1861)

Committee on Patents

Created February 12, 1861
Walter Brooke, chair
William S. Wilson
David P. Lewis
Benjamin H. Hill
Duncan F. Kenner
Henry C. Jones (replaced Lewis, April 29, 1861)
Jehu A. Orr (replaced Wilson, April 29, 1861)

Reorganized July 29, 1861
Walter Brooke, chair
Henry C. Jones
Benjamin H. Hill
Duncan F. Kenner
Jehu A. Orr
Thomas D. S. McDowell
Charles W. Russell

Committee on Pay and Mileage

Created May 6, 1861
Josiah A. P. Campbell, chair
Nicholas Davis Jr.
William B. Ochiltree

Reorganized July 29, 1861
Josiah A. P. Campbell, chair
Nicholas Davis Jr.
William B. Ochiltree
Henry C. Jones (added August 21, 1861)

Committee on Permanent Constitution

Created February 9, 1861
Robert B. Rhett, chair
Richard W. Walker
Robert H. Smith
Jackson Morton
James B. Owens
Robert Toombs
Thomas R. R. Cobb
Alexandre DeClouet
Edward Sparrow
Alexander M. Clayton
Willy P. Harris
James Chesnut Jr.

Reorganized July 29, 1861
Robert B. Rhett, chair
James Chesnut Jr.

Richard W. Walker
Robert H. Smith
Jackson Morton
James B. Owens
Robert Toombs
Thomas R. R. Cobb
Alexandre DeClouet
Edward Sparrow
Willy P. Harris

COMMITTEE ON POSTAL AFFAIRS

Created February 12, 1861

William. P. Chilton, chair
William W. Boyce
Benjamin H. Hill
James T. Harrison
Jabez L. M. Curry
William B. Ochiltree (added March 6, 1861)
Albert Rust (added May 18, 1861)

Reorganized July 29, 1861

William. P. Chilton, chair
William W. Boyce
Benjamin H. Hill
James T. Harrison
Jabez L. M. Curry
William B. Ochiltree
Albert Rust
William N. H. Smith
Robert Johnston
Cornelius Robinson (added December 9, 1861)
Thomas W. Freeman (added December 9, 1861)

COMMITTEE ON PRINTING

Created February 12, 1861

Thomas R. R. Cobb, chair
James T. Harrison
W. Porcher Miles
William P. Chilton
John Perkins Jr.

Reorganized July 29, 1861

Thomas R. R. Cobb, chair
James T. Harrison
W. Porcher Miles
William P. Chilton
John Perkins Jr.
Roger A. Pryor
Alexander Boteler (added December 9, 1861)
William H. DeWitt (added December 9, 1861)

COMMITTEE ON PUBLIC LANDS

Created February 12, 1861

Henry Marshall, chair
Willy P. Harris
Thomas Fearn
J. Patton Anderson
Augustus R. Wright
Nicholas Davis Jr. (replaced Fearn, April 29, 1861)
George T. Ward (replaced Anderson, May 2, 1861)
Augustus H. Garland (added May 18, 1861)

Reorganized July 29, 1861
Henry Marshall, chair
Willy P. Harris
Augustus R. Wright
Nicholas Davis Jr.
George T. Ward
Augustus H. Garland
Charles W. Russell
Alexander B. Bradford (added December 9, 1861)
Caspar W. Bell (added December 9, 1861)

Committee on Rules

Created February 4, 1861
Alexander H. Stephens, chair
Laurence M. Keitt
Jabez L. M. Curry
James T. Harrison
John Perkins Jr.

Committee on Territories

Created February 12, 1861
James Chesnut Jr.
Henry Marshall
Josiah A. P. Campbell
Eugenius A. Nisbet
Thomas Fearn
William B. Ochiltree (added March 6, 1861)
Nicholas Davis Jr. (replaced Fearn, April 29, 1861)
Hugh F. Thomason (added May 20, 1861)
Williamson S. Oldham (added May 3, 1861)

Reorganized July 29, 1861
James Chesnut Jr.
Josiah A. P. Campbell
Henry Marshall
Eugenius A. Nisbet
William B. Ochiltree
Nicholas Davis Jr.
Williamson S. Oldham
Hugh F. Thomason
Walter Preston
William H. DeWitt (added December 9, 1861)
Caspar W. Bell (added December 9, 1861)

Committee on the Inauguration

Created February 15, 1861 (Provisional Government)
William P. Chilton
J. Patton Anderson
Augustus H. Kenan
Alexandre DeClouet
William S. Barry
Robert B. Rhett Sr.

Created February 7, 1862 (Permanent Government)
William H. MacFarland
Colin J. McRae
William W. Watkins
Jackson Morton
Thomas M. Forman
Samuel H. Ford
Duncan F. Kenner
James T. Harrison

George G. Vest
Robert H. Smith
William W. Boyce
David M. Currin
William B. Ochiltree
Walter Brooke (replaced Harrison, February 11, 1862)
Augustus H. Garland (replaced Watkins, February 11, 1862)

COMMITTEE ON THE JUDICIARY

Created February 12, 1861
Alexander M. Clayton, chair
John Hemphill, chair (added March 13, 1861)
Thomas J. Withers
Stephen F. Hale
Thomas R. R. Cobb
Willy P. Harris
Williamson S. Oldham (added March 6, 1861)
Robert H. Smith (added March 13, 1861)
John W. Brockenbrough (added May 10, 1861)
Stephen F. Hale (replaced Clayton, May 13, 1861)

Reorganized July 29, 1861
Stephen F. Hale
Thomas R. R. Cobb
Willy P. Harris
Williamson S. Oldham
John W. Brockenbrough
Robert H. Smith
Robert E. Scott
Francis B. Craige
Augustus H. Garland
Thomas B. Monroe (added December 24, 1861)

COMMITTEE TO ARRANGE FOR GOVERNMENT BUILDINGS

Created February 9, 1861
John Gill Shorter
William P. Chilton
Colin J. McRae

Reorganized July 29, 1861
John Gill Shorter
William P. Chilton
Colin J. McRae
Alexander Boteler (added November 27, 1861)

COMMITTEE TO ORGANIZE THE EXECUTIVE DEPARTMENT

Created February 12, 1861
Alexander H. Stephens, chair
Charles M. Conrad
William W. Boyce
John Gill Shorter
Walter Brooke

Reorganized July 29, 1861
Alexander H. Stephens, chair
Charles M. Conrad

William W. Boyce
John Gill Shorter
Walter Brooke

Committee to Report a Plan for a Provisional Government

Created February 5, 1861

Richard W. Walker
Robert H. Smith
J. Patton Anderson
James B. Owens
Alexander H. Stephens
Eugenius A. Nisbet
John Perkins Jr.
Duncan F. Kenner
William S. Barry
Willy P. Harris
Christopher G. Memminger
Robert W. Barnwell

CONGRESSIONAL SESSIONS

FIRST SESSION

(MONTGOMERY, ALABAMA, FEBRUARY 4, 1861, TO MARCH 16, 1861)

Monday, February 4, 1861

(Charleston *Mercury,* February 7, 1861; Montgomery *Weekly Advertiser*, February 6, 1861)

The Congress met in the Senate Chamber, which at an early hour was thronged with members of the Legislature of Alabama and numerous spectators. The importance of the occasion was fully appreciated, and there was not a heart that did not throb proudly in anticipation of the success and glory to be achieved in a Southern Confederacy.

At half-past twelve o'clock, the Congress was called to order by Mr. CHILTON, of Alabama, who nominated Hon. ROBT. W. BARNWELL, of South Carolina, for temporary Chairman.

The question being put, Mr. BARNWELL was chosen by unanimous vote.

Mr. BARNWELL, on taking the Chair, thanked the Congress for the honor conferred upon him as their presiding officer, and stated that the deliberations of the body would be opened with prayer by the Rev. Mr. MANLY,[1] formerly of South Carolina.

Rev. Mr. MANLY then offered up the following petition:

THE PRAYER[2]

> Oh Thou great Spirit of the universe; Thou madest all things; Thou madest man upon the universe; Thou has endowed him with reason and the capacity of government. We thank Thee that Thou hast here established a free government, and a pure form of religion. We thank Thee for all the holy memories connected with our father's history. Thou wert the God of our fathers; Oh! be Thou our God. Let it please Thee to vouchsafe Thy secret presence in this assembly. Oh our Father, we trust we can appeal to the heart searching God for the purity and sincerity of our motives. If it were in rebellion against Thee, if it were in violation of any compact still obligatory upon us, that these southern portions of this great country are now withdrawing from the government our fathers instituted and proposing to set up a new one, if it were in rebellion against God and in profanation of any principle of piety or duty, we could hope for Thy presence or blessing. But oh! Thou heartsearching God, conscious as we

are of our sins, impurity, and imperfections, we, as a people, feel that we are in pursuit only of our rights—those rights guaranteed to use by solemn compact, and cemented by the blood of our fathers—those rights which the God of the universe, whose are all things, has been pleased to bestow upon us. And now, our Father, we humbly recognize Thy hand in all providences which have brought this Southern Congress together; and since it is in Thy good pleasure that it has met agreeably to appointment, oh! Thou Spirit of Wisdom, endow Thy servants with all necessary grace, with every gift, with deliberation, and with purpose; and grant that they may have wisdom adapted to the trying contingencies imposed upon all, and for all that vast condition of affairs that they are now to consider and dispose of. Oh! let it please Thee to direct their minds in all these elevated matters and holy purposes that should control the minds of legislators. Direct them all, we pray Thee, that they may immolate all the claims of ambition, or the lusts of spoils, or the desire of office and power—that they immolate every private and personal consideration, and all party feelings, in one pervading desire for the welfare of this great people. Oh! God, assist them, we pray Thee, to preserve republican institutions and the purity of the forms of religion, without interference from the civil government; and bestow upon each one of them health and strength of body, and soundness and equanimity of mind, and calm and rational state of feeling and purpose—aiming directly at the glory of God, and aiming at the welfare of the whole people. And, Oh! Father, let each one be prepared to stand by the claims of duty, whatever may come; and in all the hours of trial which are to supervene, Oh! God, we pray Thee to preserve them—to enable them to stand up with this great people in the exercise of their proper forbearance—in all grace, prudence and wisdom, and with a just regard for the welfare of their several constituencies. And God grant that the union of these Southern States, and of all that may come into the Union thereof, may be based upon such principles as shall be perpetual, and as long as the sun and moon endure. Oh! may the government now formed continue to endure.

And now, oh! God, preside over this body in its organization—in the distribution of its duties, and in its various labors. Let this momentous era—this stirring occasion—be so regarded by the Father of Mercies, the God of the universe, that it may be the commencement of a glorious reign of truth, of duty, of equal rights, and of a just apportionment of all the principles and benefits pertaining to government. And now, Father in heaven, we acknowledge Thee as our God. Oh! do Thou rule in us, do Thou sway us; do Thou control this body, and all the people they represent; and let the blessing of Thy Son and Holy Spirit rest upon them, now and forever. Amen.

The PRESIDENT. The first business in order is to provide for the permanent organization of the body. Have Deputies any propositions to submit?

Mr. RHETT, of South Carolina. Mr. President, would it not be proper first to call upon the various delegations to present their credentials, and thus let us ascertain by that instrumentality who are the members of this Congress? But prior to that we might elect a Secretary.

The PRESIDENT. If it is first ascertained who are the members of the Convention, we will then know who have a right to vote for Secretary.

Mr. SMITH, of Alabama. I received a dispatch from Mobile, stating that the Louisiana delegation and a part of the Mississippi delegation were on their way, and would be here this morning. The boat has arrived, but I am not informed yet of their attendance, and I would suggest that the permanent organization of the body be deferred until they have an opportunity to be present.[3]

Mr. KEITT, of South Carolina. The delegates have arrived and assumed their seats.

Mr. MEMMINGER, of South Carolina. Mr. President, I suggest that some gentleman be selected to act as temporary Secretary until the body is organized.

Mr. SHORTER, of Alabama, moved that Mr. A. R. LAMAR be appointed such secretary, which motion was agreed to.[4]

Mr. MEMMINGER, of South Carolina. I move that the Deputies from the several States, in alphabetical order, present their credentials to the Secretary, and also sign their names to the roll of the Convention. Adopted.

The credentials of the several delegations were accordingly read, and the deputies signed the roll. The following is the list:[5]

South Carolina—R. B. Rhett, Sr., R. W. Barnwell, L. M. Keitt, James Chesnut, Jr., C. G. Memminger, W. Porcher Miles, Thomas J. Withers and W. W. Boyce.

Florida—Jackson Morton, J. P. Anderson and J. B. Owens.

Alabama—R. W. Walker, R. H. Smith, J. L. M. Curry, W. P. Chilton, S. F. Hale, Colin J. McRae, John Gill Shorter, David P. Lewis and Thomas Fearn.

Mississippi—Willy P. Harris, Walter Brooke, W. S. Wilson, A. M. Clayton, W. S. Barry, J. T. Harrison and J. A. P. Campbell

Georgia—Robert Toombs, Howell Cobb, Francis S. Bartow, Martin J. Crawford, Eugenius A. Nisbet, Benj. H. Hill, A. R. Wright,[6] Thomas R. R. Cobb, Augustus H. Kenan and Alex. H. Stephens.

Louisiana—John Perkins, Jr., A. DeClouet, Charles M. Conrad, D. F. Kenner, Gen. Edward Sparrow and Henry Marshall

The PRESIDENT. The deputies have all signed the roll. What business will the Congress now enter upon? Is it proposed now to proceed to the election of a Secretary for the Congress?

Mr. RHETT, of South Carolina. I think, Mr. President, our proper course is to elect a permanent President, and I beg leave, on the part of the Delegation from South Carolina, to nominate a gentleman for that high and distinguished office—one who has been as illustrious in the service of government—one whose reputation is coequal with the extent of our great Confederacy—I nominate HOWELL COBB, of Georgia [*Applause*]

The PRESIDENT. It may be proper to take some preliminary action in regard to the manner of voting. South Carolina proposes that the vote shall be taken by States—each State casting one vote.

Mr. RHETT, of South Carolina. Mr. President, I am sure that the Congress is unanimous, and I propose that the vote shall be taken by acclamation. [*Applause*]

There being no objection, the question was decided by acclamation, and Mr. COBB was unanimously chosen President of the Provisional Congress.

Mr. RHETT, of South Carolina. I move that a committee of three be appointed to conduct the President elect to the Chair.

The question being put, the motion was agreed to.

The President then appointed on this committee Messrs. RHETT, of South Carolina, WALKER, of Alabama, and ANDERSON, of Florida, who conducted Mr. COBB to the Chair.

Mr. COBB, on assuming the Chair, was greeted with a round of heavy applause. He spoke as follows:

ADDRESS OF THE PRESIDENT

Accept gentlemen of the Convention, my sincere thanks for the honor you have conferred upon me. I shall endeavor, by a faithful and impartial discharge of the duties of the Chair, to merit, in some degree at least, the confidence you have reposed in me.

The occasion which assembles us together is one of no ordinary character. We meet as representatives of sovereign and independent States, who by their solemn judgment have dissolved the political association which connected them with the Government of the United States. Of the causes which have led to this decision, it is unnecessary now to speak. It is sufficient to announce that, by the judgment of our constituents, they have been pronounced ample and sufficient. It is now a fixed and irrevocable fact. [*Applause*] The separation is perfect, complete and perpetual. [*Applause*]

The great duty is now imposed upon us of providing for these States a government for their future security and protection. We can and should extend to our sister States—our late sister States—who are identified with us in interest, feeling, and institutions, a cordial welcome to unite with us in a common destiny—desirous at the same time of maintaining with the rest of our former confederates, as with the world, the most peaceful and friendly relations, political and commercial. [*Applause*]

Our responsibilities, gentlemen, are great; and I doubt not we shall prove equal to the occasion. [*Applause*] Let us assume all the responsibility which may be necessary for the successful completion of the great work committed to our care—placing before our countrymen and the world our acts and their results, as the justification for the course we may pursue and the policy we may adopt. With a consciousness of the justice of our cause, and with the confidence in the guidance and blessings of a kind Providence, we will this day inaugurate, for the South, a new era of peace, security, and prosperity. [*Applause*]

After a pause—

The PRESIDENT. Will the Convention proceed to complete its organization?

Mr. CHILTON, of Alabama. I move that we proceed to the election of a Secretary.

The question being taken, it was agreed to.

The PRESIDENT. How will the Congress proceed in this election? By nomination, by ballot, or *viva voce*?

Mr. CHILTON, of Alabama. I suggest that we proceed by nomination, and if that be agreeable to the body, I ask leave to put in nomination Mr. JOHNSON J. HOOPER.[7] [*Applause*] Mr. HOOPER, Mr. President, is a gentleman well known to all of you, and it is unnecessary to say anything more.

Mr. TOOMBS, of Georgia. I move that the vote be taken by acclamation. [*Applause*]

No objection was made.

The PRESIDENT. Before putting the motion, the Chair will request that there may be no further applause during the sittings of the Congress. It is certainly unnecessary to do more than to make this request.

The question was then taken, and Mr. HOOPER was unanimously elected Secretary.

Mr. WALKER, of Alabama, then moved that the body proceed to the election of Door-keeper.

Mr. WITHERS, of South Carolina. Mr. President, I trust the Chair will be authorized to appoint the Door-keeper, and all the other officers which may be necessary. I move that the Chair be authorized to appoint the remaining officers.

The motion of Mr. WITHERS was then agreed to.

Mr. STEPHENS, of Georgia. I move, Mr. President, that a Committee of five be appointed by the Chair, to report the rules for the government of this Congress.[8]

The question being taken, the motion was agreed to.

The President subsequently appointed the following gentlemen: Messrs. STEPHENS, of Georgia; Mr. KEITT, of South Carolina; CURRY, of Alabama; HARRIS, of Mississippi, and PERKINS, of Alabama.

And then, at half past one o'clock, p.m., the Congress adjourned till 12 o'clock, m., to-morrow.

Tuesday, February 5, 1861

(Charleston *Mercury*, February 8, 1861; Montgomery *Weekly Advertiser*, February 13, 1861)

The Congress met at 12 o'clock m. and was called to order by the President, Hon. HOWELL COBB, of Georgia.

Prayer was offered by Rev. Mr. MITCHELL, of St. Johns' Church:[9]

> Oh Lord, our Heavenly Father—the high and mighty ruler of the universe—who from thy throne behold all the dwellers upon the earth—most heartily do we beseech thee to look with favor upon these representatives of sovereign independent States in thy presence assembled. Save them from all error, ignorance and pride. Endow them with wisdom, moderation and justice. Let nothing be done through strife or vain glory, but may all things be done in thy fear and with a view to thy glory. And do thou be pleased so to order all the deliberations of this body, that they conduce to the safety, honor and welfare of the people; and that all the principles of Government they may adopt, shall be settled upon the best and surest foundations of justice and right, and that they may advance the peace and happiness, the prosperity and security, and the piety and religion of the whole people, so that God in all things may be honored and glorified. These supplications we present not in our name or for our own righteousness; but in the name and for the sake of Christ our Lord—Amen.

Mr. SHORTER, Alabama. Mr. President, there are additional officers needed for preserving the records of this Congress. I move that the body dispense with the formality of an election, and that the Secretary be authorized to appoint an Assistant and a Journalizing Clerk for the Congress.[10]

The question being taken, the motion was agreed to.

Mr. STEPHENS, of Georgia. The Committee on Rules have authorized me to make a report. I will state, Mr. President, that I have the rules as prepared printed, in order that the members can read them at their desks and understand them better than if they were read in manuscript. I will further state that some of the rules have been taken from the rules of the House of Representatives of the United States Congress, part from the rules of the Senate, part from the Manual,[11] and one or two of them are original; all of which the Committee are of the opinion will best accomplish the object of the body. I move, Mr. President, that they be taken up.

Before the rules were read, the President stated that they would be considered as adopted—as read, unless a vote was asked upon such as might be objected to. The rules were then read as follows:

I. The vote upon all questions in this Congress, except as hereafter otherwise provided, shall be taken by States; each State shall be entitled to one vote. A majority of all the States represented shall be necessary to carry any question. The delegates from each State may designate the member to cast the vote for their State, and upon the motion of any member seconded by one-fifth of the members present, or at the instance of any one State, the yeas and nays of the entire body shall be spread upon the Journal upon any question.

II. Any number of members from a majority of the States now represented or hereafter to be represented by duly accredited delegates from States seceding from the late United States of America, shall constitute a quorum to transact business.

III. The President having taken the Chair, and a quorum being present, the Journal of the preceding day shall be read, and any mistakes in the entries shall, upon motion, then be corrected.

IV. No member shall speak to another, or otherwise interrupt the business of the Congress while the Journals or public papers are being read, or when any member is speaking in debate.

V. Every member when he speaks shall address the Chair standing in his place, and when he has finished shall sit down.

VI. No member shall speak more than twice in any one debate on the same question, and on the same day, without leave of a majority of the members present.

VII. When two or more members rise at the same time the President shall name the person to speak, but in all cases the member who shall first rise and address the Chair shall speak first.

VIII. The President shall preserve order and decorum; may speak to points of order in preference to other members, rising from his seat for that purpose; and shall decide questions of order subject to an appeal by any one State; and may call any member to the Chair to preside temporarily not to extend beyond that day's session. He may participate in the debates.

IX. When any member is called to order by the President or any member, he shall sit down, and every question of order shall be decided by the President without debate, subject to an appeal to the body.

X. If any member be called to order by another member for words spoken, the exceptional words spoken shall immediately be taken down in writing, that the President may be better able to judge the matter.

XI. No member shall in debate use any language reflecting injuriously upon the character, motives, honor or integrity of any other member.

XII. No motion shall be debated until the same shall receive a second; and when a motion shall be made and seconded, it shall be reduced to writing, if desired by the President, or any member, delivered in at the table, and read before the same shall be debated.

XIII. Any motion or proposition may be withdrawn by the mover at any time before a decision, amendment, or other action of the body upon it, except a motion to reconsider, which shall not be withdrawn without leave of the body.

XIV. When a question has been once made and carried in the affirmative or negative, a motion to reconsider shall be entertained at the instance of any State, if made on the same day on which the vote was taken, or within the two next days of actual session. When a motion to reconsider shall be made, its consideration shall take precedence of the regular order of business unless a majority of the members present shall fix some other time.

XV. When a question is under debate no motion (except one to reconsider some other question passed upon) shall be received but to adjourn, to lie on the table, to postpone indefinitely, to postpone to a day certain, to commit or amend, which several motions shall have precedence in the order they stand arranged, and the motion to adjourn shall always be in order, and decided without debate.

XVI. If the question for decision contain several parts, any member may have the same divided, but on a motion to strike out and insert, it shall not be in order to move for division of the question; but the rejection of a motion to strike out and insert one proposition shall not prevent a motion to strike out and insert a different proposition, nor prevent a subsequent proposition simply to strike out, nor shall the rejection of a motion simply to strike out, prevent a subsequent motion to strikeout and insert.

XVII. In filling up blanks the largest sum and longest time shall be first put.

XVIII. The unfinished business in which the Congees may be engaged on adjournment, shall be the first business in order on the next day's sitting.

XIX. After the Journal is read, and the unfinished business, if any, of the previous day's sitting is disposed of, the regular order of business shall be as follows:

1. The call of the States, alphabetically, for memorials, or any matter, measure, resolution, or proposition, which any member may desire to bring before the Congress.
2. The call of Committees for reports—the call of the Committees to be made in the order of their appointment—such reports of Committees as may not be otherwise disposed of when made, shall be

numbered in the order in which they are presented and be placed in that order on the Calendar of the regular orders of the day.

3. The Calendar, or the regular orders of the day, shall then be taken up, and every resolution, proposition, or measure, shall be disposed of in the order in which it there stands. No special order shall be made against this rule, except by a vote of a majority of the States, and such majority may, at any time, change the order of business.

XX. Every resolution or measure submitted for the action of the Congress, shall receive three readings previous to its being passed; the President shall give notice at each reading whether it be the first, second or third reading. No resolution or measure shall be committed or amended until it shall have been twice read, after which it may be subject to motion to amend or to refer to a committee. And all such matters, on second reading, shall first be considered by the Congress in the same manner as if the Congress were in Committee of the Whole; the final question on the second reading of any matter not referred to a committee, shall be "whether it shall be engrossed and read a third time," and no amendment shall be received after the engrossment for a third reading has been ordered. But it shall at all times be in order before the final passage or action of any matter, to move its commitment; and should such commitment take place, and any amendment be reported by the committee the whole shall be again read a second time, and considered, as in Committee of the Whole, and then the aforesaid question shall be again put.

XXI. After any matter is ordered to be engrossed and it has been read a third time, the question shall be, shall the resolution (or the matter, whatever it may be) now pass?

XXII. All resolutions, or other matter on the second and third reading, may be read by the title, unless the reading of the whole shall be desired by a majority of these present.

XXIII. The titles of resolutions and other matters submitted, and such parts thereof only as shall be affected by proposed amendments, shall be inserted on the Journals.

XXIV. No motion for the previous question shall be entertained, but upon the call of any member for The Question. If seconded by a majority of the members present, the vote shall be immediately taken on the pending question, whatever it may be, without further debate.

XXV. A motion to lay any amendment on the table prevailing, shall carry with it only the amendment, and not the original proposition or matter.

XXVI. Stenographers and Reporters of the Press, wishing to take down the proceedings of the Congress, may be admitted by the President, who shall assign such places to them on the floor, to effect their object, as shall not interfere with the convenience of the members when in open session.

XXVII. On motion, made and seconded by another member, to close the doors on the discussion of any business which may in the opinion of a member require secrecy, the President shall direct the doors to be closed and the gallery to be cleared, and during the discussion of such question, no one shall be permitted to remain upon the floor, but the members of the body and its officers.

XXVIII. Any officer or member of the Congress, convicted of disclosing any matter directed by the body to be held in confidence, shall be liable, if an officer, to dismissal from service, and in case of a member, to suffer expulsion from the body.

XXIX. All cases that may arise in the proceedings of this Congress not provided for in the foregoing rules, shall be governed by the general principles of parliamentary law, as laid down in Jefferson's Manual.

Mr. MEMMINGER, of South Carolina. I ask leave of the Congress to recur to the twentieth rule for the purpose of making inquiry of the honorable Chairman of the Committee who reported them.

The rule reads:

> Every resolution or measure submitted for the action of the Congress, shall receive three readings previous to its being passed; the President shall give notice of each reading, whether it be the first, second, or third reading. No resolution or measure shall be committed or amended until it shall have been twice read, after which, it may be subject to motion to amend or to refer to a committee.

Of course, Mr. President, these words embrace every thing; but I presume it was not intended by the Committee that it should embrace questions raised upon the disposition of business, motions to adjourn, &c. I suggest whether it would not be well to insert some exceptions. The words as written seem to embrace every thing.[12]

Mr. STEPHENS. It was intended only to cover written matter. That word might very properly be added, but I think the words "every resolution or measure," covers it any how. One of the rules says, "shall be reduced to writing if the President desires." I do not see any difficulty on that point.

Mr. MEMMINGER. If that be the understanding I have no objection. I move, sir, that the Rules be printed in pamphlet form.

Mr. WALKER, of Alabama. Mr. President, I beg leave to call attention to the second Rule. It reads:

> Any number of members from a majority of the States now represented, or hereafter to be represented by duly accredited delegates from States seceding from the late United States of America, shall constitute a quorum to transact business.

It seems to me, sir, that that Rule, literally interpreted, will constitute four delegates to this Congress a quorum to transact business.[13]

Mr. STEPHENS. These rules, sir, are based upon the principle that this is a Congress of States; sovereign, independent States, and that all questions are to be determined by States, one member from each delegation casting the vote of the State that he represents. If all retire, therefore, and leave the authority of the State entirely in the hands of one man, making a quorum of States, they would constitute a quorum under these rules; and upon the principle on which these rules are based—a principle of our organization—I take it that it is right. We are to vote as States, one member casting the vote, and the vote of a State is represented by one and none other, and that one is entitled to cast the vote; and if a majority of the States are present, there is a quorum present. This is a Congress of States.

Mr. PERKINS, of Louisiana. With the understanding and explanation as made by the Chairmen of the Committee on Rules with reference to Rule number two, I beg leave to call his attention to Rule number twenty-four, in relation to the previous question. I would suggest to the gentleman that the words "members present," be stricken out, and that the words "majority of the States represented," be inserted. If we vote by States, we certainly ought to do so in calling for the previous question. Therefore I move that amendment.

Mr. STEPHENS. The object, sir, of that Rule was more in relation to the comfort and convenience of members in the event of protracted debate. It is a matter which relates to the members participating in the debates rather than to the States, and that is the reason why the Committee proposed this provision. It relates more to our business then the rights of the States. It is immaterial, however, but I think that the honorable gentleman will find that it will work better just as it is.

The PRESIDENT. Does the gentleman from Louisiana insist upon his motion?

Mr. PERKINS. Under the instructions of the State Convention of Louisiana, we feel bound to vote as a unit, and as the calling for the previous question will frequently have an important bearing upon the discussion of questions, we would desire to comply with our instructions in voting upon all important questions. We consider this an important one as a State, and I move that the rule he changed so as to read a "majority of the States present."

The PRESIDENT. The twenty-fourth rule will be amended, as suggested by the member from Louisiana, if there be no objection.[14]

No objection was made.

Mr. SMITH, of Alabama. I wish to call attention to the twenty-seventh rule. It reads as follows:

> On motion made and seconded by another member to close the doors on the discussion of any business, which may, in the opinion of a member, require secrecy, the President shall direct the doors to be closed, and the gallery to be cleared, and during the discussion of such question no one shall be permitted to remain upon the floor but the members of the body and its officers.

It may be as important, Mr. President, to have the doors closed upon the vote on a question as upon its discussion.

Mr. STEPHENS. I will state that the language covers the entire subject. That branch of it is taken from the rules of the Senate of the United States. It covers everything done in secret session, and I think no objection will be found to it.

No further amendments were proposed, and the question recurring on the motion of Mr. MEMMINGER, of South Carolina, that the rules be printed in pamphlet form, it was put, and being taken, it was decided in the affirmative. So the rules were adopted and ordered to be printed in pamphlet form.

Mr. CURRY, of Alabama. Mr. President, I ask leave to offer the following resolution:

> *Resolved*, That Messrs. SHORTER and READ be appointed Printers to this Congress while holding its sessions in Montgomery, and that all work be done in style and quality equal to that done for the State of Alabama, and to be paid for at the same rates of compensation.[15]

I will merely state that these gentlemen are Printers for the State of Alabama.

The question was taken and the resolution was agreed to.

On motion of Mr. NISBET, of Georgia, the following resolution was adopted:

> *Resolved*, That the Reverend Clergy of this city be, and they are hereby invited, to open the sessions of this Convention with prayer, and that a Committee of three be selected from the Alabama delegation and appointed by the Chair to extend to them this invitation, and to arrange with them for the performance of the service.

The PRESIDENT. The Chair will suggest to the body that it would be well in completing its organization, to fix upon a regular hour of meeting.

Mr. COBB, of Georgia. I move that the hour of 12 o'clock, m., be fixed upon until otherwise ordered by the Congress.[16]

The question was taken, and the motion was agreed to.

Mr. CHESNUT. Mr. President, I move that the States be called in their alphabetical order per resolutions.

The PRESIDENT. It would be in order, in accordance with the rules as adopted.

No objection being made, the motion was agreed to, and the States were accordingly called. The State of South Carolina being called—

Mr. MEMMINGER obtained the floor. He said Mr. President, I beg leave to offer the following resolutions:

> *Resolved*, That this Convention deems it expedient forthwith to form a Confederacy of the States which have seceded from the Federal Union, and that a Committee be appointed to report a plan of a Provisional Government for the same upon the basis of the Constitution of the United States.
>
> *Resolved*, That the committee consist of thirteen members to be appointed as follows, namely: the Chairman by the Convention, and two members to be nominated by the delegation from each State.
>
> *Resolved*, That all propositions in relation to a provisional government be referred to this committee.

I am not disposed to press the consideration of these resolutions, if any gentleman present desires to postpone them, but as it is simply a proposition to appoint a committee, and as that committee may probably consume some days in the preparation of a plan, it seems to me that in all probability the Convention will prefer to pass upon it now. I therefore, with the simple declaration that I will make no opposition to a postponement, would state that it seems to me most advisable that we should act upon it now. It will require the time of the delegations, after we adjourn, to prepare the committees which are proposed to be appointed by each delegation, and the chairman will either be appointed by the Chairman of this body or by such other means as the Convention shall see fit to declare.

Mr. STEPHENS, of Georgia. I would move to amend by inserting, wherever the word "Convention" occurs in these resolutions the word "Congress."

Mr. MEMMINGER. I have no objection to the change proposed.

The question was taken and the amendment was agreed to.

Mr. BARTOW, of Georgia. I hold in my hand a resolution which I will offer as a substitute for that offered by the gentleman from South Carolina. It is as follows:

> *Whereas*, The States of South Carolina, Georgia, Florida, Alabama, Mississippi and Louisiana, have dissevered the political ties which bound them to the compact of the Union known as the United States of America, and through duly authorized delegates are now assembled in a Congress of

> Southern States to provide for their common defence, and to promote their general welfare, and to establish an enduring Government by which their rights and social institutions may be forever maintained, looking to the concurrence of such of their late confederates as are united with them by a community of interest; and whereas this Congress is empowered to establish a Provisional Government until a permanent Government can be organized; therefore be it
>
> *Resolved*, That the President do appoint a Committee, to consist of one Delegate from each State, to report as soon as possible a form and plan of a Provisional Government, to be adopted by this Congress.

I will move to amend by increasing the Committee to two members instead of one.

The amendment was agreed to.

The PRESIDENT. The question will be upon agreeing to the amendment of the gentleman from Georgia, offered as a substitute for the proposition of the gentleman from South Carolina.

Mr. BARRY, of Mississippi. Mr. President, before that question is put, I desire to offer the following amendment to the amendment, in the nature of a substitute for the two propositions before the body.

The Clerk was about to read the amendment—

Mr. PERKINS, of Louisiana (interrupting). Mr. President, in order to—

The PRESIDENT. Will the gentleman from Louisiana allow the amendment to be reported?

Mr. PERKINS. Mr. President, I desire to move that the galleries be cleared before we proceed to the discussion of these various plans. There is diversity of opinion with reference to them, and I make that motion.

It was seconded.

The PRESIDENT. It is unnecessary for the Chair to put the question. The motion has been made and seconded.

The galleries were accordingly cleared, and the Congress proceeded to sit with closed doors.[17]

Wednesday, February 6, 1861

(Charleston *Mercury*, February 9, 1861; Montgomery *Weekly Advertiser*, February 13, 1861)

The Congress was called to order by the President, Hon. HOWELL COBB, at 11 o'clock m.

Prayer was offered by the Rev. Mr. TICHENOR, of the Baptist Church:[18]

> Our Father who art in Heaven, we rejoice for all thy mercies towards us. We bless thee that it is our privilege, guilty though we are, to come to thy

throne of grace, and ask thy forgiveness for our transgressions, and for all that grace and strength needful for us in the discharge of the duties thou hast devolved upon us. We would look up to thee this morning, realizing that thou art the giver of every good and perfect gift. We implore thy blessings on us during the hours of this day. We beseech thee that thou wouldst grant unto the Representatives of these Sovereign States, here assembled, all that wisdom, prudence and firmness, which are necessary for them to discharge the arduous and responsible duties with which they are entrusted. And do thou grant thy blessings upon the people of these Sovereign States. We thank thee for that measure of peace, prosperity and security, which they have enjoyed in days past. We pray thee continue unto them thy blessings. Spread the shield of thy protection over them—guard them by thine own right hand—and enable them to do those things which are pleasing in thy sight. And oh, we beseech thee, our Heavenly Father, if consistent with thy will, let peace be within our borders; but if thou hast in thy Providence determined otherwise—if it be needful that we should lay the foundation of this new Confederacy in tears, and cement it with blood—oh! our God, we beseech thee, that thou wouldst stand by thy servants—that thou wouldst give success to our armies in the day of battle, and that the conflict, if it must come, may be short and effectual for the preservation of the rights of this people. And now, we look to thee, our Heavenly Father, and again beseech thy blessing during the hours of this day.—Hear us, in these our petitions, and forgive our sins and save us through Christ our Redeemer—Amen.

The minutes of the preceding day were read and confirmed.

Mr. OWENS, of Florida. Mr. President, my colleague, Mr. JACKSON MORTON, who has been unavoidably detained from his seat up to this time, is now present. I will offer his credentials, and ask that he be permitted to sign the roll, and take his seat as a member of this body.[19]

No objection being made, Mr. MORTON came forward and signed the roll.

The PRESIDENT. The business first in order is the call of the States in their alphabetical order for motions, resolution, etc. The Clerk will call the States.

The States were accordingly called, but there [were] no responses; none of the Committees were ready to report, and the business on the calendar was not considered.

Mr. TOOMBS, of Georgia. I have the pleasure of presenting a communication from the Commissioners of the State of North Carolina to this body.

The PRESIDENT. The gentleman from Georgia presents a communication from the Commissioners of the State of North Carolina, addressed to the President of the Congress. The Clerk will read the communication.

The communication was then read as follows:

Montgomery, Ala., February 6, 1861.

To the Hon. Howell Cobb,
President of the Southern Congress:

The undersigned have the honor to submit to the consideration of the Southern Congress the accompanying resolutions adopted by the General Assembly of North Carolina on the 29th ult.

We are, with high consideration,
Your obedient servants

D. L. Swain
M. W. Ranson
Jno. L. Bridgers

Resolutions concerning the appointment of Commissioners to Washington City and Alabama.

1. *Resolved*, That for the purpose of effecting an honorable and amicable adjustment of all the difficulties that distract the country, upon the basis of the Crittenden resolutions, as modified by the Legislature of Virginia,[20] and for the purpose of consulting our common peace, honor and safety, the Hon. THOMAS RUFFIN, of Alamance, T. N. BARRINGER, DAVID S. READ, JOHN M. MOORHEAD, and GEORGE DAVIS, be, and they are hereby appointed Commissioners to represent North Carolina with proposed consultation to be held at Washington City, on the 4th of February, 1861.

   And whereas, the State of North Carolina has been invited by the State of Alabama, to meet at the city of Montgomery, on the 4th of February, 1861, for the purpose of framing a provisional as well as permanent government, and whereas, North Carolina, as a part of the Federal Union, has no right to send delegates for such a purpose; therefore,

2. *Resolved*, That for the purpose of effecting an honorable and amicable adjustment of all the difficulties which distract the country, upon the basis of the Crittenden resolutions, as modified by the Legislature of Virginia, and for the purpose of consulting for our common peace, honor and safety, the Hon. DAVID L. SWAIN, M. W. RANSON, and JOHN P. BRIDGERS, are appointed Commissioners to visit Montgomery, Ala., for the purposes above indicated.

3. *Resolved, further*, That His Excellency the Governor be requested immediately to inform the Commissioners of their appointment, and upon the refusal of any one of them to serve, report the same immediately to the General Assembly.

WM. T. DORTCH, S.H.C
HENRY T. CLARK, S.S.

Mr. TOOMBS. I move that the resolutions be laid on the table for the present, and that a Committee of three be appointed to invite these gentlemen to take seats on the floor of this chamber.

The question was taken, and the motion was agreed to.

Mr. KEITT, of South Carolina. Is a motion in order?

The PRESIDENT. It is.

Mr. KEITT. Then I move, sir, that HENRY BUTTS be made Engrossing Clerk of this Congress. I know him myself, and I am informed that he will make an excellent officer.

Mr. CRAWFORD, of Georgia. I desire to ask whether or not there is a necessity for an Engrossing Clerk. If there is I will make no objection; otherwise I feel compelled to do so. If the President, or the member from South Carolina, has any knowledge of such a necessity, then I will make no objection, but if there is no necessity I must object.

The PRESIDENT. The Chair is unable to answer the interrogatory of the gentleman from Georgia.

Mr. KEITT (interrupting). I will state, Mr. President—

The PRESIDENT (resuming). The Chair has inquired of the Secretary, who states that in all probability he will need an Engrossing Clerk in a few days.

Mr. CRAWFORD. I beg that the motion will be permitted to lie over for a day or two.

Mr. KEITT. I will modify my motion. I will move that the President be instructed to appoint that officer, if necessary.

The PRESIDENT. The gentleman from South Carolina moves that the President be directed to appoint Mr. HENRY BUTTS—

Mr. KEITT (interrupting). I did not intend to put any limit upon the action of the President. My intention was to leave the President free to appoint whomsoever he may please.

The question was then taken and the motion agreed to.

Mr. MEMMINGER, of South Carolina. Mr. President, I am instructed by the Committee raised yesterday to frame a Provisional Government, to ask leave of the House to continue its sittings during the sittings of the House. I move that leave be granted to that Committee.

The question was taken and the motion was agreed to.

Mr. WITHERS, of South Carolina. Mr. President, allow me to ask my colleague from South Carolina whether he can give me any conjecture as to the period of time at which that Committee will be able to report.

Mr. MEMMINGER. The Committee has been very industriously pursuing its business during the greater part of last night and all of this morning. I think I can say, that in all probability it will be prepared to report to-morrow.

Mr. WITHERS. My object in putting the question was not to indicate any impatience; but until that Committee does report, I doubt whether we will transact any business. My desire was to move a recess, if there was any possibility of having the report to-day.

Mr. MEMMINGER. I beg leave to ask the Chair to invite the Committee to retire to the Committee room, and resume their deliberations.

Accordingly, the Committee to form a Provisional Government retired from the hall.[21]

Mr. WITHERS. I move that this Congress adjourn.

Mr. CRAWFORD. I was merely going to suggest that we had received the credentials from—

Mr. WITHERS. I withdraw my motion.

Mr. CRAWFORD. I will make no motion.

Mr. WITHERS. Then I renew my motion.

Mr. TOOMBS. I propose to change the hour from 12 o'clock m., till 10 o'clock a.m.

Mr. KEITT. I hope the gentleman will say 11 o'clock. Ten o'clock is too soon.

The suggestion was accepted, and the motion was agreed to.

And then the Congress adjourned till 11 o'clock a.m. to-morrow.

Thursday, February 7, 1861

(Charleston *Mercury,* February 11, 1861; Montgomery *Weekly Advertiser*, February 13, 1861; Savannah *Daily Morning News*, February 9, 1861)

The Congress was called to order by the President, Hon. HOWELL COBB, at 11 o'clock a.m.

Prayer was offered by the Rev. G. W. H. PETRIE of the Presbyterian Church:[22]

> Almighty god, our Heavenly Father, with profound reverence do we bow before thy Divine Majesty, acknowledging thy claims upon our worship, and beseeching thee to receive our supplications, through the grace that is in Christ Jesus our Lord. Wilt thou be pleased in thine infinite goodness to bless and prosper these thy servants, the Representatives of Sovereign States, here assembled with sacred trusts, that they may be adequate to the important duties they are called upon to discharge. Bless them this day in their deliberations, and be pleased to grant that they may adopt those measures which may be promotive of the safety, honor and welfare, of the people, and which may conduce to the honor and glory of God. Avert from us all impending evils, and overrule all things so that our people may realize their highest hopes, and have their most ardent desires fulfilled. Merciful God, we beseech thee to hear us in these our supplications, and accept us in the name of the blessed Redeemer, unto whom, with thee and the holy spirit, be equal and everlasting praises—Amen.

The journal of yesterday was read and confirmed.

Mr. WITHERS, of South Carolina. Is there any business before the Congress, sir?

The PRESIDENT. None.

Mr. WITHERS. I have been informed that it is probable that the Committee (on the plan of a Provisional Government), now in session upon a matter important to this Convention, will be ready to report at 12 o'clock m. I make a motion, therefore, that we take a recess until the hour of 12 o'clock m.

The question was taken, and the motion was agreed to. So the Congress took a recess until 12 o'clock.

The hour of 12 o'clock having arrived, the President laid before the body communication from the Legislature of Alabama informing the Congress that that body had placed at its direction and control the sum of $500,000, and that seats within the bar of the House had been tendered to its members.

House of Representatives
Montgomery, Ala., Jan. 6, 1861

To the Hon. HOWELL COBB,
President of the Congress:

SIR:—The undersigned have been appointed a committee, on the part of the House of Representatives of the State of Alabama, to communicate to the Congress of Seceding States now in session in this city the enclosed act of the State of Alabama, placing at the disposal of the Congress, or the provisional government formed by them, by way of a loan, the sum of five hundred thousand dollars, for placing the Seceding States in a better condition of defence against any attack that may be made upon them by the Federal government of the United States.

We have also been directed by the same body to tender to the members of the Congress, seats on the floor of the House of Representatives.

We are very respectfully, your obedient servants,

S. F. Rice
F. S. Lyon
David Hubbard

The annexed is a copy of the act referred to in the above communication:

An act to appropriate five hundred thousand dollars to the cause of Southern independence:

SEC. 1. Be it enacted by the Senate and House of Representatives of the State of Alabama, in General Assembly convened, That the sum of five hundred thousand dollars be, and the same is hereby appropriated and placed at the disposal of the Southern Congress now is session, or of the Provisional government of the Confederacy or seceding States which the said Congress may establish, by way of a loan to said Provisional Government or Confederacy; and that the Governor be, and is hereby empowered and required to pay out the said sum of five hundred thousand dollars, in such amounts and at such times as the said Congress or Provisional government may direct, taking duly accredited receipts for the amounts so paid out: *Provided*, that it shall be left to the discretion of the Governor to pay the said amounts in coin, or in any currency of the State of Alabama, or in bonds of the State, or in the Treasury notes of this State, authorized to be issued under the authority of any law of this State.

A. B. MEEK,
Speaker House Representatives
JOHN D. RATHER,
President of the Senate
Approved 6th Feb. 1861
A. B. MOORE

Mr. HILL, of Georgia. I move that a committee of three be appointed by the Chair, to prepare and report for the adoption of this Congress a suitable response to the action of the General Assembly of Alabama, and that these papers be referred to that committee.

Mr. WITHERS. I offer the following resolution:

Resolved, That the Governor and the members of each house of the legislature be invited to occupy seats in this Congress during open sessions. Adopted

The question was taken, and the motion was agreed to.

The President appointed Mr. HILL, Mr. CONRAD and Mr. HARRIS said committee.

Mr. MEMMINGER, of South Carolina. If there is no other business that gentlemen wish to propose now in open session, I move that this Congress proceed to sit with closed doors.

No objection being made, the motion was agreed to. And accordingly the doors were closed, and the Congress proceeded to the consideration of secret business.

Congress went into secret session at 12 1/4 o'clock.

Friday, February 8, 1861

(Charleston *Mercury*, February 12, 1861; Montgomery *Weekly Advertiser*, February 13, 1861)[23]

The Congress was called to order by the President, Hon. HOWELL COBB, at 11 o'clock a.m.

Prayer was offered by Rev. A. D. PELLICER,[24] pastor of St. Peter's Catholic Church:

> O, eternal God! most holy and adorable Trinity! Father, Son and Holy Ghost—in whom we live, move and have our being—by whom we were created, redeemed and sanctified, we firmly believe that Thou art present in this assembly; and we, therefore, adore, praise and glorify Thee. We pray Thee, O God of might, wisdom and justice, through whom authority is rightly administered, laws are enacted, and judgment decreed, assist with Thy holy spirit of counsel, the representatives of these sovereign States, assembled together in Thy holy name, that, being duly impressed with their solemn representatives, they may be enabled, by Thy guidance, to frame such laws as may redound to Thy honor and glory in heaven, and to the promotion of peace and prosperity to Thy children on earth. Infuse, O, God of mercy, in the hearts of these representatives, Thy gentle spirit of love, meekness and humility.—Let the golden chain of brotherly love and union bind them firmly together, that they may speedily establish on a solid foundation a permanent government which may be cherished by all of us at home, and honored and respected abroad. Under the firmest conviction of our cause, and firmly relying on Thy divine protection, we humbly call on Thee, most merciful father, to direct the deliberations of the members of this Congress by Thy holy inspirations, and carry them on by Thy gracious assistance, that the great and glorious word for which they have assembled, in Thy name and for the independence, peace and happiness of Thy children, may always begin from Thee, and by Thee be happily ended, through Jesus Christ our Lord—Amen.

Mr. CHILTON, of Alabama, from the Committee appointed to invite the Clergy of the city of Montgomery to open the Congress with prayer, reported that the Committee had performed that duty, and that the invitation had been accepted by Rev. Mr. PETRIE in behalf of his fellow-clergymen; which was laid on the table.

> Montgomery, Ala., Feb. 6, 1861
>
> To the Hon. W. P. Chilton, J. L. M. Curry, S. F. Hale, Committee of Southern Congress—
>
> Gentlemen:—Your communication of this date to the Clergy of our city, containing a request of the Congress, to open its daily sessions with prayer, has been received by us, and it give us pleasure to inform you that we will comply. We will make arrangements among ourselves, for the regular performance of the service.
>
> With high consideration of yourselves, personally, and with fervent

desires to Almighty God for the body you represent, we are, your obedient servants,

George H. W. Petrie,
In behalf of the Clergy of Montgomery.

Mr. HILL, of Georgia, from the Committee appointed to prepare a suitable response to the communication of the General Assembly of the State of Alabama, enclosing a copy of an act, appropriating $500,000 for the cause of Southern independence, submitted a report, accompanied by the following resolutions:

Resolved, That this Congress accept the liberal offer of the General Assembly of the State of Alabama, to place at the disposal of this body the sum of $500,000 as a loan to the Government of the Confederacy now being formed.

Resolved, That this Congress places the highest appreciation on this generous and patriotic action of the State of Alabama, and realizes in it the zealous devotion of that people to the cause of Southern independence.

Resolved, That the Secretary of this body be instructed to transmit a copy of these resolutions to the General Assembly of the State of Alabama.

The question being taken, the resolutions were agreed to.

The PRESIDENT laid before the body a communication from the Judges of the Supreme Court of this state of Alabama, tendering the use of their library to the Southern Congress; which was laid on the table.

To the Hon. Howell Cobb,
President of the Southern Congress—

Sir:—The Libraries of the Supreme Court of the State of Alabama, and the State, are under the charge at the Judges of the Supreme Court. By authority of the Judges, I tender to the members of the body, over which you preside, the use of the Libraries and free access to the Library Rooms.

Very respectfully, your obedient servant,

A. J. Walker[25]
Chief Justice Supreme Court
Supreme Court Rooms
Feb. 8, 1861

Messrs. FEARN and LEWIS, deputies from Alabama, and Mr. CLAYTON, deputy from Mississippi, who were detained from reaching Montgomery, at an earlier day, appeared this morning and placed their names on the roll of the Congress.

Mr. RHETT, of South Carolina. If there is no other business before the Congress, I move that we go into secret session.

Mr. HILL. Before that is done, I desire to offer an additional resolution:

> And that a copy of the resolutions of the Congress in relation to the vote of $500,000 by the General Assembly of the State of Alabama, he communicated to that body.

The resolution was adopted.

Mr. MILES, of South Carolina. I move, sir, that the President of this Congress be requested to return the thanks of this body to the Judges of the Supreme Court of the State of Alabama, for the liberal tender of the use of their library.

The question was taken, and the motion was agreed to.

The motion of Mr. RHETT was then agreed to.[26] Accordingly, the doors were closed, and the Congress proceeded to the consideration of secret business.

Saturday, February 9, 1861

(Charleston *Mercury*, February 12, 1861; Montgomery *Weekly Advertiser*, February 13, 1861; Savannah *Daily Morning News,* February 11, 1861)

The Congress was called to order by the President, Hon. HOWELL COBB, at 11 o'clock a.m. As early as 10 o'clock, however, there was a large attendance in the Senate Chamber, attracted by the report that the Constitution had been adopted last night, and that the Deputies would this morning be sworn to support it.

Before the Congress proceeded to business, the following fervent petition was offered to Almighty God by the Rev. Dr. MANLY, formerly of Charleston:

> Almighty Father, we thank Thee for this auspicious morning, and all the happy circumstances which have attended this body in its daily deliberations. We thank Thee for the spirit of unity and concord. We thank Thee that the conflict of opinion leads only to unanimity of counsels, and we desire duly to acknowledge Thy kind and fatherly Providence in conducting the business of this important body, upon an occasion so critical and momentous, to such a state of progress as promises well for the country.
>
> Oh, our God, we know the crisis; we know the tremendous issues that are dependent upon us; we know that we have a chasm to pass, for which our strength will not be sufficient; but, "Oh God, Thou art our strength, our refuge, and a very present help in time of trouble;" and Thou hast bidden thy poor children to cast all care upon Thee, and hast promised that Thou wilt sustain them. In accordance with Thy promise, we draw nigh to Thy footstool. We confess our dependence upon Thee, and we come this morning to cast our toils and hopes and infirmities upon Thy providential guidance and blessing. Will it please Thee to own and accept all the business which has been heretofore done, and so far as the remaining business

may yet be in progress, we pray Thee to give to Thy servants who are engaged in it, strength and protection, and wisdom and power.

Oh! do Thou bestow on the officers of this body all needful impartiality, and wisdom, and self-command; and God grant that the members, individually and severally, may have purity of purpose, enlightened consciences, matured and consecrated judgments, and unfaltering resolution and will; and God be merciful and bestow upon them all such measure of Thy Holy Spirit that they may in this work obey Thy blessed will "not more, not less, not sooner, not later," than duty and the public good require; and God grant that all the events, and issues, and engagements of the day may be so formed, and accepted, and guided of God that good may be the result, and only good. And we humbly pray for our late associates, that they may not become nor attempt to become our oppressors and enemies. We pray Thee that they may be directed to such measures on their part, that while they leave us in the unrestricted enjoyment of the rights that God has given us, they may secure their own in the happiest and best manner, and may settle down into a community at once peaceful and friendly to us, as it is our purpose, our deliberate desire, to be towards them.

And now, Almighty Father, save us, if consistent with Thy will, from the horrors of war, and God grant that all matters may be so directed that a peaceful and happy settlement may be effected, and that our own sections of the country may accomplish their great purpose—the formation of a Government—that may endure as long as the sun and moon, and to the Father, Son, and ever Blessed Spirit be endless praise. Amen.

The Journal of yesterday was then read and approved.

The PRESIDENT. The business first in order this morning is the administration to the members of the Congress of the oath to support the Constitution for the Provisional Government.

In the midst of a solemn silence, and with great dignity, Judge WALKER, of the Supreme Court of Alabama, then came forward and administered the oath to the President.[27]

"You do solemnly swear that you will support the Constitution for the Provisional Government of the Confederate States of America."

Mr. MEMMINGER, of South Carolina. Mr. President, I respectfully suggest, that upon the administration of the oath, the Congress be requested to rise.

The PRESIDENT. The oath will be administered to each of the delegations separately, and, at the suggestion of the gentleman from South Carolina, the members of the Congress are requested to rise while the oath is being administered.

The States were, then called separately, and the President proceeded to administer the oath.

The State of Alabama having been called, the delegation representing it advanced to the President's chair, and placed their hands upon the Bible in his hand, the other members of the Congress at the same moment rising.

The PRESIDENT (to the Delegation). You, and each of you, do solemnly swear that you will support the Constitution of the Provisional Government for the Confederated States of America. So help you God:

To which the delegation responded: "We will," and kissed the book.

The other States were then called in their alphabetical order, South Carolina being last, and the oath to support the Provisional Government was administered to them in the same manner.

A more solemn scene has not been witnessed since the ratification of the old Constitution, and there was not a person present who did not feel relief when it was over. Hope beams on every countenance, and the general exclamation is: "We have a good Constitution, and all will be well."

The PRESIDENT. The business next in order is the call of the States in their alphabetical order, for memorials, resolutions, &c.,

The Clerk will proceed to call the roll.

The State of South Carolina having been called—

Mr. MEMMINGER said: Mr. President, I conceive this a fitting occasion to discharge a commission which has been entrusted to me, by some of my constituents in South Carolina. I have before me a model flag, which I have the honor to be requested by some of the young ladies of Charleston to present to this Congress, as the model flag for the Confederated States of the South.[28] This flag, as will be seen upon inspection, embraces the idea of a cross—a blue cross upon a red ground. No doubt, Mr. President, the idea of the cross was suggested to the imagination of these young ladies by that glorious constellation which the Great Creator has placed in the Southern heavens, as a substitute for the great constellation which is situated at the Northern pole;[29] and I have no doubt that that cross has been consecrated in the imagination of these ladies by the genius of Dante and the scientific skill of Humboldt.[30] And I have as little doubt that in their minds was also associated a religious idea. They had read of the Le Baron of Constantine,[31] and although we have not seen in the heavens the *in hoc signo vinces*,[32] yet we have seen that written by the Almighty upon the tablets of the earth, and we know it is by the aid of the revealed religion that the South has been enabled to fight the battles against fanaticism and to achieve the victory which you this day witness. It is not at all unbecoming that on such an occasion the duty of the South to the cross should be recognized, and in looking to those who first planted its standard, and first preached its doctrines, the South would recognize in these symbols those borne by its champions and defenders.

I have, also, another commission from a gentleman of taste and skill in the city of Charleston (Lieut. HAMILTON),[33] to offer another model flag, which embraces the same idea upon a different ground. The gentleman who offers this appears to be more hopeful than the ladies. They offer seven stars—six now represented in this Congress—the seventh, we trust, on her way from Texas. This flag embraces the whole fifteen. God grant that we may see them in some day. [*Applause*] But, sir, I present them to the Convention, and request that on a fitting occasion they may receive the proper consideration of the Congress.

Mr. MILES, of South Carolina. Mr. President, in continuation of the subject my colleague has introduced, I would suggest that a Committee be raised—to consist of one from each Delegation, to be chosen by the respective Delegations—to be a Committee on Selecting a Flag for the Confederated States of America.

Mr. STEPHENS, of Georgia. I second the motion.

The question was taken, and the motion was agreed to.

The PRESIDENT. The chair understands that no action will be taken, at present, in relation to the flag which has been presented.

Mr. STEPHENS. I suggest that the States be called, and the deputies select the member for the committee.

As the States were called, the following gentlemen were chosen members of the Committee: Messrs. SHORTER of Alabama, MORTON of Florida, BARTOW of Georgia, SPARROW of Louisiana, HARRISON of Mississippi, and MILES of South Carolina.

Mr. CRAWFORD, of Georgia. Mr. President, I understand that there is no business upon the calendar. I move, then, that the Congress do now go into Secret Session.

Mr. STEPHENS. I hope the gentleman will withdraw his motion for a moment.

Mr. CRAWFORD. I will.

Mr. STEPHENS. I present the following resolution:

> *Resolved*, That the President proceed to appoint the following Standing Committees, to consist of five members each: A Committee on Foreign Affairs; a Committee on Finances; a Committee on Military Affairs; a Committee on Naval Affairs; a Committee on the Judiciary; a Committee on Postal Affairs; a Committee on Commercial Affairs; a Committee on Accounts; a Committee on Engrossment; a Committee on Patents, and a Committee on Printing.

Mr. TOOMBS, of Georgia. I suggest that the Military and Naval Committees be combined in one.

Mr. STEPHENS. I accept the modification.

The question was then taken, and the resolution was agreed to.

Mr. CRAWFORD then renewed his motion which was agreed to. Accordingly, the Congress proceeded to sit with closed doors.

After remaining in secret session for about half an hour,[34] the doors were opened, and Congress proceeded to the election of a President and a Vice-President of the Confederate States of America under the provisional government.

Messrs. CURRY of Alabama, and MILES, of South Carolina, were appointed tellers to count the votes, and then the Congress proceeded to ballot for a President by States.

After some time the tellers reported that Hon. JEFFERSON DAVIS, of Mississippi, had received six votes, and he was declared unanimously elected.

The Congress then proceeded to ballot for a Vice-President, which resulted in the unanimous choice of Hon. ALEXANDER H. STEPHENS, of Georgia.

The announcement was hailed with applause on the floor and in the galleries, which brought down the gavel of the President.

Mr. TOOMBS moved that a committee of three be appointed to inform the Hon. JEFFERSON DAVIS, of Miss., of his election. Adopted.

Messrs. TOOMBS, RHETT and MORTON were appointed as the committee.

Mr. PERKINS moved that a committee of three be appointed to inform Hon. A. H. STEPHENS, of Ga., of his election. Adopted.

Messrs. PERKINS, HARRIS and SHORTER were appointed.[35]

On motion of Mr. RHETT, of South Carolina, the Congress then resumed its secret session.

Monday, February 11, 1861

(Charleston *Mercury*, February 14, 1861; Montgomery *Weekly Advertiser*, February 13, 1861; Savannah *Daily Morning News*, February 13, 1861)

The Congress was called to order by the President, Hon. HOWELL COBB, at 11 o'clock.

Prayer was offered by Rev. Mr. BATTLE, President of the Tuscaloosa Central Female Institute.[36]

> Almighty God, our Heavenly Father, we humbly recognize thy hand over us. We would humbly acknowledge thy Providence in the events of this world's history; and we would gratefully acknowledge thy kind care and providence over us at this present hour. We thank thee that thou hast permitted us to establish a new confederacy under such propitious omens. Oh! we humbly thank thee for this great mercy, and we pray thee that in thy kindness and mercy, we may continue as peaceful, prosperous States, to the remotest ages of time. We pray thee let thy blessings rest upon this body; oh, grant wisdom to their counsels and direction to their actions, so that all things may be done in accordance with thy will, and redound to the glory of thy name. Hear us, oh God; forgive our sins, and accept us through Christ Jesus our Redeemer, to whom, with the Father and the Holy Spirit, be glory everlasting—Amen.

The journals of Saturday were read and confirmed.

Mr. PERKINS, of Louisiana. Mr. President, the committee appointed to inform the Vice-President elect of his election, and invite his acceptance of the office are prepared to report. They have discharged that duty, and at the request of the committee, Mr. STEPHENS will announce his reply to their letter in person at one o'clock, at which time it is the desire of the committee that the doors be opened and that we have a public session. I now move, sir, as I understand there are some business matters which require secret session, that the galleries be cleared, and that we go into secret session.

The PRESIDENT. The motion first in order will be on the reception of the report of the Committee.

Mr. CONRAD, of Louisiana. I beg my colleague to withdraw that motion for a moment.

Mr. PERKINS. I will.

Mr. CONRAD. I beg leave to offer the following resolution.

The PRESIDENT. In connection with the report of the committee?

Mr. CONRAD. No, sir.

The PRESIDENT. Before the resolution is read, the Chair will state that the Congress has heard the report of the committee appointed to wait upon the Vice-President elect. If there is no objection, it will be ordered that at one o'clock today the Congress will receive the answer of the Vice President elect in person, at which time the doors will be opened and the proceedings will be public.

The report was received and adopted.

The gentleman from Louisiana offers the following resolution:

> *Resolved*, That a Committee composed of _____ members be appointed by the Chair, whose duty it shall be to prepare and report a Bill providing for the establishment of the Executive Departments of the Confederacy.

The PRESIDENT. Does the gentleman propose immediate action upon his resolution? If so, it will be necessary to fill the blank.

Mr. CONRAD. I move the blank be filled with the number five.

The PRESIDENT. The question will then be on the adoption of the resolution.

The question was taken, and the resolution was agreed to.

Mr. STEPHENS. Mr. President, I offer the following resolution.

> *Resolved*, That so much of the resolution passed on Saturday, as combined the Committees on Military and Naval Affairs, be reconsidered, and that the following amendments be added: a Committee on Territories, a Committee on Public Lands, and a Committee on Indian Affairs.

The Naval and Military Committees ought not to be combined. The other committees seem also to be necessary.

The resolution was agreed to.

The question was then taken on the motion of Mr. PERKINS, and it was agreed to. Accordingly, the Congress proceeded to sit with closed doors.

A little before one o'clock the doors of Congress were again thrown open, and the lobbies and galleries were soon densely filled with citizens, among whom were a large number of ladies.

The PRESIDENT. The Chair will state that he has received several patterns for a flag for the Confederate States. If there is no objection, they will be referred to the Committee on that subject.

No objection was made.[37]

The PRESIDENT. The hour has arrived, gentlemen, for hearing the response of the Vice-President elect to the communication of the Committee appointed by this body to inform him of his election.

MR. STEPHENS rose in his place and said:

> Mr. President: I have been notified by a Committee of this body of my election to the office of Vice-President under the Provisional Government, established for the Confederate States of America. The notification is in a letter, which I beg leave to read:
>
> Montgomery, Ala. February 9, 1861
>
> SIR: The Congress of the Provisional Government for the Confederate States of America have this day unanimously elected you to the office of Vice-President of the Confederate States, and we have been appointed to communicate the fact and to respectfully invite your acceptance.
>
> In performing this pleasing duty, allow us to express the hope that you will accept; and we beg to suggest that it would be most agreeable to the body we represent, as you are a member of the Congress, that you should signify to it in person your consent to serve the country in the high position to which you have been called.
>
> We have the honor to be,
> Very Respectfully, yours,
>
> JOHN PERKINS, JR.
> W. P. HARRIS
> JOHN GILL SHORTER
> To Hon. ALEX. H. STEPHENS
>
> From this it appears to be the general desire that I should in person make known to the body in a verbal response my acceptance of the high position to which I have been called.
>
> This I now do. I, in this august presence, before you, Mr. President, before the Congress and before this large concourse of people, under the bright sun and brilliant skies which now smile so auspiciously upon us—I

now take the occasion to return my most profound acknowledgements for this expression of confidence on the part of Congress. There are special reasons why I place an unusually high estimate on it. The considerations that induce me to accept it I need not state; suffice it to say, that it may be deemed questionable whether any good citizen can refuse to discharge any duty that may be assigned him by his country in an hour of need.

It might be expected that I should, at this time, indulge in some remarks upon the state of our public affairs, the dangers that threaten us, and the most advisable measures to be adopted to meet pressing exigencies. Allow me to say, that, in the absence of the distinguished gentleman who has been called to the Chief Executive chair, I think it best to forbear to say anything on such matters. We expect him here in a few days—by Wednesday, of this week, at furthest, unless providentially detained longer. When he comes we will hear from him on all these difficult questions, and I doubt not we shall cordially and harmoniously concur in the line of policy his superior wisdom and superior statesmanship shall indicate. In the meantime there are matters we may very profitably be directing our attention to; such as making provision for the transfer of the custom houses from the jurisdiction of the separate States to the Confederacy, and the imposition of such duties as will be necessary to meet present and expected exigencies. In the exercise of the power to levy duties, we are limited to the objects of revenue. A small duty, not exceeding 10 per cent., upon importations, it is believed will be sufficient. [*Applause*].

And, above all, in the interim, between this and the arrival and inauguration of the President, we can be devoting our attention to the construction of a Permanent Government, stable and durable, which is one of the leading objects of our assembling.

I am now ready to take the oath of office. [*Applause*]

At the close of the address, which was listened to with breathless attention by the immense auditory, save when a suppressed murmur of applause marked his allusion to a low standard of import duties, Mr. STEPHENS approached the President's desk, where he received the sacred volume from the hands of Mr. COBB, President of the Provisional Congress, and who administered to him the following solemn oath:

The PRESIDENT. You do solemnly swear that you will faithfully execute the office of Vice-President of the Confederate States of America, and will, to the best of your ability, preserve, protect and defend the Constitution thereof, so help you God?

To which Mr. STEPHENS responded Aye, and kissed the book, amidst the applause of the spectators.

Mr. BARNWELL, of South Carolina. Mr. President, I move that the letter addressed by the Committee of the Congress to the Hon. ALEXANDER H. STEPHENS, informing him of his election to the office of Vice-President of the Confederate States of America, together with his reply to the same, be entered upon the Journal of the Congress.

The question was then taken and the motion agreed to.

Mr. PERKINS, of Louisiana. I now move that the Congress adjourn till the usual hour to-morrow.

Mr. RHETT, of South Carolina. Congress has very little to do, except that which engages the attention of the committees. I move, therefore, that when we adjourn, we adjourn to meet to-morrow at 12 o'clock, so as to give the committees time to perfect their labors.

The motion was agreed to, and then the Congress adjourned till to-morrow.

Tuesday, February 12, 1861

(Charleston *Mercury*, February 15, 1861; Montgomery *Weekly Advertiser*, February 20, 1861)

The Congress met at 12 o'clock, m., and was called to order by the President, Hon. HOWELL COBB.

After prayer by the Rev Mr. MITCHELL, the Journal of yesterday was read and approved.

The PRESIDENT. The Chair will announce the Standing Committees he was directed to make. It is proper to state, with reference to the Committee to organize the Executive Departments, that the Chair has departed from the usual parliamentary rule, but has appointed it in accordance with the views of the gentleman from Louisiana (Mr. CONRAD).[38]

Committee to Organize the Executive Departments—Messrs. STEPHENS, CONRAD, BOYCE, SHORTER and BROOKE.

Committee on Foreign Affairs—Messrs. RHETT, NISBET, PERKINS, WALKER and KEITT

Committee on Finance—Messrs. TOOMBS, BARNWELL, KENAN, BARRY and MCRAE

Committee on Commercial Affairs—Messrs. MEMMINGER, CRAWFORD, MORTON, CURRY and DECLOUET

Committee on the Judiciary—Messrs. CLAYTON, WITHERS, HALE, THOMAS R. R. COBB and HARRIS

Committee on Naval Affairs—Messrs. CONRAD, CHESNUT, SMITH, WRIGHT and OWEN

Committee on Military Affairs—Messrs. BARTOW, MILES, SPARROW, KENAN and ANDERSON

Committee on Postal Affairs—Messrs. SHORTER, HILL, BOYCE, HARRISON and CURRY

Committee on Patents—Messrs. BROOKE, WILSON, LEWIS, HILL and KENNER

Committee on Territories—Messrs. CHESNUT, MARSHALL, CAMPBELL, NISBET and FEARNE

Committee on Public Lands—Messrs. MARSHALL, HARRIS, FEARNE, ANDERSON and WRIGHT

Committee on Indian Affairs—Messrs. MORTON, HALE, KEITT, LEWIS and SPARROW

Committee on Printing—Messrs. THOMAS R. R. COBB, HARRISON, MILES, CHILTON and PERKINS

Committee on Accounts—Messrs. OWEN, CRAWFORD, CAMPBELL, SMITH and DECLOUET

Committee on Engrossments—Messrs. SHORTER, WILSON, KENAN, MCRAE and BARTOW

The PRESIDENT. The Chair received, a few moments since, the following telegraphic dispatch, which he will lay before Congress:

New Orleans, February 9, 1861

To the Hon. HOWELL COBB,
President of the Montgomery Convention—

SIR—I am directed to communicate to you that during the session of the Convention of the State of Louisiana this morning, upon the receipt of the dispatch informing us of the election of the Hon. JEFFERSON DAVIS as President, and the Hon. ALEXANDER H. STEPHENS as Vice-President of the Provisional Government of the Southern Republic, Mr. President MORTON immediately suspended the regular business of the Convention then under consideration, and announced the agreeable intelligence to the Convention; whereupon the following resolutions were offered and unanimously adopted:

Resolved, That this Convention received, with the most cordial approval the intelligence this day received by telegraph of the election of JEFFERSON DAVIS of Mississippi, as President, and ALEXANDER H. STEPHENS, of Georgia, as Vice-President of the Provisional Government of the Southern Republic.

Resolved, That the Secretary of this Convention be instructed to communicate the foregoing resolution to the President of the Convention at Montgomery.

Very respectfully
Your obedient servant,

J. THOMAS WHEAT
Secretary of the State Convention

The PRESIDENT. What course will the Congress take with reference to this dispatch?

Mr. BARTOW, of Georgia. I move that it be placed on the Journal.

The question was taken, and the motion was agreed to.

Mr. COBB, of Georgia. I hold in my hand, Mr. President, a design for a seal and coats of arms, and a design for a flag for the Confederate States of America, sent to me by a son of Georgia. I move that it be referred to the select committee on the flag.

The designs were accordingly referred. (It may be well to state that the designs were from Mr. E. V. SHARPE, an Artist of Augusta, Georgia.)[39] [document I; image I and II]

The question was taken and the motion was agreed to.

Mr. HARRIS, of Mississippi. I offer the following resolution:

> *Resolved*, That until otherwise provided, the several offices connected with the collection of customs, duties and imposts, in the several States of this Confederacy, be and they are hereby confirmed and continued in the office in the various ports of this Confederacy.

My object, Mr. President, is to direct the attention of the Committee of Commerce at once to this subject, and therefore I move that it be referred to that Committee.

The question was taken, and the motion was agreed to.

On motion of Mr. NISBET, the following resolution was adopted:

> *Resolved*, That the Committee on Foreign Affairs be requested to inquire into the propriety and necessity of sending, so soon as the President elect shall be inaugurated, a commission to the Government of the United States of America, for the purpose of procuring the recognition of the Confederate States of America by that Government.[40]

Mr. CRAWFORD, of Georgia, would submit to his colleague whether it would not be as well to strike out the words "for the purpose of securing the recognition," &c. As instructions to a commission to any European State these words would be necessary and proper, but the commission to the Government of the United States would have other important matters in charge, and he thought, therefore, that the words which would seem to limit their powers might as well be omitted.

The resolution was then read, as follows:

> *Resolved*, That the Committee on Foreign Affairs be requested to enquire into the propriety and necessity of sending, so soon as the President elect shall be inaugurated, a commission to the Government of the United States of America.

Mr. CRAWFORD. I suggest the propriety of modifying the resolution, so as to leave out all the duties to be performed by the commission.

Mr. RHETT, of South Carolina. As it is a mere matter of enquiry, I suppose it might as well go to the Committee as it is. It is of no importance in what phraseology it is committed to that Committee.

Mr. NISBET. My object was not to invite any discussion whatever on this subject to-day. It is simply a resolution of inquiry directed to the Committee on Foreign Affairs. I think that the importance of the duties of that commission will finally be so great that perhaps it is best, in the first instance, to confine them to the mere recognition of our independence. That is a very important thing, and it is very important that it should be attended to. However, upon reflection, as the Committee will have the whole matter under consideration, I am willing to accept the modification of my colleague.

The question was then taken, and the resolution was agreed to.

Mr. STEPHENS. I move that the Clerk have printed, for the use of the Congress, one hundred copies of the Committees announced from the Chair to-day, in order that we may have them on our desk for reference.

The question was then taken, and the motion was agreed to.

Mr. STEPHENS. As the committees just announced have no business upon which to report, I move that the Congress adjourn till 12 o'clock m., to-morrow.

Mr. COBB. I hope my colleague will withdraw that motion for a moment.

Mr. STEPHENS. I do.

Mr. COBB. Then I move that we go into secret session.

The motion was agreed to, and the Congress proceeded to sit with closed doors.

Wednesday, February 13, 1861

(Charleston *Mercury*, February 16, 1861; Charleston *Courier*, February 19, 1861; Montgomery *Weekly Advertiser*, February 20, 1861)

The Congress met at 12 o'clock, m., and was called to order by the President, Hon. HOWELL COBB, of Georgia. After prayer by the Rev. Mr. J. C. DAVIS, of the Montgomery Methodist Protestant Church, the Journal of yesterday was read and adopted.

Mr. STEPHENS, of Georgia. I have received a model of a flag from Mr. J. B. PLATT, of Augusta.[41] I present it, and ask that it be referred to the Committee on Flags. [document II; image III]

The PRESIDENT. If there is no objection it will be so ordered.

No objection was made.

Mr. STEPHENS. I have also received a communication on the same subject from another source in Augusta, and also from a citizen of Richmond county.[42] I move that these papers be referred to the same Committee.

The motion was agreed to.

Mr. WRIGHT, of Georgia. Mr. President, I have received a communication which I ask leave to lay before the Congress.

The communication was read by the Clerk, as follows:

Etowah, Ga., February 11, 1861

Hon. A. R. WRIGHT, Montgomery, Ala.:

Dear SIR: As my more immediate representative in the new Congress, I write to you. The new Government must have the means of defence. It must, in the shortest time, put up an armory to cost $500,000, or it must contract with parties for a million of dollars worth of arms, to be made at home in the promptest time.

I can furnish the location the most eligible in the South or I can take the contract. This will be a great matter to the South.

MARK A. COOPER[43]

Mr. WRIGHT (resuming). I copied such portions of the letter as are of a general character, and I ask leave to make one or two observations on this subject before making a motion to refer it to the appropriate committee.

These works have been already established, and they are in successful operation. As is said in the communication, it is perhaps the most eligible site in the South. They are located on the Etowah river, three miles from the Western and Atlantic Railroad—the great trunk constructed by the State of Georgia, connecting the roads of the North and West with those of the South and Gulf. The enterprising gentleman at the head of these works has constructed, at his own expense, a railroad along the banks of [the Etowah] river to the State road, a distance of three or three and a half miles. The ore is said to be equal to any in the Union. I believe it has so proved itself. The works are extensive, and capable of turning out almost any amount of ordnance, with a little preparation that may be necessary. The site is exceedingly eligible on account of its locality. There is no point in the South with which it does not immediately communicate. The railroads of the North terminate at Chattanooga, whence various branches go to the West as well as the North. From Atlanta it is in communication with this point, with Charleston, Savannah, and soon will be with Pensacola. I cannot conceive of any site that could be more eligible than the one where these works happen to be located.

Again, sir, as to the character of the gentleman at the head of them. He is known to most of the members of this body by reputation, if not personality. He is a man of vast energy, enterprise and intellect. I doubt whether Georgia has his superior in either of these three particulars.—What he undertakes to do, he will do. What he promises, he will perform. I hope, therefore, this communication will receive a favorable reception from this body. The usual, and perhaps, the most proper committee to which to refer it, would be the Committee on Military Affairs, but I would ask leave of the House to have this referred to the Committee on Finance, not because I have any objection to the Military Committee itself, which is eminently satisfactory to myself, but from the fact that the gentleman at the head of the Committee on Finance has a personal knowledge of these works, and a personal acquaintance with the distinguished gentleman who makes the application here, and I presume would have the leisure, by diligence in his other business, to make the report.[44] From that circumstance, and also that it involves a heavy expenditure of money, I would move its reference to the Committee on Finance, with instructions to make a special report on the subject.

Mr. CURRY, of Alabama. Mr. President, I have two or three memorials relating to the same subject matter as that contained in the letter read at the instance of the gentleman from Georgia, suggesting different localities in the State of Alabama, as suitable sites for a foundry to be established for the Confederate States, defining (as the gentlemen are peculiarly interested) as geological and mineralogical surveys have demonstrated, all and probably more of what is requisite for such an establishment than those mentioned in the letter of the distinguished gentleman from Georgia. I have not them in my possession, or I would introduce them now. I will take an early occasion to do so.[45]

I rise merely to suggest that there is no special reason why this matter should not be referred to the appropriate Committee, the Committee on Military Affairs, and I apprehend that there is no Committee in this House, even that presided over by the very distinguished gentleman from Georgia (Mr. TOOMBS), to whom it is proposed to refer this subject, would be willing to undertake the final location of a matter of so much importance as this, without its first being submitted to a scientific survey or examined by a competent officer of the army. I presume this Congress will hardly undertake to locate an establishment of this sort until a survey is made. I hope the gentleman from Georgia will either refer it to the Committee on Military Affairs or ask that a Special Committee may be raised on the subject, to whom the matter may be referred. Probably that will answer his purpose quite as well as being referred to the Committee on Finance. But, as I said, I merely rise to state that at some subsequent time I will introduce memorials on the same subject matter, and to express the opinion that this Congress should, at a very early period, establish a national foundry.

Mr. WRIGHT. Mr. President, I will adhere to my propositions unless some satisfactory reasons are given for a different course. These works, as I have before remarked, are not to be constructed; they are already *in esse*.[46] They are of an extensive character, and immense quantities of railroad iron have been made at these works. They can, at short notice, turn out any amount of ordnance required. The reason why I desire it referred to the Committee on Finance is because of the personal knowledge of the gentleman at the head of that Committee, of the gentleman at the head of these works. He [Cooper] is not only a man distinguished as a civilian; he has not only served in Congress but in the field; and that, I should think, would make a great deal of difference in the action of the House, not by any means disparaging those gentlemen whom the gentleman from Alabama may present,—but

I should think it would have an important bearing on the minds of the gentlemen of this House to the character of the gentleman who proposed to execute this work. On that ground, and because the gentleman at the head of the Committee on Finance has a personal acquaintance with these works, I prefer its reference to that Committee. I shall be satisfied, however, to have it referred to any committee that the body may deem proper.

The question was then taken on the motion to refer to the Committee on Finance; and it was decided in the negative.

Mr. CURRY moved that it be referred to a select committee of five, which motion did not prevail.

On motion of Mr. CONRAD, of Louisiana, the following resolution was agreed to:

> *Resolved*, That the Committee on Military Affairs and the Committee on Naval Affairs be instructed to include in any plan they may propose in the organization of the army and the navy, suitable provision for such officers of the army and the navy of the United States as may have tendered in a resignation of their commissions in consequence of their adhesion to any or all of the States of this Confederacy.

The resolution was adopted.

Mr. CRAWFORD, of Georgia, presented a communication from Dr. HENRY M. JETER,[47] the postmaster at Columbus, Ga., conveying some important intelligence; which was referred to the Committee on Postal Affairs, without being read.

Mr. MEMMINGER. I beg leave to offer the following resolution:

> *Resolved*, That the Committee on Commercial Affairs be instructed to inquire and report upon the expediency of repealing the Navigation Laws of the Confederate States, and that they have leave to report by bill.

I will beg leave to state to the Congress that I would not be disposed to report a resolution effecting a permanent change of the government before the inauguration of the President, except in case of necessity; but by the passage of the resolution making of force the laws of the United States, the laws in regard to the enrollment and registry of vessels are now of force, and consequently any vessel coming from a foreign State without this Confederacy, has no right to be admitted without paying the tonnage duties upon foreign vessels, and no vessel has a right to carry on the internal trade without being owned by citizens of the Confederacy. This condition of affairs will remain until the President arrives and the government is permanently organized. Therefore to avoid that, I have taken leave to offer this resolution. It is one of inquiry for the committee. I trust the committee will report speedily, and that the Congress will be prepared to act speedily.

The question was taken, and the resolution was agreed to.

Mr. BROOKE, of Mississippi. Mr. President, in connection with the motion made by the delegate from Georgia (Mr. STEPHENS), on presenting the model of a flag, I propose, sir, to offer the following resolution. I think, sir, it is a matter of much importance that the subject should be acted upon immediately. It is time, sir, that we had a national flag floating from the forts and arsenals already in our possession, and the time will soon arrive when that flag should float from the fortresses of Sumter and Pickens. [*Slight applause*] In order, sir, to hasten the action of the committee on that subject, I will offer the following resolution:

> *Resolved*, That the Committee on the Flag and Seal of the Confederacy be instructed to adopt and report a flag as similar as possible to the flag of the United States of America, making only such changes as may be necessary to distinguish easily the one from the other, and to adapt the former in the arrangement of its stars and stripes to the number of States in this Confederacy.

The object of that resolution, sir, as will be perceived, is to depart in our new flag as little as possible from the old. In revolutionary times, sir, it is desirable to make as little change as possible. Those things to which the people have long been accustomed we should respect, even their prejudices. The flag of the United States is the emblem of the former glory, strength and power of the union.[48]—We, sir, as well as the Northern Confederacy, have an interest in the past. True, sir, it is an emblem; but, sir, the feelings that follow that emblem are not the result merely of custom and habit. It is the result, sir, of association. It is the ideal of the heart, around which, sir, clusters the memories of the past, which it can never efface or cause to grow dim. That flag, sir, is not associated in our recollections with any of the injuries which have precipitated this revolution upon us. It is only connected in our recollection with the victories on land and sea that we won in the last war with Great Britain. It is connected also, sir, in our recollections with the glorious Mexican war, where, sir, 'mid the flame and smoke, and roar of battle, it was baptized in blood at Buena Vista, and Monterey, and Chapultepec. There is no reason why the North should appropriate that to itself. It is eminently a Southern flag. It is connected, sir, with one of the best of our national airs ["The Star-Spangled Banner"]. It is true, sir, that air is of Irish extraction—Anacreon in Heaven[49]—but the words, sir, were written by a Southern man imprisoned on a British man-of-war, in Southern waters, in the act of bombarding a Southern fort; and we can well imagine his emotions, when through "the dawn's early light" he saw that flag floating over that fort where last he had seen it in "twilight's last gleaming." Sir, let us preserve that flag as long as we can. Let us still invoke upon it the blessings of Heaven, and let us still pray—"Long may it wave over the land of the free and the home of the brave."

Mr. MILES, of South Carolina. I trust the motion of the honorable gentleman from Mississippi will not be adopted by the Congress. Should it be, sir, I would be very much disposed, with the concurrence of my colleagues on the committee on the choice of a flag, to ask to be discharged from the further consideration of the subject. We conceived that the whole matter had been referred to us in order that we might deliberately compare our views, receive suggestions from all quarters, and make then such a report to this body as we could agree upon. Then the whole matter could be discussed, and this Congress could accept, reject or modify the report as to them might seem best. But, sir, if we are to be instructed to report a certain flag, it appears to me we are but as a committee *functus officio*.[50] All option or discretion will be taken out of our hands.

But, sir, I have, I confess, a further objection to the resolution. I do not concur in the spirit of the resolution or in the tenor of the remarks which have just been made by the honorable gentleman from Mississippi. I confess, sir, and I may be singular, that I am not one of those who can entirely separate my repugnance to a hostile government; one which has been tyrannical and oppressive, as we believe it, to such an extent that we have been compelled to throw off its authority. I cannot accept the ensign of that government.

Again, sir, I may be singular in the sentiments which I have entertained from childhood. Whenever I have seen that flag floating on the soil of my native State I have felt that it was not a friendly flag, not an ensign to which we looked for justice and protection. I admit, sir, as much as any man, the force of association, of the noble sentiments which cluster around the ensigns of one's country; but, sir, whenever a people engage in revolutionary movements they have to sever not only ties binding them politically, but many of the most endearing associations of our nature. Why, sir, in our revolution think not that our people did not abandon the glorious flag of their fathers with some reluctance, with some pain. We felt that the glories of Old England were old glories. We felt, sir, that we had a portion in the history of the mother country from Magna Carta down to the revolution of '80. We felt, sir, that the historical glories of Cressy and Agincourt were a portion of our own. Yet we abandoned that flag and adopted our flag; and does it not seem essential, when a people establish an independent political existence, that they should have some independent symbol?

The gentleman, sir, speaks of the glories which we achieved in Mexico under the flag of the United States. I trust, I can, with due modesty, say that the Palmetto regiment in Mexico bathed the Palmetto flag in blood, so gallantly borne at their head.[51]

A hearty burst of applause from the galleries.

The PRESIDENT. There must be order in the galleries.

Mr. MILES (resuming). That flag, sir, that State flag is dearer to our hearts than the ensign or flag of the United States, for it was under that flag that the battle of Fort Moultrie was fought, and the battles of Eutaw, Cowpens and King's Mountain. I have not been one of those who put a very high estimate upon the Stars and Stripes so far as they are associated with the glories of the Revolution. Most of the great battles of the Revolution were not fought under that flag, as is well known—notorious—but under separate banners of the independent sovereign States then struggling for recognition by the nations of the world.

Mr. President, I did not anticipate any such discussion as this. Sir, I am not prepared to enter upon it *in extenso*.[52] I only hope that the House will not act hastily, and allow the Committee to prepare some plan and submit it, and then the whole subject will come up for discussion.

Mr. BROOKE. Mr. President, at the suggestion of a friend I withdraw the resolution for the present.

Mr. RHETT. I move that we go into secret session.

The motion was agreed to; and accordingly, the Congress proceeded to sit with closed doors.

Thursday, February 14, 1861

(Charleston *Mercury*, February 18, 1861; Montgomery *Weekly Advertiser*, February 20, 1861)

The Congress met at 12 o'clock m., and was called to order by the President, Hon. HOWELL COBB.

After prayer by the Rev. Mr. TICHENOR, the Journal of yesterday was read and approved.

Mr. BOYCE, of South Carolina. Mr. President, I rise for the purpose of presenting to the Congress, with the view of reference to the appropriate committee, two models for the flag of our Confederacy.

One of them has been sent to me by a gentleman of Columbia, S. C., the beautiful capital of my State, the seat of refinement and intelligence, where the Southern heart beats as ardently as at any spot within our limits. [document III; image IV]

The other is sent to me by a lady, with whom I am well acquainted, a neighbor of mine, who resides in the picturesque town of Winnsboro', Fairfield District, South Carolina. She is a lady of remarkable intelligence, whose path through life has been illustrated by all those virtues which adorn the female character. I will take the liberty of reading her letter to the Congress. It is full of authentic fire. It is worthy of Rome in her best days, and might well have been read in the Roman Senate on that disastrous day when the victorious banner of the great Carthaginian was visible from Mount Aventine,[53] and I may add, sir, that as long as our women are impelled by these sublime sentiments, and our mountains yield the metals out of which weapons are forged, the lustrous stars of our unyielding Confederacy will never pale their glorious fires, though battled oppression may threaten with its impotent sword, or, more dangerous still, seek to beguile with the siren song of reconciliation:

Southern Confederacy
Winnsboro, S.C., February 10, 1861

Hon. W. W. BOYCE—

SIR: Enclosed I send to you a flag for the new Republic, designed by Mr. LADD,[54] which is simple, as all national flags should be. It is tricolored, with a red union, seven stars and the crescent moon. It was all the design of Mr. L., with the exception of the stars in a circle or wreath, and placing the crescent moon among them, which I thought would be a fit emblem of our young Republic; and by placing the stars in a wreath others could be added, forming a large wreath as the other States came in. [image V]

I am vain enough, if you please to term it so (but I term it patriotism), to feel that I would wish no greater honor than to see the slightest thing I had a hand in adopted by the Southern Confederacy.

We have three boys to give to our country. Words could not express the glow of pride that throbbed our bosoms when I saw them ready to respond to their country's call. My boys are part of a mother's jewels, freely given when needed. My next greatest glory would be to see the design adopted and flung to the breeze.

> "May it yet be unfurled,
> Floating proudly and free,
> O'er the bright sunny South
> And the dark, rolling sea."

Our great WASHINGTON fought for the principles we are now contending for, and thought he had secured them. May our young Republic honor his memory with the name of "WASHINGTON Republic," dating from the 22d of February. The day would then be kept to celebrate two great events.

Just as I finished the word "events" I heard the words that Mr. DAVIS had been elected President. *Glorious news! We are free!* We have institutions of our own—a country that we can call our own—rulers from among our own people. There is not a Southern woman, wife, mother or maid, but what feels prouder today of her country, knowing, as we do, that we have fathers, husbands, sons, and brothers, who are willing to sacrifice all to duty and honor.

In peace or war you have with you the prayers and sympathies of every woman who glories in saying, "I am a woman of the South." [*Applause.*]

Yours &c., Mrs. C. LADD[55]

I move that it be referred to the Committee on the Flag.

The question was taken, and the motion agreed to.

Mr. STEPHENS. I have now the model flag which was sent to me by Mr. PLATT, of Augusta (it was then unrolled and exhibited to the Congress,) and I have also another beautiful flag, with a letter accompanying it, (the flag was exhibited) all of which I ask to be referred to the flag committee.[56]

The question was taken, and the motion was agreed to.

Mr. WALKER, of Alabama. I hold in my hand a design of a flag, which I desire to go to the same committee. [document IV; image VI]

No objection was made.

On motion of Mr. CLAYTON, of Mississippi, the following resolution was adopted:

> *Resolved*, That the Judiciary Committee be authorized to have such matter printed as they may desire to lay before the Congress.

Mr. NISBET, of Georgia. I hold in my hand a letter from a private gentleman in our State interested in the subject of patents.[57] I believe, sir, the Committee should have this paper before them, and therefore I ask that it be referred to the Committee on Patents without being read.

The motion was agreed to.

Mr. TOOMBS. I have had sent to me a model of a flag, which I move to refer to the committee on that subject. [document V; image VII]

The question was taken and the motion was agreed to.

Mr. MEMMINGER, of South Carolina. Mr. President, the Committee on Commercial Affairs are prepared to make a report, but they deem it expedient to report in secret session, and if there is no other business in public session, I move that the Congress go into secret session.

The motion was agreed to, and accordingly the Congress proceeded to sit with closed doors.

Friday, February 15, 1861

(Charleston *Mercury*, February 19, 1861; Montgomery *Weekly Advertiser*, February 20, 1861; Charleston *Courier*, February 19, 1861)

The Congress met at 12 o'clock, m., and was called to order by the President, Hon. HOWELL COBB.

After prayer by the Rev. Mr. PELLICER, the Journal of yesterday was read and approved.

On motion of Mr. CHILTON, of Alabama, the following resolution was adopted:

> *Resolved*, That a committee of six, to consist of one Delegate from each of the States of this Confederacy, to be designated by the Delegates of said States respectively, be appointed to act in concert with the committees appointed by the public authorities of the State and of this city to make

arrangements for the reception and inauguration of the President elect of the Confederate States of America.

Subsequently, the following Committee was selected upon a call of the States: For Alabama, Mr. CHILTON; for Florida, Mr. ANDERSON; for Georgia, Mr. KENAN; for Louisiana, Mr. DECLOUET; for Mississippi, Mr. BARRY; for South Carolina, Mr. RHETT.

Mr. BROOKE, of Mississippi. Mr. President, I would ask leave of absence for my colleague, Mr. CAMPBELL, who has been called home by urgent necessity.

Leave of absence was granted.

Mr. STEPHENS, of Georgia. I have here a design and model for a seal of the Confederation from a citizen of Richmond county, Georgia. It is accompanied by no name, and is signed "A Citizen of Richmond County, Georgia." I move its reference to the Committee on Flags and Seals.

Agreed to. [document VI; image VIII]

The PRESIDENT. The Chair has received a communication on the subject of the sale of some vessels to the Provisional Government,[58] which he asks may be received and be referred to the Committee on Naval Affair. It is unnecessary to give a reading. With permission of the Congress, it is ordered to be referred to the Committee indicated.

Mr. MEMMINGER, of South Carolina. I ask leave to offer the following resolution:

> *Resolved*, That each of the Standing Committees of Congress is authorized to cause to be printed any matter which it may deem requisite for the use of the committees.

Mr. CHILTON. I move to amend the resolution so that each of the Committees shall be authorized to appoint a Clerk to aid them in their labors. I find that the labors of some of these Committees are very great. The Postal Committee, for instance, have more work to do than they can readily get through with having no assistance.

Mr. MEMMINGER. Is it not better to make that a separate resolution?

Mr. CHILTON. I would like at least to see the appointment of a Clerk to the Postal Committee. But I see there is an objection to appointing Clerks to all the Committees. So I withdraw my motion. The Postal Committee will have to employ a Clerk [even] if it is at my own expense.

The resolution was then agreed to.

Mr. SHORTER, from the Committee on Engrossment, reported as correctly engrossed a resolution in relation to the appropriation of $500,000 by the State of Alabama, and a resolution to authorize the Judiciary Committee to have such matters printed as they may desire to lay before the Congress.[59]

Mr. FEARNE, of Alabama, presented the letter of Mr. JOHN B. READ,[60] a citizen of Tuscaloosa, on the subject of a projectile, which is deemed very valuable. It has been before the public for some year or more, and has received the endorsement of scientific gentlemen connected with the military institution at West Point. I move that the letter be referred, without reading, to the Committee on Naval Affairs.

The reference was made.[61]

Mr. FEARNE, of Alabama. There is present here this morning one of the deputies from the State of Texas. The others are on their way, and are daily expected. I beg offer to the Congress an official copy of the Ordinance of Secession passed by the State of Texas, and the credentials of the deputies. As Mr. GREGG is present, I move that he be invited to take a seat in the Convention.

The PRESIDENT. Gentlemen of the Congress, the Delegate alluded to by the gentleman from Alabama has presented a copy of the proceedings of the Convention of Texas with the Ordinance of Secession. Both can be read for information, or perhaps it is better to refer it to a Committee. What action shall be taken? Shall the reference be made?

Mr. WITHERS, of South Carolina. I hope so, sir. If I am not misinformed, the Ordinance of Secession passed by the Convention of the people of Texas, has to be submitted to the vote of that State for its ratification. If this be true, I cannot see how Texas is at this time out of the Union, or how Texas can at present be represented in this Congress.

The PRESIDENT. The Ordinance and credentials are here, and can be read for the information of the Congress.

Mr. MORTON, of Florida. I should like to hear the credentials of the members read.

Mr. WITHERS. Yes, that is the better way.

The Ordinance was then read as follows:—

AN ORDINANCE TO DISSOLVE THE UNION BETWEEN THE STATE OF TEXAS AND THE OTHER STATES UNITED UNDER THE COMPACT STYLED "THE CONSTITUTION OF THE UNITED STATES OF AMERICA"

Whereas, the Federal Government has failed to accomplish the purposes of the compact of union between these States, in giving protection either to the persons of our people upon an exposed frontier, or to the property of our citizens, and whereas, the action of the Northern States of the Union is violative of the compact between the States and the guarantees of the Constitution; and, whereas, the recent developments in Federal affairs make it evident that the power of the Federal Government is sought to be made a weapon with which to strike down the interests and property of the people of Texas, and her sister slave-holding States, instead of permitting it to be, as was intended, our shield against outrage and aggression. Therefore,

SEC. 1. *We, the people of the State of Texas, by delegates in convention assembled, do declare and ordain,* That the ordinance adopted by our Convention of Delegates on the 4th day of July, A.D. 1845, and afterwards ratified by us, under which the Republic of Texas was admitted into the Union with other States, and became a party to the compact styled "The Constitution of the United States of America," be, and is hereby, repealed and annulled; that all the powers which, by the said compact, were delegated by Texas to the Federal Government are revoked and resumed; that Texas is of right absolved from all restraints and obligations incurred by said compact, and is a separate sovereign State, and that her citizens and people are absolved from all allegiance to the United States or the government thereof.

SEC. 2. This ordinance shall be submitted to the people of Texas for their ratification or rejection, by the qualified voters, on the 23rd day of February, 1861, and unless rejected by a majority of the votes cast, shall take effect and be in force on and after the 2d day of March, A.D. 1861. *Provided,* that in the Representative District of El Paso said election may be held on the 18th day of February, 1861.

Done by the people of the State of Texas, in convention assembled, at Austin, this 1st day of February, A.D. 1861.

O. M. Roberts, President
(Signed)

Edwin Waller
L. A. Abercrombie
James R. Armstrong
W. A. Allen
James M. Anderson
T. S. Anderson
Richard L. Askew
W. S. J. Adams
Wm. C. Batte
S. W. Beasley
John Box
H. Newton Burditt
James M. Burroughs
John I. Burton
S. E. Black
W. T. Blythe
Amzi Bradshaw
R. Weakley Brahan
A. S. Broaddus

Jno. Henry Brown
Robert C. Campbell
Lewis F. Casey
Wm. Chambers
T. J. Chambers
J. Green Chambers
N. B. Charlton
Geo. W. Chilton
Isham Chisum
Wm. Clark, Jr.
J. A. Clayton
Chas. L. Cleveland
A. G. Clopton
Richard Coke
James E. Cook
John W. Dancy
Tho's G. Davenport
J. J. Diamond
A. H. Davidson

C. Deen
Thos. J. Devine
Wm. W. Diamond
Jno. Donelson
Joseph H. Dunham
Edward Dougherty
H. H. Edwards
Elbert Early
John N. Fall
Drury Field
John H. Feeney
George Flournoy
Spencer Ford
John S. Ford
Thomas C. Frost
Amos P. Galloway
Charles Ganahl
Robert S. Gould
Robert Graham
Malcom D. Graham
Peter W. Gray
John A. Green
John Gregg
Wm. P. Hardeman
John R. Hayes
P. T. Herbert
A. O. W. Hicks
Thos. B. J. Hill
Alfred M. Hobby
Jos. L. Hogg
J. J. Holt
James Hooker
Edward R. Hord
Russell Howard
A. Clark Hoyl
Thos. P. Hughes
J. W. Hutcheson
Jno. Ireland
Thomas J. Jennings
F. Jones
W. C. Kelly
T. Koester
C. M. Lesuer
F. W. Latham
Pryor Lea
James S. Lester
John Littleton
M. F. Locke
Oliver Loftin
Thos. S. Lubbock
P. N. Luckett
Henry A. Maltby
Jesse Marshall
James M. Maxcy
Lewis W. Moore
Wm. Mccraven
Wm. Mcintosh
Gilchrist Mckay
Thos. M. Mccraw
Wm. Goodloe Miller
Albert N. Mills
Thos. Moore
Thos. C. Moore
Chales De Montel
B. F. Moss
John Muller
Thos. J. Nash
A. Nauendorf
T. C. Neel
Alison Nelson
James F. Newsom
W. M. Nayland
E. B. Nichols
A. J. Nicholson
E. P. Nicholson
James M. Norris
Alf. T. Obenchain
W. B. Ochiltree
W. S. Oldham
R. J. Palmer
W. M. Payne
W. K. Payne
Wm. M. Peck
W. R. Poag

Alexander Pope
David Y. Portis
D. M. Pendergast
Walter F. Preston
F. P. Price
A. T. Rainey
John H. Reagan
C. Rector
P. G. Rhome
R. S. C. Robertson
William P. Rogers
James H. Rogers
Edward M. Boss
John Rugeley
H. R. Runnels
J. C. Robertson
J. B. Robertson
E. B. Scarborough
Wm. T. Scott
Wm. Read Scurry
James E. Shepard
Sam. S. Smith
John D. Stell
John G. Stewart
Charles Stewart
F. S. Stockdale
Wm. H. Stewart
Gideon Smith
Pleasant Taylor
B. F. Terry
Nathaniel Terry
E. Thomason
James G. Thompson
W. S. Todd
James Walworth
R. H. Ward
Wm. Warren
James C. Watkins
John A. Wharton
Joseph P. Weir
Jno. A. Wilcox
A. P. Wiley
Ben Williams
Jason Wilson
Philip A. Work

R. T. BROWNRIGG, Secretary
WM. DUNN SCHOOLFIELD, Assistant Secretary
R. W. LUNDY, Assistant Secretary

Mr. FEARNE. I think it proper that this paper together with the credentials of the gentlemen, should be referred to the Committee on Credentials, or to a Select Committee, to be appointed by the Chair.

Mr. TOOMBS (interrupting). A select committee. There is none on that subject at present.

Mr. FEARNE (resuming). It does seem that the appointment is imperfect, but I hope the courtesy will be shown the gentleman here to invite him to a seat upon the floor of the Congress, merely to give him the privileges of the floor as other gentlemen are admitted. I move that the credential be referred to a Select Committee.

The PRESIDENT. Of what number?

A MEMBER. Three.

Mr. FEARN. Yes, that will do. A Special Committee of three, Mr. President.

Mr. MORTON. I would like to hear the credential read.

The PRESIDENT ordered the Clerk to read them as follows:

Austin, Texas, February 4, 1861

Resolved, That this Convention proceed forthwith to elect by ballot seven Delegates to represent the State of Texas in the Convention of Slaveholding States called to assemble at Montgomery, Alabama, on the 4th day of February, A. D. 1861, in order that the views and interests of the people of Texas may be consulted with reference to the Constitution and to the Provisional Government that may be established by said Convention.

Austin, Texas, February 8, 1861

This is to certify that the above and foregoing is a true and correct copy of the original resolution adopted by the Convention of the people of Texas on Monday, February 4th A. D. 1861.

O. M. Roberts
President of Convention
R. T. Brownrigg, Secretary to the Convention

Austin, Texas, February 4, 1861

This is to certify that the Convention of the people of Texas has elected as Delegates to the Convention of Slaveholding States called to assemble at Montgomery, Alabama, on the first Monday, and fourth day of February, A. D. 1861, the following named persons, viz: LEWIS T. WIGFALL, JOHN H. REAGAN, JOHN HEMPHILL, T. N. WARD, JOHN GREGG, W. S. OLDHAM, WM. B. OCHILTREE, who are hereby commissioned as such, and authorized to represent the State of Texas in said Convention to the extent of the powers conferred upon them by the Convention of the people of Texas.

O. M. Roberts
President of Convention
R. T. Brownrigg, Secretary to the Convention

The PRESIDENT then ordered the papers as read to be referred to the Special Committee.

Mr. TOOMBS. I move that the Delegate here, and any others that may come from Texas, be allowed the privileges of the floor.

Agreed to.

Mr. FEARN. The name of the gentleman is Mr. JOHN GREGG.

The PRESIDENT. Mr. JOHN GREGG is invited to a seat on the floor of this Congress.

The CHAIR then announced the names of Messrs. FEARN, MILES, and MARSHALL as the Special Committee on Credentials.

Mr. SMITH, of Alabama. A gentleman from Mobile has placed in my hand a model for the National Flag.[62] I move that it be referred to the Committee.

Agreed to.

Mr. WALKER. Mr. President, it is necessary that all preparations for the inauguration of the President elect should be complete. I understand that it is the design to authorize the States to make their nominations for Committee men. I, therefore, move that the roll of States be called, and that in turn each Delegation nominate its member.

The roll was called, and the following gentlemen were appointed as the Committee:—Messrs. CHILTON, of Alabama; ANDERSON, of Florida; KENNAN, of Georgia; BARRY, of Mississippi; DECLOUET, of Louisiana; RHETT, of South Carolina.

Mr. KEITT. If in order, I move that one o'clock, Monday, be fixed upon as the time for the inauguration of the President elect. He will not reach this city before Saturday, and will not be in a condition to be inaugurated before. In addition to this, some time should be given for preparation, and for the announcement of the day and hour of the ceremony.

The motion was agreed to.

Mr. RHETT. I move that the Congress do go into Secret Session.

The motion was seconded, the reporters were turned out, and the doors closed.

Saturday, February 16, 1861

(Charleston *Mercury*, February 19, 1861; Charleston *Courier*, February 19, 1861)

The Congress met at 12 o'clock m., and was called to order by the President, Hon. HOWELL COBB.

After prayer by the Rev. Mr. PETRIE, the Journal of yesterday was read and approved.

Mr. BARTOW, of Georgia. Mr. President, I have in my hand a letter from a citizen of Georgia,[63] in reference to a patent right. I move its reference to the Committee on Patents, without being read.

The question was taken, and the motion agreed to.

Mr. BARTOW. I have also received from citizens of Georgia, two models of flags, which I beg leave to refer to the Committee on Flags. [document VII; image IX and X; and document VIII]

No objection was made, and it was so ordered.

Mr. NISBET. Mr. President: The Constitution that we have adopted provides that Congress shall, by resolution, transfer the causes pending in the Circuit and District Courts of the United States, to the Courts that have been, or will be, organized under our Constitution. There are a number of cases in all the District and Circuit Courts pending within my own knowledge—a number in my own State, in the Northern and Southern Districts of Georgia. Congress is further instructed by the Constitution to provide for the protection of the judgments and fees of these Courts. As the Committee on the Judiciary should have their attention directed to these matters, I beg leave to offer the following resolution:

> *Resolved*, That the Committee on the Judiciary be instructed to report an Ordinance providing for the transfer of any causes which were pending in the Courts of the United States to the Courts of the Confederacy, and for the execution of the orders and judgments, heretofore rendered by the said Courts of the United States and for the protection of parties, their heirs and assignees, and all such decisions, orders and decrees.

Mr. SMITH, of Alabama. There may be cases pending in the Courts of the United States which can hardly be transferred. There are cases pending in the Supreme Court of the United States. I do not understand well how, without any exception at all, these cases could be reached.

Mr. HALE, of Alabama. I would say to the Congress that the Committee on the Judiciary is now considering these identical questions in reference to the cases in the district courts of the United States, in the several seceding States, and those in the Supreme Court. The Committee is endeavoring to mature their action upon the subject.

Mr. NISBET. That is sufficient, and I withdraw the resolution.

Mr. COBB, of Georgia, presented a model flag; which was referred to the Committee on that subject. [document IX]

Mr. SPARROW, of Louisiana, also presented a design of a flag; which was referred to the Committee on that subject.[64]

Mr. MEMMINGER, of South Carolina. Mr. President, I beg leave to offer some models, one of which I rather think will be the flag. It has the advantage of having the Republican tri-color, and I move the reference of that, with certain others with the stars and stripes, to the Committee on that subject. [document X; image XI]

The question was taken, and the motion was agreed to.

Mr. WITHERS, of South Carolina. Mr. President, I have not been able to manufacture a resolution, but still, I think, as everybody else near me has exercised his genius on a flag, it is my duty to announce that I received, before anybody else, a flag from a patriotic citizen of Charleston. I took the liberty of referring it myself, without the consent of Congress, to a member of the Committee on Flags.[65]

Mr. MILES, of South Carolina. Mr. President, as Chairman of the Committee on Flags, I take this occasion to say, as suggested by my colleagues on that Committee, that a very large number of models are daily submitted to us, but they are not always formally presented in the House. I merely state this in order that our patriotic citizens so industriously exercising their ingenuity may understand that we do not neglect them because no public notice is taken of them in this body. It would consume a great deal of time to notice the reception of every model offered.

Mr. HALE, of Alabama. Mr. President, I present a communication from Mr. JOHN B. READ, a citizen of this State, in reference to missiles of war, and move its reference to the Committee on Military Affairs.[66]

The question was taken, and the motion was agreed to.

Mr. CLAYTON, of Mississippi. Mr. President, the Committee on the Judiciary beg leave to report a bill on the subject of citizenship, and prescribing a uniform system of naturalization.

The CLERK then proceeded to read the bill as follows:

A BILL IN RELATION TO CITIZENSHIP, AND TO PRESCRIBE UNIFORM RULES OF NATURALIZATION

SEC. 1. The Congress—

Mr. CLAYTON (interrupting.) Mr. President, I move that the bill be not read except by its title.

The motion was agreed to, and the bill was accordingly read a second time by its title, ordered to be printed, and placed on the Calendar.

The CLERK. How many copies?

Mr. CLAYTON. A hundred.

The CHAIR. In future when no number of copies is prescribed it will be understood that a hundred are to be printed.

Mr. BROOKE, of Mississippi, from the Committee on Patents, reported the following resolution:

> *Resolved*, That J. M. WALDEN,[67] a citizen of the State of Georgia, be and he is hereby authorized to file with the Attorney General a *caveat*,[68] accompanied by suitable drawings and explanations, and setting forth the design and purpose thereof, for the protection of an improvement claimed to be made by him on railroad switches; and that said *caveat*, when so filed as aforesaid, shall be effectual to protect his right to said invention until a patent office shall be established, *Provided*, That as soon as said office is established said *caveat* shall be filed with the commissioner hereof and such proceedings had thereon as may be authorized by law.

Mr. HILL, of Georgia. I would suggest that the resolution should be amended so as to protect the rights of Mr. WALDEN from this day.

Mr. BROOKE. I would ask the Clerk to insert those words.

The resolution was then agreed to.

Mr. CONRAD, of Louisiana. Mr. President, I do not know whether it is the understanding of the Committee or the understanding of Congress, that the Committee on Patents includes a cognate subject, that of copyright. If it be not so understood by the Committee, I would move that that be included in the power of the Committee and that we nominate a Committee on Patents and Copyright. I make that motion because I have a document in regard to copyright,[69] which I wish to refer to that Committee.

The PRESIDENT. The Chair would inquire of the Chairman of the Committee on Patents, whether he regards copyright as within its jurisdiction.

Mr. BROOKE. Yes, sir; we do.

The PRESIDENT. The communication to which the gentleman refers will then be referred to that Committee.

And then on motion of Mr. SHORTER, of Alabama, the Congress went into secret session.

Monday, February 18, 1861

(Charleston *Mercury*, February 21, 1861)

The Congress met at 12 o'clock m., and was called to order by the President, Hon. HOWELL COBB, of Georgia.

After prayer by the Rev. Mr. SHEPHERD,[70] the Journal of Saturday was read and approved.

Mr. SHORTER, of Alabama. Mr. President, is it in order to make a report from the Committee on Engrossment?

The PRESIDENT. It is.

Mr. SHORTER. Then I make the following report.

The report was read as follows:

The Committee on Engrossment and Enrolled Bills have instructed me to report that they have carefully examined the enrolled copy of the Constitution of the Provisional Government of the Confederate States of America, and that the same has been correctly and handsomely enrolled on parchment in accordance with the resolution of Congress, and is now ready for the signatures of the deputies of the several States represented in the Congress at the time of its adoption.

Mr. SHORTER. Mr. President, it has been suggested that it would be proper for the Congress to sign the Constitution this morning before we proceed to the inauguration of the President elect. It is upon the desk of the Clerk, and I would suggest, if it meets the approbation of the Congress, that the deputies at once sign their names.

The suggestion was acquiesced in.

The President of the Congress then affixed his signature (Mr. HILL, of Georgia, temporarily occupying the chair), after which the deputies of the several States signed their names—South Carolina first, then Georgia, then Florida, then Alabama, Mississippi and Louisiana.

The PRESIDENT. The Constitution has been signed by all the members who are present. The Committee of Arrangements for the inauguration are absent. If it meets the approval of the Congress they will be invited to sign it when they come in.

Mr. BROOKE. Mr. President, I ask to have a bill read by its title and placed on the calendar.

Mr. HILL. I would suggest that it had better be reported in secret session.

Mr. BROOKE. I don't see why. It would have to be made public immediately.

The bill was then read by its title as follows:

A Bill To Establish A Patent Office, The Granting And Issuing Of Patents For New And Useful Inventions And Improvements

The PRESIDENT. The bill will be placed upon the calendar of the secret session.

And then the Congress proceeded to sit with closed doors.

Subsequently, upon the arrival of the President-elect, he was escorted to the chamber, by Mr. RHETT, and introduced to the Congress, which immediately adjourned to the portico, where the President delivered his inaugural and took the oath of office in the presence of a large and enthusiastic audience. Afterwards the President was reconducted to the chamber, and the Congress resumed its business.

The PRESIDENT. The Constitution has been enrolled and signed by all the members except the Vice-President and the Committee of Arrangements for the Inauguration. It is understood that at this time the opportunity is given them to sign that instrument.

The Vice-President, Hon. ALEX. H. STEPHENS, and the Committee of Arrangements, then came forward and signed the Constitution.

Mr. SHORTER. Mr. President, I move that the inaugural address of the President of the Confederate States of America, delivered to-day, be spread on the journal of this body, and that five thousand copies of it be printed for the use of the members thereof.

And then, on motion of Mr. CHILTON, the Congress adjourned till 12 o'clock to-morrow.

Tuesday, February 19, 1861

(Charleston *Mercury*, February 22, 1861)

The Congress met, at 12 o'clock m., and was called to order by the President, Hon. HOWELL COBB.

After prayer by the Rev. R. H. COBBS,[71] the Journal of yesterday was read and approved.

Mr. SHORTER, of Ala. Mr. President, I ask leave to announce this morning the arrival of Mr. WAUL, one of the delegates from Texas, who is in this hall.

The PRESIDENT. The gentleman is entitled to take his seat, as provided for by the resolution passed by the Congress.

Mr. SHORTER. The credentials of the entire delegation have been filed.

The PRESIDENT. The Chair so understands it and under the resolution of Congress, the deputies from Texas are entitled to take their seats.

Mr. BARTOW, of Ga. Mr. President, I am instructed by the Committee on Military Affairs to state that they have a bill prepared and a resolution for the consideration of the Congress, but deem it best to report it in secret session.[72]

Mr. SHORTER, from the Committee on Engrossments, reported as correctly engrossed a resolution for the enforcement of the revenue laws, a resolution for the preservation of the records of Congress, a resolution giving certain powers to the Committee on Naval Affairs, and a resolution for the relief of J. M. WALDEN, a citizen of Georgia when the President signed the same.[73]

Mr. BROOKE, of Mississippi. Mr. President, the Committee on the organization of the Executive Departments are ready to report, but they deem it better to make it in secret session. I therefore move that Congress go into secret session.[74]

Mr. CONRAD, of Louisiana. I would suggest to the gentleman from Mississippi that I see no reason why the bill—

The PRESIDENT. Debate is not in order whilst the motion to go into secret session is pending. Does the gentleman from Mississippi withdraw his motion?

Mr. BROOKE. I withdraw it for the present.

Mr. CONRAD (resuming). I suggest, then, that I see no reason why the report of these bills should be made in secret session: perhaps there are reasons why they should not. If there should arise a discussion, it is proper that the debate should take place in secret session; but probably most of them will not occasion debate.

Mr. BROOKE. I have no objection whatever.

Mr. CHILTON, of Alabama. I ask leave to lay before the Committee on the Permanent Constitution a communication which I have received from a distinguished gentleman.[75]

The PRESIDENT. If there is no objection, the communication will be so referred without being read.

No objection was made.

Mr. BROOKE then, from the Committee on the Organization of the Executive Departments, reported a bill to organize the Department of State.

> It was read. The first section provides that there shall be an Executive Department, to be denominated the Department of State, and a principal officer, to be called the Secretary of State, who shall perform and execute such duties as shall from time to time be enjoined on and entrusted to him by the President of the Confederate States relative to the commissions or instructions to or intercourse with public ministers, as well as with the Confederate States, all negotiations with public ministers from foreign States, memorials or applications from foreign ministers or other foreigners, or other matters respecting foreign affairs, as the President of the Confederate States shall assign to such Department; and said officer shall conduct the business in such manner as the President of the Confederate States shall from time to time order and instruct, and said Secretary shall be appointed by the President, by and with the advice and consent of Congress, and compensation therefor shall be made consistent with law.
>
> The second clause provides that it shall be the duty of the Secretary of State to keep and preserve all bills, orders and resolutions of Congress

having been approved and signed by the President, and carefully preserve the originals, and shall, as soon as convenient, cause every such law, order, or resolution, to be published in at least three public newspapers, published within the Confederate States, and also cause two authenticated copies of each to be sent to the Executive Department of each State; keep the great seal of the Confederate States and affix the same to all commissions approved by the President, by and with the advice and consent of Congress, provided said seal shall not be affixed to any commission before it is agreed to or signed by the President, nor to any other instrument or act without the special warrant of the President therefor; said Secretary shall also cause said Seal to be affixed to all copies of records or papers, and records or papers so authenticated shall be equally authoritative as the originals.

The third section provides for the appointment of a Chief Clerk by the Secretary, and such other clerics as may be found necessary, and may be authorized by Congress, who shall receive a compensation for their services to be fixed by law, and who shall, before entering upon the execution of their office or employment, take an oath or affirmation well and faithfully to execute the trust committed to them; and there shall be paid to said secretary the following fees of office, by the persons requiring the service to be performed, except when performed for any officer of the Confederate States: For making out authenticated copies of the records, ten cents for each hundred words, and for affixing the seal to such record or papers, one dollar. This Act to take effect from and after its passage.

Mr. NISBET. I move that the Congress do now go into secret session for the purpose of considering that bill.

The motion was agreed to, and accordingly the Congress proceeded to sit with closed doors.

Wednesday, February 20, 1861

(Charleston *Mercury*, February 23, 1861; Charleston *Courier*, February 23, 1861; Augusta *Daily Constitutionalist*, February 22, 1861)

The Congress met at 12 o'clock, a.m., and was called to order by the President, Hon. HOWELL COBB, of Georgia.

After prayer by the Rev. Mr. HEARD,[76] the Journal of yesterday was read and approved.

Mr. WRIGHT, of Georgia. Mr. President—

The PRESIDENT. The gentleman from Georgia.

Mr. WRIGHT. A few days ago, I laid before Congress a communication from Hon. MARK A. COOPER upon the subject of an armory. I have received an additional communication from him, which I desire may be read at the Clerk's desk;

and, although it will occupy twenty minutes to read it, I ask a respectful hearing for it.

The PRESIDENT. The Clerk will read the memorial.

Etowah, Ga., Feb 15, 1861

To the Members of the Congress of the Confederate States of America:

Perceiving that a communication from the undersigned to one of your honorable body, on the subject of an armory, has been laid before you, he respectfully asks the privilege of submitting the following statement of facts, to-wit:

> Twice during a period of twenty-five years last past, the subject of a National Armory at this place, has been brought before the Congress of the late Government of the United States, at Washington City, once by the late Hon. W. C. Dawson,[77] and again by the late Hon. John H. Lumpkin.[78] At the instance of that body, through an appropriate committee, the necessary examination and tests were made before the naval and war departments of that Government, of the metal at Etowah, Ga., for the purpose of an armory, and reports were made thereon, showing it to be most satisfactory. At sundry times, within the last ten years, this subject has been submitted to the Government of Georgia, with the advice and recommendation of the Governor.
>
> Appropriate committees of the Legislature have again and again reported upon the facts, showing them to be all that could be desired. This will appear by an extract of report herewith submitted. The undersigned has repeatedly had the material of Etowah tested, both in England and America, for gunnery, and for arms, and for steel cutlery. In every instance the result has proved most satisfactory, as will appear by papers herewith presented. Amongst others, a test made by Col. Sam'l Colt, one of the best, most skillful, and reliable, and well known manufacturers of arms in America, or in Europe, is a satisfactory proof that the metal here is all that can be desired.
>
> In selecting a location for an armory, after finding a concurrence of every matter needed, such as climate, water power, iron ore, fuel, accessibility, security from invasion, quick transportation to all points, one point must be demonstrated, without which an armory should not be located, to wit: the quality and adaptation of the metal must be manifest. This must require time, skill, science, and money.
>
> At Etowah you have this proof furnished to hand, gotten up during a series of twenty years experience, at the cost of one who is

a native of one of the States of your Confederacy, who is here now, was there before, and at its beginning, and here intends to remain.

In addition to this, you have also furnished in advance every preparation and machinery needed to make the iron and put it in shape for making arms. This preparation also has cost time and money, and must require years to get it up at any other place in your jurisdiction.

At this place then the facts show that you have in advance all you need for a prompt movement, and you can avail yourselves of it on better terms than elsewhere.

If you prefer to have an individual to make your arms, you can have them in process of delivery here in twelve months from the day you give us the contract. We can ship them hence by railroad, to any principal town or sea port of the Confederacy—to Charleston, Savannah, or the Grand Junction, in twenty-four hours—to Mobile and New Orleans in thirty-six hours.

All of which is respectfully submitted by the undersigned, a citizen of Cass county, Ga.

Mark A. Cooper

(The extract of the report of the committee of the Georgia Legislature, referred to in the above letter, is too long for insertion here, but we make the annexed extracts from it.)

The Etowah river and its tributaries furnish the most ample and never-failing water power for manufactures of all kinds.

Between the State road and Canton, along this valley, within a distance of fifteen miles, there are seven blast furnaces for smelting iron ore with charcoal. They have been put in operation in about fifteen years past. They are producing an aggregate of four to five thousand tons of pig metal and castings per annum, at a cost of fifteen or twenty dollars per ton. These products have, until recently, been carried by wagons to the State road, a distance of four to fifteen miles, and shipped to Cincinnati, Nashville, Decatur, Ala., and Knoxville, or to Montgomery, Columbus, Macon, and Augusta, and intermediate points; nearly all of it in the form of pig or bar iron has been carried on the State road.

At Etowah, four miles above and north of the State road, there are two blast furnaces for pig metal, a rolling mill for merchant iron of all sizes and shapes, flats, rounds, squares and ovals. It is now operating and producing from eight to ten tons per day. This rolling mill has been in operation about ten years, but for lack of transportation, has not, until a year past, made over one thousand or one thousand two hundred tons per annum.

The two blast furnaces are in operation also, producing from ten to fourteen tons of pig metal per day; charcoal iron. This is consumed at the rolling mill.

The supply of ore at Etowah is almost inexhaustible. The iron at Etowah has been sent to England and fully tested for all purposes of wrought and cast iron, for blister and cast steel, and samples of each article with files, &c., made of the steel, exhibited. The report puts it on a footing of the best English iron for such purposes. For the purpose of gunnery it has been tested at the War Department and is found to rank amongst the best.

The Secretary then read certificates from several competent and experienced gentlemen, in reference to the quality of the iron at Etowah.

A sample of Etowah iron was sent to Col. Colt, at Hartford, Connecticut, last November, with an order for a pistol and a rifle to be made of it. Early in December last a pistol was received with the following letter on the subject:

Hartford, Conn., November 28, 1860

Dear Sir:—We send to-day by Express to your address, one of our Navy or Belt Pistols, with two barrels, the lock, frame, &c., which are made from the samples of Etowah Iron, sent by you November 7th. This Iron evidently possesses great tenacity, and appears to be as free from seams and flaws as any of the brands of Norway Iron which we are now using in the manufacture of our arms. And we should say, from the test we have given it, that it compares favorably, in every respect with the best brands of Norway iron.

Wm. B. Hartley
Superintendent Colt Arms Company

Those who are informed, know that the Norway Iron is the best which is made for such purposes. In May, 1860, a sample of the Etowah Iron was sent to Sheffield, England, to be made into razor steel, and a lot of razors were ordered to be made of it. This order was executed, and twenty-three dozen razors were received and sent to Etowah by Mr. A. J. Brady, of the firm of Brady & Solomon, of Atlanta, Georgia,[79] then in New York, with the following letter from the manufacturer of Sheffield, England, to wit:

Sheffield, October 29, 1860.

Mr. A. J. Brady—Dear Sir: I have now the pleasure of waiting upon you, with the enclosed invoice of razors, shipped by Screw Steamer *Kangaroo*, from Liverpool, for your port, which will be delivered to you by Messrs. H. Leon & Co.

These razors are manufactured of the steel produced from the Etowah iron sent to me for that purpose, and the results of this trial cannot but be gratifying, as the razors produced are of a very good quality, thus attesting the superior quality of the steel, which particularly recommends itself for razors and spring cutlery, and tools in general, by reason of its high degree of malleability and elasticity, a combination of properties which peculiarly adapts your steel for the above named purposes.

Yours respectfully,
A. Leon

Mr. Hartley, Secretary of Mr. Colt's Arms Company, in the same letter above quoted, concerning the manufacture of arms, writes as follows, to wit:

The barrels, cylinders, cones and lock work of all our arms, are made of a peculiar quality of steel, that being the only metal which we consider perfectly reliable. But, from the toughness of your iron, its freedom from scoria,[80] the ease and facility with which it can be welded, and the high finish of which it is susceptible, we see no reason why it may not be used in the manufacture of any of the parts of our arms which are made of iron.

The testimonials of Mr. Leon established that the Etowah Iron makes "a superior quality of steel" possessing the properties of malleability and elasticity in a high degree. And it is known that these are the properties in steel most desirable in making the barrels, cones, and lock work, of Mr. Colt's most reliable arms.

We have, therefore, proven, from the highest testimonials, that, for iron and for steel, we have now made at Etowah all the Government can desire in metal to manufacture the most desirable arms.

For the manufacture of ordnance and cannon shot, it is also ascertained that we can make, at Etowah, metal equal to any. To prove this, reference is here made to the tests made of it, at the War and Navy Departments at Washington City, and reported to the Congress of the United States.

Touching the eligibility of this location, it will, with propriety, be submitted to Commissioners appointed for that purpose, whose fidelity and competency will be unquestioned, provided further proofs are needed. (Signed by Mark A. Cooper)

The reading of the several papers was interrupted by—

Mr. Conrad, of Louisiana. Mr. President, we might as well suspend the reading of this document. I presume no action will be taken upon it, except upon the recommendation of the War Department.

The President. The reading is nearly finished. There is only a page left. More time will be occupied in discussing this point than in conducting the reading.

The reading of the papers was then finished.

Mr. Wright. Mr. President, I am no jobber, sir, for my State or for my personal friends, nor yet for my constituents. If this is not a matter of interest for the Confederate States of America, or if I had not supposed that it was, the memorial would not have been laid before this body. If I had not considered it a matter of importance, perhaps second to none, I should not have troubled the body with its reading, but according to the view I take of our position just now it is a matter of imminent, of great concern. The probabilities are that within twenty days we shall be involved in war. We are unprepared, it seems to me, in several respects for that contingency. The most gallant people on the face of the earth can achieve nothing without arms. We are not armed.

I see no preparation for arming ourselves. Within the Confederate States there is not a single manufactory of arms; if so, it has escaped my attention. These arms might be purchased at private establishments in time of peace, or in a foreign country; but in times of war they can be purchased at neither, and no means of supplying ourselves suggests itself to my mind except by the establishment of a public armory. If the probabilities be such as I have indicated, this is the only sure means by which we can supply ourselves for defensive if not aggressive warfare. I ask if it is not a question of importance to this body? I think it is, sir; and for that reason have presented the memorial, and I ask its reference to the Committee on Military Affairs.

Mr. CONRAD, of Louisiana. Mr. President, if the gentleman's remarks are intended to apply to the motion I made, he certainly entirely misunderstood that motion and its objects. It was not my purpose to intimate that the subject is not important, or to find fault with the gentleman for having presented it to this body. On the contrary, I deem it of the greatest importance, and my motion was simply to dispense with the reading of it, and to have it referred to the appropriate committee—the very course he should have taken. I apprehend the proper course will be for that Committee to consider the memorial, and moreover to have the advice of the War Department—the proper department, the Ordnance Department of the War Department—which will be in existence in a few days, and then it can act with knowledge and experience, and bring the subject before this body. I had not the slightest intention of underrating the importance of the subject or the motives of the gentleman in bringing it before the body.

Mr. WRIGHT. I find I misapprehended the gentleman. His statement is entirely satisfactory to me.

Mr. BARTOW, of Georgia. Mr. President, I have not the slightest objection to the reference of this memorial to the Committee on Military Affairs, and I assure my colleague it will receive the most respectful consideration. The subject of providing for a national armory is one of great interest and concern to this government, but I must beg leave to differ with my colleague in another observation he has made—that in the event of a war being forced on us within a period of twenty days from this time, we are unprepared to meet it. I do not agree with him in that statement. We are prepared for any contingency of that sort that may occur within twenty days. We are not as defenseless as he supposes we are to-day. Although we have no manufactory of arms within the limits of this Confederacy, there is at this moment in the possession of every State in it a sufficient number of arms to resist any invasion that may be made upon us, and more than a sufficient number of men, all trained, disciplined, and officered, who will be enabled to protect the honor and the independence of this government, let it be assaulted from what quarter it may.

The question was then taken, and the memorial was referred to the Committee on Military Affairs.

Mr. STEPHENS, of Georgia, from the Committee on the Organization of the Executive Departments, reported the following bill, which was read the third time and passed:

> A Bill To Be Entitled "An Act To Authorize The President To Appoint A Private Secretary."
>
> *Be it enacted by the Congress of the Confederate States of America, and it is hereby enacted by the authority of the same,* That the President of the Confederate States of America be and he is hereby authorized to appoint a Private Secretary through whom to communicate with Congress, and discharge such duties as shall be assigned to him, and receive such compensation for his services as may be fixed by law.

And then, on motion of Mr. STEPHENS, the Congress went into secret session.

Thursday, February 21, 1861

(Charleston *Mercury*, February 26, 1861; Montgomery *Weekly Advertiser*, February 27, 1861)

The Congress met at 12 o'clock, m., and was called to order by the President, Hon. HOWELL COBB, of Georgia, when the Journal of yesterday was read and approved.

Mr. CHILTON, of Alabama. Mr. President, I have two communications, sent to me by a scientific gentleman,[81] one of which I desire to have referred to the Committee on Military Affairs and the other to the Committee on Patents. These communications have reference to cast iron cannon, and it is claimed that the inventor, who desires a fair experiment and explanation before the Committee, can make rifled cannon superior in force to the Armstrong piece.

The communications were severally referred without being read.

Mr. THOMAS R. R. COBB, of Georgia. I propose to offer, sir, a resolution of inquiry:

> A Resolution of Inquiry as to Export Duty on Cotton.
>
> *Resolved,* That the Committee on Finance be instructed to inquire into the expediency of laying an export duty on all cotton exported by any other channel than through the seaports of this Confederacy.

I propose, Mr. President, merely to refer it to the Committee on Finance. I do not suppose that it is necessary, this morning, to enter into any discussion as to the policy of laying such a duty. I wish to inquire through our Committee on Finance, whether it is necessary—whether the facts now existing justify such an act on our part. That we have the power to do so I have no doubt. I apprehend, Mr. President, we are all conscious of the power which these Confederate States hold in their hands, by reason of the fact of their producing so much of that staple which is so necessary to the world; and I doubt not it has entered into the minds, perhaps, of every member of Congress that this power is greater than that of armies or navies, and that by an embargo prohibiting the exportation of cotton from these States, we could soon place not only the United States but many of the European powers in the dilemma, compelling them at once to select between such a recognition of our independence as we choose to require, or domestic convulsions at home. The information seems to be sufficient to justify an inquiry as to these facts, that some portion of the cotton produced in these States already is seeking a new channel to the east. We are informed that, at Pittsburg, more than twenty thousand bales of cotton have already been received by means of the Mississippi River and its tributaries. I was reliably informed that from the city of Rome, in Georgia, more than twenty thousand bales of cotton had been sent by railroad in order to seek the ocean at Norfolk, and seek the seaboard at Alexandria. I have been informed that the directors of the railroads, communicating with the public line of our country, are concocting schemes in the reduction of freight on these roads for the purpose of enticing our cotton to market in that way. The result of such a scheme, if successfully carried out would necessarily be: first, to make the blockade of our ports a matter of no importance to foreign nations;[82] second, to destroy all the commerce of our seaports; and third, and most important, to compel us to receive all the imports and imported goods of the North, after paying duties at the ports of the United States. These considerations have induced me to offer the resolution of inquiry. I do not think it will elicit any discussion this morning; but upon the report of the Committee it will become a matter of grave consideration for this body.

The question was taken, and the resolution was agreed to.

Mr. FEARNE, of Alabama, presented a communication from Mr. SAMUEL P. L. MARSHALL,[83] on the subject of metal castings, which, without reading, was referred to the military committee.

Mr. SHORTER, from the Committee on Engrossment, reported as correctly engrossed an act to determine the salaries and fees of the different heads of Departments; an Act to organize the Department of State; an Act to establish the War Department; an Act to establish the Navy Department; an Act to organize and establish an Executive Department, to be known as the Department of Justice; an Act to establish a Post Office Department; and an Act to organize the Treasury Department; when the President signed the same.[84]

Mr. HARRIS. Mr. President, I move that we proceed to the consideration of the business on the secret calendar. I take the responsibility, therefore, of moving that the Congress resolve itself into secret session.

The latter motion was agreed to, and accordingly the Congress proceeded to sit with closed doors.

Friday, February 22, 1861

(Charleston *Mercury*, February 26, 1861; Charleston *Courier*, February 26, 1861)

The Congress met at 12 o'clock, m., and was called to order by the President, Hon. HOWELL COBB, of Georgia.

After prayer by the Rev. Mr. PELLICER, the Journal of yesterday was read and adopted.

Mr. WALKER, of Alabama, presented a communication on the subject of a flag for the Confederate States; which was referred to the Committee on that subject.

Mr. WRIGHT, of Ga. Mr. President, I ask leave to present the following bill:

A BILL TO BE ENTITLED "AN ACT TO FORM A VOLUNTEER DIVISION IN THE ARMY OF THE CONFEDERATE STATES OF AMERICA"

Be it enacted by the Confederate States of America in Congress assembled, That there shall be a division in the regular army of the Confederate States, commanded by a Major General, to be denominated the volunteer division.

SEC. 2. Said division shall be composed of two brigades; said brigades of two regiments each; said regiments of two battalions each; said battalions of___ companies each; and said companies of___ men each.

SEC. 3. From the passage of this act it shall be the duty of the Secretary of War to receive into the army of the Confederate States, for the term of enlistment established by law, any companies of infantry, artillery or cavalry, having reference to a due apportionment of the same in the formation of a proper military division.

SEC. 4. Vacancies in the rank and file of such companies after enlistment may be filled by recruits, and upon the expiration of the term of service of said companies the same shall be filled as mentioned in the aforesaid third section.

SEC. 5. Officers above the grade of Captain shall be made by appointment as in other divisions of the regular army.

SEC. 6. After the organization of said division or any of its brigades, regiments, battalions or companies, vacancies in the officers shall be filled of soldiers of the volunteer division, and the controlling considerations shall be skill and courage.

SEC. 7. Extraordinary service in battle of either officers or any of the soldiers, may be rewarded by promotion over the superior grades, and conferring such badges of honor as may be established by the War Department.

I do not propose, Mr. President, to address the Congress at length upon this bill at this time. I have presented it for the purpose of calling to the attention of Congress, and offering some reflections upon it. It will make a very important change in the regular army of the Confederate States; that is, it will make a difference in the organization of that army, from what exists at the present time in the army of the United States. The immediate occasion of this bill, sir, was an application through me to the Government of the Confederate States by Capt. GEORGE W. LEE,[85] of the city of Atlanta, to be received into the service of the new Republic. Captain LEE had organized, at his own expense, a company of one hundred men in the city, composed mostly, if not entirely, of mechanics of that city—working men—men of intelligence, men inured to toil—and having drilled these men, presented them, together with their officers, to be received, not as volunteers for a year or two into the service of the Confederate States, but to be received into the regular army of the Confederate States. When he first mentioned the subject to me, I told him there was no question of his reception, of his immediate reception, for our republic needed men, and men of the character of those who constituted the body of his company. But, sir, upon application, I found that, according to the army organization that had been established, he could not be received, neither himself nor his men. His men could not be received as volunteers, and as a company, into the service of the Confederate States, according to the rule which obtained in the army of the late United States, but they could only be received as recruits. Now, sir, there is a vast difference between a man's going into the army of the Confederate States as a recruit and going in there as a member of an organized company; and I would take this occasion to remark, sir, there would be a vast difference between the character of the men in this volunteer division, and the character of the common soldier which forms the great body of the regular army. My opinion is that the advantages will all be in favor of the men constituting this volunteer division. A recruit places himself at the disposal of the government. He may be thrown with men that he never saw before; men for whom he has no affinity, neither social, intellectual nor moral. He may be thrown into the filth of the purlieus[86] of your cities—for a large number of our recruits are formed of this character of men. Men who have proper training, mental and moral, can never consent to occupy that position. No matter how burning his patriotism, no matter how ardently he is disposed to defend his country's rights or honor, he cannot do it at such a personal sacrifice. He is to be commanded, too, by men his immediate superiors, whom he never saw. He cannot tell whether he shall be led to battle by a wise man or a fool. The bill which I have introduced, sir, proposes to obviate the defect in the regular army.

This is not a bill to receive volunteers, but a bill to create a volunteer division in the regular army; that is, a division commanded by a Major General, and composed of men who have organized themselves into companies and presented themselves to the Republic for service. You will also observe, sir, that the superior officers are appointed, as well as the officers in the regular army, from the grade of Captain up to

Major General. You will also observe, sir, that these officers may be taken from any rank in life, or from any of the Confederate States, or from the regular army that may be in the service at the time the volunteer company is formed; but, sir, that the officers composing the volunteer corps are to be made of the soldiers composing that division, and that alone.

There is another important distinction which I propose to incorporate, and that is, that promotions in this division shall be made, not as they are made in the regular army of the United States, but that the controlling consideration shall be courage and skill; that there shall be no obstacle to the promotion of a man who has won his laurels in the field of battle over his superiors; a man who, perhaps, has sought that office and obtained it from powerful and influential friends, and who, according to that organization, operates as an incubus to rising merit. I propose to obviate in this division, not in the division of the regular army, what I conceive to be a great fault in the regular service.

One other remark, Mr. President, and I will have stated all I intend to say. Without going back to history further than the wars of the Crimea, I can prove conclusively the correctness of the plan of this division. The English soldiers in the Crimea fought side by side with the French in the same cause. They had the same men to fight against. Their behavior was the subject of comment not only by the English press but by the American press, and the conclusion to which all military men came was that the difference originated in the manner in which the officers of the two armies received their appointments. In the British army these posts were filled by men who either bought them, or were placed in position by their friends of influence and power. NAPOLEON, the Third, observing the wisdom of his ancestor, and avoiding his faults, pursued the same course in appointing men in reference to their skill and courage, and the result, sir, was marked in that campaign. It was actually marked in the late campaign in Italy between the French and Austria.[87]

Sir, our government is predicated on the principle that "worth makes the man; the want of it the fellow." I propose to carry a little of this republican sentiment into the army, to make a division where this shall be the fundamental principle.

I propose to do one thing more, sir; to open up in the regular army of the Confederacy a division in which the sons of our farmers and merchants and mechanics can enter; where they can enter and feel themselves men; where they may enter, not as common soldiers enlisted for the purposes of pay, but where they can enter moved by those high and holy impulses that move men in conflicts like that ahead of us. No other way suggested itself to my mind. I do not suppose the bill is perfect, but I have introduced it at this time for reference to the Committee on Military Affairs, in the hope that they will consider it and amend its defects, if there are any.

The bill was then read a second time by its title, and referred to the Committee on Military Affairs.

On motion of Mr. BROOKE, of Mississippi, the following resolution was adopted:

> *Resolved*, That WILLIAM P. BARKER,[88] a citizen of the State of Alabama, be authorized to file in the office of the Attorney-General a specification of an invention claimed to have been made by him in the mode of casting ordnance, and that the same shall, from this date, operate as a *caveat* to protect his said invention until an application can be made for a patent according to law.

Mr. BARNWELL, of South Carolina. I move, sir, that my colleague (Mr. MEMMINGER) be excused from serving the Committee (Commercial Affairs) on which he is now placed. The organization of the department to which he has been appointed will require all his time.[89]

The question was taken, and the motion was agreed to.

And then, on motion of Mr. WALKER, of Alabama, the Congress proceeded to sit with closed doors.

Saturday, February 23, 1861

(Charleston *Mercury*, February 26 and 27, 1861)

Congress met at 12 o'clock, m., and was called to order by the President, Hon. HOWELL COBB, of Georgia.

After prayer by the Rev. Mr. SHEPHERD, the Journal of yesterday was read and adopted.

From the Journal, it appears that the vacancy in the Committee on Commercial Affairs, caused by the appointment of Mr. MEMMINGER Secretary of the Treasury, has been filled by the appointment of Hon. W. PORCHER MILES, of South Carolina.

Mr. ANDERSON, of Florida. Mr. President, I have received a communication from a member of the Florida Legislature, addressed to the delegates of Florida in this Congress, which I desire to read and spread on the Journal. It is short. The communication was read as follows:

> Montgomery, Ala., February 23
>
> To the Hon. JACKSON MORTON, JAMES B. OWENS, J. PATTEN ANDERSON, Deputies in Congress from the State of Florida:
>
> GENTS: I have the pleasure herewith to furnish you with a copy of the joint resolutions recently adopted by the General Assembly, expressive of the hearty approval of the election of the Hon. JEFFERSON DAVIS and ALEX. H. STEPHENS as President and Vice-President of the Confederate States of America.
>
> Owing to the irregularity of the mails, I have deemed it advisable to

furnish you with the same in advance of the regularly certified copy, which you will doubtless receive.

Very respectfully,
D. P. Holland

Joint Resolutions

Resolved, That the General Assembly of Florida have heard with pleasure of the selection, by the Convention at Montgomery, of the Hon. JEFFERSON DAVIS and ALEXANDER H STEPHENS as President and Vice-President of the Southern Confederation; and that in the selection of these two distinguished statesmen they recognize that burial of former political differences, which is so much to be desired by all true lovers of their country.

Resolved further, That this General Assembly recognizes the Hon. JEFFERSON DAVIS as Chief Magistrate of the Southern Confederation, and as such, as being entitled to exercise the same powers and privileges at all points, and in all respects, within the limits of the State of Florida as the President of the late United States could have exercised while Florida was a member of that Confederation.

Adopted at Tallahassee, Fla., Feb. 14, 1861.

The question was taken and the motion to spread the resolutions on the Journal was agreed to.

Mr. WRIGHT, of Georgia. Mr. President, I received by the mail yesterday a model flag from Mrs. E. G. CARPENTER,[90] a lady of my District, accompanied by an appropriate explanation for the Committee. I have no disposition to make a flag speech. If I had, the speech of the gentleman from Mississippi (Mr. BROOKE), is so much superior in sentiment and graceful in diction to anything I could say, that I will not attempt it. But permit me to call the attention of the house to this design—one of the prettiest, if not the prettiest, presented. There is a centre star with six points, representing the Confederacy, with a heart in the centre of that star, representing the hopes and affections of the people. It is surrounded by other stars, sir, representing the stars of the Border States, the stars representing the Border States, the Border Slave States. In the corner, isolated by itself, is a star, intended to represent the right of a State to pursue the path of empire by herself, if she so wills. In the left hand corner is a dove with the olive branch of peace in his mouth, which we sent to our Northern brethren. I trust, sir, they may receive him into the ark, and not drive him away with no rest for his feet. In the right hand corner is a sword, representing our purpose to act in defence, unconquerable defence of the right. There is also an eye to remind us that the eye of Omnipotence is always upon us and regards the actions of men as well as of individuals. I move its reference to the Committee on Flags. [document XI; image XII]

The question was taken and the motion agreed to.

Mr. T. R. R. COBB, from the Committee on Printings reported the following bill, which was read twice by its title and placed on the public calendar:

A BILL IN RELATION TO PUBLIC PRINTING

The Congress of the Confederate States of America do enact, That the Secretary of Congress shall, after each session, prepare for publication fair copies of all the acts passed by the Congress, and resolutions of a public nature intended to have the effect of laws, together with the Constitutions for a Provisional and Permanent Government of this Confederacy adopted by this Congress.

SEC. 2. The acts shall be arranged under appropriate titles, shall have marginal notes to each section and be fully indexed.

SEC. 3. The Secretary shall also prepare for publication copies of the public journal of the proceedings of this Congress and a full index for the same.

SEC. 4. The Acts and Journals when prepared shall be delivered to the public printers, who shall, without delay, publish three thousand copies of each in a style equal in execution and upon paper of the same quality in every respect, as the laws of the United States, annually published by Messrs. LITTLE & BROWN.[91]

SEC. 5. The Acts of Congress, thus published, shall be bound by the public printer in a style not inferior to the Acts of the General Assembly of the State of Alabama, for which service he shall receive the sum of twenty-five cents per copy.

SEC. 6. The public printer shall be entitled to receive as compensation for the publication of the laws and journal, the following prices, viz: for each page of the laws and journals, including press work, paper, pressing, folding and stitching, the sum of four dollars.

SEC. 7. For all job printing ordered by Congress, the public printers shall receive the following compensation, and no more:

I. *For bills, resolutions and reports*—For compensation per page (foolscap), one dollar and twenty-five cents; for press work, folding and stitching one hundred copies, twenty-five cents per page, and *pro rate* for all copies over one hundred.

II. *For Rules, Constitution and other Pamphlets*—For composition per page (octavo), in small pica plain, one dollar; in small pica ruled, one dollar and fifty cents; for brevier plain, one dollar and fifty cents; for brevier ruled, two dollars; for rule and figure work, on page larger than royal octavo, per one thousand ems, one dollar; for press work, including folding and stitching, per token seventy cents.

III. *For Yeas and Nays, Circular Letters, and other Miscellaneous Printing order by Congress.*—For composition, plain work, per one thousand ems, seventy cents; rule and figure work per one thousand ems, one dollar; for press-work, including folding and stitching, per token or fraction of token.

IV. For all paper on which printing is done for Congress the public printer shall be allowed the fair market cost thereof, and twenty per cent additional thereto.

V. On all work done for Congress when in secret session, the public printer shall receive an additional compensation of ten per centum on the above rates.

SEC. 8. The chief officers of the Executive Departments of the Government are hereby authorized to contract for all necessary printing in connection with their several offices; in no case, however, at higher rates of compensation than hereinbefore prescribed for work done for Congress.

SEC. 9. The Postmaster General shall contract for the publication of all post bills and other blanks connected with his office, not exceeding the following rates for compensation, including rule and figure work; per one thousand ems, fifty cents; for press work, per clean token (the sheets not to be less than sixteen by twenty six inches), fifty cents; for paper, ten per cent. on actual cost. Nothing shall be allowed for altering the name of a postmaster on a post bill, or other blank; nor shall there be an additional charge for composition when the name of the postoffice alone is changed; but the printer shall be required to keep always on hand forms for postoffice blanks, and when new orders are given the charge shall be made only for the press work and paper, and such new composition as may be necessary.

SEC. 10. All accounts for printing done for Congress, or any one of the Executive Departments, shall, before the same are allowed and paid, be sworn to by the Public Printer or contractor; shall be accompanied by vouchers, showing the cost of the paper used, and the quantity thereof; so shall be certified to be correctly made out under this law by at least two disinterested practical printers in no way connected with the office or business of the claimant.

SEC. 11. The foregoing rates and provisions do not apply to advertisements in public gazettes by order of any of the Executive Departments for which the usual fees paid by other advertisers shall be allowed, but no advertisement from any of the Executive Departments shall be inserted in more than three public gazettes in the same State.

SEC. 12. When printing on parchment is required to be done for any Executive Department, the parchment shall be purchased and furnished by such department, and a special contract made for such printing, not exceeding ten dollars per thousand copies.

SEC. 13. There shall be connected with the Department of Justice a Bureau of Printing, the chief officer of which shall be appointed by the President, by and with the advice and consent of the Congress, and shall be known as the Superintendent of Public Printing. No person shall be eligible to this office who is not skilled in and acquainted with the practical details of the business of printing—nor shall the Superintendent of Public Printing be in any manner, directly or indirectly, interested in the contracts for public printing—nor with the printing office at which the same is done—nor connected with any newspaper in any capacity whatever.

SEC. 14. It shall be the duty of the superintendent to supervise, direct, and control all the printing done by order of Congress, or under contract with any executive department, as to the quality of paper to be used, the character of type, the style of binding, and the general execution of the work, and also as to the time and order in which the same shall be completed. It shall be his duty also to report to the head of the department, at least once a year, the condition of the public printing, stating the amount paid out for the same on each contract, specifying the amount paid out under the order of each department, and giving estimates of the probable expenditure for the succeeding year, which report shall be laid before the Congress by the President, in connection with his annual message. It shall be his duty also to take from every contractor of public printing such bonds, with good security, as he may require, not exceeding the probable amount of the contract price for the printing to be done by such contractor, and conditioned for the faithful performance of his contract in every particular. Such bonds shall be renewed annually by contractors whose work shall be continuing in its character, and extends beyond the year continuing its commencement.

SEC. 15. All accounts for printing done when rendered, as hereinbefore provided, shall be audited and endorsed by the Superintendent of Public Printing before the same shall be paid. If the superintendent shall refuse to receive any work done, or shall refuse to allow any accounts rendered, the printer or contractor may appeal from such decision to the head of the department, whose decision on the appeal shall be final and conclusive.

SEC. 16. All laws or parts of laws militating against the provisions of this Act are hereby repealed.

And then, on motion of Mr. WALKER, of Alabama, the Congress went into secret session.

Monday, February 25, 1861

(Charleston *Mercury*, February 28, 1861)

The Congress met at 12 o'clock, m., and was called to order by the President, Hon. HOWELL COBB, of Georgia.

After prayer by the Rev. Dr. MANLY, the Journal of Saturday was read and adopted.

Mr. SHORTER, of Alabama. Mr. President: I ask leave to present the following resolution:

> *Resolved*, That the Committee on Public Lands be instructed to inquire into the present condition of the public lands lying within the limits of the Confederate States, and also into the expediency of declaring by the Confederate States all title and right in the same in favor of the states respectively in which any of the public lands may be situated; and that the committee have leave to report by bill or otherwise, as they deem expedient.

Mr. President, the States of Mississippi and Louisiana have taken some action with respect to the public lands within their own limits. Georgia and South Carolina are the only original States within which there are no public lands, now comprised within the Confederate States. We trust other States will join us at some future day. The opinion prevails to a very large extent that the best disposition that could be made of the public lands in which the Confederate States may feel that they have an interest, is to put them in charge of the States respectively in which they may lie. As a source of revenue they cannot be looked to or relied upon to any extent. The expense of disposing of them would be very nearly as great as the amount that could be realized from their sale. In consultation with the Chairman of the Committee on Public Lands, I thought it expedient to introduce that resolution, and particularly because inquiries made of me by officers in the land offices of the State of Alabama, as to what direction would be given by Congress to this matter. I trust, therefore, that the resolution will be adopted, and the Committee be charged with the inquiry.

Mr. WRIGHT, of Georgia. Mr. President, the question submitted by the gentleman from Alabama is a very grave question, or the one embodied in his resolution, and has formed the subject of some reflections with me as a member of the Committee on Public Lands, but I do not know that I have any objection to the course the gentleman indicates, that the resolution be referred to the committee for its consideration, to make such report as they think the circumstances require.

The question was then taken and the resolution was agreed to.

Mr. CHESNUT, of South Carolina, presented the petition of GEORGE FOX and JOHN C. THORNTON,[92] citizens of the State of Georgia, in relation to patents; which was referred to the Committee on Patents.

Mr. WAUL, of Texas, presented a memorial from Mr. HENRY WINSLOW, a citizen of New Mexico,[93] which was referred to the Committee on Territories without being read.

Also, a communication from the President of the Texas Convention,[94] which was also referred to the Committee on Indian Affairs, without being read.

Mr. RHETT, of South Carolina. Mr. President, I rise merely to state to the Congress that the labors of the Committee on the Permanent Constitution are nearly brought to a close, and on last Friday it was placed in the hands of the printer, but not up to this time completed. We hope, however, to lay the Constitution before the body by Wednesday morning next.

The body then proceeded to consideration of the bill to make certain provisions in relation to printing the first on the calendar.

Mr. T. R. R. COBB, of Georgia. Mr. President, I propose that that bill lay over for a day. The Committee desire one more interview with the public printer before action is taken on it.

The bill was accordingly laid over.

Mr. MEMMINGER, of South Carolina, presented the application of Mr. SIMPSON BOBO, of South Carolina,[95] offering a site for an armory; which was referred to the Committee on Military Affair.

And then, on motion of Mr. BARNWELL, the Congress proceeded to sit with closed doors.

Tuesday, February 26, 1861

(Charleston *Mercury*, March 1, 1861)

The Congress met at 12 o'clock, m., and was called to order by the President, Hon. HOWELL COBB, of Georgia. After prayer by the Rev. Mr. MITCHELL, the Journal of yesterday was read and approved.

Mr. WALKER,[96] of Alabama, presented a communication from a citizen of Alabama, in reference to a flag for the Confederacy; which was referred to the Committee on Flags. [document XII; image XIII and XIV]

Mr. CURRY, of Alabama, presented two letters containing suggestions in reference to the flag; which were referred to the Committee on that subject. [documents XIII and XIV; images XV and XVI]

Mr. HILL, of Georgia. Mr. President—

The PRESIDENT. The gentleman from Georgia.

Mr. HILL. During my absence, sir, from Congress, a lady of great taste and genius in the city of La Grange sent to me a model flag for the new Confederacy, which I design to present to Congress, and I present it with a remark or two, because the letter was miscarried, and is not here at hand for the information of the committee. I will simply remark that the flag combines three very important ideas: first, simplicity—it is easily made, very easily; second, its originality—there is no flag of any nation even approaching it; and, thirdly, its expressiveness. I will simply say there is not a figure or a design of that flag that does not in itself represent some fundamental idea in the history or character, or the supposed destiny of this Confederacy, and in the combined effect representing the combined character and destiny of the Republic. I move, sir, that it be referred to the Committee on Flags, and hope the late hour will not prevent its receiving the consideration which it may merit.

The motion was agreed to.

Mr. NISBET, of Georgia. Mr. President, I hold in my hand a memorial from the Chamber of Commerce of the city of Macon,[97] the place of my residence, which I beg leave to offer to the consideration of Congress, and move to refer it to the Committee on Commerce; and I ask indulgence for one moment to state the object of these memorialists. Last fall, it is known to our people—perhaps not generally—that a cotton fair (as it was called) was held at Macon, and it was numerously attended.[98] The object was to invite the co-operation of foreign State capitalists in the hopes of inaugurating a free trade with our States. That fair was partially successful, sir, but in order to aid in the views of that fair, by an act of the Federal Government the city of Macon was declared, for the special purpose, a port of entry. The memorial I hold in my hand asks the consideration of this Congress, whether or not it is proper to declare that city, by act of Congress, a free port and port of entry. There are some advantages for making the city of Macon a port of entry. For example, it occupies, geographically, the centre of the State of Georgia, which her sister States have been pleased to honor with the appellation of the Empire State of the South. It is on the border of the great cotton region of our state, with a population of some eight to ten thousand, very enterprising in its character—a body of merchants, possessing large capital, and diligence, and enterprise in the pursuit of their avocation. In addition to that, it is accessible to the Atlantic ocean; to this city by railroad; by navigation to the Chattahoochee river, and is in direct communication west by railroad leading to Memphis. There is, however, one single thought that I venture to present in the hearing of Congress which may commend these facts to them, and that is this: It is known to all of us that the ports of our Southern coast are subject, at intervals, to the scourge, yellow fever, and other autumnal diseases and epidemics, which has had the effect, as at Norfolk, Charleston, Savannah and New Orleans, to repel the investment of capital to some extent. Now, sir, it is supposed by many that if a port of entry is established at Macon, it will not necessarily interfere with the business of the seaboard beyond the matter in view, but it will have the effect of inviting capital to a location not embarrassed by the causes to which I have just now adverted. It is the opinion of intelligent gentlemen, merchants and others, that the increase of revenue to the Confederate States of America, by reason of the establishment of a port of entry at such a location, would greatly enhance the revenues of the Confederacy. I invite respectfully the consideration of the Committee of Commerce to the application of the citizens of Macon.

Mr. CRAWFORD. Mr. President, the passage of a resolution renders unnecessary the reference of the communication from the city of Macon to the Committee on Commerce. The action of this body will render it necessary for the honorable member of the Macon District of the State of Georgia, to present the claims of that city to the Secretary of the Treasury. The Secretary of the Treasury has the regulation and direction of the ports of entry and delivery within the Confederate States; therefore, it will be proper for him to withdraw the communication and refer it to the Secretary of the Treasury.

Mr. NISBET. Do I understand my colleague to say that a law has been passed conferring that power upon the Secretary of the Treasury?

Mr. CRAWFORD. Yes, sir.

Mr. NISBET. That being the case, Mr. President, I withdraw the memorial and refer it to the proper department.

Mr. RHETT, of South Carolina. Mr. President, I beg leave to say that the Committee on the Permanent Constitution have come to a conclusion of their labors, and I have now before me the Constitution proper and, as soon as convenient, I shall move to go into secret secession for the purpose of considering it.

Mr. SHORTER, of Alabama, from the Committee on Engrossment, reported as correctly enrolled, an Act to define more accurately the exemption on certain goods from duty; an Act to modify the Navigation Laws, and repeal the discriminating duties on ships and vessels; an Act in relation to the slave trade, and to punish persons offending therein; an Act for the establishment and organization of a general staff for the army of the Confederate States of America, and an Act to authorize the Secretary of the Treasury to establish additional ports and places of entry and delivery, and appoint officers therefor, when the President signed the same.[99]

The PRESIDENT. The Clerk will report the first Bill in the public calendar.

The Clerk accordingly reported the Bill in relation to public printing.

The section being reported in relation to binding, stitching, &c.—

Mr. COBB moved that the compensation be increased from $4 to $6. I am (said he) satisfied that price is not sufficient compensation.

The amendment was agreed to.

The section in relation to composition per page having been reported—

Mr. COBB said: For the same reason, Mr. President, I move to strike out "twenty" in the fourth line, and insert "seventy"; so that it will read for composition per page $1.75. I am satisfied that is not too much.

Mr. WITHERS, of South Carolina. Mr. President, I must ask the gentleman (I do not know whether or not my memory is correct) whether at the time the public printer was employed, it was not resolved that he should receive such compensation as was received by the public printer of the State of Alabama? If my recollection is correct, these are the terms upon which the public printer was chosen.

Mr. COBB. It is true; sir, that the resolution embraced that provision. The difficulty is—and the Committee on Printing discovered it very early—that the laws of Alabama do not provide sufficiently for the case, and the compensation given by these laws is not proper under the circumstances. This bill has been submitted to the printers under that resolution, and with the amendments I have offered, and shall offer, meets their approbation. It makes the regulations permanent, and meets the cases not met under the laws of Alabama. The law of Alabama provides for the publication of so many copies of the laws passed by the Legislature, and gives so much per page; and this compels this Congress to publish the same number of copies; and give the same compensation. The printers, themselves, are satisfied with this compensation. It puts them on a better basis—a more permanent basis, and it ought to be adopted.

Mr. WITHERS. Mr. President, this body very well knows that whenever I have had to do with the business of salaries or compensation, I have endeavored to confine this body, not to a parsimonious, but to a fair and economical administration of the funds of the Government, whenever we have any. I speak of the future—we have nothing now. I do not know whether or not the terms established between the printers of the Legislature of Alabama really do accord to the printer a full compensation for his services. I never can be made to understand that, sir, because I am not a practical printer, but I think I understand this, that the respectable gentlemen appointed by this Congress to do their public printing, know their own business—that they are much more likely to know what is a fair compensation than this Congress is likely to know, and if they have undertaken the work on the terms specified by this Congress, I know of no reason why we should depart from them. If they find they have been uninformed—

Mr. COBB, (interrupting.) Mr. President, one word will satisfy the delegate. The prices fixed by the bill are lower than those fixed by the Alabama law, and the printers have given up an advantage.

Mr. WITHERS, (resuming.) I am opposed, then, to that bill for that very reason. If it is lower than the contract made, it is derogatory to the reputation of this body. I understand that the particular motion before the body is to enlarge the compensation for the particular work specified beyond that given by the Legislature of Alabama. My proposition is to adhere to the bargain made, and, whether good or bad, let the printers have the compensation we agreed to give them.

Mr. COBB. Mr. President, I hope the Congress and the gentleman will be satisfied with the explanation I will now give. It is impossible for the printers to do their work under that resolution and not leave a great many matters unsettled, and necessary to be settled hereafter. First, it includes all work required by this Congress that was not required of the printers of the Legislature of Alabama; and second, there are no terms or prices specified in that bill. The printers are satisfied with the general scope of this bill, and although it is true it diminishes the price on certain of the laws in general and in the printing of bills and resolutions, yet it gives them ample compensation, and fixes the compensation for those other kinds of printing not provided for in the Alabama law. It is clearly our duty to leave nothing unsettled in this matter, but at once to arrange the law so as not only to control the printers for Congress, but the printers for the Executive Departments. Delegates will perceive that the subsequent sections of the bill prescribe that the same prices shall be allowed to the printers for Congress and the printers for the Executive Departments. It is exceedingly important that the bill should be passed.

The amendment was agreed to.

The bill was then read the third time and passed.

And then, on motion of Mr. BROOKE, the Congress proceeded to sit with closed doors.

Wednesday, February 27, 1861

(Charleston *Mercury*, March 2, 1861)

The Congress met at 12 o'clock, m., and was called to order by the President, Hon. HOWELL COBB, of Georgia.

After prayer by the Rev. Mr. CAPERS,[100] the Journal of yesterday was read and adopted.

Mr. WRIGHT, of Georgia, presented a model flag; which was referred to the Committee on the Flag.

Mr. WRIGHT. Mr. President, I also offer the following resolution:

> *Resolved, by the Confederate States in Congress assembled,* That whenever Congress may enter upon the consideration of the Permanent Constitution, it shall be done in open session.

I do not propose to press a vote upon it now, or make any remarks upon it at this time. I move that it be placed upon the proper calendar, and in the meantime I ask the consideration and reflection of the members upon it.

Mr. CHILTON, of Alabama. I ask leave, Mr. President, to offer the following resolution:

> *Resolved,* That the Committee on Naval Affairs be instructed to inquire into the propriety of constructing, by this Government, two iron-plated frigates, and such iron-plated gunboats as may be necessary to protect commerce and provide for the safety of this Confederacy.

The question was taken and the resolution was agreed to.

Mr. CONRAD, of Louisiana. Mr. President, I beg leave to present the memorial of Messrs. GRATIAA & CO.,[101] a respectable commercial house in New Orleans, respecting a case arising out of the action of our recently passed revenue laws, which appears to be one of great hardship, and I beg that it be referred, without reading, to the Committee on Finance. I believe, sir, there is no Committee on Claims, and that the Committee on Finance is the proper one.

No objection being made, the memorial was referred.

Mr. CHESNUT, of South Carolina. Mr. President, I ask leave to present a communication from Mr. WM. GLAZE,[102] of Columbia, So. Ca., in relation to a manufactory of arms, and ask that it be referred to the Committee on Military Affairs without being read.

No objection being made, it was so referred.

Mr. WITHERS, of South Carolina. Mr. President, I have a communication addressed to me here by a citizen of South Carolina, Dr. JNO. M. PITTS,[103] making known to me that he has recently taken out a patent in relation to movable or portable fences, I believe, and another in relation to some invention concerning surgical instruments. He desires such course taken as will protect his rights in this Confederacy. I do not know what better to do with it than to offer it to Congress, with a motion to refer it to the Committee on Patents. I do not ask its reading.

No objection being made, it was so referred.

Mr. WAUL, of Texas, presented a communication from JAMES E. HARRISON;[104] which was referred to the Committee on Indian Affairs without being read.

Mr. WILSON, of Mississippi, from the Committee on Engrossment, reported, as correctly engrossed, an Act in relation to public printing; when the President signed the same.[105]

Mr. CHESNUT. Mr. President: There seems to be nothing on the public calendar, and Congress does not seem disposed to do any other business; I now move that we proceed to sit with closed doors.

The motion was agreed to; and, accordingly, the Congress proceeded to sit with closed doors.

Thursday, February 28, 1861

(Charleston *Mercury*, March 5, 1861)

The Congress met at 11 o'clock, and was called to order by the President, Hon. HOWELL COBB, of Georgia, when the journal of yesterday was read and approved.

Mr. CHILTON, Alabama. Mr. President.

The PRESIDENT. The gentleman from Alabama.

Mr. CHILTON. I am requested to present a memorial signed by all of our merchants, except two or three who are absent, praying that Montgomery be made a port of entry. I ask its reference—it is not necessary to read it. I ask its reference to the Committee on Commercial Affairs.

The PRESIDENT. It will be so ordered, unless objection be made.

Mr. CURRY, of Alabama. I have a letter, sir, which I ask to be referred to the Committee on Naval Affairs.[106]

The letter was so referred, without being read.

Mr. CURRY. Mr. President. I hold in my hand, also, several designs, for—I won't call it a national flag, for I do not think the term national properly applicable to this government;—but for a flag for the Confederate States of America, which I desire to ask a reference of to the appropriate Committee. Several of them, I think, are worthy of attention; one of them especially, Mr. President, I invite the attention of the Committee on Flags to. The conception is that of a distinguished gentleman of rare intellectual culture, varied attainments, and unquestioned taste for the beautiful.[107] On a field of blue is an eagle in its upward flight, with a cluster of stars representing the Confederate States. The remainder of the flag also preserves the historical white and red, not in horizontal stripes, but in perpendicular lines. The flag, in my judgment, is unique and emblematical, blending the historical associations of the past, and stimulating the hopes of the future. It also preserves our Republican emblem—the red, the white and the blue, with the eagle which we all know, on Roman, French and American standards is everywhere regarded as the bird of liberty. I propose to refer it also to the appropriate Committee. [images XVII and XVIII]

The President. It will be so ordered, unless objection be made.

Mr. T. R. R. Cobb, of Georgia. I desire to report a bill, sir. Although I do not wish it to be placed on its passage, I hope it will be read in full. It is very short; and after it is read, I will move its reference to the appropriate Committee.

The bill was accordingly read, as follows:

A Bill to Define The Jurisdiction Of The Federal Courts In Certain Cases

Sec. 1. *The Congress of the Confederate States do enact,* That in the event of a conflict of arms between the Confederate States and the United States, or of a refusal on the part of the authorities of the United States to recognize the Independence of the Confederate States, or to receive the Commissioners sent by the latter to treat with the former, in relation to the several matters of controversy existing between them, the courts of the Confederate States shall not take cognizance of any civil cause in which the plaintiff is or may be either the said United States, or either one of them, or any citizen or citizens thereof.

Sec. 2. All pending cases, in which the plaintiff shall be in either of the classes aforesaid, shall, upon the happening of either of the contingencies aforesaid be dismissed on motion; and all process, mesne or final, which shall have been issued at the suit of such plaintiffs, shall be arrested and declared inoperative.

Mr. Cobb. Mr. President, I would desire to put that bill on its passage, but according to our regular rule it is better that it should pass through our standing committees. I move, therefore, its reference to the Committee on the Judiciary.

The President so ordered, unless objection be made.

Mr. Hill of Georgia, presented a model flag, designed by an excellent lady of Northern Georgia; which was referred to the Committee on Flags.[108]

Mr. CHESNUT, of South Carolina, presented a memorial from Mr. GEORGE T. SINCLAIR,[109] praying that a *caveat* be issued for the protection of a magazine until he can get a patent; which was referred to the Committee on Patents, without being read.

Mr. OCHILTREE, of Texas, presented a communication from JNO. C. ROBERTSON,[110] of the Committee of Safety appointed by the State Convention of Texas, containing most important suggestions; which was referred to the Committee on Military Affairs, without being read.

Mr. CURRY presented a letter regarding a tariff,[111] which was referred to the Committee on Finance, without being read.

Mr. CHILTON, from the Committee on Postal Affairs, reported the following bill, which was read three times and passed:

AN ACT SUPPLEMENTAL TO AN ACT TO REGULATE THE RATES OF POSTAGE AND FOR OTHER PURPOSES[112]

SEC. 1. *The Confederate States of America do enact,* That until postage stamps and stamped envelopes can be procured and distributed; the Postmaster-General may order the postage of this Confederacy to be prepaid in money, under such rules, regulations and restrictions as he may adopt.

SEC. 2. *Be it further enacted,* That until otherwise provided by law, the Postmaster-General may contract with any line of steamers for the transportation of mail matter between the ports this Confederacy and the ports of foreign governments. *Provided,* that the rates of postage shall not exceed the rates allowed by the present laws of the United States for similar service, and the compensation to be paid shall not exceed the income from postage on such matter.

Mr. SHORTER, of Alabama, from the Committee on Engrossments, reported, as correctly engrossed, an Act to raise money for the support of the Government, and to provide for the defence of the Confederate States of America and an Act to raise provisional forces for the Confederate States of America, and for other purposes; when the President signed the same.[113]

And then, on motion of Mr. NISBET, the Congress went into secret session.

Friday, March 1, 1861

(Montgomery *Weekly Advertiser*, March 6, 1861)

Congress met to-day at 10 o'clock, a.m. As no public business was offered, the body went into secret session.

Saturday, March 2, 1861

(Charleston *Mercury*, March 5, 1861; Montgomery *Weekly Advertiser*, March 6, 1861)

The Congress met at 10 o'clock, a.m., and was called to order by the President, Hon. HOWELL COBB, of Georgia, when the Journal of yesterday was read and approved.

Mr. CURRY, of Alabama. Mr. President, I have a memorial from a citizen of this State in reference to the establishment of an armory and a foundry.[114] I desire to present it, and have it referred to the Committee on Military Affairs. I took occasion to express the other day, Mr. President, my opinion that such an establishment was very much needed by the Confederate States of America. I believe from the administration of General WASHINGTON, down to the present administration of the United States Government, every single one of them, from the Executive to some of the heads of departments, urged the necessity of an establishment of this kind for the Government of the United States. While the old government had armories for the construction of small arms, I believe they were compelled, and are yet, to rely upon individual manufactories for their cannon. It seems to me, Mr. President, that the Confederate States have neither armories nor foundries, neither of a public nor of a private character. We ought to take prompt and efficient measures for the establishment of some such enterprise. A foundry especially is necessary, in my judgment at least, to test the metals, analyze them, and furnish standards and patterns, for cannon may be needed by the Government. States and Governments are almost the sole purchasers of cannon, as individuals have very little use for them; but as it is a weapon of much more importance than small arms, the issues of battle being almost entirely dependent upon them, the necessity and importance of having an enterprise of this kind is so much greater. I do not propose, however, to go into an elaborate statement of the necessities for such an establishment. I desire more particularly to call the attention of the Committee on Military Affairs and this Congress to some of the requisites which I think are essentially necessary in determining the location of an establishment of this sort. It should have healthfulness; that being indispensable. There should be an ample supply of coal, iron ore and wood, and it should be so conveniently situated as to be free from attack by a foreign power. It should also, of course, have an easy means of transportation to the seaboard, and be accessible to all parts of the Confederate States. The location which is designated in the memorial I have presented, combines all these indispensable requisites. The country is remarkable for its salubrity; iron ore, inexhaustible, and of the finest qualities, exists right at the spot. In close proximity there are invaluable coal mines and innumerable quantities of wood. It is also free from access by foreign powers except from the United States. It is now in close and intimate connection with the seaboard, and when the railroad from Montgomery to Decatur is completed, and the railroad from Jacksonville to Dalton is completed, connection with the States east of us will be established. I do not think, Mr. President, that either this Congress or any Committee that may be appointed by this Congress, are competent to select a place for a foundry, for they have not the requisite information and knowledge of the subject. Every one familiar with the subject knows that there are possibly a hundred different kinds of iron adapted to the various necessities of such an establishment. He then read from a report of the Secretary of the Treasury of the United States Government, on the properties of iron, remarking that samples of the iron submitted to that department by the memorialists showed the least oxidation when exposed to water. This report (said he) shows the tendency to form new combinations and the necessity for chemical purity. Hence, I remark, that neither the Committee nor this Congress are competent to make a selection of a suitable place for a foundry for this Government, and I think the Committee on Military Affairs ought to report—so urgent and imperative is the necessity for an establishment of this kind—ought to report a small sum of money, requiring that a full, thorough and accurate survey should be made of the different localities which may be offered as competing points by disinterested and competent scientific officers of the army or of the navy. Some such process, it seems to me, ought to be adopted, before the final location of an establishment of so much importance as this. I ask that the memorial may be referred to the Committee on Military Affairs.

The PRESIDENT. It will be so ordered, if there be no objection.

Mr. HARRIS, of Mississippi. Mr. President, I offer the following resolution:

> *Resolved*, That the Committee on Finance be instructed to enter upon a revision of the present tariff as early as practicable, with a view to a gradual reduction of the rates of duties and enlargement of the free list, by exemption of such dutiable articles as occasion an expense and trouble in the collection of duties disproportionate to the revenue arising therefrom.

Mr. President, at the very commencement of the session of this body under the Provisional Government, I introduced a bill which was passed, putting in force the body of federal laws so far as applicable to our condition and not inconsistent with our Constitution. When that was done, the friends of free trade met me with the objection that, notwithstanding all our professions to the country on that subject, we had put down upon it the tariff of '57—a tariff wholly inapplicable to our condition and contrary to the principles we professed. The answer given was, that, for the time being, we must have some law in force, and it was understood that the Congress would at once enter upon the revision of that body of laws, and especially upon a revision of the tariff law. With a view to that policy—that is, to enable the great Northwest to get a market cheaper than those of Boston and New York, to enable the country merchants of the Confederate States on the extended line of contact with the United States to undersell the country merchants of the United States, and thus throw the onus of illicit traffic on their shoulders—a policy that is to put the crown of commercial supremacy upon the South—which is to achieve, sir, one of the great positive advantages of a separation from the unfriendly States of North America—to wit: commercial independence. I do not distrust the committee, sir. This resolution is not to be taken as evidence that this body distrusts that committee. My object is to invite from them a public response, to give them a chance to make a public response upon that subject this morning, in order to satisfy the country on this matter. All I desire is to have a public expression on the part of Congress of our purpose in respect to this tariff. It will be perceived that the object of this resolution is to instruct that committee to make such a response to it. As the latter is unnecessary now, I ask that the resolution be put on its passage.

The resolution was accordingly read a second time.

Mr. TOOMBS, of Georgia. I will remark, sir, that that Committee have had under consideration the vexed question of duties upon imports, and a public report will be made at an early day. I rather think that it is better that there should not be any instructions upon the subject.

Mr. CONRAD, of Louisiana. Read the resolution.

The PRESIDENT. The gentleman from Georgia is on the floor.

Mr. TOOMBS. Mr. President, if the resolution is one of instruction, as I understand it to be, I am opposed to its passage.

The PRESIDENT. The Clerk will again report the resolution.

The resolution was accordingly read again.

Mr. TOOMBS. My objection, Mr. President, is to the reduction of duties in the present condition of the Confederate States. It is very important that we should raise a large revenue necessary for the maintenance of the government—to raise armies and defend our liberties; and surely the existing tariff is the best mode of doing so. The rate of duties under the existing tariff is the best mode of raising revenue, and it ought to be done in that way. The present tariff, which received the unanimous vote of the whole of the Confederate States, of the entire representation of the slaveholding States, was a tariff found inadequate, according to the extravagant habits of the old Government, to maintain at all its expenditures. Then while entering into a revolution in which it is possible we may have to fight for our rights, will you instruct your committee to reduce the tariff? I think it unwise.

Mr. BARNWELL, of South Carolina. Mr. President, my views are different from those of the gentleman from Georgia. It is my opinion we can make large and substantial reductions in the rate of duties imposed by the tariff of '57, and yet provide ample revenues. But whilst I differ on that point, I do not know that it is necessary for the House to instruct the Committee on the form of that resolution. It seems too precise in its language; and that Committee ought to be allowed a wider scope in the consideration of this question. I do not think that the bill of '57 is proper. It was decidedly a bill for protection. It remains, then, for protection, and that, I think, neither meets the wishes nor the wants of the country. I think we ought to make large reductions in the duties, and still be able to maintain the Government; and I only object to the resolution because its terms are too precise, and do not allow the Committee that latitude of expression that ought to be allowed to them.

Mr. HARRIS. Mr. President, it occurs to me that the resolution admits of a wide range of discussion both as to the time and manner of the report from the Committee. It provides that as early as practicable they shall provide for the gradual—not sudden—the gradual reduction of the Tariff. Well, now, if satisfactory to the country, perhaps, this reduction will begin six, eight, or twelve months hence. It will be perceived by Congress that this resolution gives a wide discretion to the committee. That is all it does. It specifies nothing, except what commends itself to the good sense of the financier, that we ought to enlarge the free list so as to put upon it all those articles involving expenses in their collection. My object in introducing the resolution was to get some public expression from this Congress in order to satisfy the country that we are earnestly and honestly engaged in an effort to secure for it one of the great advantages it promised itself in this movement—that is, a low duty.

Mr. McRae, of Alabama. Mr. President, I think the Committee will report a bill on Monday morning next. The resolution, therefore, is scarcely necessary.

Mr. Miles, of South Carolina. Mr. President, I am one of those who always supposed that the Southern slaveholding States desire the near approximation of free-trade, and at as early a period as practicable. I always supposed there was throughout these slaveholding States now united in this Government, a very decided opposition to the Tariff of 1857. I cannot agree in the views my friend from Georgia (Mr. Toombs) expressed, and there is one point I desire to call attention to, and that is, that the United States are now a foreign government in reference to this government. We import from those States immense quantities of manufactures which are paying, of course, into the treasury of this Confederacy the regular rates. We can, therefore, reasonably expect to raise a great deal more money at a reduction of the rates, importing as we do, so largely from States from which we heretofore imported free. In reference to this tariff of '57, I have supposed that it was universally considered very protective. The free list itself was really a compromise with the manufacturing interest. The free list was practically for the protection of the manufacturers. I daily receive from Charleston letters from merchants, complaining, bitterly complaining, I am almost compelled to say, of this tariff. They are willing, of course, Mr. President, to have duties imposed upon goods coming from the United States, or any quarter of the world; but they believe, and I believe, a duty of ten or fifteen per cent. to be sufficient. We expect our trade to be largely increased, and our imports to swell to such proportions that we will raise quite as large a revenue by a low duty as by a high one. I trust the Committee will, as I understand they are desirous of doing, report some decided reduction of the present tariff.

Mr. Withers. Mr. President, I have not heard a proposition in this Congress that I approve of more than that of the gentleman from Mississippi (Mr. Harris). I do not know whether it is in my power to throw out the idea of enlarging the free list to any very great extent. I am aware that he confines the proposition to that description of articles, the collection of the duty upon which will not be in due proportion to the expenses of the collection; but the best and most just tariff, of which

I can conceive, is one very horizontal, so as to enable every consuming interest (so far as there is a distinction in the consumption of the various articles by the various description of people) equal—equal and proportionate to the necessities of the Government. Well, when a man looks at the subject through South Carolina eyes, he regards this matter of low duties to be one of essential importance as affecting the liberties and enjoyment of the proper political rights of the people of the Confederate States. That is the way we look at the question, and those who passed through the scenes of '28 and '32 in South Carolina know well what was the fixed opinion of that day.[115] I have seen no occasion to change my views from that day to this, and I had some humble part in the scenes of that crisis. We were willing to go to the extent of enlarging the powers of the Federal Government to support free trade—not meaning, thereby, that no tariff should be levied upon imports, but that a tariff should be strictly and honestly for the purposes of revenue, and should not be poisoned with the protection of one interest at the expense of another. It is said to be an improper course to give instruction to the Committee on Finance. I see no objection to the kind of instruction contained in that resolution—that they should enter upon the gradual reduction of the duties and the enlargement of the free list in respect to those articles, the collection of the duties on which do not bear their proper proportion of the expense of collection. The expression of the opinions entertained by members of this body are invited by this resolution. Their expression is invited in public. I am glad of it. It is fit that we should express our views upon a question of so much importance as that. And, let me call attention to one view of this question. You believe that you have it in your power, by a judicious course of policy on the part of the government of these Confederate States, to command the amiable view and the amiable sentiments of fraternal regard of certain powerful governments in Europe. How do you expect to command it? King Cotton, say you, is the power; and you have decided upon this subject by laying upon his majesty the expense of the government, intended mainly for his protection. How do you expect to gain the good will of foreign governments of any people? Do you expect to gain it upon a theory inconsistent with the well established doctrines of political economy, or of moral philosophy? You never can secure the good will of nations upon grounds of that kind. If Mammon gets ten thousand worshipers for one of the living God; if it is true that nations look to interest—and such I believe to be undeniably the fact—in respect to individuals and classes of individuals, how to you expect to command the regard you desire for the commissioners you will send to Europe? How do you expect to command for them the gracious consideration of these powers? Give them to understand, by adopting a resolution of this kind, that our policy is fixed; that there shall be a gradual reduction of your tariff of duties. Think you it will not attract the attention of Lord Palmerston and Louis Napoleon? Do you not put in the possession of your commissioners the power of commanding the respect of those who control the destinies of these great countries? Let us then express the opinion, and it will be in the power of your commissioners to point to this resolution and say to Louis Napoleon—"We desire to consult the interest of the people you rule, and to accept the olive branch extended to us." Here is a foundation—a foundation of national interest, which alone will control any people, and whereby we may establish a relation of amity, which at the same time will terminate in the good will and highest interests of the country. I believe such will be the natural fruit of the adoption of this resolution.[116]

Mr. BOYCE, of So. Carolina. I am very anxious, Mr. President, to take up this tariff. I look upon the tariff of 1857 as but a temporary measure. I think it ought to be considered with as little delay as possible, and that we ought to adopt simply a revenue tariff—one looking merely to the raising of money for the public treasury, and nothing else. I have in this regard, sir, differed from my honorable friend from Georgia, and I think the present tariff susceptible of reduction.

Mr. HARRIS. Mr. President, I have been informed that it is the intention of the Committee to report a bill on Monday, and as this discussion will be raised then, I withdraw this resolution.

Mr. TOOMBS. I hope he will not act upon that assurance. I do not give any myself. I do not know that the Committee will report in a week. I hope the gentleman will not act under a wrong impression.

Mr. HARRIS. I understand so from a member of that committee, who gave me the information in order that I might withdraw this resolution. I shall be willing to take it up at an early day, and I hope a measure will be reported corresponding in its features to this resolution.

Mr. TOOMBS. I shall not make one corresponding to that resolution, so far as I am concerned. I am for revenue, and I would like to make a tariff exclusively to raise revenue. These protective articles furnish the best revenue tariff that can be devised, because they lead to the transfer now of money from the pockets of the manufacturers to our treasury. But this is a question I decline going into further at this time. Free-trade and protection is not the issue before this Congress. It is whether or not we will raise money by duties upon imports. I think the duties upon imports are the best, especially now, and the duties of the Tariff of 1857 are purely revenue duties. You may take the articles of brandy and wine under the Tariff of 1816, and they were taxed exclusively for revenue. Gentlemen are mistaken as to the benefits to result from an extension of the free list. While the free list is made for the purpose of protecting manufactures, we will get none of them, because we are not engaged in that branch of industry. So far as foreign Governments are concerned, I think we will make a great mistake by consulting their interest instead of our own. Fifty millions in the Treasury and one hundred thousand armed men are the best recommendation to send abroad and the best security at home. Seek to buy foreign opinion. We will get their contempt, and deserve it; that's worse. We must take care of the interests of our people. I am for the freest trade consistent with the best mode of collecting the revenue. I will not put burdens upon our industry for the purpose of protecting another. This idea of gentlemen that we will get a great deal of revenue by charging a low duty is mistaken. We might just as well get direct taxes by charging cents instead of dollars. There is, in my opinion, not one dollar's increase of revenue by a reduction of the duty on the larger articles. I am opposed to charging all alike as nearly as possible. It is unjust to labor. Suppose the whole revenue was raised upon the articles of salt and coffee, of which the poor man consumed as much as the wealthy man. Then you would receive more from poverty than from wealth, and that would be wrong. The true basis is that property shall pay according to its amount. Hence you would make out of the articles of general consumption a fruitful source of revenue. In England the beer drinkers—the very dregs of poverty itself—pay the very largest duty. It is unjust. Luxuries ought to pay higher duties than the necessaries of life. If the reduction of the present tariff from nineteen to ten per cent. should be adopted and become a failure, I do not wish to be held responsible for it.

Mr. WITHERS. I have but a word to say in reply. I wish to explain myself on one point, and not to get into any argument with the gentleman from Georgia, upon the virtue of what may be called the horizontal system. If the poor man drinks coffee and eats salt, I do not see why he should not pay his proportion as well as the rich man. The rich man pays for silks and satins at least, and his wines and brandies. But let that pass. I shall not enter into that subject, but to what has fallen from him on another subject I wish to call attention, because he is a double character. He is a member of this body, and he is Secretary of State. Now, sir, he says what I agree to as a general proposition. I would by no means recommend to this people to enlist the favor of foreign governments by sacrificing their own interest or their own honor. Not I. That is not the temper of my people. The gentleman seems to think that this resolution was to be placed in the hands of the Commissioners, and announced to the European powers by way of humble supplication that they would grant the light of their countenances to this young Confederacy. Not so. He says the way to command their respect is to have fifty millions in the treasury, and one hundred thousand armed men. God forbid that it should be necessary for this Executive department to attain to such magnitude; but if we get into war, let there be a million muskets, and five hundred millions in the treasury.

Mr. MILES. Mr. President, I concur in what has fallen from my colleague. I confess that I think that it will not do for us to imagine that we are to impress foreign nations, or procure their good will or amity, by a full treasury or a large standing army. Now, I cannot see what part we in this Confederacy can possibly claim in European affairs. We cannot take any part at all in the matters distracting European Courts. We are an agricultural people. We desire to trade with the countries of the Old World. The only means, therefore, which we have of ensuring their good will, or of making favorable treaties with them, is through their commerce. Thorough military preparations on the part of our people will not influence them. They wish to deal with us as an agricultural people, and therefore it seems to me that we should present to them facilities for trading with us by imposing no duties on their manufactures. I differ entirely with the gentleman from Georgia, as to whether high duties will give us more revenue than low ones. There is a fundamental difference between us. I believe that if we have lower duties we will have more revenue; and with reference to the discrimination between the poor man and the rich man, I think my colleague (Mr. WITHERS), who has just spoken, addressed himself sufficiently to that point. Even in the tariff of '57, which he seems to approve, we have discrimination in favor of the rich against the poor. We find, sir, in the tariff of '57 that silk manufactures are only put down at 10 per cent., whilst the manufactures composed wholly of cotton are taxed 24 per cent. Now surely this cotton is more used by the poor than by the rich. And so I might specify other articles—woollens and other articles. But, Mr. President, we must lay the greatest stress upon the fact that we are now importing from the United States immense quantities of things which formerly came in free of duty. Why, take the article of glass. Glass in the tariff of '57 is put down at 24 per cent. We get, I suppose, the most of our glass from the Northern States. This, at a duty of 10 per cent., will give us a considerable amount.

Mr. TOOMBS. I would ask the gentleman if he supposes that this duty of 24 per cent. on cotton had any effect upon these manufactures?

Mr. MILES. The gentleman has misapprehended me. I instanced the duty of 24 per cent. to show that cotton was taxed higher than silk, a fabric used mainly by the rich. That which I intend to impress upon this Congress is the fact that we are now getting daily from the United States immense quantities of goods, some of them at 24 per cent. and others 19 per cent., upon which we could, if we assessed a duty of 10 per cent., get a very large amount of money into our Treasury, and it would be a clear gain.

Mr. TOOMBS. By the tariff of '57 there was a reduction of 25 per cent. upon all the articles of the tariff of '46, except such articles as were transferred to the free list. The principle was not altered except in that respect, and when a duty of 25 per cent. was put on cotton goods it was not to raise the price of the article.

Mr. MILES. The point incidentally mentioned was not the point I was elaborating at all. Now, the fact is this, we both want revenue; we both wish a tariff for revenue purposes, and as large as necessary for common defence and carrying on the common Government. The question is can you raise that revenue more readily by tolerably high duties or tolerably low duties? My impression is by low duties, because I find it is the experience of all countries that by diminishing the rates of duties you increase the importation so much more largely in proportion, that the result is a greater amount of revenue.

Mr. RHETT, of South Carolina. Mr. President, I do not think it important what kind of a tariff bill we pass for this year. This is a provisional government that will last but one year. We are in a transitory condition. What we do in this transitory condition is not of very much importance excepting as it reflects upon the future and our permanent condition. Sir, if the gentleman from Georgia (Mr. TOOMBS) over the way will join me in putting into the permanent constitution, which we have under consideration, a clause emphatically denying the power of this

Congress to lay duties for protection—for the protection of one branch of industry at the expense of another. I would not care what tariff he reported then.—I would vote for it because it would be nothing more than a temporary provision, adopted under the Provisional Constitution. That Constitution is but a temporary one; it is a revolutionary one; and the people everywhere will make allowances for any sort of legislation under it. But if gentlemen will not join me in putting that prohibition of the protective policy to the permanent Constitution, I say it will prove disastrous not only to our whole people, but to all our relations with foreign nations. It is in vain, sir, to suppose that foreign nations have no interest in this great movement. There can be no question that our progress is opening the door for the free access of foreign nations. Liberal commercial intercourse with England and France will secure the peace of the world and the prosperity of the people. It is in this view, sir, that this tariff will be met. But I say to the gentleman from Georgia, that I do not go for the fifty millions in the treasury or the one hundred thousand men. I do not see their necessity. I do not believe there will be a war. I do not believe in a standing army as the best instrument of preserving the liberties of the people.

Mr. CONRAD, of Louisiana. Mr. President, I think this discussion is premature. We are discussing the policy of a tariff before a tariff bill is reported. I submit therefore to the gentlemen to wait until a practical measure is before Congress before they engage in discussion. I move, therefore, that this resolution be laid over for the present.

The motion was agreed to.

Messrs. OLDHAM and REAGAN, of the Texas delegation, appeared and took their seats.

On motion of Mr. STEPHENS, of Georgia, the Congress then went into secret session.

Monday, March 4, 1861

(Charleston *Mercury*, March 7, 1861)

The Congress met at 10 o'clock, a. m, and was called to order by the President, Hon. HOWELL COBB, of Georgia. After prayer by the Rev. Mr. MANLY, the Journal of Saturday was read and adopted.

On motion of Mr. T. R. R. COBB, of Georgia, the following resolution was adopted:

> *Resolved*, That the members of the Alabama State Convention be invited to seats in this Hall during the public sessions of the Congress.

Mr. CURRY. Mr. President—

The PRESIDENT. The gentleman from Alabama.

Mr. CURRY. I have been requested, sir, by three citizens of the State of Alabama,[117] residents of the County of Talladega, to present to you, as President of the Congress of the Confederate States of America, this inkstand, manufactured by them from Alabama marble. As an inkstand, it may remind us that, while sitting as a Convention, we should not rely on unwritten law to define the powers of this Government, or the relations between it and the several States, but that the delegated powers should be so clearly expressed as to avoid all dangerous or latitudinous construction and interpretation. It seems to me, Mr. President, to be not altogether fanciful that the material of which that inkstand is constructed represents, in some degree, our present political condition. Marble is of such consistency as to yield readily to the delicate touch of the artist, moulding it into a thing of beauty, but yet not so yielding as to moulder away before the touch of time, or to dissolve by exposure to the elements. Our Government will yield readily to the suggestions of wisdom, friendship and peace, but will resist like a rock the red shock of battle or the more silent and dangerous attacks of treason and corruption. In the Constitution, true republican principles, like the constituent elements of marble, will crystalize into form, and be so durable that they will last for ages to come. This marble may indicate the strength and indissolubility of our Government and the duration of our Union. In its polish we may see the importance, and progress, and prosperity that spread out so invitingly before us; in its present form, the inducement to liberalize and extend our commerce; in its present form also, the insecurity of every institution without popular intelligence; in its Parian whiteness and purity,[118] the inseparable connection between virtue and freedom; in its origin, our dependence upon a common Creator, for whose glory all things exist.

It will not be improper for me, in this connection, Mr. President, to state that whilst Alabama is the first cotton producing country in the world, agriculture is not her sole reliance. Immense water power exists at points where it can be cheaply and profitably applied to machinery. No equal area probably possesses a greater amount and variety of valuable minerals than that portion of the State of Alabama lying between the Tennessee River and the line of latitude drawn twenty miles north of this place. Besides, she has slate, sandstone, granite, gold, copper, lead, and porcelain clay. She has iron ore inexhaustible in quantity, and equal, if not superior, to any in North America. Bituminous coal of the richest specimens covers an area of hundreds of square miles. Limestone exists in various localities, and Alabama lime, which is now displacing Northern lime and furnishing lucrative commerce. Marble, white, black, and variegated, invites the touch of genius and enterprise to spring forth into architectural decorations of rarest beauty, or statues of imperishable marble. May it ever be applied to pursuits of peace and science, and not be marred into monuments of war or tyranny.

I am honored, Mr. President, in being the medium of presenting this testimonial. I am rejoiced that to you personally, to whom an emancipated South is so much indebted for her present freedom from thralldom and Abolition domination, I am privileged to bear this token of confidence and esteem.

The PRESIDENT. The President of the Congress requests the gentleman from Alabama to return his sincere thanks to his constituents for the compliment paid to the official position to which he has been elevated by the partiality and kindness of this Congress.

Mr. CHILTON, of Alabama. Mr. President, I have just received from two young ladies of decided genius and taste, several models for a flag for these Confederate States, and I know the House will indulge me in a few remarks explanatory of the patriotic designs of the fair contributors. They are but school girls, sir, yet they have early imbibed the spirit, which animated the matrons of the Revolution. These models have been produced by them in the prosecution of their studies in the Art Department of the Tuskegee Female College; and I submit; sir, that several of them, for originality of design and the artistic skill displayed in their execution, reflect great credit upon the excellent institution of which they are members. These young ladies are not singular in their devotion to our new Republic. They hail from the county of Macon, a people among whom I have long lived, and, where, I feel confident, not a man, woman or child can be found who would be willing to endanger our liberties by a longer submission to Northern domination—a people who have been preparing, by the erection of schools and colleges equal to any in the late Union, for Southern emancipation from the anticipated thralldom of sectional numerical majorities for Southern independence. When I say this for the county of Macon, allow me, sir, to say that the same love of equal rights; the same devotion to the cause of independence; the same, unwavering faith that the Confederacy which you have formed will secure the blessings of well regulated liberty, and transmit them to our latest posterity, animates and inspires the hearts of the great mass of the people of our State.

Sir, as the State I have the honor, in part, to represent, has been represented as divided and disloyal to our new government,[119] if the time shall ever come (as I pray God it never may) when our infant liberties must be baptised in the blood of our people, I take this occasion to say, in the language of a gallant commander, spoken of the soldiers of my native State, Kentucky, "none will repair to the post of danger with more alacrity; fight more bravely, or bleed more freely, than the brave and patriotic sons of Alabama."

Our fair artists assure us that their efforts at originality were rendered difficult by constantly recurring visions of the "stars and stripes which floated so proudly over the late United States." Sir, you must not understand this expression as I see some of the papers in the North did the speech made a short time since, in this body, by the honorable gentleman from Mississippi (Mr. BROOKE),[120] as containing in its under-tone a desire for a reconstruction with the United States Government. Mr. President, no one had a more sincere attachment for the Union which our fathers gave us, or rejoiced more in the triumphs of that banner which symbolized its glory and its greatness, than the humble individual who now addresses you. No one strove more earnestly to preserve its integrity, and to allay the sectional agitation which foreshadowed its destruction. But the sectional issue was at last forced upon us, and a policy affirmed at the ballot box denying us equality, endangering our security, and destructive of the chief ends for which that Union was formed. Since that period I have had no hope of preserving the structure of Southern society, and of carrying out the grand scheme of civilization so deeply imbedded in its frame-work, except by the formation of a confederacy of States whose peoples are homogeneous, and whose institutions, interests and pursuits are so closely allied and harmoniously blended as to prevent that attrition from jars and discordant elements in the operation of the government as would ultimately destroy it. That government, in its primeval structure, has been formed, and is now in full operation. We have passed the Rubicon, and if there be one individual connected with it, in either of its departments, who contemplates a reconstruction with the United States, even the finger of rumor has not pointed him out. No, sir, I believe this government possesses as many of the elements of perpetuity as any the sun now shines upon, and will pass into its permanent organization without a jar.

This is the day when our Northern brethren inaugurate their President—the grand gala day which consummates their triumph and enables them to carry on their Government without being partakers of what they esteem our sin of African servitude, but which we regard as the God-ordained auxiliary to Christianity and civilization. We bid them Godspeed, and wish them all the blessings they are capable of enjoying. We are brethren; and since we cannot harmoniously live together, let us part in peace. We tender them the olive-branch, and upon them will be thrown the terrible responsibility of rejecting it, if it be rejected. Here is the letter to which I have referred:

> Tuskegee, Ala., March 1, 1861
>
> SIR: The undersigned, pupils to the Art Department of the Tuskegee Female College, conscious of weakness, but ardently desirous to do something for their country, have employed their pencils to produce various designs for a flag for a Southern Republic. They have found a pleasure in trying the patriot's with the artist's flame. You will appreciate the difficulty of their task when you reflect that amidst all their efforts at originality, there has ever danced before them visions of the star-gemmed flag with its parti-colored stripes that floated so proudly over the late United States.
>
> In the design submitted, we have endeavored to secure implicity, with an intelligible symbolism and striking perspicuousness of color.
>
> Let us snatch from the eagle of the cliffs our idea of independence, and cull from the earth diamonds and gems from the heavens to deck the flags of the Southern Confederacy. With Cotton for King, there are seven States bound by a chain of sisterly love, that will be strengthened by time as onward, right onward, they move up the glorious path of Southern independence.

No. 1. The seven seceding States represented by seven rings, bound together by golden links.
No. 2. The opposite side of the above a large cotton bale.
No. 3. Field gules, eagle in Or,[121] and blue shield, bearing in its beak a scroll with our representative political ideas.
No. 4. Eagle, vest, seven eagles, representing seven seceded States
No. 5. An eagle perched upon a lone rock in the midst of a tempestuous ocean; star in semi-circle, sun rising.
No. 6. Eagle on a field of blue, diamond shaped; olive branch in one claw, arrows in the other; scales in his beak.
No. 7. A circle; within it seven diamonds tangent, forming a seven pointed star; in the centre a cotton bale.

With our best wishes, respectfully,

REBECCA C. FERGUSON.[122]
MOLLIE A. D. SINCLAIR.[123]

P.S.—We would beg to observe in addition that, should either of the designs meet the approval of the Committee, we will cheerfully connect, recombine, or modify them in any desired manner, as well as engage to produce a seal corresponding to the Flag.

Very respectfully &c.

REBECCA C. FERGUSON.
MOLLIE A. D. SINCLAIR.

Mr. President, I move that the models and the letter be referred to the Committee on Flags.

The question was taken, and the motion was agreed to,

Mr. T. R. R. COBB, of Georgia. Mr. President, I offer the following resolutions:

Resolved, That the Mint at New Orleans and Dahlonega be continued, and proper arrangements made as soon as possible to procure suitable dies for the coin of the Confederate States.

Resolved, That the Secretary of the Treasury be requested to estimate and report to Congress the lowest amount of appropriation necessary to carry out the above resolution.

Mr. KENNER, of Louisiana.[124] Mr. President, I think it would probably be the better policy to have these resolutions referred to the Committee on Finance. I move, therefore, unless the gentleman has some special desire to have it adopted forthwith, that it be so referred.

Mr. COBB. I would have moved its reference to the Committee on Finance if it contained any but a single idea. The only idea in the resolution is the fact that these mints will be continued. I am aware of the fact that there is a suspicion in the minds of some of my constituents that the mint at Dahlonega will be discontinued. I am informed that a similar suspicion or feeling exists in the minds of some of the citizens of New Orleans. I think it is right not only to our constituents, but especially to those interested as depositors at these mints, that the question should be put at rest so far as their continuance is concerned. I believe, from what I have heard and know, that so far as the mint at Dahlonega is concerned, it may be continued at less expense than heretofore by the United States, and I suppose the Secretary of the Treasury is the best officer to investigate, decide upon and report that matter to Congress. Hence, the second resolution refers that to that Department rather than to the Committee on Finance. If my friend still desires to have it referred to the Committee on Finance, I have no objection to its taking that course. My desire was to settle the question this morning, so that it would be known that both mints would be continued.

The question was then taken, and the resolutions were agreed to.

Mr. HILL, of Georgia. Mr. President, I have received another model flag for the Confederacy. It may be too late to present it, but from the remarks accompanying it, and the evident taste and intelligence displayed by the lady, it ought to receive some attention. The design of the flag is different from any yet presented. I will not detain the Congress by any remarks upon it. I will simply give one feature. She preserves the stars of course, and while any number of stars may be added, so arranged as to be equally beautiful with the first six States that seceded. She has succeeded in giving these six States a position conspicuous in the foreground. I will not read the whole communication. I do not think it necessary. She is a lady of intelligence and taste, and large learning upon this subject, residing in Darien, Georgia. In the design of her flag, while she seems to have a great regard for the fifteen slaveholding States, she has a greater regard for the six States that first seceded, and a very especial regard for that State which first all led in the work—the State represented by the gentlemen from South Carolina.

I move its reference to the Committee on Flags.

The motion was agreed to; and then the Congress went into secret session.

Tuesday, March 5, 1861
(Charleston *Mercury*, March 8, 1861)

The Congress met at 10 o'clock, a.m., and was called to order by the President, Hon. HOWELL COBB, of Georgia. After prayer by the Rev. Mr. MITCHELL, the Journal of yesterday was read and adopted.

The PRESIDENT laid before the body a communication on the subject of patents; which will be referred to the Committee on Patients.

Mr. NISBET presented a letter on the subject of postage; which was referred to the Committee on Postal Affairs, without being read.

Also, a letter from Isaac Scott, President of the Macon and Western Railroad in relation to the transit of goods through the State of Georgia to Tennessee;[125] which was referred to the Committee on Commercial Affairs without being read.

Mr. OCHILTREE, of Texas presented a resolution, which was appropriately referred.

Mr. WAUL, of Texas, presented a communication from the Hon. JOHN HEMPHILL; which was referred to the Committee on Commercial Affairs.

Mr. MILES, of South Carolina. Mr. President, in consequence of an omission of Congress, yesterday, I beg leave, from the Committee on the Flag of the Confederacy, to submit the following report:

> The Committee appointed to select a proper flag of the Confederate States of America beg leave to report:
>
>> That they have given the subject due consideration and carefully inspected all the designs and models submitted to them. The number of these has been immense, but they all may be divided into two great classes:
>
> *Firstly*, those which copy and preserve the principal features of the United States flag, with slight and unimportant modifications:
>
> *Secondly*, those which are very elaborate, complicated or fantastical. The objection to the first class is, that none of them, at any considerable distance, could easily be distinguished from the one which they imitate. Whatever attachment may be felt, from association, for "the stars and stripes," (an attachment which your committee may be permitted to say they do not all share,) it is manifest that in inaugurating a new government, we cannot retain the flag of the government from which we have withdrawn with any propriety, or without encountering very obvious practical difficulties. There is no propriety in retaining the ensign of a government which, in the opinion of the States composing this Confederacy, had become so oppressive and injurious to their interests as to require their separation from it. It is idle to talk of "keeping" the flag of the United States when we have voluntarily seceded from them. It is superfluous to dwell upon the practical difficulties which would flow from the fact of two distinct and probably hostile governments both employing the same or very similar flags. It would be a political and military solecism. It would produce endless confusion and mistakes. It would lead to perpetual dispute. As to "the glories of the old flag," we must bear in mind that the battles of the revolution, about which our fondest and proudest memories cluster, were not fought beneath its folds; and although in more recent times—in the war of 1812, and in the war with Mexico—the South did win her fair share of glory, and shed her full measure of blood under its guidance, and in its defence, we think the impartial page of history will preserve and commemorate the

fact more imperishably than a mere piece of striped bunting. When the colonies achieved their independence of the "mother country" (which, up to the last, they fondly called her), they did not desire to retain the British flag, or anything at all similar to it. Yet, under that flag they had been planted and nurtured and fostered; under that flag they had fought in their infancy for their very existence, against more than one determined foe; under it they had repelled and driven back the relentless savage, and carried it further and further into the decreasing wilderness as the standard of civilization and religion: under it the youthful WASHINGTON won his spurs in the memorable and unfortunate expedition of BRADDOCK, and Americans helped to plant it on the Heights of Abraham, where the immortal WOLFE fell covered with glory in the arms of victory.[126] But our forefathers, when they separated themselves from Great Britain—a separation not on account of their hatred of the English Constitution, or of English institutions, but in consequence of the tyrannical and *unconstitutional* rule of Lord NORTH's administration and because their destiny beckoned them on to independent expansion and achievement—cast no lingering, regretful looks behind. They were proud of their race and lineage, proud of heritage in the glories and genius and language of Old England, but they were influenced by the spirit of the motto of the great HAMPDEN, "*Vestigia nulla retrorsum.*"[127] They were determined to build up a new power among the nations of the world. They, therefore did not attempt to "keep the old flag." We think it good to imitate them in this comparatively little matter, as well as to imitate them in greater and more important ones.

The committee, in examining the representations of the flags of all countries, found that Liberia and the Sandwich Islands had flags so similar to that of the United States, that it seemed to them an additional, if not in itself a conclusive reason why we should not "keep," copy, or imitate it. They felt no inclination to borrow at second hand what had been pilfered and appropriated by a free negro community and a race of savages. It must be admitted, however, that something was conceded by the committee to what seemed so strong and earnest a desire to retain at least a suggestion of the old "stars and stripes." So much for the mass of models and designs, more or less copied from or assimilated to the United States flag.

With reference to the second class of designs, those of an elaborate and complicated character (but many of them showing considerable artistic skill and taste), the committee will merely remark, that however pretty they may be, when made up by the cunning skill of a fair lady's fingers, in silk, satin and embroidery, they are not appropriate as flags. A flag should be something simple, readily made, and, above all, capable of being made upon bunting. It should be different from the flag of any other country, place, or people. It should be significant. It should be readily distinguishable at a distance. The colors should be well contrasted and durable. And lastly, and not the least important point, it should be effective and handsome.

The Committee humbly think that the flag which they submit combines these requisites. It is very easy to make. It is entirely different from any national flag. The three colors of which it is composed, red, white and blue, are the true republican colors. In heraldry, they are emblematic of the three great virtues of valor, purity and truth. Naval men assure us that it can be recognized and distinguished at a great distance. The colors contrast admirably, and are lasting. In effect and appearance, it must speak for itself.

Your committee therefore recommend that the flag of the Confederate States of America shall consist of a red field, with a white space extending horizontally through the centre, and equal, in width to one-third the width of the flag. The red spaces above and below to be of the same width as the white. The union blue extending down through the white space, and stopping at the lower red space. In the centre of the union a circle of white stars corresponding in number with the States in the Confederacy. If adopted, long may it wave over a brave, a free, and a virtuous people. May the career of the Confederacy whose duty it will then be to support and defend it, be such as to endear it to our children's children, as the flag of a loved, because a just and benign government, and the cherished symbol of its valor, purity, and truth.

Respectfully submitted.

WILLIAM PORCHER MILES,
Chairman.

Mr. WITHERS, of South Carolina. I move that the report be received, and entered on the Journal with the proceedings of yesterday.

The motion was agreed to.

Mr. BROOKE, of Mississippi. Mr. President, I wish just here, sir, to ask permission of this House to make somewhat of a personal explanation. I was pained yesterday to learn, sir, from the reference which a distinguished representative of Alabama was pleased to make to a few remarks that I had the honor of submitting on this floor some weeks ago, that those remarks had been so understood in certain quarters, or had been understood as indicating an undertone of reconstruction here, or in the State which I have the honor in part to represent upon this floor. What, sir, I may think or say, humble as I am, may be a matter of very little importance; but, sir, if understood to be the representative of the sentiments of any party in my State, it may, sir, become a matter of some importance and some consideration. I did have the honor, sir, to belong to what is called the Co-operation party of the State of Mississippi—a party large and respectable, both in point of numbers and ability; but, sir, I can say, with truth and confidence, that the Co-operation party of the State of Mississippi never was, in any sense of the term, a thoroughly Union party. It differed, sir, with what was called the immediate secession party only on the questions of time and the mode of action. This question, sir, has long gone by, and that party, with the Secession party, now stand, sir, upon the same platform. I am not authorized, sir, to speak their sentiments on this floor, but from what I have learned, from information received from reliable sources, I can say, sir, my belief is that that party, to a man, will say as you (the President of the Congress), sir, said in taking that chair, that our separation from the North is "perfect, complete, and perpetual," and that they will also say, with our distinguished President, that "reconstruction is neither practicable nor desirable." I have no doubt, sir, that that flag, which yesterday was given so gracefully to the breeze, I saw floating, sir, in my gallant State from many a hill and housetop, and while, sir, the tear may glisten upon the eyelid of many who witnessed it, at the diminished number of stars and stripes, yet, sir, they are only the tears shed in tribute to the memory of the past, to be succeeded by smiles and hopes of a brighter and better future. And, sir, however my former associates may have regarded our old Government, whatever lingering feelings or regard and affection they may have for it, I believe now, sir, that, like Othello, they will say:

> Thus all my fond love do I blow to heaven:
> 'Tis gone.

Mr. CURRY, from the Committee on Commercial Affairs, reported a bill to establish and organize a Lighthouse Bureau; which was read twice and placed on the calendar.

Mr. DECLOUET, of Louisiana, also from the Committee on Commercial Affairs, reported adversely upon the memorial of citizens and merchants of Montgomery, praying the Congress to constitute the city of Montgomery a port of entry and delivery, and asked to be discharged from its further consideration.

Mr. SHORTER. Mr. President, as the honorable gentleman who presented that memorial is absent this morning, I would suggest that the body take no action upon the report, out of courtesy to him, and I move that the report be laid on the table for the present.

The question was taken, and the motion was agreed to.

Mr. DECLOUET, also from the Committee on Commercial Affairs, reported a bill to provide for the registration of vessels owned in whole or in part by citizens of the Confederate States.

Mr. MILES. I have no desire to hurry the bill through; but I hardly think there will be any dismission or difference of opinion upon it.

The PRESIDENT. The bill will be read at length. [The bill was accordingly read. Its title fully indicates the nature of its provisions.]

Mr. MILES. The committee left a blank for the Congress to fill. They were uncertain whether a third or a fourth ownership should be recognized; but since the repeal of the navigation laws by this Congress, it becomes necessary to make some laws for the registration of vessels.

The PRESIDENT. How would the gentleman fill the blank?

Mr. MILES. I would suggest, sir, that it be made to read so that a fourth of each ship at least shall be owned by a citizen of the Confederate States.

The amendment was adopted, and then the bill was read a third time and passed. And then the Congress went into secret session.

Wednesday, March 6, 1861

(Charleston *Mercury*, March 9, 1861; Montgomery *Weekly Advertiser*, March 13, 1861)

The Congress met at 10 o'clock, a.m., and was called to order by the President, Hon. HOWELL COBB, of Georgia.

After prayer by the Rev. Dr. RALLS,[128] the Journal of yesterday was read and approved.

On motion of Mr. CURRY, the following resolution was adopted:

> *Resolved*, That the Committee on the Judiciary be instructed to inquire into the expediency of prohibiting the importation of slaves from the United States into the Confederate States, except by persons emigrating thereto for the purpose of actual settlement or residence.[129]

The Congress then proceeded to the consideration of the bill to establish and organize a Bureau in connection with the Department of the Treasury, to be known as the Light House Bureau.

On motion of Mr. CURRY, the bill was amended to read as follows:

> SEC. 1. *The Congress of the Confederate States do enact*, That there shall be established, in connection with the department of the treasury, a Bureau, to be known as the Light House Bureau. The chief officer of such Bureau shall be a captain or commander of the navy, detailed for this service by order of the President of the Confederate States, who shall receive as his compensation the same pay allowed to officers of the same rank in the navy. There shall be appointed also a chief clerk, with a salary of twelve hundred dollars, and an accounting clerk with a salary of one thousand dollars.
>
> SEC. 2. All light houses, light vessels, buoys, and other aids to navigation, all the officers connected therewith, and all matters connected with the construction, repair, illumination, inspection and government thereof, and all duties appertaining to the administration of light house affairs

shall be under the direction and control of the Light House Bureau hereby established, subject at all times to the superintendence of the Secretary of the Treasury.

SEC. 3. The chief of the bureau shall, as soon as possible, divide the sea coasts of the Confederate States into districts not exceeding five in number, as the Secretary of the Treasury may deem expedient, and over each of these districts the president shall appoint an Inspector, to be selected from the lieutenants in the navy, who shall discharge all the duties of inspection, survey or otherwise which may be required of him by the chief of the bureau. For these services the Inspectors shall receive only their regular pay in the navy.

SEC. 4. The President of the Confederate States may, from time to time, at the request of the Secretary of the Treasury, detail one or more of the officers of the Engineer Corps of the army, to be employed under the direction of the Light House Bureau, in superintending the construction or repair of light houses or other necessary structures in connection with the light house establishment, or other similar duty assigned by the Light House Bureau, in connection therewith.

SEC. 5. The chief of the bureau shall at least once every year make a full report to the Secretary of the Treasury, giving a full statement of the operations of the Light House Establishment. He shall also, from time to time, give such information to the Secretary of the Treasury as he may require in reference to his Bureau.

On motion of Mr. CURRY, an additional section was added repealing all laws or parts of laws inconsistent with the above; and then the bill was read the third time and passed.

Mr. CURRY. Mr. President, I ask leave, at the request of citizens of Montgomery, to withdraw from the files of the Congress a memorial presented by my friend [Mr. CHILTON] in reference to the establishment of Montgomery as a port of entry and delivery, in order that the papers may be referred to the Treasury Department.

The PRESIDENT. There being no objection, it will be so ordered.

Mr. MILES, of South Carolina, presented the memorial of the Swedish Iron Manufacturing Company, of South Carolina,[130] which was referred to the Committee on Military Affairs.

And then the Congress went into secret session.

Thursday, March 7, 1861

(Charleston *Mercury*, March 11, 1861; Savannah *Daily Morning News*, March 9, 1861)

The Congress met at 10 o'clock, a.m., and was called to order by the President, Hon. HOWELL COBB, of Georgia.

Prayer was offered up by the Rev. Mr. JENKINS.[131]

The Journal of yesterday was read and approved.

On motion of Mr. T. R. R. COBB, of Georgia, the following resolution, in relation to international copyrights, was adopted:

> *Whereas,* Great Britain, France, Prussia, Saxony, and other European powers, have passed laws to secure to authors of other States the benefit and privileges of their copyright laws upon condition of similar privileges being granted by the laws of such States to authors, the subjects of the powers aforesaid; Therefore be it
>
> *Resolved, by the Congress of the Confederate States,* That the President be and he is hereby authorized to instruct the Commissioners appointed by him to visit the European powers, to enter into treaty obligations for the extension of international copyright privileges to all authors, the citizens and subjects of the powers aforesaid.

Mr. CLAYTON, of Mississippi, from the Committee on the Judiciary, reported the following bill, to define the jurisdiction of the Federal Courts in certain cases; which was read twice and placed on the calendar:

> *The Congress of the Confederate States do enact,* That in the event of a conflict of arms between the Confederate States and the United States, or of refusal on the part of the authorities of the United States to recognize the independence of the Confederate States, or to receive the Commissioners sent by the latter to treat with the former in relation to the several matters of the controversy existing between them, the Congress of the Confederate States shall not take cognizance of any civil case in which the plaintiffs or may be, either the said United States or either one of them, or any citizen or citizens thereof, or the assignee or assignees, or endorser or endorsee of any such person.
>
> SEC. 2. All pending cases in which the plaintiff shall be in either of the classes aforesaid, shall, upon the happening of either of the contingencies aforesaid, be dismissed, on motion, and all process *mesne* or final which shall have been issued at the suit of such plaintiff, shall be arrested and declared inoperative.

And then the Congress went into secret session.

Friday, March 8, 1861
(Charleston *Mercury*, March 12, 1861)

The Congress met at 10 o'clock a.m., and was called to order by the President, Hon. HOWELL COBB, of Georgia.

After Prayer by Rev. Mr. PELLICER, the Journal of yesterday was read and approved.

Mr. WRIGHT, of Ga. Mr. President, I received a communication yesterday from a gentleman of New York stating that he had completed a war implement of great power, and proposing the use of it by the Confederate States.[132] I move its reference, without reading, to the Military Committee.

The PRESIDENT. It will be so ordered, if there be no objection.

Mr. CLAYTON, of Miss., from the Committee on the Judiciary, reported a bill to establish a Court of Admiralty and Maritime Jurisdiction at Key West, in the State of Florida; which was read twice and placed on the calendar.

The Congress then proceeded to the consideration of the bill reported yesterday, to define the jurisdiction of the Federal Courts in certain cases.

Mr. T. R. R. COBB. Mr. President, I do not think it necessary to take up that bill this morning, and I move that it be continued on the calendar.

The motion was agreed to.

Mr. WAUL, of Texas. Mr. President, the Texas delegation are now ready, and desire to sign the Constitution.

The PRESIDENT. The opportunity will be afforded to them.

The Constitution was accordingly produced, when it was signed by Messrs. WAUL and OLDHAM. The other delegates will be permitted to sign at their convenience.

Mr. SPARROW, of Louisiana. Mr. President, I offer the following resolution:

> *Resolved*, That the Committee on Commerce be instructed to inquire and report the present condition of the Custom House at New Orleans; what repairs, if any, are immediately necessary to preserve the same from damage; and also to report a bill providing accommodations for the Federal Courts, and for the preservation of the records thereof.

I will state, Mr. President, that I am informed that the Custom House is in a condition to require attention. The ceiling is damaged from the effects of the weather, and I am also informed that no provision is made for the records. This resolution is to provide some remedy. I move that it be referred to the Committee on Commerce.

Mr. CLAYTON. I beg leave to say to my friend that the Judiciary bill provides for the preservation of the records of the courts.

Mr. SPARROW. I will state that the building which the United States Courts hold, was vacant on the first day of this month, the lease having expired, and there is now no place for these records. It may be some time before the Judiciary bill is passed, and this is merely a temporary matter.

Mr. CLAYTON. I have no objection to it at all, sir.

Mr. CONRAD, of Louisiana. Mr. President, I have received from a distinguished friend a communication in regard to some changes that it is expedient and necessary should be made in the law of Congress regarding steamboats, principally on the Mississippi River. The change is made necessary by the change in the Government. I will simply introduce this document, with the request that it be referred to the Committee on Commerce. [document XV]

The PRESIDENT. So ordered, if there be no objection.

And then the Congress went into secret session.

Saturday, March 9, 1861

(Charleston *Mercury*, March 15, 1861)

Without transacting any business in public session, the Congress proceeded to sit with closed doors.

Monday, March 11, 1861

(Charleston *Mercury*, March 15, 1861)

The Congress met at 10 o'clock a.m., and was called to order by the President Hon. HOWELL COBB, of Ga.

After prayer by the Rev. Dr. MANLY, the Journal of Saturday was read and approved.

The PRESIDENT laid before the body a communication from Mr. LAMAR, Secretary of the Georgia State Convention,[133] communicating the following resolution:

> *Resolved*, That the people of Georgia, in Convention assembled, most heartily approve of the election by the Congress at Montgomery, of JEFFERSON DAVIS, of Mississippi, as President, and ALEX. H. STEPHENS, of Georgia, as Vice-President, of the Provisional Government of the Confederate States of America, the duties of which position their distinguished public service and acknowledged abilities eminently qualify them to discharge.

Mr. WRIGHT, of Georgia. Mr. President, I move that the resolution of the State Convention of Georgia be spread upon the Journal of Congress.

The question was taken and the motion was agreed to.

Mr. WRIGHT, of Ga. Mr. President—Mr. Stebbs,[134] a citizen of Savannah, is here with an invention of a breech loading cannon, which he has submitted to military and naval gentlemen. He has requested me to ask permission of Congress to place a model which he has, at the Clerk's desk tomorrow morning, that Congress may have an opportunity of examining it, and take what action to them seems proper. I ask that permission for him.

No objection was made.

Mr. KENNER, of Louisiana. Mr. President—I have not a resolution, but I desire to call attention to an Ordinance just passed by the Convention of the State of Louisiana—an Ordinance which is exceedingly gratifying to the delegates of that State on this floor, and which they think ought to be equally gratifying to the Congress at large, and the whole Confederacy, as an evidence of the patriotism of the people of that State. I will read the Ordinance, Mr. President, and then proceed to make one or two observations upon it:

AN ORDINANCE TO TRANSFER CERTAIN FUNDS TO THE GOVERNMENT OF THE CONFEDERATE STATES OF AMERICA

SEC. 1. *It is hereby ordained*, That the sum of $389,267.46, now in the hands of A. J. GUIROT,[135] State Depository, and known as the bullion fund, be transferred to the Government of the Confederate States of America, and that said State Depository be, and is hereby authorize and instructed to pay such sums, upon the order of the Secretory of the Treasury of the said Confederate States.

SEC. 2. *It is further ordained*, That the sum of $140,519.66, being the balance received by the said State Depository from the customs since the 31st of January last, be transferred to the said Government, and paid by said Depository upon the order of said Secretary of the Treasury of the Confederate States.

Mr. President, it will be recollected that when Louisiana seceded, she found a certain amount of money in the Mint belong to the United States, on deposit, the Mint being near New Orleans. It will be recollected also, that there was a large amount of goods bonded in her warehouses liable to duty. From the period of that secession, to wit, the day when Louisiana, by her action, through her delegates upon this floor, became one of the Confederate States of the Southern Confederacy, the sums received in the way of duties have been strictly consecrated and set apart for the benefit of this Confederacy. Now, sir, this may look very much as a matter-of-course thing, but I wish to call attention to-day, sir, to two points of view, in which that action may be regarded. The first is, that she is the only State that has seen proper to pursue this policy. We are the people, sir, who have held the duties received by the Custom House for the benefit of the Confederacy at large. I would state, also, sir, its connection with this, that it would not at all have been improper for Louisiana to have taken this money and made of it for the purposes of defence, considering the condition in which she found her defences when she seceded. The forts protecting her commerce when she seceded, we found to be in a dilapidated—probably that is saying too much, but they were found by no means in a good—condition. They had been very much neglected. While the forts protecting the commerce of New York and other ports of the North were prepared for immediate defence against an enemy, our forts were neglected. The cannon were not mounted, and the fact is that it required a large expense to put them in a good condition to render them serviceable. Now, sir, Louisiana did not appropriate this money. She put her hands in her own pocket and appropriated $500,000 for the purpose of arming and equipping her people, and another $500,000 more to put the forts in a state of defence. It is in connection with this fact, that I wish to call attention to this subject, because no fair and candid man will say that Louisiana would have done an improper thing had she taken this money for her own defence, for in defending her own borders, she defended the Confederacy of the Southern States. Now, Mr. President, I also wish to make this remark. The object, sir, which I have in calling attention to the conduct of our State in this particular, is put solely to gain your approbation. We think it worthy of your praise, and as such, present our conduct to your consideration, but, sir, the great object I have in view is to call the attention of the President and Chief Executive to the spirit in which this thing is done, and for one, sir, I hope that it may be met in a corresponding spirit by the Chief Executive of our Confederacy. I am one of those, Mr. President, who has had serious misgivings about war. I have thought, until the inaugural of President Lincoln, we would not have war; but, sir, the delusion, as far as I am concerned is dispelled. I admit candidly, after a careful reading, that it is a virtual declaration of war. I say it with the deepest regret, because I know that if we have war, the interests of my State will suffer more than any other State in the Confederacy; but, sir, I hold it to be one of the principles of wisdom to look danger fully in the face and be prepared to meet it.

Now, as we have, with a spirit of liberality, appropriated all the money in our hands for the benefit of our Confederacy, I hope and trust this Confederacy will meet our gift in a corresponding spirit, and take such measures as will protect the commerce of New Orleans and the Valley of the Mississippi from blockade, or other injury that Mr. Lincoln may attempt to impose upon it. I hope, sir, this will be the especial object and care of our President, should such a state of things require it. But, Mr. President, I have no misgivings on this subject. I do not ask this because I think President DAVIS would be careless of our condition or negligent of our interest. He is not a Louisianian, it is true. He is not a resident of our State, but he is the next thing to it; he resides next to us, and will care for our interest as if he were a Louisianian himself.

I don't know, sir, that any action should be taken upon the Ordinance which I have just read. I do not desire that any action should be taken, but thought it proper to call the attention of Congress to this subject.

Mr. WITHERS, of South Carolina. Mr. President, I beg leave to offer the following resolution:

> *Resolved*, That Congress accept, with a high sense of the patriotic liberality of the State of Louisiana, the funds so generously tendered to the Treasury of the Confederate States, specified in the Ordinance of her Convention.

Mr. President, I am deeply penetrated with the liberality of that State, though it is no more than I expected from the conception I had of the character of her people. I desire, however, to say one word in regard to my own State on that subject. The income of the customs at the port of Charleston is not large. I believe it is entirely expended in keeping up buoys and light houses on the coast, and supporting those aids to navigation indispensable at a port of that kind. I am very sure, sir, that the State of South Carolina would follow the illustrious example of the State of Louisiana, if she occupied the same situation; but it is known to this Congress, I am sure, that the condition of affairs in the State of South Carolina at the time of her secession, the 20th day of December, 1860, was such as to make it indispensable that she should apply every possible fund which she could commend to meet the exigencies for the defence of her port and her people. Very large expenditures had been made for the purpose of defending that port, and the other purpose of securing what she and the Confederate States ought to have—the possession and occupancy of Fort Sumter. So far as the Sub-Treasury is concerned, there was a fund of some $45,000 belonging to the Government of the United States of America, said fund having been collected under the authority of that Government, but up to the 31st of December, it was paid out in checks drawn upon it at Washington. Our Convention thought it was due to a proper conception of the rights of individuals, to release all claim to that fund which these drafts from Washington called for. Under these circumstances, and in view of the large taxation which has been saddled upon our people in consequences of our necessities, I hope it will be understood by this Congress that it is not the want of such a spirit of liberality that has prevented our tendering any thing we possessed to the Treasury of the Confederacy, but our necessities, which required that the money should be appropriated for other purposes.

Mr. KENNER. Mr. President, I hope the gentleman will not think I had any disposition to disparage the action of any sister States. I had no such intention.

Mr. WITHERS. I do not think anything of the kind, sir.

The PRESIDENT. The Chair will suggest that, if the resolution is adopted, the ordinance should be placed on the journal.

The question was then taken, and the resolution was adopted, and the ordinance was ordered to be placed on the Journal.

Mr. HARRISON, of Mississippi, presented a communication from A. M. DOWLING,[136] which was referred to the Committee on finance without being read.

On motion of Mr. OCHILTREE, the following resolution was adopted:

> *Resolved,* That the Committee on Finance be instructed to inquire into the expediency of exempting from duty all railroad cars, tenders, iron chairs, spikes, road cars, and generally all the fixtures necessary for building and keeping up railroads, which were purchased for the benefit of railroads in the Confederate States prior to the 28th day of February, 1861.

Mr. HEMPHILL, a Deputy from the State of Texas, appeared and was qualified to take his seat as a member of the Congress.

And then the Congress proceeded to sit with closed doors.

Tuesday, March 12, 1861

(Charleston *Mercury*, March 15, 1861)

The Congress met at 10 o'clock and was called to order by the President, Hon. HOWELL COBB, of Georgia. After prayer by the Rev. Mr. COBBS (Mr. CHESNUT, of South Carolina, in the chair), the Journal of yesterday was read and approved.

Mr. WRIGHT. Mr. President—

The PRESIDENT. The gentleman from Georgia.

Mr. WRIGHT. I hold in my hand, sir, a communication from a gentleman in Washington City, who is a member of an incorporated company, distinguished as the [New] Mexican Railway Company. In the spring of 1860, the Territorial Legislature of New Mexico incorporated a company by that name, for the purpose of erecting a railroad through the Territory of New Mexico, in the direction of California. The gentleman has forwarded to me, by mail, the charter of that Company, together with a rough draft of a bill granting a donation of lands from the Territory of New Mexico, and asking me to lay it before this Congress; and, in the name of the Company, ask a donation of lands for the purpose of forwarding the enterprise for which the Company was incorporated.[137] I feel it my duty, sir, with due courtesy to the gentleman with whom I am well acquainted, to lay the communication before the House and ask its reference to the Committee on Territories. But, sir, that I may not be understood, I desire to make one or two remarks before I make that motion.

When I had the honor to be a member of Congress from the State of Georgia, the 35th Congress, I took occasion, during the session of that Congress, to express my disapprobation of these grants of public lands to railroads and other companies.[138] My opinion was then, and is yet, that the best possible disposition that can be made of the public lands, is their gratuitous distribution among actual settlers; that the material wealth of a country, and its power, is increased in that way, and by that disposition of its public lands better than by any other. My opinions on that subject, sir, have undergone no alteration.

One word more, sir, as to the right of this Congress to legislate on this subject, because the application made to this Congress involves the right to legislate upon and dispose of public lands in the Territory of New Mexico. Have we that right? Have we any right in the territory of the late Government of the United States? If the theory of secession be true, upon which we have practiced and put this Government into operation, incontestably we have not lost our right to public lands. I, for one, never will consent while this Government has an arm to defend its right; I never will consent to the loss of these rights which the six or seven Confederate States have already acquired in the public lands, and more especially in this territory. I can never, as a Southern man, agree to relinquish our rights. It was emphatically the purchase of Southern treasure and Southern blood. It is true that the expense of that war were borne out of the national treasury; but if we are correct in our theory as to who pays the duties of the Government, by far the largest proportion has been paid by the South. Upon one subject there can be no doubt: that so far as the purchase of that territory at a sacrifice of human life is concerned, it belongs to us; it was Southern men who won that territory, and who won the laurels acquired in the Mexican war. Sir, it would not comport well with my opinions of right and justice, nor with the honor of the Confederate States to relinquish our rights to this territory, when the very man who turned the battle of Buena Vista in our favor presides over the six Confederate States. [A voice—"seven!"] That battle was lost when the Mississippi hero entered, turned the tide of battle, and wrung victory from the very grasp of defeat.

But, sir, I make these observations that I may not be misunderstood. It may be wise and prudent for the Government of the Confederate States not to touch this subject until all means are exhausted by negotiation to settle the question of the public property. But, sir, I ask the reference of the memorial to the Committee on Territories, that it may take such action as it may think proper.

The PRESIDENT. If there be no objection it will be so ordered.

Mr. WITHERS. Mr. President—

The PRESIDENT. The gentleman from South Carolina.

Mr. WITHERS. The only thing I have been able to produce out of my brain, in behalf of the State of South Carolina, is the following resolution:

> *Resolved*, That when the printers of the Congress shall have prepared an edition of the laws and resolutions directed to be published, the Secretary of the Congress do transmit one copy of the same to each member of this body.

By that means, Mr. President, I will be able to find out what I have been doing, and have an opportunity of reporting the sins and iniquities I have committed.

The question was taken, and the resolution was agreed to,

The Congress then proceeded to the consideration of the bill to define the jurisdiction of the Federal Courts in certain cases.

On motion of Mr. CLAYTON, of Mississippi, it was laid over for the present.

And then, the Congress went into secret session.

Wednesday, March 13, 1861

(Charleston *Mercury*, March 16, 1861)

The Congress met at 10 o'clock a.m. and was called to order by the President Hon. HOWELL COBB, of Georgia. After prayer, the journal of yesterday was read and approved.

Mr. CHILTON, of Alabama, asked and obtained leave to record his vote in favor of the Constitution, not being present when the vote was taken.

Mr. CURRY, of Alabama, presented several accounts; which were referred to the Committee on Accounts.

On motion of Mr. SPARROW, of Louisiana, his colleague, Mr. DECLOUET, was excused from serving as Chairman of the Committee on Accounts and Chairman *pro tempore* of the Committee on Commercial Affairs.

The PRESIDENT stated that he would fill the vacancies thus caused at some subsequent period.

Mr. CLAYTON, of Mississippi. Mr. President, I have a letter which I desire read to the House.

The letter was accordingly read as follows:

> Salem, Miss., March 9, 1861
>
> JUDGE CLAYTON: I notice that the Montgomery Congress has just authorized a loan, but have seen nothing further on the subject. I have just tendered to Gov. PETTUS $5000 for the use of the State, and I have about the same amount in the hands of H. APPERSON & Co.,[139] which is at the service of the Confederate States if needed.
>
> Yours, truly, F. T. Leake.[140]

Mr. CLAYTON. As a just appreciation of that gentleman, I ask that his letter be spread upon the Journal.

The PRESIDENT. It will be so ordered.

Mr. BARRY, of Mississippi. Mr. President, I have a resolution which I desire to submit for the purpose of reference. It is in these words:

> *Resolved*, That the Committee on Finance be instructed to inquire into the expedience of imposing an ad valorem duty on negro slaves imported into the Confederacy from the slaveholding States of the United States, and report as early as convenient by bill or otherwise.

Mr. President, the purpose of the resolution is simply one of reference. The Constitution authorizes the Congress to exclude entirely the introduction of new negros from the slaveholding States of the old Union. It may not be expedient at the present time to exercise that power in full, but it is entirely proper that so large a branch of commerce as the importation of slaves from the border States, stimulated as that importation doubtless will be for the next year or two, should be made to contribute its full share towards the support of this Government. It is not introduced with a design to coerce those States, or to exercise any influence, directly or indirectly, in inducing them to join this Confederacy. It is designed, and will be acted upon, as a measure of revenue. A trade involving as that does fifty millions a year, should contribute its full share to the public support. Why should we tax New England manufactures and Pennsylvania iron and adopt a different policy with regard to the border States slave trade? The trade from New England in shoes and cloth and from Pennsylvania in iron is subject to the operation of the tariff. I know that some have said that such a policy would be regarded by them as coercion. Some have said it would induce them to come in; others that it would induce them to remain out by arousing their pride. I do not think we are justified in looking upon either as likely to occur; nor, should either occur, do I think we are responsible for it. We tax all other products on the principle of revenue. We have excepted certain articles, not out of regard for anything but our interest; but I see no reason why this interest should not contribute its full share to the support of the Government. There are political reasons which had great force in suggesting the mode of raising the revenue, but I believe that it is well that these States should understand that it is the inexorable policy of this Confederacy not to permit the introduction of African slaves from these States, if they continue to refuse to become members of this Confederacy. This section of the continent would not be made the recipient of their slaves when they have an Abolition Government, with property in slaves insecure. They should not be permitted to get rid of the institution, by sending two millions of slaves to us, and thus bring the Black Republican territory on our border, and leave us dependent upon so large a population of that description. I think that we should, as a measure of self-protection, exclude them, and if this country is in need of two millions of slaves, we will bring them from Africa, instead of buying them from Virginia and other border States. We will give two or three hundred dollars for African slaves, instead of giving Virginia, North Carolina and other states, one thousand dollars, although it would be some injury to the native Africans to introduce among them wild Africans. There are, on the other hand, political considerations, and that is, that we will not allow these States, as a matter of policy to themselves, to depopulate themselves by sending abroad their negro population, doubling our own, and in a very short time become the enemies to us and our institutions, which the States further North have become under the same process. I trust the Congress. I trust that this Congress will act upon this resolution. It is one of inquiry, merely of reference, and I desire the Committee to give it that attention which they deem it to merit.

Mr. Clayton, of Mississippi. Mr. President, I do not wish to raise an objection or throw obstacles in the way of the object the gentleman has in view. I rise simply to state that a resolution of somewhat similar in character has been passed and referred to the Committee on the Judiciary Committee.[141] That Committee has not yet come to any conclusion or made any report on the subject. I beg leave, therefore, to ask that the resolution heretofore referred to the Judiciary Committee, may also go to the Finance Committee in order that they may have the whole subject before them.

The President. The Chair will inform the gentleman that the discussion is not proper, as the resolution has not been acted upon in open session.

Mr. RHETT, of South Carolina. Mr. President—the merits of the resolution offered by the gentleman from Mississippi, are not properly before the convention, for until the Committee thinks its expedient to act upon it, it is not strictly before us. Yet I will say I have no objection to its going before the Committee. I will say also that I think that any action upon that subject at present would be exceedingly unwise. Everything in the frontier States is in a changing position. They do not know themselves where they will be. Circumstances are operating upon them, and if we desire them to unite with us we should do nothing at all to alienate, or exasperate, or disparage them. This resolution cannot but have that effect. On that account, and on account of expediency, I think it very unwise to take any action upon that subject. I shall not, however, oppose its reference to the Committee, where it will doubtless receive the consideration required.

Mr. PERKINS, of Louisiana. Mr. President, I move that we go into secret session.

The question was agreed to and without taking final action on the resolution the Congress proceeded to sit with closed doors.

Thursday, March 14, 1861

(Charleston *Mercury*, March 19, 1861; Montgomery *Weekly Advertiser*, March 20, 1861)

The Congress met at 10 o'clock, a.m., and was called to order by the President, Hon. HOWELL COBB, of Ga.

After Prayer offered by the Rev. Mr. O. R. BLUE,[142] the Journal of yesterday was read and approved.

Mr. OCHILTREE, of Texas, presented a communication from JOHN SIDNEY SHERMAN,[143] in command at Galveston, Texas; which was referred to the Committee on Military Affairs.

Mr. CLAYTON, of Miss. Mr. President, I ask leave to report a bill to establish a Court of Admiralty and Maritime Jurisdiction in the State of Mississippi, in the counties bordering on the Mississippi river. It is essentially the same bill as that for the establishment of a Court of Admiralty and Maritime Jurisdiction at Key West. There are no changes except such as are necessary to designate the difference of locality.

The bill was read three times, and the question being on its passage—

Mr. HALE, of Alabama, said: Mr. President, it seems to me that that bill should go to the Committee on the Judiciary. I cannot see, myself, the necessity of establishing a second Court of Admiralty in Mississippi. The District Courts of the Confederate States have admiralty jurisdiction, and, as I understand it, that bill proposes to establish an additional Court. Well, I see no more necessity for an additional Court in Mississippi than in other State—for example, in Alabama. Why not establish a separate Court of Admiralty in the city of Mobile, wholly distinct from the District Court of Alabama? So with reference to other States. With these reasons, I move that the bill referred to the Committee on the Judiciary.

Mr. CLAYTON. I beg leave to say that that bill is the production of the Judiciary Committee. The gentleman has been absent from the sittings of the Committee very much, and the bill was drawn by the Chairman of the Committee under the instruction of a majority of the Committee in attendance at the sitting. So much for that part of his argument, sir. I think there is every great necessity for a Court of Admiralty on the Mississippi river, that river showing the border of the State for about five hundred miles. It is wholly impossible to collect the revenue unless we have a judge residing at some point on the river, with court always open, to punish offences against the revenue laws. A judge in the interior of the State would be wholly incompetent to discharge the duties that would be required of him, and unless some tribunal clothed with the necessary powers is established, it will be wholly impossible to make the revenue laws efficient.

Mr. HALE. Mr. President, I can only say that I was not aware of the action of the Committee. I have never seen the bill or heard of it as a member of the Committee; and so far as he refers to the enforcement of the revenue laws of the State of Mississippi, and the necessity of a Judge residing on the bank of the Mississippi, I can say that there are no stronger reasons for this than there is to have a Judge residing at Mobile, or in any other part of the State. It was indicated by the gentleman from Mississippi, or some other gentleman, that the business of the District Court of the State of Mississippi had been heretofore almost a sinecure, and that the bulk of the business would be the maritime business on the Mississippi river. There was then no more necessity for the establishment of an additional Court, solely charged with that purpose, than to establish a Court at Mobile, Savannah or Charleston. To this way of indefinitely increasing the number of Courts having the jurisdiction of the District Courts, I am opposed. It seems to me wholly unnecessary, and not demanded by the exigencies of the times. For that reason I will insist upon my motion, that the bill be further considered.

Mr. SMITH, of Alabama. Well, Mr. President, a Court of Admiralty should be held at the place indicated in the bill, but at the same time I do not see the necessity, unless the chairmen can point it out, of having another Judge appointed especially for that purpose. We have limited the Jurisdiction of the District Court to five thousand dollars. Mississippi had but one seaport when in the United States, and I think the testimony will establish the fact that the duties of the Judge were quite nominal. The great bulk of the business has arisen from maritime business. I concur with my colleague, that there is no necessity to appoint a judge, specially to reside there, though I differ with him as to the necessity of having a Court there.

Mr. HALE. (interrupting) I grant the necessity to have the Court, but I contend that there is no necessity to have a District Judge.

Mr. SMITH. (resuming). I agree on that point. I cannot see the necessity for having a Judge residing in the interior holding a nominal office, especially when the Jurisdiction is cut down so as to exclude him from all cases above five thousand dollars. It seems very important that this should be the point for the District Court, and that the Judge of the District Court for Mississippi may be required to hold his Admiralty Court there. But I do not see why the Judge for Mississippi cannot discharge all these duties.

Mr. CLAYTON. I have no objection to have the bill sent back to the judiciary Committee.

Mr. HALE. Then I will modify my motion. I move that it be placed on the calendar and printed.

Mr. CLAYTON. I have no objection to that.

The motion was agreed to.

The PRESIDENT laid before the body a communication from the Secretary of the Treasury, containing estimates for the Post Office Department; which was referred to the Committee on Finance.

Mr. WAUL, of Texas, presented a communication, which was referred to the Committee on Military Affairs without being read.

Mr. SPARROW, of Louisiana, from the Committee on Military Affairs, reported the following resolution, which was agreed to:

> *Resolved*, That the communication of H. A. GERICKE,[144] of Louisiana, in relation to new caps for firing cannon, be referred to the Secretary of War, with instructions to have said caps tried, and report thereon.

And then the Congress went into secret session.

Friday, March 15, 1861

(Charleston *Mercury*, March 19, 1861; Montgomery *Weekly Advertiser*, March 20, 1861)

The Congress met at 12 o'clock, m., and was called to order by the President, Hon. HOWELL COBB, of Georgia. After prayer, the Journal of yesterday was read and approved.

Mr. WRIGHT, of Georgia. President, I hold in my hand a communication from B. F. JONES, Esq., of the firm of WHITLOCK & CO., importers of New York city,[145] on the subject of the tariff. This gentleman was formerly a citizen of the State of Georgia, resident in my town. He is now of this house in the city of New York, and addressed this communication to me for the purpose of having it laid before this Congress. It is a subject in which I do not feel myself skilled at all and I shall move its reference to the Committee on Finance, which is, I believe, the proper Committee. The communication I know is in good faith, and contains, what appears to me, to be good practiced common sense. The writer is one of those old and chronic cases of fire-eaters, that has devoted much study to the tariff question, and his mind, at present, is much exercised upon the subject. [document XVI]

The motion was agreed to.

Mr. WAUL, of Texas. I send to your desk, Mr. President, a communication from the President of the Convention of the people of Texas, and an ordinance adopted by her people in Convention assembled, by which that State has become a member of this Confederacy.[146]

The people of that State, sir, did not know, at the time of the adoption of that ordinance, of the confidence which this Congress had reposed in their fidelity and devotion to the rights of the South; they did not know that you had already admitted the members of that State to a seat to your counsels and deliberations; and that even before the communication which is submitted was made, her delegates were admitted to all the privileges of members upon the floor of this Congress. The people of Texas will not soon forget such confidence reposed in their patriotism: they will ever remember with pride the fact that before the proclamation of their secession was issued their State was already represented by one of the stars that shine in the galaxy of this Confederacy.

The people of Texas began, sir, the revolution which has so gloriously resulted in the Confederacy of States, under the guidance of those principles contained in the Declaration of Independence under which our fathers maintained their liberty, that all governments must derive their just authority from the consent of the governed.

This revolution, like the torrents down the mountain side, gathered as they flowed, until, as a mighty river, it swept irresistibly all before it. The voice of the people came up like the roar of many waters, drowning the gurgling brooks and babbling rills that attempted to swell their notes in opposition. It is known that a distinguished citizen of Texas was unfortunately at the helm of State, and in this hour of triumph, e'er the song of victory has died from our ears, I would do injustice to Texas and to my own feelings, did I attempt to pluck one leaf from the wreath that surrounds his brow, or place one blot upon the page of history illuminated by his name.[147] He and the people of his State have differed. He appealed to their generosity, and no man ever made it in vain. He was elected our Governor. Let us hope that it was devotion to a union that he moved not wisely but too well, that placed him in opposition to a people who had ever honored him.

When news fell upon the ears of our people that Lincoln was elected; when it was known that South Carolina, the farthest from us in distance, would secede; that she stood like a knight in armor from head to heel, with visor down and lance in rest—another Curtius ready to spring into the yawning chasm[148]—willing to sacrifice himself for the liberties of his country, Texas became thoroughly aroused, and like the well trained, high mettled war steed when the charge is sounded, who swells beyond the measure of his girth, throws the feeble horseman and with his bit in his teeth, rushes to the van of battle, so Texas sought her place in the grand array of Southern chivalry. When she permitted her territory to be divided in 1851,[149] many of her bold sons felt the humiliation, and when she bowed her proud neck and passed under the yoke, and permitted the fetters to be placed on her free limbs, believe not, sir, that she was less sensitive to encroachments on her rights than now. She felt that she was a new member of the Confederacy, and should err, if at all, on the side of peace; and was unwilling to embroil her sisters in a quarrel that was chiefly her own; but mistaken in deed were they who supposed that her supineness then would become submission now. No, sir, as soon as the call went forth, "Samson, the Philistines are upon thee!" she sprang forth, bursting the green and slender withes, and stood like a young Samson, with his unshorn locks, reveling in his manhood, his beauty and his power.

Nor is Texas ignorant of the position she occupies by her act of secession. Seven hundred miles of frontier is left without protection from the most warlike, cruel and ferocious race of savages on the continent.[150] On her western boundary is a nation whose life is revolution, and whose support is depredation. From the mouth of the Sabine to the Rio Grande, there is hardly one mounted gun, to defend her against such enemies as would attack them from their home on the deep. Texas knows all this, has counted the cost, and comes a willing member to this Confederacy, choosing to share all the perils of a new government, then be less than equal amidst her former peers.

I am satisfied that the Constitution that has been unanimously adopted by this Congress for a permanent government, will meet with the universal approbation of our State. You will perceive by the documents forwarded, that the desire was that a government should be formed based upon the Constitution of the United States. That has been done. In addition, the experience of seventy years has exposed some dangers and misconstructions, which we have avoided, or attempted to shun.

The patronage of the government, which, like the Maelstroms, drew within its vortex all that approached its attraction, we have attempted to check.

We have locked, bolted, barred and guarded the treasury.

We have greatly curtailed the expense of legislation, destroyed extra allowances, and saved the country to a great extent from jobbers and speculators. Taxes are to be collected for the uses of the government alone, leaving industry free to pursue that channel best suited to the tastes and habits of our people. Indeed, much has been done to commend it to the people of the whole South, and no change from the old Constitution that can with reason be condemned.

Texas has taken her place, and locks her shield with yours—her eyes are to the front, and she casts no glance backward. Reconstruction upon any terms is never dreamed of within her borders—as that confidence that holds nations as well as individuals together is wanting. And, sir, we have learned from history that a nation once divided, never, never reunites upon terms of equality. They have too vividly before their minds the example of the first secession that occurred in history under Jeroboam. When Jeroboam was asked to yield to the clamor of the people for justice, and a reduction of their taxes, he gave an answer after being consulted with the young men instead of with the aged and wise, that "my father made your yoke heavy, but I will add thereto; my father chastised you with whips, but I will chastise you with scorpions." After this the people answered the King saying, "what portion have we in David? And have we no inheritance in the son of Jesse; every man to your tents O, Israel, and now David see to this own house."[151] And every man went to his tent, the ten tribes went forth, and never, never has that breach been healed. And never, never will the people of Texas consent again, upon any terms, to live with a people from whom such injustice and oppression has been manifested. I hope, sir, the strife of that nation will find no parallel in this. We would go in peace, but if our adversaries desire war, so be it. If the old stars and stripes are threatened as the banner to force our degradation, even so

> Free be their banner flung; we are loth
> Its silken folds should seed the moth.[152]

And we will strike at the tall crests of those who fight under its folds, as your fathers and grandfathers fought those who rallied under the banner of St. George—associated as it was with their historic memories and gallant associations. We pay our devotions to the banner spread before us, and whether it dallies in the sunbeam, wantons on the breeze, or plays with its bright reflections in the waters.—Texas will offer its love, and, sir, should it float over the crashes of armies and the tide of battle, bathed in the red current that baptizes nations, while a shred remains aloft, or a man to fight for it, there by his side you will find a Texas seeking glory or a grave.

Texas has embarked for the voyage in the ship you but launched the other day. All her life, humanity and liberty are with you, and though the storm rages, and the timbers break beneath the swelling waters; "though the strained mast quiver as a reed and the rent canvass fluttering strew the gale,"[153] no Texan's cheek will blanch or heart grow faint. My life for it, she will ride out the storm, and make the port with her freight of human happiness and liberty. I move, sir, that the proclamation and ordinance be placed upon the journals of this body.

The motion was agreed to.

On motion of Mr. CURRY, of Alabama, the following resolutions, reported from the Committee on Accounts, were agreed to:

> *Resolved*, That the disbursement of the contingent fund of Congress be placed under the direction and control of the Secretary, subject to the approval of the Committee on Accounts.
>
> *Resolved further*, That estimates shall regularly be submitted by the Secretary, and no disbursement of the contingent fund shall hereafter be audited by the Committee on Accounts, except in accordance with such estimates.

> *Resolved further*, That the Secretary, at the next meeting of Congress, shall submit a detailed and particular statement of the payments made and authorized by loan from the contingent fund of Congress.

And then the Congress went into secret session.

Saturday, March 16, 1861
(Charleston *Mercury*, March 19, 1861)

The Congress met at 12 o'clock, m., and was called to order by the President, Hon. HOWELL COBB, of Georgia. After prayer by Rev. Mr. HENDERSON,[154] the Journal of yesterday was read and approved.

Mr. HALE, of Alabama, introduced a bill supplemental to an act to fix the pay of the officers of Congress, providing that the receipt of the officer receiving a salary under said act shall be a sufficient voucher to the proper officer of the Treasury.

Mr. HALE explained that in his judgment there was no necessity for the passage of this bill, but as there was some difference of opinion as to the construction of the act in question, in order to remove all difficulty he had introduced the bill, which he desired to have put upon its passage.

The bill was accordingly read three times and passed.

Mr. HALE, of Ala. Mr. President, I introduce the following resolution:

> *Resolved, by the Congress of the Confederate States of America*, That the Hon. WM. P. CHILTON, resident member of the Committee on Accounts, together with the Secretary of Congress, be authorized to audit and allow the accounts against Congress; and claims thus audited and allowed, shall be paid upon the order of said WM. P. CHILTON, countersigned by said Secretary, and this resolution only to operate during the recess of Congress.

The only object of the resolution is simply this: There is a great number of outstanding claims against Congress not audited and allowed. The parties want the money, and desire to get it during the recess.

Mr. CHILTON. Mr. President: That is putting a great deal of responsibility upon myself and the Secretary. Although I shall not decline to accept it, I only desire to say that it is not of my seeking.

The resolution was then adopted.

On motion of Mr. RHETT, of South Carolina, the following resolution was adopted:

> *Resolved*, That as soon as the signatures of the members of this Congress are placed on the enrolled Constitution of the Confederate States, the President of this Congress shall cause the same to be lithographed, and copies thereof to be sent to each of the Confederate States.

Mr. CLAYTON, of Mississippi, from the Committee on the Judiciary, reported a bill to prohibit the introduction of slaves from any State not a member of this Confederacy; which was read a first time by its title.

Mr. CLAYTON said: Mr. President, out of deference to the opinions of many members here, I do not propose to put the bill on its passage now, although I am in favor of its immediate passage. The object of the bill is to put a stop to the introduction of slaves into any of the Confederate States from any other State. This bill is to be followed up by a similar bill in relation to the introduction of slaves from Africa. We wish it to be distinctly understood, that whilst we have undertaken this movement to protect our own property in slaves, we desire to make it incumbent upon all others to take care of their own slaves, and to prevent the possibility of their throwing their slaves upon us, in order that, at some future time, they may be able to join another confederacy, the policy of which is hostile to ours. I have no wish to put the bill on its passage now. I simply ask that it may be read a second time and placed upon the public calendar.

The bill was accordingly read the second time and placed on the calendar.

Mr. WILSON, of Mississippi, from the Committee on Patents, reported back sundry letters and memorials on the subject of patents, which had been referred to them, and asked to be discharged from the further consideration of the same.

There being no objection, it was so ordered.

And then the Congress proceeded to sit with closed doors.

SECOND SESSION

(MONTGOMERY, ALABAMA, APRIL 29, 1861, TO MAY 21, 1861)

Monday, April 29, 1861

(Charleston Mercury, May 2, 1861; Montgomery *Weekly Advertiser*, May 1, 1861; Savannah *Daily Morning News*, May 1, 1861)

The Congress met at 12 o'clock, m., and was called to order by the President, Hon. HOWELL COBB, of Georgia. The following prayer was then delivered by the Rev. Mr. MANLY, formerly of South Carolina:

> Almighty Father, we thank Thee for the preservation of life and health, and that Thou has granted the members of this body a prosperous journey hither. We thank Thee, Father, for all the auspicious circumstances which have attended the noble struggle in which we are engaged, and we would especially recognize Thy hand in that bloodless victory which has attended the first hostile conflict of arms.[1] Oh God, we know it is to Thee we must look for power to resist them, and that all combinations of men acting in contravention of Thy will must fail. We humbly invoke, therefore, thy patience, our Heavenly Father. Let Thy wisdom control the counsels of this body, and not their own human wisdom. Let Thy providence so present all events and all subjects that the path of duty may be plain and straight before them. And we pray Thee to give them such a maturity and clearness of judgment, that they may see the right, and such a firmness of resolve that they may pursue it at whatever cost. And God grant us Thy gracious protection and blessing. Oh God, assist us with Thy will and wisdom, and dispose our enemies to a peaceful adjudication of matters and difficulties on equitable terms. Thou sittest in Heaven, judging the earth; Thou art an impartial Judge between these contenting parties. Oh, our Father, we should not have ventured to engage in a conflict without the feeling—the satisfying feeling—that we are asserting the rights Thou hast given us. We pray Thee to arbitrate between us, and if we must resort to the arbitrament of the sword, God bless fair young men, and let success attend their arms; cover their heads in the day of battle, and grant that if this controversy must come to a hostile conflict, that it may speedily terminate as bloodless as possible. Now, Oh God, bless this body; preserve the lives

of its members, and preserve their families during their absence. Forgive and accept us, for Christ's sake. Amen.

The roll was then called, when the following gentlemen answered to their names:

Alabama
Walker, R. W.
Smith, R. H.
Curry, J. L. M.
Chilton, W. P.
Hale, S. F.
Mcrae, Colin J.
Shorter, John Gill
Jones, H. C.
Davis, N. L.

Florida
Morton, Jackson
Anderson, J. P.
Owens, J. B.

Georgia
Toombs, Robert
Cobb, Howell
Bartow, Francis S.
Crawford, Martin J.
Nisbet, Eugenius A.
Hill, Benj. H.
Wright, A. R.
Cobb, Thomas R. R.
Kenan, Augustus H.
Stephens, Alex. H.

Louisiana
Perkins, Jr., John
DeClouet, A.
Conrad, Charles M.
Kenner, D. F.
Sparrow, Gen. Edward
Marshall, Henry

Mississippi
Harris, Willy P.
Brooke, Walker
Orr, J. A.
Clayton, A. M.
Barry, W. S.
Harrison J. T.
Campbell, J. A. P.

South Carolina
Rhett, Sr., R. B.
Barnwell, R. W.
Keitt, L. M.
Chesnut, Sr., James
Memminger, C. G.
Miles, W. Porcher
Withers, Thomas J.
Boyce, W. W.

Texas
Wigfall, Louis T.
Reagan, John H.
Hemphill, John
Waul, T. N.
Gregg, John
Oldham, W. S.
Ochiltree, Wm. B.

The PRESIDENT stated that a quorum was present, and that Congress was now ready to transact business.

Mr. WALKER, of Alabama, stated that there were some new members present from his State who had not been qualified, and moved that they now have an opportunity of doing so. He referred to Messrs. H. C. JONES and NICH. DAVIS, JR., who had been elected to fill the vacancies created by the resignations of Messrs. DAVID P. LEWIS and THOMAS FEARN.

Mr. OCHILTREE, of Texas, said that Mr. LOUIS T. WIGFALL was present, and he had not been qualified.

Mr. CLAYTON, of Mississippi, announced that Mr. J. A. ORR, (the successor of Mr. W. S. WILSON,) was also present, and moved that all these gentlemen be requested by the President to come forward and be qualified.

Messrs. DAVIS, JONES, WIGFALL, and ORR came forward, and took the oath and subscribed to the constitution.

On motion of Mr. T. R. R. COBB, of Georgia, the following gentlemen were appointed a Committee to wait upon the President and inform him that a quorum of members had appeared, in obedience to his Proclamation, and were now ready to receive any communication he might be pleased to make: Messrs. T. R. R. COBB, CHESNUT, and PERKINS. Subsequently the Committee reported that they had discharged their duty, and that the President informed them that he would communicate presently with the Congress, in writing.

On motion of Mr. T. R. R. COBB, the following resolution was adopted:

> *Resolved, by the Confederate States of America*, That the Secretary of the Congress be authorized to appoint an Assistant in the place of A. B. CLITHERALL,[2] resigned.

The PRESIDENT laid before Congress the following communication from citizens of Arizona:

> Messilla, March 18, 1861
>
> To the Hon. Howell Cobb, President of the Congress of the Confederate States of America:
>
> SIR: In pursuance of a resolution adopted at a Convention of the citizens of that portion of New Mexico known as Arizona, held at this place on the 16th inst., I have the honor and herewith to transmit the enclosed preamble and resolutions unanimously adopted, with the hope and request that you will lay them before the Congress of the Confederate States of America for their consideration. Signed by the President and Secretary.

Mr. CHESNUT, of South Carolina. Mr. President, I move that the further reading of the paper be dispensed with, and that it be referred to the Committee on Territories.

The motion was agreed to.

Mr. OCHILTREE, of Texas. Mr. President: I have a communication from the

Provisional Governor of the Territory of Arizona, transmitting a copy of the Provisional Constitution, with the request that it be laid before this body.

The paper was received, and referred to the Committee on Territories.

THE PRESIDENT'S MESSAGE.

The Doorkeeper having announced the arrival of Mr. JOSSELYN,[3] the Private Secretary of the President, that gentleman came forward, and said:

Mr. PRESIDENT: I am instructed by the President to deliver to the Congress a Message in writing, with the accompanying documents.

Mr. WITHERS. Before the Message is read, I will ask a member of the Cabinet whether or not it is proper to read it in open session.

Mr. TOOMBS. There is no objection to its being read in open session,

The Message was accordingly read in a very distinct tone by Mr. DIXON,[4] as follows:

Gentlemen of the Congress:

It is my pleasing duty to announce to you that the Constitution framed for the establishment of a permanent Government for the Confederate States has been ratified by conventions in each of those States to which it was referred. To inaugurate the Government in its full proportions and upon its own substantial basis of the popular will, it only remains that it should be held for the designation of the officers to administer it.

There is every reason to believe that at no distant day other States, identified in political principles and community of interests with those which you represent, will join this Confederacy, giving to its typical constellation increased splendor—to its Government of free, equal, and sovereign States a wider sphere of usefulness, and to the friends of constitutional liberty a greater security for its harmonious and perpetual existence.

It was not, however, for the purpose of making this announcement that I have deemed it my duty to convoke you at an earlier day than that fixed by yourselves for your meeting. The declaration of war made against this Confederacy by Abraham Lincoln, the President of the United States, in his proclamation issued on the fifteenth day of the present month, rendered it necessary, in my judgment, that you should convene at the earliest practicable moment to devise the measures necessary for the defense of the country.[5]

The occasion is indeed an extraordinary one. It justifies me in a brief review of the relations heretofore existing between us and the States which now unite in warfare against us, and in a succinct statement of the events which have resulted in this warfare; to the end that mankind may pass intelligent and impartial judgment on its motives and objects.

During the war waged against Great Britain by her colonies on this continent, a common danger impelled them to a close alliance, and to the formation of a Confederation, by the terms of which the colonies, styling themselves States, entered "*severally* into a firm league of friendship with each other for their common defense, the security of their liberties, and their mutual and general welfare, binding themselves to assist each other against all force offered to or attacks made upon them, or any of them, on account of religion, sovereignty, trade, or any other pretense whatever."

In order to guard against any misconstruction of their contract, the several States made explicit declaration, in a distinct article, that "*each* State *retains its* sovereignty, freedom and independence, and every power, jurisdiction, and right, which is not by this Confederation *expressly delegated* to the United States in Congress assembled."

Under this contract of alliance, the war of the Revolution was successfully waged, and resulted in the treaty of peace with Great Britain in 1783, by the terms of which the several States were, *each by name*, recognized to be independent.

The articles of confederation contained a clause whereby all alterations were prohibited, unless confirmed by the Legislatures of *every State*, after being agreed to by the Congress; and in obedience to this provision, under the resolution of Congress of the 21st of February, 1787, the several States appointed delegates who attended a Convention "for the *sole and express purpose* of revising the articles of confederation, and reporting to Congress and the several Legislatures such alterations and provisions therein as shall, when agreed to in Congress, *and confirmed by the States*, render the Federal Constitution adequate to the exigencies of government and the preservation of the Union."

It was, by the delegates chosen, by the *several States*, under the resolution just quoted, that the Constitution of the United States was framed in 1787, and submitted to the *several States* for ratification, as shown by the 7th article, which is in these words:

"The ratification of the *Convention of nine States* shall be sufficient for the establishment of this Constitution BETWEEN *the States* so ratifying the same."

I have italicized certain words made in the quotations just made, for the purpose of attracting attention to the singular and marked caution with which the States endeavored, in every possible form, to exclude the idea that the separate and independent sovereignty of each State was merged into one common government and nation; and the earnest desire they evinced to impress on the Constitution its true character—that of a *compact* between INDEPENDENT States.

The Constitution of 1787 having, however, omitted the clause already recited from the articles of Confederation, which provided, in explicit terms, that each State *retained* its sovereignty and independence, some alarm was felt in the States when invited to ratify the Constitution, lest this omission should be construed into an abandonment of their cherished principle, and they refused to be satisfied until amendments were added to the Constitution, placing beyond any pretense of doubt the reservation, by the States, of all their sovereign rights and powers—not expressly delegated to the United States by the Constitution.

Strange, indeed, it must appear to the impartial observer, but it is none the less true, that all these carefully worded clauses proved unavailing to prevent the rise and growth in the Northern States of a political school which has persistently claimed that the government thus formed was not a compact *between* States, but was in effect a National Government, set up *above* and *over* the States. An organization, created by the States to secure the blessings of liberty and independence against *foreign* aggression, has been gradually perverted into a machine for their control of their *domestic* affairs—the *creature* has been exalted above its *creators*; the *principals* have been made subordinate to the *agent* appointed by themselves.

The people of the Southern States, whose almost exclusive occupation was agriculture, early perceived a tendency in the Northern States to render the common Government subservient to their own purposes, by imposing burdens on commerce as a protection to their manufacturing and shipping interests. Long and angry controversies grew out of these attempts, often successful, to benefit one section of the country at the expense of the other. And the danger of disruption arising from this cause was enhanced by the fact that the Northern population was increasing by immigration and other causes in a greater ratio than the population of the South. By degrees, as the Northern States gained preponderance in the National Congress, self-interest taught their people to yield ready assent to any plausible advocacy of their right as a majority to govern the minority without control: they learned to listen with impatience to the suggestion of any constitutional impediment to the exercise of their will; and so utterly have the principles of the Constitution been corrupted in the Northern mind, that in the inaugural address delivered by President Lincoln in March last, he asserts as an axiom which he plainly deems to be undeniable, that the theory of the Constitution requires that in all cases the majority shall govern; and in another memorable instance the same Chief Magistrate did not hesitate to liken the relations between a State and the United States to those which exist between a county and the State in which it is situated and by which it was created. This is the lamentable and fundamental error on which rests the policy that has culminated in his declaration of war against these Confederate States.

In addition to the long-continued and deep-seated resentment felt by the Southern States at the persistent abuse of the powers they had delegated to the Congress, for the purpose of enriching the manufacturing and shipping classes of the North at the expense of the South, there has existed for nearly half a century another subject of discord, involving interests of such transcendent magnitude as at all times to create the apprehension in the minds of many devoted lovers of the Union, that its permanence was impossible.

When the several States delegated certain powers to the United States Congress, a large portion of the laboring population consisted of African slaves imported into the colonies by the mother country. In twelve out of the thirteen States negro slavery existed, and the right of property in slaves was protected by law. This property was recognized in the Constitution, and provision was made against its loss by the escape of the slave. The increase in the number of slaves by further importation from Africa was also secured by a clause forbidding Congress to prohibit the slave-trade anterior to a certain date; and in no clause can there be found any delegation of power to the Congress authorizing it in any manner to legislate to the prejudice, detriment, or discouragement of the owners of that species of property, or excluding it from the protection of the Government.

The climate and soil of the Northern States soon proved unpropitious to the continuance of slave labor, whilst the converse was the case at the South. Under the unrestricted free intercourse between the two sections, the Northern States consulted their own interests by selling their slaves to the South, and prohibiting slavery within their limits. The South were willing purchasers of a property suitable to their wants, and paid the price of the acquisition without harboring a suspicion that their quiet possession was to be disturbed by those who were inhibited, not only by want of constitutional authority, but by good faith as vendors, from disquieting a title emanating from themselves.

As soon, however, as the Northern States that prohibited African slavery within their limits had reached a number sufficient to give their representation a controlling voice in the Congress, a persistent and organized system of hostile measures against the rights of the owners of slaves in the Southern States was inaugurated, and gradually extended. A continuous series of measures was devised and prosecuted for the purpose of rendering insecure the tenure of property in slaves; fanatical organizations, supplied with money by voluntary subscriptions, were assiduously engaged in exciting amongst the slaves a spirit of discontent and revolt; means were furnished for their escape from their owners, and agents secretly employed to entice them to abscond; the constitutional provision for their rendition to their owners was first evaded, then openly denounced as a violation of conscientious obligation and religious duty; men were taught that it was a merit to elude, disobey and violently oppose the execution of the laws enacted to secure the performance of the promise contained in the constitutional compact; owners of slaves were mobbed and even murdered in open day solely for applying to a magistrate for the arrest of a fugitive slave; the dogmas of these voluntary organizations soon obtained control of the Legislatures of many of the Northern States, and laws were passed providing for the punishment, by ruinous fines and long-continued imprisonment in jails and penitentiaries, of citizens of the Southern States who should dare ask aid of the officers of the law for the recovery of their property.

Emboldened by success, the theater of agitation and aggression against the clearly expressed constitutional rights of the Southern States was transferred to the Congress; Senators and Representatives were sent to the common councils of the nation, whose chief title to this distinction consisted in the display of a spirit of ultra fanaticism, and whose business was not "to promote the general welfare or insure domestic tranquility," but to awaken the bitterest hatred against the citizens of the sister States by violent denunciation of their institutions; the transaction of public affairs was impeded by repeated efforts to usurp powers not delegated by the Constitution, for the purpose of impairing the security of property in slaves, and reducing those States which held slaves to a condition of inferiority.

Finally a great party was organized for the purpose of obtaining the administration of the Government, with the avowed object of using its power for the total exclusion of the slave states from all participation in the benefits of the public domain, acquired by all States in common, whether by conquest or purchase; of surrounding them entirely by States in which slavery should be prohibited; of thus rendering the property in slaves so insecure as to be comparatively worthless, and thereby annihilating in effect property worth thousands of millions of dollars. This party, thus organized, succeeded in the month of November last in the election of its candidate for the Presidency of the United States.

In the meantime, under the mild and genial climate of the Southern States, and the increasing care and attention for the well-being and comfort of the laboring class, dictated alike by interest and humanity, the African slaves had augmented in number from about 600,000 at the date of the adoption of the constitutional compact, to upward of 4,000,000. In moral and social condition they had been elevated from brutal savages into docile, intelligent, and civilized agricultural laborers, and supplied not only with bodily comforts but with careful religious instruction.

Under the supervision of a superior race, their labor had been so directed as not only to allow a gradual and marked amelioration of their own condition, but to convert hundreds of thousands of square miles of the wilderness into cultivated lands, covered with a prosperous people; towns and cities had sprung into existence, and had rapidly increased in wealth and population under the social system of the South; the white population of the Southern slave-holding States had augmented from about 1,250,000, at the date of the adoption of the Constitution, to more than 8,500,000 in 1860; and the productions of the South in cotton, rice, sugar, and tobacco, for the full development and continuance of which the labor of African slaves was, and is, indispensable, had swollen to an amount which formed nearly three-fourths of the exports of the whole United States, and had become absolutely necessary to the wants of civilized man.

With interests of such overwhelming magnitude imperiled, the people of the Southern States were driven, by the conduct of the North, to the adoption of some course of action to avert the danger with which they were openly menaced. With this view, the Legislatures of the several States invited the people to select delegates to conventions to be held for the purpose of determining for themselves what measures were best adapted to meet so alarming a crisis in their history.

Here it may be proper to observe that from a period as early as 1798 there had existed in *all* of the States of the Union a party, almost uninterruptedly in the majority, based upon the creed that each State was, in the last resort, the sole judge as well of its wrongs, as of the mode and measure of redress. Indeed, it is obvious, that under the law of nations, this principle is an axiom as applied to the relations of independent sovereign States, such as those which had united themselves under the constitutional compact. The Democratic party of the United States repeated, in its successful canvass in 1856, the declaration made in numerous previous political contests, that it would "faithfully abide by and uphold the principles laid down in the Kentucky and Virginia resolutions of 1798, and in the report of Mr. Madison to the Virginia Legislature in 1799; and that it adopts those principles as constituting one of the main foundations of its political creed."

The principles thus emphatically announced, embrace that to which I have already adverted, the right of each State to judge of and redress the wrongs of which it complains. These principles were maintained by overwhelming majorities of the people of all the States of the Union at different elections, especially in the elections of Mr. Jefferson in 1805, Mr. Madison in 1809, and Mr. Pierce in 1852.

In the exercise of a right so ancient, so well established, and so necessary for self-preservation, the people of the Confederate States, in their Conventions, determined that the wrongs which they had suffered, and the evils with which they were menaced, required that they should revoke the delegation of powers to the Federal Government which they had ratified in their several Conventions. They consequently passed Ordinances, resuming all their rights as sovereign and independent States, and dissolved their connection with the other States of the Union.

Having done this, they proceeded to form a new compact amongst themselves by new Articles of Confederation, which have been also ratified by the conventions of the several States with an approach to unanimity far exceeding that of the Conventions which adopted the Constitution of 1787. They have organized their new Government in all its departments; the functions of the executive, legislative, and judicial magistrates are performed in accordance with the will of the people as displayed, not merely in a cheerful acquiescence, but in the enthusiastic support of the Government thus established by themselves; and but for the interference of the Government of the United States in this legitimate exercise of the right of a people to self-government, peace, happiness and prosperity would now smile on our land.

That peace is ardently desired by this Government and people, has been manifested in every possible form. Scarce had you assembled in February last, when, prior even to the inauguration of the Chief Magistrate you had elected, you passed a resolution expressive of your desire for the appointment of commissioners to be sent to the Government of the United States "for the purpose of negotiating friendly relations between that Government and the Confederate States of America, and for the settlement of all questions of disagreement between the two Governments upon principles of right, justice, equity, and good faith."

It was my pleasure as well as my duty to co-operate with you in this work of peace. Indeed, in my address to you on taking the oath of office and before receiving from you the communication of this resolution, I had said "as a necessity, not a choice, we have resorted to the remedy of separation, and henceforth our energies must be directed to the conduct of our own affairs and the perpetuity of the Confederacy which we have formed. If a just perception of mutual interests shall permit us peaceably to pursue our separate political career my most earnest desire will have been fulfilled."

It was in furtherance of these accordant views of the Congress and the Executive, that I made choice of three discreet, able and distinguished citizens, who repaired to Washington.[6] Aided by their cordial co-operation, and that of the Secretary of State, every effort compatible with self-respect and the dignity of the Confederacy was exhausted before I allowed myself to yield to the conviction that the Government of the United States was determined to attempt the conquest of this people and that our cherished hopes of peace were unattainable.

On the arrival of our Commissioners in Washington, on the 5th of March they postponed, at the instigation of a friendly intermediary, doing more than giving in formal notice of their arrival.[7] This was done with a view to afford time to the President, who had just been inaugurated, for the discharge of other pressing official duties in the organization of his Administration, before engaging his attention in the object of their mission. It was not until the 12th of the month that they officially addressed the Secretary of State, informing him of the purpose of their arrival, and stating in the language of their instructions their wish "to make to the Government of the United States overtures for the opening of negotiations, assuring the Government of the United States that the President, Congress and people of the Confederate States earnestly desire a peaceful solution of these great questions; that it is neither their interest nor their wish to make any demand which is not founded on strictest justice, nor do any act to injure their late confederates."

To this communication no formal reply was received until the 8th of April. During the interval the commissioners had consented to waive all questions of form. With the firm resolve to avoid war if possible, they went so far, even, as to hold during that long period, unofficial intercourse, through an intermediary, whose high position and character inspired the hope of success, and through whom constant assurances were received from the Government of the United States of peaceful intentions; of the determination to evacuate Fort Sumter; and further, that no measure changing the existing *status* prejudicially to the Confederate States, especially at Fort Pickens, was in contemplation, but that in the event of any change of intention on the subject, notice would be given to the commissioners. The crooked paths of diplomacy can scarcely furnish an example so wanting in courtesy, in candor and directness, as was the course of the United States Government toward our commissioners in Washington. For proof of this I refer to the annexed documents marked ____, taken in connection with further facts, which I now proceed to relate.[8] [document XVII]

Early in April the attention of the whole country, as well as that of our Commissioners, was attracted to extraordinary preparations for an extensive naval and military expedition in New York and other Northern ports. These preparations, commenced in secrecy, for an expedition whose destination was concealed, only became known when nearly completed, and on the 5th, 6th, and 7th of April, transports and vessels of war, with troops, munitions and military supplies sailed from Northern ports, bound Southwards. Alarmed by so extraordinary a demonstration, the commissioners requested the delivery of an answer to their official communication of the 12th of March, and thereupon received on the 8th of April, a reply dated on the 15th of the previous month, from which it appears that, during the whole interval, whilst the Commissioners were receiving assurances calculated to inspire hope of the success of their mission, the Secretary of State and the President of the United States had already determined to hold no intercourse with them whatever; to refuse even to listen to any proposals they had to make, and had profited by the delay created by their own assurances, in order to prepare secretly the means for effective hostile operations.

That these assurances were given has been virtually confessed by the Government of the United States by its sending a messenger to Charleston to give notice of its purpose to use force, if opposed in its intention of supplying Fort Sumter. No more striking proof of the absence of good faith, in the conduct of the Government of the United States toward this Confederacy can be required than is contained in the circumstances which accompanied this notice. According to the usual course of navigation, the vessels composing the expedition designed for the relief of Fort Sumter, might be expected to reach Charleston harbor on the 9th of April; yet, with our Commissioners actually in Washington, detained under assurances that notice should be given of any military movement, the notice was not addressed to *them*, but a messenger was sent to Charleston to give the notice to the Governor of South Carolina, and the notice was so given at a late hour on the 8th of April, the eve of the very day on which the fleet might be expected to arrive.

That this maneuver failed in its purpose was not the fault of those who contrived it. A heavy tempest delayed the arrival of the expedition, and gave time to the commander of our forces at Charleston to ask and receive the instructions of this Government. Even then, under all the provocation incident to the contemptuous refusal to listen to our Commissioners, and the tortuous course of the Government of the United States, I was sincerely anxious to avoid the effusion of blood, and directed a proposal to be made to the commander of Fort Sumter, who had avowed himself to be nearly out of provisions, that we would abstain from directing our fire on Fort Sumter if he would promise not to open fire on our forces unless first attacked. This proposal was refused, and the conclusion was reached, that the design of the United States was to place the besieging force at Charleston between the simultaneous fire of the fleet and the fort. There remained, therefore, no alternative but to direct that the fort should at once be reduced.

This order was executed by Gen. Beauregard with the skill and success which were naturally to be expected from the well-known character of that gallant officer, and, although the bombardment lasted but thirty-three hours, our flag did not wave over its battered walls until after the appearance of the hostile fleet off Charleston. Fortunately not a life was lost on our side, and we were gratified in being spared the necessity of a useless effusion of blood by the prudent caution of the officers who commanded the fleet in abstaining from the evidently futile effort to enter the harbor for the relief of Major Anderson. I refer to the report of the Secretary of War and the papers which accompany it for further details of this brilliant affair.[9]

In this connection, I cannot refrain from a well deserved tribute to the noble State, the eminent soldierly qualities of whose people were so conspicuously displayed in the port of Charleston. For months they had been irritated by the spectacle of a fortress held within their principal harbor, as a standing menace against their peace and independence. Built in part with their own money, its custody confided with their own consent to an agent who held no power over them other than such as they had themselves delegated for their own benefit, intended to be used by that agent for their own protection against foreign attack, they saw it held with persistent tenacity as a means of offense against them by the very Government which they had established for their protection.

They had beleaguered it for months—felt entire confidence in their power to capture it—yet yielded to the requirements of discipline, curbed their impatience, submitted without complaint to the unaccustomed hardships, labors and privations of a protracted siege; and when at length their patience was rewarded by the signal for attack, and success had crowned their steady and gallant conduct—even in the very moment of triumph—they evinced a chivalrous regard for the feelings of the brave but unfortunate officer who had been compelled to lower his flag. All manifestations of exultation were checked in his presence.

Their commanding general, with their cordial approval and the consent of his Government, refrained from imposing any terms that could wound the sensibilities of the commander of the fort.[10] He was permitted to retire with the honors of war—to salute his flag, to depart freely with all his command, and was escorted to the vessel in which he embarked, with the highest marks of respect from those against whom his guns had been so recently directed. Not only does every event connected with the siege reflect the highest honor on South Carolina, but the forbearance of her people, and of this Government, from making any harsh use of a victory obtained under circumstances of such peculiar provocation, attest to the fullest extent the absence of any purpose beyond securing their own tranquility and the sincere desire to avoid the calamities of war.

Scarcely had the President of the United States received intelligence of the failure of the scheme which he had devised for the re-enforcement of Fort Sumter, when he issued the declaration of war against this Confederacy which has prompted me to convoke you. In this extraordinary production, that high functionary affects total ignorance of the existence of an independent Government, which, possessing the entire and enthusiastic devotion of its people, is exercising its functions without question over seven sovereign States—over more than five millions of people—and over a territory whose area exceeds over half a million of square miles. He terms sovereign States "combinations, too powerful to be suppressed by the ordinary course of judicial proceedings or by the powers vested in the marshals by law." He calls for an army of seventy-five thousand men to act as a *posse comitatus* in aid of the process of the courts of justice in States where no courts exist whose mandates and decrees are not cheerfully obeyed and respected by a willing people. He avows that "the *first* service to be assigned to the forces called out," will be, not to execute the process of courts, but to capture forts and strongholds situated within the admitted limits of this Confederacy, and garrisoned by its troops; and declares that "this effort" is intended "to maintain the perpetuity of popular government." He concludes by commanding "the persons composing the combinations aforesaid," to wit: the five millions of inhabitants of these States, "to retire peaceably to their respective abodes within twenty days."

Apparently contradictory as are the terms of this singular document, one point is unmistakably evident. The President of the United States called for an army of seventy-five thousand men, whose *first* service was to be to capture our forts. It was a plain declaration of war which I was not at liberty to disregard because of my knowledge that under the Constitution of the United States the President was usurping a power granted exclusively to the Congress. He is the sole organ of communication between that country and foreign powers. The law of nations did not permit me to question the authority of the Executive of a foreign nation to declare war against this Confederacy. Although I might have refrained from taking active measures for our defense, if the States of the Union had all imitated the action of Virginia, North Carolina, Arkansas, Kentucky, Tennessee, and Missouri, by denouncing the call for troops as an unconstitutional usurpation of power to which they refused to respond, I was not at liberty to disregard the fact that many of the States seemed quite content to submit to the exercise of the power assumed by the President of the United States, and were actively engaged in levying troops to be used for the purpose indicated in the Proclamation.

Deprived of the aid of Congress at the moment, I was under the necessity of confining my action to a call on the States for volunteers for the common defense, in accordance with the authority you had confided to me before your adjournment.[11] I deemed it proper, further, to issue a proclamation inviting application from persons disposed to aid our defense in private armed vessels on the high seas, to the end that preparations might be made for the immediate issue of letters of marque and reprisal, which you alone, under the Constitution, have power to grant.[12] I entertain no doubt you will concur with me in the opinion that in the absence of a fleet of public vessels, it will be eminently expedient to supply their place by private armed vessels, so happily styled by the publicists of the United States, "the militia of the sea," and so often and justly relied on by them as an efficient and admirable instrument of defense warfare. I earnestly recommend the immediate passage of a law authorizing me to accept the numerous proposals already received.

I cannot close this review of the acts of the Government of the United States without referring to a proclamation issued by their President, under date of the 19th instant, in which, after declaring that an insurrection has broken out in this Confederacy against the Government of the United States, he announces a blockade of all the ports of these States, and threatens to punish as pirates all persons who shall molest any vessel of the United States under letters of marque issued by this Government.[13] Notwithstanding the authenticity of this proclamation, you will concur with me that it is hard to believe it could have emanated from a President of the United States. Its announcement of a mere paper blockade is so manifestly a violation of the law of nations that it would seem incredible that it could have been issued by authority—but conceding this to be the case so far as the Executive is concerned, it will be difficult to satisfy the people of these States that their late confederates will sanction its declarations, will determine to ignore the usages of civilized nations, and will inaugurate a war of extermination on both sides, by treating as pirates, open enemies acting under the authority of commissions issued by an organized government. If such proclamation was issued, it could only have been published under the sudden influence of passion, and we may rest assured mankind will be spared the horrors of the conflict it seems to invite.

For the details of the administration of the different departments, I refer to the reports of the Secretaries, which accompany this message.[14]

The State Department has furnished the necessary instructions for three commissioners who have been sent to England, France, Russia and Belgium, since your adjournment, to ask our recognition as a member of the family of nations, and to make with each of those powers treaties of amity and commerce.[15] Further steps will be taken to enter into like negotiations with the other European powers, in pursuance of your resolutions passed at the last session. Sufficient time has not yet elapsed since the departure of these commissioners for the receipt of any intelligence from them. As I deem it desirable that commissioners or other diplomatic agents should also be sent at an early period to the independent

American powers south of our Confederacy, with all of whom it is our interest and earnest wish to maintain the most cordial and friendly relations, I suggest the expediency of making the necessary appropriations for that purpose.

Having been officially notified by the public authorities of the State of Virginia that she had withdrawn from the Union and desired to maintain the closest political relations with us which it was possible at this time to establish, I commissioned the Hon. Alexander H. Stephens, Vice-President of the Confederate States, to represent this Government at Richmond. I am happy to inform you that he has concluded a convention with the State of Virginia, by which that honored Commonwealth, so long and justly distinguished among her sister States, and so dear to the hearts of thousands of her children in the Confederate States, has united her power and her fortunes with ours, and become one of us. This Convention, together with the Ordinance of Virginia, adopting the Provisional Constitution of the Confederacy, will be laid before you for your constitutional action. I have satisfactory assurances from other of our late confederates, that they are on the point of adopting similar measures, and I cannot doubt that ere you shall have been many weeks in session the whole of the slave-holding States of the late Union will respond to the call of honor and affection, and by uniting their fortunes with ours, promote our common interests and secure our common safety.

In the Treasury Department, regulations have been devised and put into execution for carrying out the policy indicated in your legislation on the subject of the navigation of the Mississippi river, as well as for the collection of revenue on the frontier. Free transit has been secured for vessels and merchandise passing through the Confederate States; and delay and inconvenience have been avoided as far as possible, in organizing the revenue service for the various railways entering our territory. As fast as experience shall indicate the possibility of improvement in these regulations, no effort will be spared to free commerce from all unnecessary embarrassments and obstructions.

Under your act authorizing a loan, proposals were issued inviting subscriptions for five millions of dollars, and the call was answered by the prompt subscription of more than eight millions by our own citizens, and not a single bid was made under par. The rapid development of the purpose of the President of the United States to invade our soil, capture our forts, blockade our ports, and wage war against us, induced me to direct that the entire subscription should be accepted. It will now become necessary to raise means to a much larger amount to defray the expenses of maintaining our independence and repelling invasion. I invite your special attention to this subject, and the financial condition of the Government, with the suggestion of ways and means for the supply of the Treasury, will be presented to you in a separate communication.

To the Department of Justice you have confided not only the organization and supervision of all matters connected with the courts of justice, but also those connected with patents and with the bureau of public printing.

Since your adjournment all the courts, with the exception of those of Mississippi and Texas, have been organized by the appointment of Marshals and District Attorneys, and are now prepared for the exercise of their functions.[16]

In the two States, just named, the gentlemen confirmed as Judges declined to accept the appointment, and no nominations have yet been made to fill the vacancies. I refer you to the report of the Attorney-General, and concur in his recommendation for immediate legislation, especially on the subject of patent rights. Early provision should be made to secure to the subjects of foreign nations the full enjoyment of their property in valuable inventions, and to extend to our own citizens protection, not only for their own inventions, but for such as may have been assigned to them, or may hereafter be assigned by persons not alien enemies.

The patent office business is much more extensive and important than had been anticipated. The applications for patents, although confined under the law exclusively to citizens of our Confederacy, already average seventy per month, showing the necessity for the prompt organization of a bureau of patents.

The Secretary of War, in his report and accompanying documents, conveys full information concerning the forces, regular, volunteer and provisional, raised and called for under the several Acts of Congress, their organization and distribution. Also, an account of the expenditures already made, and the further estimates for the fiscal year ending the 18th of February, 1862, rendered necessary by recent events.[17] I refer to his report also for a full history of the occurrences in Charleston harbor, prior to and including the bombardment and reduction of Fort Sumter, and of the measures subsequently taken for the common defense, on receiving the intelligence of the declaration of war against us made by the President of the United States. There are now in the field at Charleston, Pensacola, Forts Morgan, Jackson, St. Philip and Pulaski, nineteen thousand men, and sixteen thousand are now *en route* for Virginia. It is proposed to organize and hold in readiness for instant action, in view of the present exigencies of the country, an army of one hundred thousand men. If further force should be needed the wisdom and patriotism of Congress will be confidently appealed to for authority to call into the field additional numbers of our noble-spirited volunteers who are constantly tendering service far in excess of our wants.

The operations of the Navy Department have been necessarily restricted by the fact that sufficient time has not yet elapsed for the purchase or construction of more than a limited number of vessels adapted to the public service. Two vessels purchased have been named the "Sumter" and "Machree," and are now being prepared for sea at New Orleans with all possible dispatch.[18] Contracts have also been made at that city with two different establishments for the casting of ordnance, cannon shot and shell, with the view to encourage the manufacture of these articles, so indispensable for our defense, as at many points within our territory as possible.[19]

I call your attention to the recommendation of the Secretary for the establishment of a magazine and laboratory for preparation of ordinance stores, and the necessary appropriation for that purpose. Hitherto such stores have usually been prepared at the navy yards, and no appropriation was made at your last session for this object.

The Secretary also calls attention to the fact that no provision has been made for the payment of invalid pensions to our own citizens. Many of these persons are advanced in life, they have no means of support, and by the secession of these States have been deprived of their claim against the Government of the United States. I recommend the appropriation of the sum necessary to pay those pensioners, as well as those of the army, whose claims can scarcely exceed seventy thousand dollars per annum.

The Postmaster-General has already succeeded in organizing his department to such an extent as to be in readiness to assume the direction of our postal affairs, on the occurrence of the contingency contemplated by the act of March 15, 1861, or even sooner if desired by Congress. The various books and circulars have been prepared, and measures taken to secure supplies of blanks, postage stamps, stamped envelopes, mail bags, locks, keys, &c. He presents a detailed classification and arrangement of his clerical force and asks for its increase. An auditor of the Treasury for this department is necessary, and a plan is submitted for the organization of his bureau. The great number and magnitude of the accounts of this department require an increase of the clerical force in the accounting branch in the Treasury. The revenues of this department are collected and disbursed in modes peculiar to itself, and require a special bureau to secure a proper accountability in the administration of its finances.

I call your attention to the additional legislation required for this Department; to the recommendation for changes in the law fixing the rates of postage on newspapers, periodicals, and sealed packages of certain kinds, and specially to the recommendation of the Secretary, in which I concur, that you provide at once for the assumption by him of the control of our entire postal service.

In the military organization of the States provision is made for brigadier and major generals, but in the Army of the Confederate States the highest grade is that of brigadier-general. Hence it will, no doubt, sometimes occur that where troops of the Confederacy do duty with the militia, the General selected for the command, and possessed of the views and purposes of this Government, will be superseded by an officer of the militia not having the same advantages. To avoid this contingency in the least objectionable manner, I recommend that additional rank be given to the General of the Confederate Army, and concurring in the policy of having but one grade of generals in the Army of the Confederacy, I recommend that the law of its organization be amended so that the grade be that of general.

To secure a thorough military education, it is deemed essential that officers should enter upon the study of their profession at an early period of life, and have elementary instruction in a military school. Until such school shall be established, it is recommended that cadets be appointed and attached to companies until they shall have attained the age and have acquired the knowledge to fit them for the duties of lieutenants.

I also call your attention to an omission in the law organizing the army, in relation to military chaplains, and recommend that provision be made for their appointment.

In conclusion, I congratulate you on the fact, that in every portion of our country, there has been exhibited the most patriotic devotion to our common cause. Transportation companies have freely tendered the use of their lines for troops and supplies. The presidents of the railroads of the Confederacy, in company with others who control lines of communication with States that we hope soon to greet as sisters, assembled in convention in this city, and not only reduced largely the rates heretofore demanded for mail service, and conveyance of troops and munitions, but voluntarily proffered to receive their compensation at these reduced rates in the bonds of the Confederacy, for the purpose of leaving all the resources of the Government at its disposal for the common defense. Requisitions for troops have been met with such alacrity that the numbers tendering their services have, in every instance greatly exceeded the demand. Men of the highest official and social position, are serving as volunteers in the ranks. The gravity of age and the zeal of youth, rival each other in the desire to be foremost for the public defense, and though at no other point than the one heretofore noticed, have they been stimulated by the excitement incident to actual engagement, and the hope of distinction for individual achievement, they have borne what for new troops is the most severe ordeal, patient toil and constant vigil, and all the exposure and discomfort of active service, with a resolution and fortitude such as to command approbation and justify the highest expectation of their conduct when active valor shall be required in place of steady endurance.

A people thus united and resolved cannot shrink from any sacrifice which they may be called on to make, nor can there be a reasonable doubt of their final success, however long and severe may be the test of their determination to maintain their birthright of freedom and equality as a trust which it is their first duty to transmit, undiminished, to their posterity.

A bounteous Providence cheers us with the promise of abundant crops. The fields of grain, which will, within a few weeks be ready for the sickle, give assurance of the amplest supply of food for man; whilst the corn, cotton, and other staple productions of our soil, afford abundant proof that up to this period the season has been propitious.

We feel that our cause is just and holy; we protest solemnly in the face of mankind that we desire peace at any sacrifice save that of honor and independence; we seek no conquest, no aggrandizement, no concession of any kind from the States with which we were lately confederated; all we ask is to be let alone, that those who never held power over us, shall not now attempt our subjugation by arms. This we will, this we must, resist to the direst extremity.

The moment that this pretension is abandoned, the sword will drop from our grasp, and we shall be ready to enter into treaties of amity and commerce that cannot but be mutually beneficial. So long as this pretension is maintained, with a firm reliance on that Divine Power which covers with its protection the just cause, we will continue to struggle for our inherent right to freedom, independence, and self-government.

Jefferson Davis
Montgomery, April 29, 1861

The reading of the Message having been concluded—

The PRESIDENT inquired what disposition should be made of the accompanying documents; when—

Mr. TOOMBS, remarking that it was not decided that the accompanying documents should be read in open session, moved that the Congress proceed to sit with closed doors; which motion was agreed to. Congress shortly thereafter adjourned.

Tuesday, April 30, 1861

(Charleston *Mercury*, May 3, 1861)

The Congress met at 12 o'clock, m., and was called to order be the President, Hon. HOWELL COBB, of Georgia. After prayer by the Rev. Mr. MITCHELL, the journal of yesterday's proceedings was read and approved.

Mr. CHILTON, of Alabama, presented a communication from A. HATCHETT of Tennessee,[20] containing important information in relation to military affairs; which was referred to the Committee on Military Affairs without being read.

Mr. WRIGHT, of Georgia. Mr. President, I do not rise for the purpose of offering any resolution, or bill, or memorial, but for the purpose of making an inquiry of the Military Committee. During the last session of this body I introduced a bill proposing to form a volunteer division in the regular army of the Confederate States. The bill was referred to the Military Committee. They have made no report upon the subject. I rise for the purpose of enquiring of the Chairman of that Committee whether or not it is their purpose to report upon the subject of the bill to the House.[21]

Mr. BARTOW, of Georgia. Mr. President, the bill, of which the gentleman speaks, was referred to the Committee on Military Affairs, and my recollection is, that the Committee considered it, and my remembrance also is, that they instructed me to report unfavorably on it. But I am not so clear upon that subject. I do not remember precisely that instruction, or whether it was laid over for further consideration. I myself was called away from Congress, to attend the session of the Convention of the State of Georgia at Savannah, and I do not know what action the Committee on Military Affairs took in reference to that matter during my absence, or whether they took any action at all. I presume there was a great deal of unfinished business laid over until the reassembling of Congress, and this bill may be among the unfinished business. That is all the information I can give on the subject.

Mr. WRIGHT. I will simply say it is the duty of the Military Committee to consider the bill. It is certainly one of sufficient importance to engross their attention. I trust they will consider it, and report to the House for or against it, so that I can again bring it before the body. I hope the report will be favorable, for the subject deserves it. If the Committee reports in a reasonable time, I shall wait, otherwise I shall endeavor to get the bill before the House in some other way.

Mr. BARTOW. I will assure the gentleman there is no disposition on the part of the Committee on Military Affairs to stifle this bill—none in the world. I am perfectly willing to report it. It was the intention of the Committee to report it. But I do not think at present it required the immediate attention of the Committee. The military bills are all passed organizing the army, and this matter is left for further consideration. No doubt the Committee will give it the attention it merits; certainly they will report it back.

Mr. T. R. R. COBB, of Georgia, presented a memorial from certain clergymen in relation to chaplains for the Army; which was referred to the Committee on Military Affairs without being read.[22]

Mr. OCHILTREE, of Texas, presented the memorial of certain citizens [J. P. NASH, R. P. CRUMP, and others] of Texas,[23] praying the establishment of an armory in Marion county, in that State; which was referred to the Committee on Military Affairs without being read.

And then, on motion of Mr. RHETT, of South Carolina, the Congress proceeded to sit with closed doors.

Wednesday, May 1, 1861
(Charleston *Mercury*, May 4, 1861)

The Congress met at 12 o'clock m., and was called to order by the President, Hon. HOWELL COBB, of Georgia. After prayer by the Rev. Mr. DAVIS, the Journal of yesterday was read and approved.

The President then laid before the Convention the following communication, received by mail from the President of the Baptist State Convention of Georgia:

Athens, Geo., 29th April, 1861

SIR: I have the honor of transmitting to you the accompanying resolutions, *unanimously* passed on Saturday last by the Baptist Convention of the State of Georgia, with the request that you will present them to the Congress over which you preside.

That God will direct and bless the counsels of the Congress and the Confederate Government, is the prayer of the Baptist Conference of Georgia, and of none more sincerely than your obedient servant,

N. M. Crawford,[24]
Chairman of Committee

Howell Cobb,
President of Congress.

At the meeting of the Baptist Convention of the State of Georgia, the following preamble and resolutions were unanimously passed:

Whereas, the State of Georgia, in the legitimate exercise of her sovereignty, has withdrawn from the Confederacy known as the United States of America, and for the better maintenance of her rights, honor and independence, has united with other States in a new Confederacy, under the title of the Confederate States of America and whereas Abraham Lincoln, the President of the United States, is attempting by force of arms to subjugate these States in violation of the fundamental principles of American liberty: Therefore,

1. *Resolved*, By the members of the Baptist Convention of the State of Georgia, that we consider it to be at once a pleasure and a duty to avow that, both in feeling and in principle, we approve, endorse, and support the Government of the Confederate States of America.
2. *Resolved*, That while this Convention disclaims all authority, whether ecclesiastical or civil, yet as citizens we deem it but a duty to urge the union of all the people of the South in defense of the common cause; and to express the confident belief that, in whatever conflict the madness of Mr. Lincoln and his Government may force upon us, the

Baptists of Georgia will not be behind any class of our fellow-citizens in maintaining the independence of the South by any sacrifice of treasure or of blood.

3. *Resolved*, That we acknowledge, with devout thankfulness to Almighty God, the signal favor with which, up to this time, he has blessed our arms and our policy; and that the Baptist Church of this State be requested to observe the first and second days of June next as days of fasting and prayer that God will deliver us from all the power of our enemies, and restore peace to our country.
4. *Resolved*, That the Confederate Government be requested to invite the Churches of all denominations within the Confederacy, to unite in observing said days of fasting and prayer.
5. *Resolved*, That copies of these Resolutions be sent to President DAVIS, the Confederate Congress, and the Governor of Georgia.

Mr. WRIGHT, of Georgia. Mr. President: I move that the resolutions, together with the letter of the accomplished President of the Convention, be spread upon the journals of this Congress.

The question being taken, the motion was agreed to.

On motion of Mr. SHORTER, of Alabama, the following resolution was adopted:

Resolved, That one hundred copies of the Acts and Resolutions of the Congress, passed up to, and inclusive of, the 16th of March, and from which the injunction or secrecy has been removed, be printed for the use of the Congress during the present session.

Mr. KENNER, of Louisiana. Mr. President: I move to amend by including the Provisional and Permanent Constitutions.

Mr. SHORTER. I will accept the amendment.

The question was then taken, and the resolution, as modified, was agreed to.

On motion of Mr. CLAYTON, of Mississippi, the following resolution was adopted:

Resolved, That so much of the report of the Attorney-General as relates to the administration of justice be referred to the Judiciary Committee, and that so much as relates to the matter of printing be referred to the Committee on Printing.

Mr. OCHILTREE, of Texas, introduced a bill to be entitled "An Act to establish a port of entry at Sabine Pass, in the State of Texas, and to provide for the appointment of a Collector for the same;" which was referred to the Committee on Commerce.

Mr. HEMPHILL, of Texas. Mr. President: During the recess, I received the following communication from the President of the Convention of the people of Texas, enclosing resolutions, expressing the profound satisfaction of that body on receiving intelligence of the election of JEFFERSON DAVIS and ALEXANDER STEPHENS to the offices of President and Vice-President. I move that the resolutions be read and entered on the Journal of Congress:

City of Austin, Texas, Friday, March 16, 1861

Messrs. JOHN GREGG, WILLIAM E. OCHILTREE, T. N. WAUL, and W. S. OLDHAM, M.C. [member of Congress].

GENTLEMEN: By instruction of the people of Texas, I transmit to you the enclosed resolution, this day adopted in Convention.

To-day the additional returns of the votes upon the Ordinance of Secession were transmitted, with the following result, in round numbers: Total vote received 54,000; majority for secession, 31,500 votes.

Truly, your friend,

R. T. BROWNRIGG,[25]
Secretary of the Convention.

Resolved, That this Convention has heard with profound satisfaction of the election of JEFFERSON DAVIS, of Mississippi, and ALEXANDER H. STEPHENS, of Georgia, to the offices of President and Vice-President of the Provisional Government of the Confederate States of America, and that in their well known ability, experience and patriotism, the country possesses ample guarantees that the high and important functions confided to them will be so administered in these times of peril as will redound to the safety, security, and best interests of the people.

Resolved further, That a copy of the foregoing resolutions be communicated to our members of Congress at Montgomery.

Adapted in Convention, at the city of Austin, on the 15th day of March, 1861.

R. T. BROWNRIGG, Secretary of the Convention.

The question being taken on the motion of Mr. HEMPHILL, it was agreed to.

Mr. BARTOW, of Geo. Mr. President: I ask, leave to report the following resolution from the Committee on Military Affair:

Resolved, That the Committee on Military Affairs have permission to print such portion of the report of the Secretary of War, and as many copies thereof, as they may deem necessary.

The question being taken, the resolution was adopted.

And then, on motion of Mr. RHETT, of South Carolina, the Congress proceeded to sit with closed doors.

Thursday, May 2, 1861
(Charleston *Mercury*, May 7, 1861)

The Congress met at 12 o'clock, m., and was called to order by the President, Hon. HOWELL COBB, of Georgia. After prayer, the journal of yesterday was read and approved.

A NEW MEMBER

Mr. MORTON, of Florida, announced the arrival of his colleague, Mr. GEORGE T. WARD, elected to fill the vacancy caused by the resignation of Mr. ANDERSON. Mr. WARD was accordingly qualified, and took his seat as a member of Congress from the State of Florida.

Mr. MORTON then moved that the vacancies on the several standing committees created by Mr. ANDERSON's resignation be filled by the name of Mr. WARD.

THE PUBLIC DEFENCE

Mr. WRIGHT, of Georgia. Mr. President, I desire to introduce the following bill:

> *A Bill Further to Provide for the Public Defence.*
> *Whereas*, the Confederate States of America are menaced with war, and an invasion of their territory; and whereas, the public welfare and safety may require the reception of volunteer corps, companies, battalions and regiments, either mounted or on foot, into the service of said Confederate States, without formality and delay of a call upon the States.
>
> *Be it therefore enacted by the Confederate States in Congress assemble*, That the Secretary of War, by and with the advice and consent of the President, be authorized to receive into the service of such States such corps, companies, battalions or regiments, either mounted or on foot, as may be tendered, and the public welfare and safety may require, without the delay of a formal call upon the respective States.
>
> Sec. 2. *Be it further enacted*, That where troops as aforesaid may have been received, they may be attached to the regular army of volunteers, or be ordered upon such independent service as the President may deem proper for the public welfare.

Mr. President, I introduce that bill with some degree of reluctance, and I desire to put it upon its passage this morning, if it suits the temper of the House to do so. I introduce it with reluctance for two reasons. One is an apprehension that the object of the bill may be misunderstood. I have no purpose to interfere with the sovereignty of the States or with the rights of the respective representatives of the States, nor would I have it believed by any one that I did not entertain for the chief executive officers of the different States the highest respect, so far as I know them personally. For each one, individually and officially, I entertain the very highest respect. So far as I know them, their official conduct has been satisfactory to me, and, I believe, has been to the country. And the second consideration why I introduce the bill with some degree of reluctance, is the peculiar attitude I occupied with reference to the parties which divided the country heretofore. I do not desire to appear officious in the execution of the public business; and I have introduced the bill from a sense of duty, believing that the public necessity required the passage of such a law. The act authorizing the President to call out one hundred thousand volunteers used this language:

"The President be and he is hereby authorized to employ the militia, military and naval forces of the Confederate States of America, and to ask for and accept the services of any number of volunteers not exceeding one hundred thousand."

Upon conversation with the Secretary of War, I find he construes that act to mean that companies could only be received upon a formal call upon the Governors of the respective States, and he came to this conclusion upon consultation with the President; and although the Secretary in that conversation expressed a very great desire to receive the companies applying and required for the public service, he felt the hands of his Department tied by the language of the law—"ask for and accept"—that the volunteers must be formally asked for before they can be accepted by the Government of the Confederate States. Well, sir, the only question which arises is, whether the public necessity, or, in the language of the bill, "the public welfare and the public safety requires," that this discretion shall be vested in the President, or, if you please, in the Secretary of War, with the advice and consent of the President of the Confederate States. It seems to me that our public interests require it, and absolutely require it. The preamble of the bill states that we are menaced with war. My distinguished colleague said (perhaps in secret session) yesterday in his place upon this floor, that war existed, and that it was useless for gentlemen to talk about menaces of war or threats of war—that it existed in fact. Well, so it appears to me, sir, at all events. We are menaced with war. We are, beyond controversy, menaced with an invasion of our territory. From the President's Message, I learned that he sent sixteen thousand troops to Virginia. He has not given any information in that Message, nor is it perhaps proper that the President should do so, as to the number of troops which may be needed there: but, for whatever number may be needed, he is dependent upon the respective States, and can only receive them, under the construction which he puts upon this act, upon a formal call. Why, sir, the city of Richmond may be taken and demolished before we can bring our forces into the field. An expert enemy, like that with whom it seems we have to contend, directed with energy and dispatch, may immediately pour down, upon us such a force as to be perfectly irresistible by the forces we now have in the field. As the law now stands, the President has no legal authority to accept the services of a single volunteer company for the purpose of repelling that invasion until he can issue a formal call for them. Is this just to the "public service and the public safety," and more especially to the safety of those States which are in more imminent danger than we are? We, perhaps, at this distance from the scene of action, do not properly appreciate the troubles and anxieties under which our friends on the border labor. Besides, sir, I conceive that, it may be necessary upon various occasions that the President of the Confederate States should have organized companies for special independent service, such as will present itself after a few moment's reflection to the minds of every gentleman in this House. He may need scouting parties, parties for the purpose of reconnoitering the position and conduct of the enemy, and I think we may safely trust the head of our new Republic with this discretion. All the danger that is to be apprehended is the want of the exercise of a proper discretion by the Chief Magistrate of the Confederate States. Well, sir, I am no worshipper of man, and not in the habit of complimenting much those in power, but duty requires that I should "render unto Caesar those things which are Caesar's;" and in my place I can declare, with truth, so far as my observation has gone, that he has done all things well, and we need not fear to trust him with this power. I believe the public necessity requires such an act, and for that reason I have introduced it. I ask, therefore, the permission of the Congress now to put it upon its passage.

Mr. MORTON. Mr. President, I believe one single objection will prevent the immediate concerns of the bill, and I make it. I move that it be referred to the Committee on Military Affairs.

The question was taken, and the motion was agreed to.

ENDORSEMENT OF GEN. BEAUREGARD

On motion of Mr. BARTOW, the following resolutions were unanimously adopted:

A RESOLUTION OF THANKS TO BRIGADIER-GENERAL G. T. BEAUREGARD, AND THE ARMY UNDER HIS COMMAND, FOR THEIR CONDUCT IN THE AFFAIR AT FORT SUMTER

Be it unanimously resolved by the Congress of the Confederate States of America, That the thanks of the people of the Confederate States are due, and through this Congress are hereby tendered to Brig. Gen. G. T. BEAUREGARD, and his officers, and to the gallant troops of the State of South Carolina, for the skill, fortitude and courage, by which they reduced and caused the surrender of Fort Sumter, in the harbor of Charleston, on the 12th and 13th days of April, 1861; and the commendation of Congress is also hereby declared of the generosity manifested by their conduct towards a brave and conquered foe.

Be it resolved, That a copy of this resolution be communicated by the President to Gen. BEAUREGARD, and through him to the army now under his command.

Defence of Tampa Bay

Mr. Morton presented a memorial from certain citizens of Florida in relation to the defence of Tampa Bay; which was referred to the Committee on Military Affairs.

Chaplains for the Army

Mr. Bartow, of Georgia, from the Committee on Military Affairs, reported the following bill; which was read three times and passed:

A Bill to Provide for the Appointment of Chaplains in the Army

The Congress of the Confederate States of America do enact, that there shall be appointed by the President such number of chaplains, to serve with the Army of the Confederate States during the existing war, as he may deem expedient; and the President shall assign them to such regiments, brigades, or posts as he may deem necessary; and the appointments made aforesaid shall expire whenever the existing war shall terminate.

Sec. 2. The monthly pay of these chaplains shall be eighty-five dollars, and such pay shall be in full of all allowance whatever.

A New Rule

On motion of Mr. Shorter, of Alabama, the following amendment to the standing rules was adopted:

> *Resolved*, That all propositions affecting our foreign relations, or looking to the public defences, be submitted to the Congress while in secret session.

And then, on motion of Mr. Hill, of Georgia, the Congress proceeded to sit with closed doors.

Friday, May 3, 1861

(Montgomery *Weekly Advertiser*, May 8, 1861)

Congress met to-day at noon. Prayer was offered by the Rev. Mr. Pellicer, of the Catholic Church.

The journals of yesterday were read and approved.

Mr. Ochiltree, of Texas, presented a design for the seal of the Confederate States, sent to him Mr. A. B. Collins of Henderson, Texas.[26] The design embraces a portion of the seals of the several Confederate States, and grouped together, exhibits taste and artistic ability. The design was referred to the Committee on Flag and Seal.

Mr. SHORTER, of Alabama, from the Committee on Public Buildings, reported the following, which was unanimously adopted:

> *Resolved*, That the President of Congress communicate, in behalf of this body, to his Excellency Andrew B. Moore, Governor of Alabama, their thanks for the tender made by him of the Hall of the House of Representatives, for the use of Congress, and inform him that his courteous invitation to occupy the same is accepted by Congress.
>
> *Resolved*, That when Congress adjourns this day it adjourn to re-assemble in the Hall of the House of Representatives in the State Capital.

On motion of Mr. CHESNUT, of S. C., and made at the request of the Committee, the President was requested to add another member to the Committee on Territories. The motion was agreed to.

Mr. T. R. R. COBB, from the Committee on Public Printing, to whom was referred a resolution relative to the printing of extra copies of the acts and resolutions of the first session of Congress, reported in favor of printing one thousand extra copies of said acts and resolutions for general distribution.—The report was agreed to.

Mr. SHORTER, of Ala., reported as duly enrolled "An act to provide for the appointment of chaplains in the army," and "a resolution of thanks to BRIG. GENERAL G. T. BEAUREGARD and the army under his command for their conduct at Fort Sumter," which were then signed by the President.

On motion of Mr. HILL, of Ga., Congress went into secret session.

Saturday, May 4, 1861

(Montgomery *Weekly Advertiser*, May 8, 1861)

Congress met to-day at noon and was opened by prayer. The journals of yesterday were read and confirmed.

No business being offered, Congress went into secret session.

Monday, May 6, 1861

(Charleston *Mercury*, May 9, 1861; Montgomery *Daily Advertiser*, May 8, 1861)

Congress met to-day at noon. Prayer was offered by the Rev. BASIL MANLEY.

The journals of Saturday were read and confirmed.

The PRESIDENT asked leave to present the following communication:

> Near Pensacola, Fla. May 1861
>
> Hon. HOWELL COBB, President &c. Montgomery, Ala.
>
> SIR—On the 8th of April last, I addressed to you a communication formally resigning the seat in the body over which you preside, which I

had the honor of holding from the State of Florida. I have this day learned that up to a late date that communication had not been received. I desire, therefore, to repeat its tenor as indicated.

The new relations I have voluntarily assumed with another branch of the government render this course proper that a successor may supply my place in the Congress.[27]

With many of the liveliest and most pleasing recollections of my brief association with the memorable body over which you worthily preside, and with sentiments of the highest regard for you personally,

I am sir,
Very respectfully,
Your obedient servant,
J. Patton Anderson.

Mr. MORTON, of Florida, moved that the communication be spread upon the journals of Congress.

Mr. CURRY, of Alabama, presented two bills, one to fix the time for the election of representatives to Congress; and another to provide for the election of President and Vice-President under the Permanent Constitution, were referred to the Judiciary Committee.

Mr. PERKINS, of Louisiana, presented a resolution adopted at East Feliciana, Louisiana, on the 22d of April, by a large meeting of citizens. Mr. Perkins said that the question had been frequently asked what course would be pursued by those of our citizens who opposed the secession movement. The response of East Feliciana may be regarded as the voice of all that class. It is not a large parish, but small as it is, it has already placed at the disposal of the government 300 soldiers, and at the meeting referred to $12,000 was subscribed, and the lists were still open, and if fifty thousand dollars should be needed that sum will freely be subscribed. The resolution fully expressed the feeling of the citizens of East Feliciana, and he believed they are the sentiments of the people of Louisiana. He said he had no motion to make, but simply asked that the resolutions be read at the desk. It is as follows:

Resolved, by the planters of the Parish of East Feliciana, in general meeting assembled, That we hereby stand pledged to tender to the State of Louisiana and to the Government of the Confederate States should they be needed, the whole of the annual proceeds of our crops, deducting only what may be necessary for our current expenses, during, the continuance of the present hostilities.[28]

Mr. PRESIDENT. What motion does the gentleman have?

Mr. PERKINS. Mr. President, I make no motion. I simply desire the favor of having the resolution read at the desk.

Mr. MORTON, of Florida. I beg leave to present a memorial of the Pensacola and Georgia Railroad Company, and I ask that the memorial, together with the accompanying papers, be referred to the Committee on Finance. The memorial is not to remit the duties but to obtain credit for the railroad iron now in bond in the Custom House.[29]

The question being taken, the motion was agreed to, and the memorial was accordingly referred without being read.

Congress then went into secret session.

Tuesday, May 7, 1861

(Charleston *Mercury*, May 10, 1861)

The Congress met at 12 o'clock, m., and was called to order by the President, Hon. HOWELL COBB, of Georgia. After prayer by the Rev. Mr. COBBS, the Journal of yesterday was read and approved.

THE VIRGINIA COMMISSIONERS

Mr. BROOKE, of Miss. Mr. President, before proceeding to call the States, I wish to present to the House the Ordinance of the State of Virginia, adopting and ratifying the Provisional Constitution of the Confederate States of America, and also a resolution of the Convention of Virginia, appointing the following delegates to represent the State of Virginia in this body: Messrs. HUNTER, REEVES, BROCKENBROUGH, STAPLE, and CAMERON. Two of these gentlemen are now present, Messrs. BROCKENBROUGH and STAPLES, and I move they be invited to take their seats upon this floor, and take the oath to support the Constitution.

Mr. RHETT, of S.C. Mr. President, I move that the Congress go into secret session, and that the gentleman from Virginia be requested to attend that session with us.

The motion was agreed to, and accordingly Congress proceeded to sit with closed doors.

Wednesday, May 8, 1861

(Charleston *Mercury*, May 11, 1861)

The Congress met at 12 o'clock, m., and was called to order by the President, Hon. HOWELL COBB, of Georgia. After prayer by the Rev. Mr. HEARD, the Journal of yesterday was read and approved.

SECESSION OF ARKANSAS

The PRESIDENT. The Chair will ask leave to have read to the Congress a telegraphic dispatch from the Commission of Georgia to Arkansas, though the information doubtless is known to all the members.

The dispatch was accordingly read as follows:

Little Rock, May 6, 1861

Hon. H. Cobb: Through you I with pleasure announce that Arkansas this day passed an unconditional Ordinance of Secession, by a unanimous vote.

D. P. Hill[30]
Commissioner of Georgia

Chaplains for the Navy

On motion of Mr. Morton, of Florida, the following resolution was adopted:

> *Resolved*, That the Committee on Naval Affairs be instructed to inquire into the propriety of appointing Chaplains in the Navy of the Confederate States.

Payment of Disbursing Officers

Mr. Ochiltree, of Texas, on leave, introduced a bill, to be entitled, "An Act to provide for the compensation of the disbursing officers of the several Executive Departments," which was read twice, and referred to the Committee on Finance.

A New Committee

Mr. Conrad, of Louisiana. Mr. President: I have received from one of my constituents a claim for some money, which should be referred to some committee. I believe, sir, there is no Committee on Claims.

The President. No, sir.

Mr. Conrad. I do not know, sir, that there is a committee to which it can properly be referred; and I suggest, therefore, the propriety of having a Committee on Claims raised. I make that motion. I understand there are other gentlemen who have claims to present, and I desire there shall be a committee to which they can be referred.

The question was taken, and the motion agreed to. So the President is authorized to appoint a Committee on Claims, to consist of six members.

And then the Congress went into secret session.

Thursday, May 9, 1861

(Montgomery *Weekly Advertiser*, May 15, 1861)

Congress met to-day at noon. After prayer the journals of the preceding day were read and approved.

Mr. Wright, of Georgia, said he had received a communication in relation to the public defense from Mr. Pleasant Stovall,[31] a gentleman who resides in Georgia, and sustains a high social position. He asked to have the communication referred to the military committee, which was accordingly done.

No other public business being presented, Congress went into secret session.

Friday, May 10, 1861

(Charleston *Mercury*, May 13, 1861)

The Congress met at 12 o'clock m., and was called to order by the President, Hon. HOWELL COBB, of Georgia, when the Journal of yesterday was read and approved.

AMENDMENTS TO THE CONSTITUTION

Mr. MORTON, of Florida. Mr. President, the Florida delegation have had several acts of the Florida Convention forwarded to them, amongst others an act ratifying the Permanent Constitution; but I am advised by the Chair that no other acts of ratification have been presented. Therefore, the delegation will take the responsibility of withholding it for the present. But the following resolution I beg leave to present, and after being read, I move that it be ordered to be spread on the Journal.

> *Resolved*, That while the people of Florida heartily approve in the main of the Constitution of the Confederate States of America, and have given evidence of that approbation by the unanimous vote of this Convention on its ratification, yet there are certain parts thereof, which, in the opinion of this Convention, should, at an early day, be amended. With the view, therefore, of giving a proper expression of the sentiments of the people of this State, it is hereby suggested that the said Constitution would be greatly improved by the following amendments, to wit:
>
> That the third clause of the second section of the first article should be altered by striking out after the word "determined," in the fourth line, to the word "slaves," inclusive, and inserting the words "by the whole number of inhabitants within the State."
>
> That the first clause of the third section of article four should be amended by inserting the word "States" in the third, and the words "and no State shall be admitted into this Confederacy unless the institution of slavery shall be distinctively and clearly recognized in its constitution, and in actual operation under its laws," and by striking out the word " but" next following in the same line.
>
> That the seventh clause of the eighth section of the first article should be amended by striking out the remainder of the clause after the word "rights," in the first line.
>
> Done in open Convention at the Capitol, in the city of Tallahassee, Saturday, the 27th day of April, A. D., 1861.
>
> J. C. McGehee, Pres't of the Convention.[32]
>
> [Attest:] Wm. H. Harris, Secretary.

The question was then taken, and the motion of Mr. MORTON was agreed to.

PRESENTATION OF A CLAIM

Mr. CONRAD, of Louisiana, on leave, presented the claim of J. H. GURLEY;[33] which was referred to the Committee on Claims.

Provision for the Indians

On motion of Mr. OCHILTREE, of Texas, the following resolution was adopted:

> *Resolved by the Congress of the Confederate States of America,* That the Committee on Indian Affairs be instructed to inquire into and report upon the propriety of this Government taking cognizance of, and making provision for, the Indians located upon the reserves situated in the State of Texas, which were under the control of the late United States, and that they report upon the same at the earliest date, by bill or otherwise.

CARE OF THE PUBLIC BUILDINGS

Mr. SHORTER, of Alabama, from the Committee on Public Buildings, reported the following resolution; which was adopted:

> *Resolved,* That the Secretary of the Treasury be authorized and directed to employ sufficient night watch to guard the Executive building; also that he be directed to report estimates of appropriation which may be found needful to defray the expenses of the same; and also to pay for the gas light in the Executive Building.

ADDITIONS TO THE COMMITTEES

On motion of Mr. BARNWELL, of South Carolina, the President was authorized to add another member to the Committee on Finance.

On motion of Mr. STEPHENS, of Georgia, the President was authorized to add another member each to the Committee on the Judiciary and the Committee on Military Affairs.

PATENTS AND THE PATENT OFFICE

Mr. BROOKE, of Mississippi, from the Committee on Patents, reported a Bill to be entitled "An Act to establish a Patent Office, and to provide for the granting and issuance of patents for new and useful discoveries, inventions, improvements and designs" which was read twice by its title and ordered to be placed on the public calendar.

And then the Congress proceeded to sit with closed doors.

Saturday, May 11, 1861
(Charleston *Mercury*, May 14, 1861; Montgomery *Weekly Advertiser*, May 15, 1861)

The Congress met at 12 o'clock, m., and was called to order by the President Hon. HOWELL COBB, of Ga.

After Prayer by the Rev. Mr. MONTGOMERY,[34] the Journal of yesterday was read and approved.

NEW COMMITTEE MEMBERS

From the Journal it appears that Mr. HUNTER, of Va., has been added to the Committee on Finance; Mr. BROCKENBROUGH, of Va., to the Committee on the Judiciary, and Mr. STAPLES, of Va., to the Committee on Military Affairs.

CLAIMS AGAINST THE CONFEDERATE STATES

Claims against the Government were severally presented by Messrs. MCRAE and SHORTER, of Ala. [on the behalf of Cade M. Godbold, former United States marshal for the southern district of Alabama, for being a census taker in 1860], and CONRAD, of Louisiana, [on behalf of Nathan Stephens] and referred to the Committee on Claims and Finance.[35] [see document XX]

ADMIRALTY COURT FOR TEXAS

Mr. GREGG, of Texas. Mr. President, I hold in my hand a copy of a joint resolution passed by the Legislature of the State of Texas, which I ask to have read and referred to the Committee on the Judiciary.

The joint resolution was accordingly read as follows, and referred to the Committee on the Judiciary:

A JOINT RESOLUTION IN RELATION TO THE ESTABLISHMENT OF AN ADMIRALTY COURT FOR THE STATE OF TEXAS, AT GALVESTON, AND SUCH OTHER PLACES ON THE COAST AS COMMERCE REQUIRES

SECTION 1. *Be it Resolved by the Legislature of the Stale of Texas,* That the Government of the Confederate States of America, be, and is hereby, respectfully requested to establish an Admiralty Court for the State of Texas, at the city of Galveston, and such other places on the coast, in this State, as commerce requires.

SEC. 2. The delegates of the State of Texas, in the Congress of the Confederate States, are here by requested to use all proper efforts to accomplish the measures meditated in the foregoing resolution, and that the Governor cause a duly certified copy of these resolutions to be transmitted to those delegates; and this joint resolution shall be in force from its passage.

Approved, February 6, 1861.

The President, after the call on the committees for report, without response, stated that the only business on the public calendar was the bill to establish a patent office. As the bill had not been printed, and no other business offering, Congress went into secret session.

Monday, May 13, 1861

(Montgomery *Weekly Advertiser*, May 15, 1861)

Congress met to-day at noon, and after prayer by the Rev. Mr. HILL, the journals were read and approved.

Mr. RHETT, of South Carolina, moved that an additional member be added to the Committee on Foreign Affairs, which was agreed to.

Mr. HALE, of Alabama, moved that the President appoint a member to fill the vacancy caused by the resignation of Mr. CLAYTON on the Committee on the Judiciary.

Congress then went into secret session.

Tuesday, May 14, 1861

(Charleston *Mercury*, May 16, 1861)

The Congress met at 11 o'clock, m. and was called to order by the President, Hon. HOWELL COBB, of Georgia. After prayer, the journal of yesterday was read and approved.

Mr. THOMAS R. R. COBB offered the following:

A RESOLUTION IN REFERENCE TO A DAY OF FASTING AND PRAYER

The dependence of nations, as of individuals, upon an overruling Providence, at all times, we fully recognize. But when perils surround, and national existence is threatened, it particularly becomes a people to manifest their submission to the will and guidance of the omnipotent Ruler of the Universe. If the cause be righteous, and the quarrel just, we may confidently rely on Him who reigneth alike over the armies of Earth and the hosts of Heaven. At the same time we recognize our duty to appeal humbly to Him who hath said "I will be inquired of, of my people." To the end, therefore, that the whole people of these Confederate State may, in unison, and with one accord, approach the Throne of the Most High, to invoke his blessing upon us in our defensive struggle for the right of self-government, and the enjoyment of the liberty He vouchsafed to our fathers, and to protect us from those who threaten our home with fire and sword—our domestic circles with ruthless lust—our father's graves with invader's feet, and our altars with infidel desecration:

Resolved, by the Congress of the Confederate States, That the President be requested to issue his Proclamation appointing a day of

> Fasting and Prayer, in the observance of which all shall be invited to join who recognize our dependence upon God, and the happiness and security of that People whose God is the Lord.

The preamble and resolution were unanimously adopted.

Mr. OLDHAM, of Texas, offered the following which was adopted:

> *Resolved*, That the Committee on Commercial Affairs be directed to inquire into the expediency of making the city of Houston, in the State of Texas, a port of entry and delivery, and that they report by bill or otherwise.

Mr. CLINGMAN, the Commissioner from the State of North Carolina, presented the following preamble and resolutions, and stated that the Government of the United States had declared war against his State. North Carolina has proclaimed that she is an independent Commonwealth, and has determined to co-operate with the Confederate States. He desired the preamble and resolution read and entered on the journals.

> RESOLUTIONS AUTHORIZING THE GOVERNOR TO USE ALL THE POWERS OF THE STATE, CIVIL AND MILITARY, CONSISTENT WITH THE CONSTITUTION, TO PROTECT THE PERSONS AND PROPERTY OF OUR CITIZENS, AND TO MAINTAIN AND DEFEND THE HONOR OF NORTH CAROLINA
>
> *Whereas* the Constitution of the United States has been entirely subverted, and its Government has been converted into a military despotism by the usurpations of the Administration of ABRAHAM LINCOLN; and, whereas, the said ABRAHAM LINCOLN has promulgated a proclamation declaring the ports of North Carolina in a state of blockade, and directing our ships engaged in lawful commerce to be seized; and, whereas such measures are, by the laws of civilized nations, only to be resorted to against a foreign State, and one against which war has been declared; and, whereas North Carolina has no alternative, consistent with her safety and honor, but to accept the position thus assigned to her as that of an independent and foreign State: Therefore, be it
>
> *Resolved*, That the Governor is hereby authorized to use all the powers of the State, civil and military, consistent with the Constitution, to protect the persons and property of our citizens, and to maintain and defend the honor of North Carolina.
>
> A true copy from the minutes of the house of commons of North Carolina.
>
> Edward Cantwell, C.H.C.

The preamble and resolution were ordered to be entered upon the journals of Congress.

The PRESIDENT. The only business on the public calendar is the bill to organize a Patent office, but as the Chairman is absent, Congress will now go into secret session.

Wednesday, May 15, 1861

(Charleston *Mercury*, May 18, 1861; Montgomery *Weekly Advertiser*, May 22, 1861)

The Congress met at 11 o'clock, a.m. and was called to order by the President, Hon. HOWELL COBB, of Georgia. After prayer by the Rev. Mr. SIMMONS,[36] the journal of yesterday was read and approved.

COURT FOR VIRGINIA

On motion of Mr. SMITH, of Alabama, the following resolution was adopted:

> *Resolved,* That the Committee on the Judiciary be instructed to report a bill establishing and organizing a Court of the Confederate States for the State of Virginia.

INDIAN TRIBES

Mr. KEITT, of S.C., from the Committee on Indian Affairs, reported a bill to be entitled "An Act for the protection of certain Indian tribes." The Clerk commenced reading the bill, and it appeared that the provisions of it extended protection over the Indian Territory South of Kansas.

On motion of Mr. KEITT, the further reading was suspended, and on his motion Congress went into secret session.

Thursday, May 16, 1861

(Charleston *Mercury*, May 20, 1861)

The Congress met at 11 o'clock, a.m., and was called to order by the President, Hon. HOWELL COBB, of Georgia. After prayer by the Rev. Mr. PETRIE, the Journal of yesterday was read and approved.

MESSAGE FROM THE PRESIDENT

The President laid before Congress the following Message from the President of the Confederate States, received at the hands of Mr. JOSSELYN, the Private Secretary, which, together with the accompanying documents, was referred to the Committee on Military Affairs.

Executive Department, May 16, 1861

Hon. Howell Cobb, President of the Congress:

SIR: I herewith transmit to Congress additional estimates of the Secretary of War.[37]

[signed] Jefferson Davis

THE PATENT OFFICE AND PATENTS

The Congress then proceeded to the consideration of the Bill to be entitled "An Act to establish a Patent Office, and to provide for the granting and issuance of patents for new and useful discoveries, inventions, improvements and designs"—the question being on its engrossment. The bill was accordingly read by sections, for amendment.

[Editorial note: The reading of sections one through twenty-nine of the patent legislation, printed in full by the Charleston *Mercury*, is omitted here. Researchers should be aware of slight differences in verbiage between the draft version reported by the *Mercury* and the final version reported in the *Statutes at Large*.[38]]

Mr. SMITH, of Ala. Mr. President, I move that the thirtieth section of the Bill be stricken out, simply because we want the money for gunpowder and ball, and because, if it is expended in the collection of agricultural statistics, and other agricultural purposes, it will lead to the old seed arrangement of the old government, which, I think, was a nuisance. The following is the section referred to:

> SEC. 30. *And be it further enacted*, That a sum of money, not exceeding one thousand dollars, be, and the same is hereby, appropriated, out of the Patent Fund, to be expended by the Commissioner of Patents, in the collection of agricultural statistics, and for other agricultural purposes for which the said Commission shall account in the next annual report.

Mr. WITHERS, of South Carolina. I second the motion. It is very true that this appropriation is made for a specific purpose; but I think if my friend from Mississippi [Mr. BROOKE], who reported this bill, will consider the subject, he will perceive that when this information is collected and reported to Congress, a very large drain will be made upon the funds of the Government to print it. I think I am not mistaken in saying that the printing of this matter is paid for out of the funds of the Treasury of the United States, and if I am not mistaken the Treasury has been bled most freely and copiously for the circulation of books of this description, which are read by no man. I have had occasion to look into this, and even the pictures of race horses and various animals from regions beyond civilization, are very poor production. And the letters collected from person[s] in Iowa and Indiana as to the number of bushels of wheat and the quality of corn produced, are very unreliable, and will not apply to any other place. I think the experience of members of this body will demonstrate the truth of this. In conclusion, Mr. WITHERS said he had planted the seed sent him from the United States Agricultural Bureau, but all that came up was some turnip seed, which was of no account. If any gentleman had in his own experience derived benefit from these seed and would so state to the body, he would be inclined to withdraw his objection.

Mr. REAGAN, of Texas, said the Agricultural Bureau was a most unmitigated humbug. Not only was it throwing money away, but it led to appointing of a Bureau to come into competition with seed stores of the country. Besides the franking privilege was abolished, and there would be no facilities for the distribution of these seed. Sometimes rare seed and rare cuttings were brought from abroad; but in the main their introduction never compensated for their expense.

He hoped the section would be stricken out.

Mr. BROOKE. I have not said a word about seed. This clause simply makes a small appropriation, not out of the Treasury, but out of the Patent Office fund, for the purpose of collecting the statistics and information that will be valuable to the people. I do not propose to publish it. A thousand dollars would not answer for that purpose if I did. It is simply to have this information in the Patent Office, where persons desirous of obtaining it may go for that purpose.

Mr. HEMPHILL, of Texas. I agree with the remarks of the gentleman from Mississippi. These Patent Office Reports have been very valuable and acceptable to the people of the country. I have distributed a great many; and have received many letters of thanks for the book. I have received more thanks for that book than any other I have sent to my constituents. I know very little about agriculture myself, but I never sent one of these books that was not acceptable to the person to whom it was sent. We all know that one single seed will change the whole face of agriculture.

Mr. WITHERS said the *Sorghum Sucre* had been tried in South Carolina under the most favorable circumstance. It was tried by Senator HAMMOND; but so far as that was concerned, it had done no good—none at all.[39] But he objected to the proposition. According to the theory of the Constitution, the Government did not design to become the patron of any class in it. Of all classes in a republican county, his understanding had been that the tillers of the earth stand most erect and most independent of the Government. His understanding was that those who were the foundation of all society, those upon whom rest the prosperity of the Government and the prosperity of society, in all its developments—the tillers of the earth—have elevated themselves by their own hands to a condition in which they need none of your assistance. All they ask of the Government is, to protect them in their rights, and leave them to manage their own affairs in their own way. The moment the Government protected one class, how could they keep out the contrivers of patents and the manufacturing interests.

The question was then taken, and the motion of Mr. SMITH was agreed to. So the thirtieth section was stricken out.

SEC. 31. *And be it further enacted*, That the provisions of the 15th section of this act shall extend to all cases where patents are refused for any reason

> whatever, either by the Commissioner of Patents or by the Attorney-General, upon appeals from the decision of said Commissioner, as well as where the same shall have been refused on account of, or by reason of, interference with a previously existing patent; and to all cases where there is no opposing party a copy of the bill shall be served upon the Commissioner of Patents, when the whole of the expenses of the proceeding shall be paid by the applicant, whether the final decision shall be in his favor or otherwise.
>
> SEC. 32. *And be it further enacted*, That the Treasurer of the Confederate States be, and he hereby is authorized to pay back, out of the Patent Fund, any sum or sums of money to any person who shall have paid the same into the Treasury, or to any receiver or depositary to the credit of the Treasurer, as for fees accruing at the Patent Office through mistake, and which are not provided to be paid by existing laws, certificate thereof being made to the said Treasurer by the Commissioner of Patents.

Mr. OCHILTREE, of Texas. Mr. President, I desire to offer the following additional section to come in at this point. Before the amendment is read, I will simply say that I have frequently known persons who have made valuable inventions unable themselves to pay the fees accruing to the Patent Office, and therefore compelled to divide their patents with some speculator or sharper. It is to provide for that class of inventors that I propose the following section:

> *And be it further enacted*, That in every instance where an applicant for a patent, under the provisions of this act, shall make oath that, by reason of poverty, he is unable to pay the fees required, then he shall be entitled to all the benefits of this act as if he had paid the same.
>
> Mr. BROOKE of Mississippi. I hope the amendment will not be adopted. The question was then taken, and the section was rejected.
>
> SEC. 33. *And be it further enacted*, That the oath required for applicants for patents may be taken when the applicant is not, for the time being, residing in the Confederate States, before any minister plenipotentiary, charge d'affaires, consul or commercial agent holding commission under the Government of the Confederate States, or before any notary public of the foreign country in which such applicant may be.

On motion of Mr. T. R. R. COBB, of Georgia, the following proviso was adopted:

> *Provided*, Such foreign States shall have recognized the independence of the Confederate States, and shall be at the time in amity with them.

[Editorial note: The reading of sections thirty-four through fifty of the patent legislation, printed in full by the Charleston *Mercury*, is omitted here. Researchers should be aware of slight differences in verbiage between the draft version reported by the *Mercury* and the final version reported in the *Statutes at Large*.[40]]

> SEC. 51. *And be it further enacted*, That all patents heretofore granted and issued by the United States to any person or persons now a citizen or citizens of either of the States of this Confederacy, or the States of Tennessee, Arkansas, or North Carolina, or now held by assignment by any such citizens or citizens, shall continue in force for the term for which they were issued yet unexpired, and if assigned in part only to any citizen of this Confederacy, or the States aforesaid, shall continue in force for such part.

Mr. SMITH, of Alabama. Mr. President. I move to strike the following clause from the fifty-first section:

> [And all patents granted by the said United States prior to the 20th day of December, 1860, to any person or persons other than a citizen or citizens of this Confederacy, and not now owned by any such citizen, in whole or in part, shall be in force for their unexpired term from the time when the government, or governments, to which such person or persons may owe allegiance, shall be at peace with and recognize the independence and sovereignty of this Confederacy.]

Mr. BARRY, of Mississippi. Mr. President, I want a distinct declaration by this Congress that no patent of the United States will be recognized. I believe it is right in principle, and I hope this Congress will carry out the doctrine. We are a new Government, and we get nothing in return. I desire a distinct declaration that the patents granted by the old Union shall be of no force or effect in the Confederate States.

Mr. STEPHENS, of Georgia. Mr. President, I prefer the original motion of the gentleman from Alabama.

Mr. BARRY. My motion is to strike out the following words: "In force for their unexpired term from the time when the Government or Governments to which such person or persons may owe allegiance, shall be at peace with and recognize the independence and sovereignty of this Confederacy," and insert the following words: "Shall be of no force and effect in these Confederate State."

Mr. WITHERS. I am very decidedly in favor of the amendment of the gentleman from Mississippi. Why, sir, while these people are now in arms against us—when they are in arms to put to death the citizens of these States and overturn their rights, will you pass a law and refuse to leave it to a treaty as to what shall be done with these people? I submit to the Chairman of the Committee, and to this Congress, that the better plan is to leave this subject to a treaty. I trust, then, that the motion of the gentleman from Mississippi will be adopted.

Mr. TOOMBS (interrupting). Mr. President, I move that the Congress go into secret session.

The motion was agreed to; and accordingly, the Congress proceeded to sit with closed doors.

The following are the sections of the bill not considered:

> *Provided*, That patents provided for in this section shall be recorded in the Patent Office of the Confederate States, and there also shall be deposited in said office such models and descriptive drawings as may be necessary to identify and explain the subject matter of said patents and all person claiming the benefit of this section shall pay to the Commissioner of Patents the sum of twenty dollars, for the use of the Patent Fund; unless such patents are so filed for record, with such drawings or models as aforesaid, within nine months from the date of publication of this act, they shall be considered as abandoned and shall be null and void. And it shall be the duty of the Commissioner to endorse on each patent so filed for record, the date of such filing, and also a certificate under the seal of this office that said patent has been recorded, which certificate shall be evidence of the fact in any court of justice, whether of the State or of the Confederacy, and of the rights of the owner thereof to use said patent; and such patents shall, after they are recorded, be returned to the owner thereof.
>
> SEC. 52. *And be it further enacted*, That if any citizens of this Confederacy should, at the close of the war now existing between this Confederacy and the United States of America, be in the use or exercise of any patent rights, belonging in whole or in part to an alien enemy or enemies, or engaged in the manufacture of any article or fabric by machinery or composition, covered and protected by any such rights, such citizens or citizens shall have the right to continue such use and manufacture, notwithstanding such patent may be recorded as hereinbefore provided for: *Provided*, That the citizens of the slaveholding States of the United States shall not be considered as alien enemies, within the meaning of this act, so long as their respective States shall refuse to assist the said United States in its war against this Confederacy, with troops, provisions, or munitions of war; and any citizen of any such slaveholding States desiring to avail himself of the privileges of this act during said war, shall, with his application, file an affidavit or statement in writing, under oath, admitting the

independence of this Confederacy, and disclaiming all sympathy with the said United States in their war aforesaid.

Friday, May 17, 1861
(Charleston *Mercury*, May 21, 1861; Montgomery *Weekly Advertiser*, May 22, 1861)

Congress met at 11 o'clock a.m., and was called to order by the President, Hon. HOWELL COBB. After prayer, the Journal of yesterday was read and approved.

TEXAS AND NEW ORLEANS RAILROAD

Mr. OCHILTREE of Texas, presented a memorial from the Texas and New Orleans Railroad Company. He said he did not desire the memorial read but simply have it referred to the military committee. It was unanimously adopted.

RAILROAD IRON

Mr. CONRAD, of Louisiana, presented a memorial on behalf of certain railroad companies in New Orleans, together with a bill to be entitled, "An Act to exempt from duty certain cars purchased by the New Orleans and Carrolton Rail Road Company, and the New Orleans City Railroad Company;" which were severally referred to the Committee on Finance. [document XVIII]

BAPTIST CONVENTION OF GEORGIA

The PRESIDENT laid before the body the report of the Baptist Convention of Georgia in relation to the state of the country; and it was ordered to be spread upon the Journal. This Convention held its session at Savannah, and its report has already appeared in the newspapers.

Mr. T. R. R. COBB, of Georgia, moved that the report and proceedings be entered on the journals, without being read. [document XIX]

Mr. CONRAD, of La., presented a claim for services rendered to the Government.[41] It was referred to the Committee on Claims.

THE PATENT OFFICE

The Congress then resumed the consideration of the bill to be entitled "An Act to Establish a Patent Office, and to Provide for the Granting and Issuance of Patents for New and useful Discoveries, Inventions, Improvements and Designs," the question being on the amendment of Mr. BARRY, of Mississippi, to the fifty-first section, as will be seen by reference to the report in *The Mercury* of yesterday; and then the motion of Mr. SMITH, of Alabama, to strike out the entire clause in reference to patents granted by the United States.

Mr. BROOKE, of Mississippi. Mr. President, I think I have the right, having reported the bill, to accept the amendment of the gentleman from Alabama [Mr. SMITH] offered yesterday.

The PRESIDENT. The gentleman from Mississippi cannot accept the amendment. The bill is in the possession of the House.

Mr. BROOKE. Then I will state, sir, that I am perfectly willing that that amendment should be adopted.

The amendment referred to was then reported—to strike out the following:

> And all patents granted by the said United States, prior to the 20th day of December, 1861, to any person or persons other than a citizens or citizens of this Confederacy, and not now owned by any such citizen, in whole or in part, shall be in force for their unexpired term from the time when the Government or Governments to which such person or persons may owe allegiance, shall be at peace with, and recognize the independence and sovereignty of this Confederacy.

The amendment of Mr. BARRY, of Miss., was then reported—to strike out the following words:

> In force for their unexpired term from the time when the government or governments to which such person or persons may owe allegiance, shall be at peace with, and recognize the independence and sovereignty of this Confederacy.

And insert—

> Be of no force or effect within these Confederate States.

The question was then taken on the amendment of Mr. BARRY, and it was rejected.

The question recurring on the amendment of Mr. SMITH, it was taken, and decided in the affirmative. So this clause of the bill was stricken out.

Mr. WITHERS, of South Carolina, moved to amend the fifty-first section by adding the following proviso after the word "part" in the sixth line:

> *Provided*, That such assignment has been made prior to the 4th day of February 1861.

The question was taken, and the Amendment adopted, so that the portion of the Bill reads as follows:

> *And be it further enacted*, That all patents heretofore granted and issued by the United States to any person or persons now a citizen or citizens of either of the States of this Confederacy, or of the States of Tennessee, Arkansas or North Carolina, or now held by assignment by any such citizen

of citizens, shall continue in force for the term for which they were issued yet unexpired; and if assigned in part only to any citizen of this Confederacy, or the States aforesaid shall continue in force for such part; *Provided*, That such assignment has been made prior to the 4th day of February 1861.

On motion of Mr. BROOKE, the following additional proviso was added to this part of the bill:

Provided, That nothing contained in this act and bill be considered to recognize any removal of a patent by the United States heretofore made.

On motion of Mr. BROOKE, the last section of the bill, the fifty-second, was stricken out. It reads as follows:

And be it further enacted, That if any citizens of this Confederacy should, at the close of the war now existing between this Confederacy and the United States of America, be in the use or exercise of any patent rights, belonging in whole or in part to an alien enemy or enemies, or engaged in the manufacture of any article or fabric by machinery or composition, covered and protected by any such rights, such citizens or citizens shall have the right to continue such use and manufacture, notwithstanding such patent may be recorded as hereinbefore provided for: *Provided*, That the citizens of the slaveholding States of the United States shall not be considered as alien enemies, within the meaning of this act, so long as their respective States shall refuse to assist the said United States in its war against this Confederacy, with troops, provisions, or munitions of war; and any citizen of any such slaveholding States desiring to avail himself of the privileges of this act during said war, shall, with his application, file an affidavit or statement in writing, under oath, admitting the independence of this Confederacy, and disclaiming all sympathy with the said United States in their war aforesaid.

Mr. BROOKE. Mr. President: I wish the body to reconsider section thirty-eight, fixing the salaries of the officers of the Patent office. I move to amend by making the salaries of the examiners $2000 instead of $1800. I am satisfied that we can obtain competent examiners for that sum. I wanted to reduce the pay to some extent, but I learned this morning that the salaries at Washington were $2500. I hope the motion will be agreed to. We may require two examiners; possibly not more than one.

The question was taken and the motion was agreed to, and then the motion to increase the pay of the examiners of patents was agreed to.

Mr. HEMPHILL, of Texas. Mr. President: I move to reconsider the vote yesterday, upon an amendment I proposed, to strike out all that portion of the 13th section which gives the judges of the courts the power to increase the damage which may be given in a case, to three times the amount of the verdict. It seems to me that that is in direct contravention of the Constitution of the Confederate States. In the case of Texas, the jury tries all cases, whether in equity or law. This is not the case in some other States.

Mr. BROOKE said the power to increase the damages returned had always been vested in the courts, and this provision has been in force in the United States ever since the Patent Office had been organized. This was the first time any constitutional objection had ever been made to it. It had always operated well for the advancement of justice, and I have not seen a single objection rising out of it. I hope, therefore, the objection of the gentleman from Texas will not prevail. The clause is intended as a protection to the inventor, and to raise a barrier between him and the influence of popular prejudice.

Mr. SPARROW, of Louisiana, said this clause would be expressly violated in Louisiana, where the whole judgment of the Court must conform itself to the verdict of the Jury.

Mr. GREGG, of Texas, said it seemed to him that the clause was absurd in more than one point of view. Juries were more competent than the judges of the courts.

Mr. HARRIS, of Mississippi, sustained the bill. There was no constitutional objection to the clause. A patent was a monopoly, and monopolies were always odious, and because of this peculiar right the law had wisely and properly given this distinction to the judges. He thought the provision wise, wholesome, and just.

The question was then taken, and the motion to reconsider prevailed.

The question recurred on the amendment—

Mr. HILL, of Georgia, said he trusted it would not be adopted. It had always been a portion of the patent laws. No man could point to an instance where it had worked bad, and it never before had been complained of. It could not be in contravention of any law of Louisiana either, because that State had no law regulating the subject of patents. The law of patents in this country belonged to the United States, and now, of course, to the Confederate States. The law of Louisiana to which the gentleman referred, had nothing to do with it.

Mr. SPARROW. I will ask the gentleman if he does not know that the Judiciary Bill adopted by us requires that the action of the Confederate Courts should conform to the practice of the State Courts. Now, the practice of the State Courts of Louisiana is that the judgment of the Court must conform to the verdict of the jury.

Mr. HILL. That does not alter the case for the rule to which the gentleman refers; it exists only where there is no rule of the Confederate States in contravention of it. The law of Louisiana can have nothing to do with the question of patents. That belongs to the Confederate Courts and the Confederate Government.

The debate was further continued by Messrs. SMITH, of Alabama, and CAMPBELL, of Mississippi, when the question was taken and the motion to strike out prevailed.

The following are the words stricken out:

> It shall be in the power of the Court to render judgment for any sum above the amount found by such verdict as the actual damages sustained by the plaintiff, not exceeding three times the amount thereof.

On motion of Mr. BROOKE, the following additional section was adopted:

> *And be it further enacted*, That this Act shall take effect, and be in force, from and after its passage.

On motion of Mr. T. R. R. COBB, of Georgia, the 28th section was stricken out, and the following inserted:

> All applications by aliens to obtain patents for inventions by patentees from foreign countries, shall be made within six months of their taking out a patent in their own country; nor shall letters patent be granted to any alien whose government is at war with the Confederate States.

On motion of Mr. HEMPHILL, of Texas, an additional section was adopted, providing for the patenting of inventions by slaves.[42]

The bill was then ordered to be engross, and being engrossed, it was read the third time, and passed.[43]

And then, on motion of Mr. KEITT, of South Carolina, the Congress proceeded to sit with closed doors.

Saturday, May 18, 1861

(Charleston *Mercury*, May 21, 1861)

The Congress met at 11 o'clock, a.m., and was called to order by the President, Hon. HOWELL COBB, of Georgia. After prayer, the Journal of yesterday was read and adopted.

ADMISSION OF ARKANSAS

Mr. STEPHENS, of Georgia. Mr. President: I beg leave to offer the following bill:

> A BILL TO BE ENTITLED "AN ACT TO ADMIT THE STATE OF ARKANSAS INTO THE CONFEDERACY"
>
> The people of the State of Arkansas, in Sovereign Convention, having passed an Ordinance dissolving their political connection with the United States, and another Ordinance adopting and ratifying the Constitution for the Provisional Government of the Confederate States of America, therefore,

> *The Congress of the Confederate States of America do enact*, That the State of Arkansas be and is hereby admitted into this Confederacy upon an equal footing with the other States, under the Constitution for the Provisional Government of the same.

I move, Mr. President, that the bill be put upon its passage, and that the vote be taken by States.

Mr. WITHERS, of South Carolina. As to my own personal belief, that is all true. Arkansas has done what is there recited, but I would like to inquire whether the evidence of the act is amongst our records?

Mr. STEPHENS. Yes, sir.

The PRESIDENT. The gentleman from Georgia has in his possession the Ordinance of secession, and the Ordinance adopting the Provisional Constitution.

Mr. WITHERS. It is sufficient for me to know that the papers are here.

The question was then taken, and all the States having voted in the affirmative, Arkansas was admitted without a dissenting voice.

THE OATH OF ALLEGIANCE

Mr. STEPHENS. Mr. President, the delegation from Arkansas are present. I move that they be sworn in.

The motion was agreed to, and accordingly the oath was administered to Messrs. R. W. JOHNSON, A. RUST, A. H. GARLAND, W. W. WATKINS and H. F. THOMASSON. The latter named delegate has not arrived, but is expected on Monday.

ADDITIONAL COMMITTEES

On motion of Mr. STEPHENS, the President was authorized to appoint additional committeemen—one each to the Committees on Indian Affairs, the Postoffice Department, Public Lands, and Commerce.

And then, on motion of Mr. KENNER, of Louisiana, the Congress proceeded to sit with closed doors.

Monday, May 20, 1861

(Montgomery *Weekly Advertiser*, May 22, 1861)

Congress met this forenoon at 11 o'clock. Prayer was offered by Rev. BASIL MANLY.

The journals of yesterday were read and confirmed.

On motion Mr. THOMASSON, of Arkansas, was duly qualified and took his seat as one of the members from Arkansas.

Mr. SHORTER, of Alabama, gave notice that he would move to reconsider the Patent Office bill, which notice was ordered to be placed on the journal.

Mr. RHETT, of South Carolina, offered the following resolution, which was adopted:

Resolved, That the ordinances of the States constituting the Confederacy, ratifying and adopting the Permanent Constitution of the Confederate States, shall be recorded and filed away in the State Department.

No other business being on the public calendar, Congress went into secret session.

Tuesday, May 21, 1861
(Montgomery *Weekly Advertiser*, May 22, 1861)

Congress assembled this morning at 11 o'clock.—Prayer was offered by Rev. Mr. MITCHELL.

After the reading and confirmation of the minutes of the previous day—

Mr. SHORTER, of Alabama, withdrew his notice of intention to reconsider the Patent Office bill. He said at the time he had not fully examined the bill, but now he was satisfied with it, and consequently withdrew his notice for a reconsideration.

No other business was offered, and Congress went into secret session, and continued until 3 o'clock, when it adjourned to meet at 5 o'clock P.M.

THIRD SESSION

(RICHMOND, VIRGINIA, JULY 20, 1861, TO AUGUST 31, 1861)

Saturday, July 20, 1861
(*Richmond Daily Dispatch*, July 22, 1861; Richmond *Examiner*, July 22, 1861; New Orleans *Times-Picayune*, July 26, 1861)

The Congress was called to order in the Hall of the House of Delegates at the Capitol, precisely at 12 o'clock m.

Hon. HOWELL COBB, in the Chair, called the Assembly to order.

The Rev. Dr. S. K. TALMADGE,[1] of Georgia, then offered up an affecting prayer:

> O Lord, Thou art the Lord God, merciful and gracious, long suffering and abundant in goodness and truth, whilst Thou, by no means, clearest the guilty, Thou art glorious in thy holiness, fearful in thy punishment of sinners; Thou art our Creator, our Preserver, our kind and gracious Benefactor. Thou openest Thine hand, and we are filled with good; Thou hidest Thy face, and we are troubled; Thou takest away our breath, we die and return to our dust. We desire to feel our entire dependency on Thee, personally and socially, civilly and religiously. It is the Lord only that can bless us. It is not man that walketh to direct his steps; the "race is not to the swift or the strong." We would look to Thee at all times for Thy assistance and Thy guidance in our duties. We would look to Thee, especially, our kind Father in Heaven, at this time—this solemn crisis in our history. We pray God to smile propitiously upon our youthful Republic, and give success to our efforts. Bless all who are connected with the government of the Southern Confederacy. Bless Thy servant, the President of the Southern States, and aid him plenteously with wisdom from on high. Hold him in the hollow of Thy hand. Give him energy, and endurance, and boldness, and faithfulness in the discharge of the awfully solemn duties devolving upon him. Bless our Vice-President, and bless thy servants here, who have met together for the solemn purpose of laying the foundation of our precious republic. O, make them instrumental in rescuing the temple of liberty, bought by the toils, and the tears, and the sufferings of our father, and cemented by their blood. O, make them instrumental in rescuing it from

all the evils that have threatened the precious cause of American liberty. Save us from despotism; save us from tyranny; save us from oppression; save us from anarchy and those thousand evils into which we are in danger of being plunged. And, O God, grant that all our laws may be devised in wisdom, may be founded in truth, and that the smiles of Heaven ever may graciously rest upon us. Bless our beloved soldiery in the field of battle, periling their lives and their all to defend our land. Support and protect them. Cover their heads in the day of battle. Be their bulwark and their fortress, and give them abundant success. Confound our enemies and blast their councils, if it please Thee, for we believe they are wrong. Thou art the God of justice and of truth. O, do Thou aid us to do our duty, and do Thou humble us in the dust, and bring us to a sense of our unworthiness.

Save us from the national sins and crimes that bring down the vengeance of Heaven. Save us from the sin of Sabbath breaking, from the sin of profanity, from the vile sin of intemperance, and let virtue, and piety, and intelligence and learning abound. Make this a Government of thine own planting, and of thine own gracious guardian care. May the liberties which we are defending be transmitted by our fidelity to the latest posterity. Save us from pride and self-dependence. O, let us not rise in a sense of self-importance, and say with one of old, "is not this Babylon that I have builded by the might of my power and the majesty of my strength?" lest the curse of heaven come upon us. Father in heaven, we commit these thy servants to thy faithful care. Direct their judgements, their intellects, their hearts, and give them a solemn sense of their responsibility before Thee. Let the deliberations of this meeting be such as Thou wilt own and bless; and let all the councils of this Congress redound to the glory of God and the temporal and eternal welfare of mankind. We pray Thee to bless us, and guide us through the trials of this earthly pilgrimage, and when our short journey is ended, lead us, through the rich grace of the blood of Christ, into the brighter and better world "where the wicked cease from troubling and the weary are at rest" and the praise of our salvation shall be ascribed to the throne of God, Father, Son and Holy Spirit, forevermore. Amen.

By direction of the President, the roll of the Confederate States was called alphabetically, and the following named members were ascertained to be present:

From Alabama—R. R. Smith, J. L. M. Curry, Nich. P. Davis and H. O. Jones.

From Arkansas—Robert W. Johnson, H. F. Thomasson, A. H. Garland and W. W. Watkins.

From Florida—None.

From Georgia—ROBERT TOOMBS, HOWELL COBB, EUGENIUS A. NISBET, BENJAMIN H. HILL, A. R. WRIGHT and AUGUSTUS H. KENAN.

From Louisiana—JOHN PERKINS, JR., A. DECLOUET, CHARLES M. CONRAD, D. S. KENNER and HENRY MARSHALL.

From Mississippi—WILEY P. HARRIS, WALKER BROOK and J. T. HARRISON

From South Carolina—L. M. KEITT, C. G. MEMMINGER and W. W. BOYCE.

From Texas—LOUIS T. WIGFALL, JOHN H. REAGAN, JOHN HEMPHILL, T. N. WAUL and W. P. OCHILTREE.

From Virginia—J. W. BROCKENBROUGH and WALTER R. STAPLES.

On motion of Mr. BROCKENBROUGH, the following named newly appointed delegates from Virginia came forward, presented their credentials, and took the oath of office: JAMES A. SEDDON, WM. BALLARD PRESTON, WM. H. MACFARLAND, CHARLES W. RUSSELL and ROBERT JOHNSON.

Mr. TOOMBS. I believe the members elect from the State of North Carolina, whose credentials have been filed are present.

The PRESIDENT. They will please come forward and take the oath of office.

Accordingly, the following named gentlemen, members elect from North Carolina, came forward and were sworn in—GEORGE DAVIS, W. W. AVERY, W. N. H. SMITH, A. W. VENABLE, J. M. MOREHEAD, R. C. PURYEAR, and E. A. DAVIDSON.

Mr. PERKINS, of Louisiana. As the House is now organized, I move the appointment of a committee to inform the President that a quorum is present and ready to receive any communication he may be pleased to make.

The motion being sustained, the Chair appointed Messrs. PERKINS, of Louisiana, BROCKENBROUGH, of Virginia, and JOHNSON, of Arkansas, to constitute such committee.

During the absence of the committee, Mr. TOOMBS, from the Committee on Ways and Means, introduced a bill entitled an act to authorize the appointment of agents to sign treasury notes, which was read in due order and passed.

The committee appointed to inform the President of the organization of the House, returned and reported that the President would send in a communication in writing.—A few moments thereafter, the following message was received from his Excellency, President DAVIS, by his Private Secretary, and ordered to be read, together with accompanying documents:

To the Congress of the Confederate States of America

GENTLEMEN: My message, addressed to you at the commencement of the session, contained such full information of the state of the Confederacy as to render it unnecessary that I should now do more than call your attention to such important facts as have occurred during the recess, and to matters connected with the public defense.

I have again to congratulate you on the accession of new members to our Confederation of free, equal, and sovereign States. Our loved and honored brethren of North Carolina and Tennessee have consummated the action, foreseen and provided for at your last session, and I have had the gratification of announcing, by proclamation, in conformity with law, that those States were admitted into the Confederacy.

The people of Virginia also, by a majority previously unknown in her history, have ratified the action of her convention, uniting her fortunes with ours. The States of Arkansas, North Carolina, and Virginia have likewise adopted the Permanent Constitution of the Confederate States, and no doubt is entertained of its adoption by Tennessee at the election to be held early next month.

I deemed it advisable to direct the removal of the several Executive Departments, with their archives, to this city, to which you had removed the seat of government, immediately after your adjournment. The aggressive movements of the enemy required prompt and energetic action. The accumulation of his forces on the Potomac sufficiently demonstrated that his efforts were to be directed against Virginia; and from no point could the necessary measures for her defense and protection be so efficiently directed as from her own capital.

The rapid progress of events for the last few weeks has fully sufficed to strip the veil behind which the true policy and purposes of the Government of the United States had been previously concealed; their odious features now stand fully revealed; the message of their President and the action of their Congress during the present month, confess the intention of subjugating these States by a war, whose folly is equaled by its wickedness; a war by which it is impossible to attain the proposed result, whilst its dire calamities, not to be avoided by us, will fall with double severity on themselves.

Commencing in March last, with an affectation of ignoring the secession of the seven States which first organized this Government; persisting in April in the idle and absurd assumption of the existence of a riot which was to be dispersed by a *posse comitatus* continuing in successive months the false representation that these States intended offensive war, in spite of the conclusive evidence to the contrary, furnished as well by official action as by the very basis on which this Government is constituted; the President of the United States and his advisers succeeded in deceiving the people of those States into the belief that the purpose of this Government was not peace at home, but conquest abroad; not the defense of its own liberties, but the subversion of those of the people of the United States.

The series of maneuvers by which this impression was created, the art with which they were devised, and the perfidy with which they were executed, were already known to you; but you could scarcely have supposed that they would be openly avowed and their success made the subject of boast and self-laudation in an executive message. Fortunately for the truth of history, however, the President of the United States details with minuteness the attempt to reinforce Fort Pickens in violation of an armistice, of which he confesses to have been informed, but "only by rumors too vague and uncertain to fix attention;" the hostile expedition dispatched to supply Fort Sumter, admitted to have been undertaken with a knowledge that its success was impossible; the sending of notice to the governor of South Carolina of his intention to use force to accomplish his object, and then quoting from his inaugural address the assurance that there could be no conflict, unless these States were the aggressors, he proceeds to declare that his conduct, as just related by himself, was a performance of this promise, "so free from the power of ingenious sophistry as that the world should not be able to misunderstand it;" and in defiance of his own statement that he gave notice of the approach of a hostile fleet, he charges these States with becoming the assailants of the United States, "without a gun in sight or *in expectancy* to return their fire, save only the few in the fort." He is indeed fully justified in saying that the case "is so free from the power of ingenious sophistry that the world will not be able to misunderstand it."

Under cover of this unfounded pretense that the Confederate States are the assailants, that high functionary, after expressing his concern that some foreign nations "had so shaped their action as if they supposed the early destruction of our National Union was probable," abandons all further disguise, and proposes "to make this contest a short and decisive one," by placing at the control of the Government for the work *at least* 400,000 men and $400,000,000. The Congress concurring in the doubt thus intimated as to the sufficiency of the force demanded, has increased it to half a million of men. These enormous preparations in men and money for the conduct of a war on a scale more gigantic than any which the New World has ever witnessed, is a distinct avowal in the eyes of civilized man that the United States are engaged in a conflict with a great and powerful nation; they are at last compelled to abandon the pretense of being engaged in dispersing rioters and suppressing insurrections, and are driven to the acknowledgment that the ancient Union has been dissolved. They recognize the separate existence of these Confederate States by the interdiction, embargo, and blockade of all commerce between them and the United States, not only by sea, but by land; not only in ships, but in rail cars; not only with those who bear arms, but with the entire population of the Confederate States. Finally they have repudiated the foolish conceit that the inhabitants of this Confederacy are still citizens of the United States, for they are waging an indiscriminate war upon them all with a savage ferocity unknown to modern civilization. In this war, rapine is the rule; private residences in peaceful rural retreats are bombarded and burnt; grain crops in the field are consumed by the torch; and when the torch is not convenient, careful labor is bestowed to render complete the destruction of every article of use or ornament remaining in private dwellings after their inhabitants have fled from the outrages of a brutal soldiery.

In 1781 Great Britain, when invading her revolted colonies, took possession of the very district of country near Fortress Monroe now occupied by troops of the United States.[2] The houses then inhabited by the people, after being respected and protected by avowed invaders, are now pillaged and destroyed by men who pretend that the victims are their fellow-citizens.

Mankind will shudder to hear the tales of outrages committed on defenseless females by soldiers of the United States now invading our homes. Yet these outrages are prompted by inflamed passions and the madness of intoxication. But who shall depict the horror with which they will regard the cool and deliberate malignity which, under pretext of suppressing an insurrection, said by themselves to be upheld by a minority only of our people, makes special war on the sick, including the women and the children, by carefully devised measures to prevent their obtaining the medicines necessary for their cure? The sacred claims of humanity, respected even during the fury of actual battle by careful diversion of attack from the hospitals containing wounded enemies, are outraged in cold blood by a Government and people that pretend to desire a continuance of fraternal connections.

All these outrages must remain unavenged, save by the universal reprobation of mankind, in all cases where the actual perpetrators of the wrongs escape capture. They admit of no retaliation. The humanity of our people would shrink instinctively from the bare idea of waging a like war upon the sick, the women, and the children of the enemy.

But there are other savage practices which have been resorted to by the Government of the United States which do admit of repression by retaliation. I have been driven to the necessity of enforcing this repression. The prisoners of war taken by the enemy on board the armed schooner *Savannah*, sidling under our commission, were, as I was credibly advised, treated like common felons, put in irons, confined in a jail usually appropriated to criminals of the worst dye, and threatened with punishment as such. I had made an application for the exchange of these prisoners to the commanding officer of the enemy's squadron off Charleston Harbor, but that officer had already sent the prisoners to New York when the application was made.[3] I therefore deemed it my duty to renew the proposal for the exchange to the constitutional Commander in Chief of the Army and Navy of the United States, the only officer having control of the prisoners. To this end I dispatched an officer to him under a flag of truce, and in making the proposal I informed President Lincoln of my resolute purpose to check all barbarities on prisoners of war by such severity of retaliation on the prisoners held by us as should secure the abandonment of the practice.

This communication was received and read by the officer in command of the Army of the United States, and a message was brought from him by the bearer of my communication that a reply would be returned by President Lincoln as soon as possible. I earnestly hope that this promised reply, which has not yet been received, will convey the assurance that prisoners of war will be treated, in this unhappy contest, with that regard to humanity which has made such conspicuous progress in the conduct of modern warfare. As a measure of precaution, however, and until the promised reply is received, I still retain in close custody some officers captured from the enemy whom it had been my pleasure previously to enlarge on parole, and whose fate must necessarily depend on that of the prisoners held by the enemy.

I append a copy of my communication to the President and Commander in Chief of the Army and Navy of the United States and of the report of the officer charged to deliver it, marked Doc. A.

There are some other passages in the remarkable paper to which I have directed your attention, having reference to the peculiar relations which exist between this Government and the States usually termed the border slave States, which cannot properly be withheld from notice.

The hearts of our people are animated by sentiments toward the inhabitants of those States which found expression in your enactment refusing to consider them as enemies or to authorize hostilities against them. That a very large portion of the people of those States regard us as brethren; that if unrestrained by the actual presence of large armies, the subversion of civil authority, and the declaration of martial law, some of them at least would joyfully unite with us; that they are with almost entire unanimity opposed to the prosecution of the war waged against us are facts of which daily recurring events fully warrant the assertion.

The President of the United States refuses to recognize in these our late sister States the right of refraining from attack on us, and justifies his refusal by the assertion that the States have no other power "than that reserved to them in the Union by the Constitution, *no one of them having ever been a State out of the Union.*"

This view of the constitutional relations between the States and the

General Government is a fitting introduction to another assertion of the message that the Executive possesses the power of suspending the writ of habeas corpus and of delegating that power to military commanders at his discretion;[4] and both these propositions claim a respect equal to that which is felt for the additional statement of opinion in the same paper that it is proper in order to execute the laws that "some single law, made in such extreme tenderness of the citizens' liberty that practically it relieves more of the guilty than the innocent, should to a very limited extent be violated."

We may well rejoice that we have forever severed our connection with a Government that thus tramples on all the principles of constitutional liberty and with a people in whose presence such avowals could be hazarded.

The operations in the field will be greatly extended by reason of the policy which, heretofore secretly entertained, is now avowed and acted on by the United States. The forces hitherto raised proved ample for the defense of the seven States which originally organized the Confederacy, as is evinced by the fact that, with the exception of three fortified islands,[5] whose defense is efficiently aided by a preponderating naval force, the enemy has been driven completely out of those States; and now, at the expiration of five months from the formation of the Government, not a single hostile foot presses their soil. These forces, however, must necessarily prove inadequate to repel the invasion by half a million of men, now proposed by the enemy, and a corresponding increase in our forces will become necessary. The recommendations for the raising and efficient equipment of this additional force will be contained in the communication of the Secretary of War, to which 1 need scarcely invite your earnest attention.

In my message delivered in April last, I referred to the promise of abundant crops, with which we were cheered. The grain crops generally have since been harvested, and the yield has proven to be the most abundant known in our history. Many believe the supply adequate to two years' consumption of our population. Cotton, sugar, and tobacco, forming the surplus production of our agriculture, and furnishing the basis of our commercial interchanges, present the most cheering promise, and a kind Providence has smiled on the labor which extracts the teeming wealth of our soil in all portions of our Confederacy.

It is the more gratifying to be able to give you this assurance because of the need of a large and increased expenditure in the support of our Army. Elevated and purified by the sacred cause they maintain, our fellow-citizens of every condition of life exhibit the most self-sacrificing devotion. They manifest a laudable pride in upholding their independence, unaided by any resources other than their own, and the immense wealth which a fertile soil and genial climate have accumulated in this Confederacy of agriculturists could not be more strikingly displayed than in the large revenues which, with eager zeal, they have contributed at the call of their country. In the single article of cotton the subscriptions to the loan proposed by the Government cannot fall short of fifty millions of dollars, and will probably largely exceed that sum; and scarcely an article required for the consumption of the Army is provided otherwise than by subscription to the produce loan so happily devised by your wisdom. The Secretary of the Treasury, in the report submitted to you by him, will give you the amplest details connected with that branch of the public service. [document XXI]

But 'tis not alone in their prompt pecuniary contributions that the noble race of freemen who inhabit these States evince how worthy they are of the liberties which they so well know how to defend. In numbers far exceeding those authorized by your laws they have pressed the tender of their services against the enemy. Their attitude of calm and sublime devotion to their country, the cool and confident courage with which they are already preparing to meet the threatened invasion in whatever proportions it may assume, the assurance that their sacrifices and their services will be renewed from year to year with unfaltering purpose until they have made good to the uttermost their right to self-government; the generous and almost unquestioning confidence which they display in their Government during the pending struggle, all combine to present a spectacle such as the world has rarely if ever seen.

To speak of subjugating such a people, so united and determined, is to speak in a language incomprehensible to them. To resist attacks on their rights or their liberties is with them an instinct. Whether this war shall last one, or three, or five years is a problem they leave to be solved by the enemy alone; it will last till the enemy shall have withdrawn from their borders—till their political rights, their altars, and their homes are freed from invasion. Then, and then only, will they rest from this struggle, to enjoy in peace the blessings which with the favor of Providence they have secured by the aid of their own strong hearts and sturdy arms.

Jefferson Davis

After the reading of the Message, by request of Mr. Perkins, of Louisiana, the following correspondence was read by the Clerk. The subject being in relation to a matter about which there has been a great deal of anxiety felt, to wit: the mission of Col. Taylor to President Lincoln,[6] under a flag of truce from President Davis, we lay it before our readers this morning, with the assurance that it will be read with that interest which the subject demands:

Richmond, 6th July 1861[7]

To ABRAHAM LINCOLN, President and Commander in Chief of the Army and Navy of the United States:

Sir:—Having learned that the schr. *Savannah*, a private armed vessel in the service and sailing under a commission issued by authority of the Confederate States of America, had been captured by one of the vessels forming the blockading squadron off Charleston harbor, I directed a proposition to be made to the officer commanding that squadron for an exchange of prisoners of war held by this Government "according to number and rank"—To this proposition, made on the 19th ult., Capt. MERCER, the officer in command of the blockading squadron, made answer on the same day that "the prisoners (referred to) are not on board of any of the vessels under my command."[8]

It now appears, by statements made without contradiction in newspapers published in New York, that the prisoners above mentioned were conveyed to that city, and have there been treated not as prisoners of war, but as criminals: that they have been put in irons, confined in jail, brought before the Courts of Justice on charges of piracy and treason, and it is even rumored that they have been actually convicted of the offenses charged, for no other reason than that they bore arms in defense of the rights of this Government and under the authority of its commission.[9]

I could not with grave discourtesy have made the newspaper statements above referenced to, the subject of this communication, if the threat of treating as pirates the citizens of this Confederacy, armed for its service on the high seas, had not been contained in your proclamation of the ___ April last.[10] That proclamation, however, seems to afford sufficient justification for considering these published statements as not devoid of probability.

It is the desire of this Government so to conduct the war now existing as to mitigate its horrors as far as may be possible; and, with this intent, its treatment of the prisoners captured by its forces has been marked by the greatest humanity and lenience consistent with public obligation: some have been permitted to return home on parole, others to remain at large under similar conditions within this Confederacy, and all have been furnished with rations for their subsistence, such as are allowed to our own troops. It is only since the news has been received of the treatment of the prisoners taken on the *Savannah*, that I have been compelled to withdraw these indulgences, and to hold the prisoners taken by us in strict confinement.

A just regard to humanity and to the honor of this Government now requires me to state explicitly, that painful as will be the necessity, this Government will deal out to the prisoner held by it, the same treatment and the same fate as shall be experienced by those captured on the *Savannah*; and if driven to the terrible necessity of retaliation by your execution of any of the officers or the crew of the *Savannah*, that retaliation will be extended so far as shall be requisite to secure the abandonment of a practice unknown to the warfare of civilized man; and so barbarous as to disgrace the nation which shall be guilty of inaugurating it.

With this view, and because it may not have reached you, I now renew the proposition made to the commander of the blockading squadron, to exchange for the prisoners taken on the *Savannah*, an equal number of those now held by us, according to rank.

I am, sir, yours, &c.

JEFFERSON DAVIS,
President, and Commander-in-Chief of the Army and Navy of the Confederate States

---

To His Excellency JEFFERSON DAVIS,
President of the Confederate States:

SIR: In obedience to your instructions, I left the city of Richmond on the morning of the 7th July, at 6 o'clock A.M., as bearer of dispatches to His Excellency ABRAHAM LINCOLN, President of the United States. At Manassas I received from General BEAUREGARD a letter to General MCDOWELL, commanding the U.S. forces at Arlington.[11] From Manassas I proceeded to Fairfax Court-House, where I was furnished, by General BONHAM,[12] an escort of fourteen cavalry, under the command of Lieut. BRECKINRIDGE,[13] of the Virginia cavalry. Proceeding on the direct road to Alexandria, I met a detachment of cavalry under the command of Colonel PORTER, USA,[14] about three miles from the junction, from which place I sent back my escort. Captain WHIPPLE, USA,[15] accompanied me to Arlington, where I arrived about 4 o'clock P. M., Monday, the 8th. Gen. MCDOWELL not being at Arlington, my arrival was telegraphed him to Washington City. About 9 o'clock P.M., Col. VAN RENSLAER, senior aid-de-camp to Gen. SCOTT,[16] was sent to convey me to Gen. SCOTT's headquarters, where I found Gen. MCDOWELL, to whom I delivered Gen. BEAUREGARD's letter. After reading Gen. B's letter he passed it to Gen. SCOTT, who being informed in this letter, that I desired to deliver your communication in person received it of me—After reading your communication to Mr. LINCOLN, General SCOTT informed me that a reply would be returned by Mr. LINCOLN as soon as possible—and at the same time instructed me to return to Arlington with Gen. MCDOWELL, thence to proceed in the morning back to our lines, which I did, under an escort of twenty United States cavalry, commanded by Lieut. PUTNAM.[17]

In my intercourse with Gen. SCOTT and the other officers of the United States Army, I have to say that I was received with marked consideration and attention, and with that courtesy and kindness which should ever characterize the diplomatic relations of great nations, in war as well as in peace. Understanding that the object of my mission was the delivery of your letter to Mr. LINCOLN, I have the honor to state that it was done, and subscribe myself

Your obedient servant,

Thos. H. Taylor
Capt. Cavalry C.S.A.
and Lt. Col. 1st Ky. Regiment[18]

On motion of Mr. WIGFALL, of Texas, five thousand copies of the President's Message were ordered to be printed.

On motion of Mr. KEITT, of South Carolina, the Committee on Printing was instructed to inquire into the expediency of electing a Public Printer.

Congress then adjourned to meet Monday at 12 o'clock, M.

Monday, July 22, 1861

(Richmond *Enquirer*, July 23, 1861; Richmond *Whig*, July 23, 1861)

Congress met at 12 M.

The Hon. HOWELL COBB in the Chair. Prayer was offered by the Rev. J. L. BURROWS, of the First Baptist Church, of Richmond.[19] The journal of Saturday was read and approved.

On motion, ROBERT E. SCOTT and WALTER PRESTON, of Va., and T. MCDOWELL, of North Carolina, newly elected members, came forward and took the oath of office

Mr. MEMMINGER, of South Carolina. Mr. President, I beg leave to interrupt the order of business by bringing to the attention of Congress the intelligence that has been received at this place from the seat of war. I present the following dispatch which I ask the Secretary to read:

Manassas, July 21, 1861

Mrs. JEFFERSON DAVIS:—We have won a glorious, though dear-bought victory. Night closed on the enemy in full flight and closely pursued.

(Signed) JEFFERSON DAVIS

I beg leave to present an official dispatch received since that:

Manassas, July 21, 1861

To Gen. S. COOPER, Adj. Gen. Richmond:

Night has closed upon a hard fought field. Our forces have won a glorious victory. The enemy was routed and fled precipitously, abandoning a very large amount of arms, munitions, knapsacks and baggage. The ground was strewn for miles with those killed, and the farm houses and the grounds around were filled with his wounded. The pursuit was continued along several routes towards Leesburg and Centreville, until darkness covered the fugitives. We have captured several field batteries and regimental standards, and one United States flag. Many prisoners have been taken. Too high praise cannot be bestowed, whether for the skill of the principal officers, or for the gallantry of all the troops. The battle was mainly fought on our left, several miles from our field works; our force engaging them not exceeding fifteen thousand; that of the enemy estimated at thirty-five thousand.

(Signed) JEFF. DAVIS

This announcement, continued Mr. MEMMINGER, informs Congress that the invader of our soil has been driven back, that our altars have been purified and our houses secured for the ruthless hand of an unprincipled foe. But, sir, it has been at a cost that will bring sorrow into many families; wet with burning tears the cheeks of many widows and orphans, and into many happy homes bring grief and desolation; and I presume, sir, Congress will be little disposed on such an occasion to go on with their usual business. I have therefore taken the liberty of offering a series of resolutions, which I will submit to the attention of Congress, and ask their adoption.

Resolved, That we recognize the hand of the Most High God, the King of Kings and Lord of Lords, in the glorious victory with which He hath crowned our arms at Manassas; and that the people of these Confederate States are invited, by appropriate services on the ensuing Sabbath, to offer up their united thanksgivings and prayers for this mighty deliverance.

Resolved, That we deeply deplore the necessity which has washed the soil of our country with the blood of so many of her noblest sons, and that we offer to their respective families and friends our warmest and most cordial sympathies, assuring them that the sacrifice made will be consecrated in the hearts of our people, and will there enshrine the names of the gallant dead, as the champions of free and Constitutional Government.

Resolved, That we approve of the prompt and patriotic efforts of the Mayor of the City of Richmond to make provisions for the wounded,[20] and that a committee of one member from each State be appointed to cooperate in the plan.

Resolved, That Congress do now adjourn.

The resolutions were unanimously adopted, and Congress adjourned to meet to-morrow at 12 M.

The Speaker announced the following committee in pursuance of the 3rd resolution:

> Hon. W. H. MACFARLAND, of Virginia; Hon. A. W. VENABLE, of North Carolina; Hon. JACKSON MORTON, of Florida; Hon. THOMAS R. R. COBB, of Georgia; Hon. N. P. DAVIS, of Alabama; Hon. J. T. HARRISON, of Mississippi; Hon. HENRY MARSHALL, of Louisiana; Hon. A. G. GARLAND, of Arkansas; and Hon. B. OCHILTREE, of Texas.

Tuesday, July 23, 1861

(*Richmond Daily Dispatch*, July 24, 1861; Richmond *Examiner*, July 24, 1861)

Congress met at 12M., pursuant to adjournment, and was opened with prayer by the Rev. MOSES D. HOGE, of the Presbyterian church,[21] thanking God that the first official act of the Congress had been the recognition of His Almighty hand in the affairs of their country. Hon. HOWELL COBB in the chair.

The Journal of the preceding day was read and approved.

On motion of Mr. BROCKENBROUGH,[22] Messr. THOMAS S. BOCOCK, of Virginia, and BURTON CRAIGE, of North Carolina, newly elected members from their respective States, presented their credentials and took the oath of office.

REPORT OF THE SECRETARY OF THE TREASURY

President COBB presented the report of the Secretary of the Treasury; which on motion, was, without being read, referred to the Finance Committee.[23]

PETITIONS, MEMORIAL, &C.

Mr. PERKINS, of Louisiana, presented a memorial in relation to the resources of the south, which, on motion, was referred to the Committee on Finance.

By the same.—The following resolution of inquiry, which was adopted

> *Whereas*, the Government of the United States is exerting all its energies and employing its army and navy, and every agency within its power, to prevent the exportation of our great staples cotton, tobacco, &c., to any other country, except through its own ports, or by its permission, thereby securing the complete commercial subjugation of the Confederate States, and causing the industrial and manufacturing interests of all other countries sustained by these products to be dependent upon them for their supply: Therefore, be it
>
> *Resolved*, That the Committee on Finance be instructed to inquire into

> the expediency of at once conferring upon the Government of the Confederate States the power to control the Cotton and Tobacco crops of this country by receiving whatever supplies in kind or by purchase from individuals, at a price fixed, or by such an advance upon their value in Treasury Notes or Confederate bonds, as may enable the Government to make their possession the basis of credit and negotiation abroad.

The resolution was agreed to.

Mr. HARRIS, of Mississippi, said that there had been placed in his hands a communication touching the public service. It related to the disposition of the cotton subscribed to the Government, and contained a plan of finance to be acted upon by Congress. He might say that the communication was from an intelligent and very able citizen of the Confederate States. He moved its reference, without being read, to the Committee on Finance. The communication was so referred.

Mr. OCHILTREE, of Texas, offered the following resolution, which was adopted:

> *Resolved,* That the Committee on Finance be instructed to inquire into the expediency of collecting all duties imposed by the laws now in force on goods, wares, merchandise and commodities of every description whatever imported into these Confederate States during the existence of the present war, and that they report at an early day by bill or otherwise.

Mr. RIVES, of Virginia, submitted the petition of Lieut. Col. SAMUEL JONES,[24] late of the United States army, but now in the Confederate service, asking that the wages due him by the United States Government be paid out of the funds lately belonging to the United States, but now in possession of the Confederate States. Referred to the Committee on Military Affairs.

No business on the calendar.

The list of Committees was called through, and no business appearing on the public calendar, Congress resolved itself into secret session.

Wednesday, July 24, 1861

(*Richmond Daily Dispatch,* July 23 and 25, 1861; Richmond *Examiner,* July 25, 1861; Richmond *Whig,* July 26, 1861)

Congress met at 12 M. Appropriate prayer was offered by Rev. Mr. WOODBRIDGE, of the Episcopal Church.[25]

THE VIRGINIA DELEGATES

Mr. BOCOCK, of Va., announced the presence of Mr. JAMES M. MASON, of that State, who was ready to qualify as a delegate of the Congress. The presence of Mr.

ROGER A. PRYOR was also announced; whereupon the gentlemen were sworn in at the Secretary's desk.

APPROPRIATION FOR CARE OF THE WOUNDED

Mr. MACFARLAND, of Va., submitted a report, with accompanying resolution, from a Select Committee, appointed to co-operate with the Mayor of Richmond in making provisions for the wounded.

> The committee to whom was referred the resolutions, approving the prompt and patriotic efforts of the Mayor of the city of Richmond in behalf of the wounded in the glorious victory at Manassas, and tendering the co-operation of Congress in his beneficent plan, respectfully report that, in a public meeting of the citizens of Richmond, convened by the Mayor on Monday, the 22d inst., the following proceedings were had:
>
> The intelligence from the army of a brilliant victory, achieved by the Confederate forces at Manassas, over the ruthless enemies of public liberty and constitutional law, is an occasion of devout thanksgiving to Almighty God; and the citizens of Richmond here assembled reverently acknowledge His goodness and mercy. They acknowledge, moreover, that it is a sacred and patriotic duty to manifest their grief for the loss of the noble men who fell in the arduous struggle and were disabled, and to console with and relieve the sufferers and their families.
>
> *Resolved*, That a committee of _____ citizens be appointed to proceed to Manassas and confer with the commanding generals of the posts in reference to the removal and transportation to this city of such wounded soldiers as can be safely removed; also
>
> *Resolved*, That a committee of citizens be appointed to confer with the citizens of the city of Richmond and vicinity, to ascertain how many wounded soldiers can be nursed and comfortably provided for by the several families in the city and vicinity, and in aid of that committee the citizens report to the mayor the number of the wounded that they can respectively provide with comfortable accommodations.
>
> *Resolved*, That said committee do also provide and fit up, at the expense of the city, such additional rooms as may be necessary for the comfortable accommodation of the wounded; and that said committee do provide all necessary means of conveyance of the wounded to the places designated.
>
> *Resolved*, That a committee be appointed to solicit subscriptions of money for the above purpose.
>
> These proceedings meet the exigency in a spirit of broad and considerate sympathy.—There is no duty to which our fellow citizens or their

representatives and agents, are prepared to respond more spontaneously and liberally than that which summons them to the consolation and relief of their intrepid defenders. It would not become the Congress of the Confederate States to permit the city of Richmond to take to herself the whole charge of providing for the wounded and sick of the army, which, under the blessing of Providence, triumphed gloriously at Manassas.

It behooves Congress to provide the funds necessary to meet the outlay which may attend the execution of their beneficent design; therefore

Resolved, That the sum five thousand dollars be placed at the disposal of the Secretary of the Treasury, to be expended in securing the comfort of the officers and men of the army, who were in the battle of Manassas, and may be removed to the city of Richmond under the resolutions of the Common Council.

The resolution passed unanimously.

RESPECT TO THE MEMORY OF COLONEL BARTOW, OF GEORGIA[26]

Mr. T. R. R. COBB, of Georgia. I rise, Mr. President, to announce facts too well known to all the members of this Congress, and which the saddened faces before me convince me are deeply felt by all of this body. The mortal remains, sir, of our late beloved colleague, FRANCIS S. BARTOW, of Georgia, lie in the other end of this Capitol, which has been temporarily made a charnel house for the illustrious dead.[27]

I confess, sir, that this is one of the saddest duties of my life, and one which I must acknowledge my incompetency to discharge. To indulge in formal generalities would illy comport with the feelings of the House, and to give utterance to the suppressed feelings of my heart would scarcely be appropriate in such presence. The deceased was my friend, and loved me as Jonathan did David. You, Mr. President, knew him long, but I knew him longer, and, therefore, loved him better.

The speaker eloquently recited an incident that had taken place between himself and his deceased colleague, at the time that Congress was in session at Montgomery. The deceased had been the Chairman of the Committee on Military Affairs, and in this important position had brought many valuable measures before the House, which he (Mr. COBB) had the greatest confidence and pleasure in assisting by his enfeebled powers. Once only he had differed from him in a single point, and on leaving the session of the Congress in which the difference had occurred, the speaker, in jest, made a remark to his friend, which he instantly saw wounded him. Deeply regretting that he had given the wound, he begged him to forget it.—Again that night he saw him, and his friend still seemed distressed by the remembrance of the wounding remark. The Speaker retired to bed in pain and uneasiness at the unpleasant incident in a life-long friendship. At last he sought the chamber of Colonel BARTOW; he found him also restless under the recollections of the day; but the gallant deceased divining the mission of his friend to be again to ask forgiveness, rose and without a word, and in a gush of tears, silently clasped him in his arms. Such continued the speaker, was our friendship. Such, Mr. President, was my loss.

Mr. COBB continued in an eloquent recital of the life of the illustrious deceased. He was born on the 11th day of September, 1816, and would have been forty-five years of age on his next birth day. He was a native of Georgia; had graduated at the University of that state, and had proceeded to the study and practice of law, in which he distinguished himself for ability and a remarkable order of eloquence. He had never been much in public life, until he had been called to represent the people of Georgia in the Confederate Congress. He had been twice forced by the importunities of his party—that party headed by the great man whose fame had been commemorated in marble in the enclosure of the Capitol—to serve in the Legislature of his State; and, in one of his terms of service, had almost, by his own unaided efforts, urged and accomplished the completion, by the State of Georgia, of the great internal improvement that was the basis of her prosperity.

The circumstances of the death of the gallant deceased were told by the speaker in eloquent conclusion of his remarks. While the battle was raging, Col. BARTOW had ridden up to Gen. BEAUREGARD and said: "Show me what now is to be done, and if human effort can accomplish it, I will do it." The General replied; with pointed finger, "that battery must be taken." Instantly seizing the standard of his own Regiment, and accompanied by the Virginia forces, Col. BARTOW led the van of the gallant and desperate assault. A ball wounded him slightly and killed his horse. Again mounted, he led and cheered his men. The next wound was a ball, which entered his heart. His last words were memorable: *"They have killed me, but never give up the field!"*

Mr. COBB concluded the affecting tribute to the deceased by saying that, in a few days, he hoped to be himself in the field, and to follow in the footsteps of his beloved friend, sustained by that same Christian faith in which Col. BARTOW had lived and acted and died.

[We but express the unanimous sense of the House, and of all who listened to Mr. COBB's remarks, that they were most eloquent and effecting; and we had intended to obtain a full copy of the address from Mr. C. for publication, and had, therefore, made but meagre notes of it, but understand that it was entirely extempore, and delivered without note, or any effort whatever of the pen.]

The following resolutions of respect to the memory of the deceased were moved by Mr. COBB:

> *Resolved*, That Congress has heard, with unfeigned sorrow, of the death of Hon. FRANCIS S. BARTOW, one of the delegates from the State of Georgia; that the national exultation for a glorious history, achieved by our arms, is checked by the heavy loss sustained by the Confederacy in the death of one of her most efficient Commanders; and that, as his

colleagues, we feel a peculiar loss to ourselves in one who had won our esteem and gained much of our affection.

Resolved, That with pleasure we record our admiration of his heroic defense on the field of battle; of the action of this Congress in which he participated so largely; and find some consolation for his death in the conviction that his noble self-sacrifice will serve to establish the work which he so boldly aided to begin.

Resolved, That we appreciate the loss which Georgia, his native State, has sustained in the death of one of her noblest sons; and that we tender to the bereaved the sympathy of hearts, to some extent, stricken by the same blow which has crushed their own.

Resolved, That a copy of these resolutions be communicated to the family of the deceased.

Resolved, That in respect for his memory the Congress do now adjourn.

Mr. HILL, of Georgia, made a speech of some length, paying an eloquent tribute to the illustrious dead! He said that Colonel BARTOW had been distinguished in his devotion to the Union. A member of the old Whig party, the Union had been his idol, and his mind was closely and long-wedded to the idea that the Union of the United States was inseparable from the civil liberty of the country. But the later development of events and the policy of the Washington Administration decided him to another opinion; and, at the time of the separation of Georgia, that State had no more ardent or devoted Secessionist within her borders.

Mr. MASON, of Virginia, was anxious to testify to his happy estimation of the chance that had introduced him to the prized acquaintance of Col. BARTOW when the forces that he commanded were in the neighborhood of Winchester; and in his house there, the deceased had been a welcome and honored inmate. No mere courage or bravery had made Col. BARTOW a soldier; a sentiment of even higher devotion than these—a sentiment of noblest patriotism—stimulated his soul; and though any man might die, it had been given to him they mourned to show now a hero could surrender his life to his country.

Mr. CHESNUT, of South Carolina, said that the cloud that darkened Georgia in the loss of her illustrious son would extend its shadow over the whole land of the South. He had known the deceased. He had seen his dead form on the field at Manassas, the burning eye of courage draped in the sleep of death and the cold form lying still and insensate in the atmosphere that swelled with the sounds of the victory he aided to obtain. No tribute of admiration, no expression of sorrow; no offering of tears could be given to the brave and noble deceased to which his own heart did not make the fullest response.

The resolutions of respect referred to were then put to the vote and unanimously adopted.

Congress adjourned until to-morrow.

Thursday, July 25, 1861
(Richmond *Examiner*, July 26, 1861)

Congress met at twelve o'clock, and the opening prayer was made by Rev. T. A. WARE.[28] In a portion of the prayer, the reverend gentleman, referring to the thanks ascribed to God for our late victory, besought that He would so impress the hearts of the people with a sense of his providence and goodness that the name "Manassas" should always remind them of its scriptural signification, which was: "*God hath made us to forget all our troubles.*"

Mr. THOMAS RUFFIN, one of the delegates elected from North Carolina, appeared, was sworn in, and took his seat.

The House was then called by States for resolutions.

THE TRIBUTE OF RESPECT TO COL. BARTOW

Mr. GARLAND, of Arkansas, offered the following resolution, which was unanimously adopted:

> *Resolved*, That the Secretary be, and he is hereby and directed to have, as soon as possible, the proceedings of Congress on the announcement of the death of the Hon. FRANCIS S. BARTOW, together with the several speeches made on the occasion, printed in pamphlet form, and that 3,500 copies of the same be printed for the use of Congress.

PROHIBITION OF THE PAYMENT OF NORTHERN DEBTS

Mr. SMITH, of Alabama, said that the act heretofore passed by Congress, to prohibit the payment of sums of money due by citizens of the Confederate States to those of the United States, was defective in an important particular. It provided no penalty to secure its prohibition. Under the construction of the common law, where it made a penal offence, but prescribed no penalty, the offence was to be considered and punished as a misdemeanor. But, under our constitutional law, and under the decisions of the Supreme Court, which had enlightened the point, it was considered that no penalty could be attached unless prescribed in the body of the statute. The omission of a penalty in the law referred to had formerly escaped his notice, and it was an omission that should be cured. He offered the following resolution, which was adopted:

> *Be it resolved by the Congress of the Confederate States,* That the Committee on the Judiciary be instructed to report a bill amending an act, approved May 21, 1861, entitled an act "to authorize certain debtors to pay the amounts due by them into the Treasury of the Confederate States," so as to provide suitable penalties for violations of the prohibitions contained in said act.

The Blockade—Purchase of Naval Steamers &c

Mr. Hill, of Ga., said that he had received a copy of the proceedings of a meeting held at Marietta, in his State, on the 17th instant, which had come to him probably with the desire that it should be communicated to Congress. The subjects of which it treated were of great importance; and the gentlemen who had principally participated in the meeting were well acquainted with these subjects, and had made them a particular study. The communication recommends to Congress the propriety of throwing open our ports to the shipping and commerce of neutral nations, by granting to those who succeeded in running or breaking the blockades remission of duties. It also suggests the propriety of a plan to purchase ocean steamers, by some sort of assurance from Congress to the owners of those vessels, suitable for war purposes—that upon their successful entry into our ports they would be purchased for our navy, after examination by a commission, &c. The communication was referred to the Committee on Finance. [document XXII]

A General Confiscation Bill[29]

Mr. Kenner, of Louisiana, offered the following preamble and resolution, which were agreed to:

> *Whereas,* the Congress of the United States has passed a law providing for the confiscation of the property of all rebels found in arms against the United States; and[30]
>
> *Whereas,* it is known by the public official declarations of the Executive and Congress of the United States that the intent and meaning of said act is the confiscation, not of the property of the rebel citizens of the United States, but of the citizens of this Confederacy, who are now enemies of the United States; and,
>
> *Whereas,* the confiscation aforesaid is, in effect, a general seizure of the property of all the inhabitants of these Confederate States, inasmuch as they are all in arms against the United States; and,
>
> *Whereas,* this additional resort by the Government of the United States to means of warfare repudiated by the usages of civilized nations can only be repelled and resisted by that just retaliation, which is the legitimate weapon of defense against such barbarities as the United States have inaugurated in this war, to the disgrace of this Government and people: Therefore,
>
> *Resolved,* That the Committee on the Judiciary be instructed to inquire into the propriety and necessity of adopting means of retaliation by a general confiscation bill, and make report, by such bill or otherwise, as early as practicable.

FREE TRAVEL FOR THE SICK SOLDIERS

Mr. PERKINS, of La. offered the following communication, which was referred to the Military Committee:

Office Petersburg R. R. Co.,
July 23, 1861

Hon. JOHN PERKINS, JR.:

In pursuance of your suggestion, I have addressed letters to the several railroad companies in the State, calling their attention to the case of persons in the military service, on furlough, or leave by reason of sickness, and who may wish to travel for the sake of health, and desiring to know whether such persons will be allowed to travel free of charge. All of the companies from which replies had been received have responded favourably. A list of them is appended, to which my own company is added. To prevent imposition, the party to avail himself of this privilege should present a certificate from the Surgeon of his Regiment, countersigned by the Regimental commander, stating the reason of the furlough.

As I explained to you, this class of cases did not occur to any of us in the Convention of the 26th of June.[31]

Very truly, &c,
Wm. T. Joynes, President

The following is the list of railroad companies referred to in the above letter: Virginia Central Railroad Company, Richmond, Fredericksburg & Potomac Railroad Company, Richmond & York River Railroad Company, Richmond & Petersburg Railroad Company, Southside Railroad Company, Norfolk & Petersburg Railroad Company, and the Petersburg Railroad Company.

THE PUBLIC FINANCE

Mr. BROOKE, of Mississippi, presented a communication from M. J. ZUNTS,[32] of New Orleans, proposing a plan to Congress of financial policy, to make the crops of cotton, sugar and tobacco subservient as gold and silver, to create a currency, with a basis of credit in the issue of $300,000,000 Treasury notes; which was referred to the Committee on Finance. [document XXIII]

MEMORIALS TO CONGRESS

Mr. MILES, of South Carolina, presented a memorial from Edgerton & Richards, of Charleston,[33] petitioning Congress for a change in the patent law touching an interest held by them in "Wheeler & Wilson's Sewing Machine." Referred to Committee on Patents.

Mr. SCOTT, of Virginia, presented the memorial of Mr. HENRY CLAY PATE,[34] for payment for certain extra military services. Referred to Military Committee.

CLAIMS OF THE STATES FOR ADVANCES IN THE WAR

Mr. RUSSELL, of Virginia, offered the following resolution which was adopted:

> *Resolved*, That the Committee on Finance inquire into the expediency of providing for, auditing and the adjusting [of] the claims of the respective States against the Confederate States for expenditures and advances made, and to be made for carrying on the war, so that the amounts may be ascertained, while the evidence is accessible; and of providing for a time and the mode of satisfying such claims.

TREASURY NOTES

A message was received from the President returning, with his approval, an act "to authorize the appointment of agents to sign Treasury notes."[35]

THE CHURCH DEVOTIONS FOR THE WOUNDED SOLDIERS

Mr. MEMMINGER, of South Carolina, said that, with relation to the provision for the wounded,[36] a report had been made by the Secretary of the Treasury previous to the action had by Congress, on that of the select committee, and that he wished to recall the attention of the House to it by proposing a resolution to pay the expenses incurred for the comfort of the wounded out of a particular fund. He made the following report:

> Richmond, July 24, 1861
>
> Hon. HOWELL COBB, President Congress:
> Sir:
>
> A clergyman from the State of Georgia proposed, through the newspapers, that, on the Fast Day appointed by Congress, collections should be taken up in aid of the Government. [document XXIV] The proposal was acted upon without further concert, and up to this time the sum of $5,278.88 has been paid into the Treasury from their contributions. When it is considered that the proposal was made so late that it could not be known at all in many of the churches, and in none of them could previous notice have been given, the amount may be regarded as a spontaneous and gratifying indication of the sympathies of the religious communities with the Government. The source from which the money has come would make it peculiarly appropriate that it should be devoted to some object consistent with the sick and wounded. Upon some of the donations, this character has been already impressed by the donors.

I would, therefore, respectfully recommend that the amount be set apart as a fund for the use of the sick and wounded, and to that end be paid over to the committee raised by Congress to co-operate with the Mayor of Richmond in taking care of the wounded in the late battle. All of which is respectfully submitted.

C. G. Memminger
Secretary of the Treasury

The accompanying resolution, making the appropriation was adopted.[37]

There being no reports from the standing committees, the House resolved itself into secret session.

Friday, July 26, 1861

(Richmond *Examiner*, July 27, 1861, Richmond *Daily Dispatch*, July 27, 1861)

Congress met pursuant to adjournment, at 12 M., and was opened with prayer, by the Rev. Mr. JOSHUA PETERKIN,[38] of the Protestant Episcopal Church. Hon. HOWELL COBB in the Chair.

THE CHOWAN BAPTIST ASSOCIATION ON THE WAR

President COBB announced that during the recess he had received a communication from Rev. G. C. MOORE,[39] Moderator of the Chowan Baptist Association of North Carolina, conveying resolutions adopted by that body on the 18th of May, 1861, with respect to the subject of the existing war.

The resolutions were read. They concur in the action of the Baptist State Convention of Georgia, to recommend a day of humiliation and fast; and declare their confidence in the justice and moderation of the Confederate Government and the arms of our volunteer soldiers.[40]

On motion of Mr. WRIGHT, of Georgia, the resolutions were received and ordered to be spread on the journal.

THE PATENT LAWS

Mr. CURRY, of Alabama, presented the memorial of M. G. RHODES,[41] with reference to the amendment of the patent law on the subject of the revalidation of patents. Referred to the Committee on Patents.

ORGANIZATION OF THE ARMY

Mr. WRIGHT, of Georgia, asked leave to introduce a bill to amend the 8th section of an act entitled an act to provide for the public defence.

Mr. OCHILTREE, of Texas. I rise to a question of order. I think there is a resolution now in force requiring all such bills to be acted on in secret session.

The PRESIDENT. It depends upon the character of the bill.

Mr. WRIGHT. There is nothing in the bill requiring concealment. Again, the original bill has already been published.

After examining the bill, the President said it might be introduced. The bill provides that the 8th section of the original bill be amended by the addition of the following paragraph, viz: "And that, in cases where said Battalion shall consist of more companies than five, and less than ten, the President may appoint such additional officer or officers as he may deem necessary to its proper organization"

Mr. WRIGHT said the amendment provided for a difficulty the original bill failed to meet. It often happened there were companies left over after the organization of a regiment, sufficient to make a battalion. There supernumerary companies having no officer to command them, are kept inactive in the field until enough additions can be obtained to form a regiment. The amendment provided for rendering such battalions immediately serviceable by the appointment of proper officers to take charge of them.

Mr. SMITH, of Alabama. I do not believe, sir, that this House should take action on any bill affecting the organization of the army, without it being first referred to the Military Committee.

Mr. WRIGHT. I would say that the bill has the approval of the War Department. I have no objection to its reference, if the committee will report it at once.

Mr. CHESNUT moved that the bill be referred and also printed. He wished to offer some amendments to it. The bill was referred to the Military Committee.

THE CONFEDERATE LOAN

Mr. WRIGHT. Mr. President, I had intended this morning to ask the honourable Secretary of the Treasury an important question on the subject of the Confederate loan; but as I do not see him in his seat, I shall defer the subject.

MEMORIAL

Mr. PERKINS, of La., presented a memorial of Dr. P. M. ENDERS,[42] late surgeon in the U. S. Army, petitioning pay for a war warrant on the U.S. Government that that Government had refused to pay. Referred to the Committee on Claims.

Mr. BOCOCK, of Virginia, presented the memorial of Dr. A. Y. P. GARNETT,[43] petitioning an amendment of the act concerning officers of the Confederate Navy.

Mr. BOCOCK said that he would state some facts that the memorialist had omitted to state, on account of his modesty. Doctor GARNETT had, some years ago, been Assistant Surgeon in the United States Navy; but, after his marriage, removed to Washington city. He had there made himself conspicuous as an object for the distrust and annoyance of the creatures of a vile Administration, who had, at last, proceeded to the extremity of surrounding his house, menacing his life and threatening his family. Doctor GARNETT had been a devoted and fearless advocate of the Southern cause, as every member of the House, who had ever been in Washington, could attest. When he left that city, where he had obtained a position and acquired a practice, second to that of no other physician, and came to Virginia,

Gov. LETCHER had commissioned him as a Surgeon in the Navy. The act, however, of the Confederate Congress, on the subject of the reinstatement in the Confederate service of resigned United States naval officers did not embrace his case, as he had resigned his position in the Federal service some years ago. The design of the amendment asked for was to have the law extend to his case, which, he believed, was individual. He hoped it would be done; for there was no more meritorious, worthy, able and accomplished gentleman deserving the recognition of the Government than the memorialist.

The memorial was referred to the Committee on Naval Affairs.

INDEMNITY FOR SLAVES TAKEN BY THE ENEMY

Mr. SEDDON, of Virginia, offered the following resolution; which was referred to the Committee on the Judiciary:

> *Resolved by the Congress,* That the Committee on the Judiciary be instructed to inquire and report on the expediency of prescribing, by law, while the facts are fresh and susceptible of proof, some uniform mode of taking, authenticating and preserving the evidence of the abduction or reception by the enemy of slaves owned in any of the Confederate States, as also of the ages, sex and value of such slaves, to the end that indemnity may hereafter be exacted from the enemy.

THE FRANKING PRIVILEGE

Mr. RUSSELL, of Virginia, offered the following resolution; which was appropriately referred:

> *Resolved,* That the Committee on Postal Affairs inquire into the expediency of conferring the franking privilege on JOHN TYLER, formerly President of the United States.[44]

THE MEDICAL DEPARTMENT

Mr. STAPLES, of Virginia, offered the following resolutions; which were separately referred to the Military Committee:

> *Resolved,* That the Committee on Military Affairs inquire into the expediency of amending the law as to authorize officers of the Medical Department to exercise command over all enlisted men, like other commissioned officers.
>
> *Resolved,* That the Committee on Military Affairs inquire into the expediency of so amending the law; as to authorize the Secretary of War to employ a messenger for the office of the Surgeon-General.

PROVISIONS FOR FEDERAL NAVAL OFFICERS FORMERLY RESIGNED

Mr. AVERY, of North Carolina, said that, with reference to the memorial of Dr. GARNETT, offered by the gentleman from Virginia, his was not an individual case. Among the officers in the Federal naval service, who had resigned some years ago, not in consequence of the secession of their States, were a number of citizens of North Carolina, who had been appointed by the Governor of that State to their former ranks, before North Carolina had surrendered her Navy to the Confederate Government. He proposed to introduce a bill to include such cases, and to settle their relative ranks in the Confederate naval service; and he asked that it be referred to the Committee on Naval Affairs.

AN ACT TO FURTHER AMEND AN ACT TO PROVIDE FOR THE REORGANIZATION OF THE NAVY, APPROVED MARCH 16, 1861

The Congress of the Confederate States of America do enact, That the President be and is hereby authorized to nominate, and by and with the consent of Congress to appoint all officers of the navies of any of the States of this Confederacy, who have been officers of the United States Navy, and who may be fit for active service, to the same rank and position in the Navy of the Confederate States which they would have held in the Navy of the United States, by the ordinary course of promotion therein, if they had remained in the said United States Navy until the date of their said appointment in the Confederate Navy: *Provided, however,* that no such officer shall be appointed to a higher rank or position than he has held in the State Navy to which he has been attached and, *Provided further,* That no such officer shall be appointed a captain, commander, lieutenant, or sailing-master in the line of promotion, who did not hold, at the time of leaving the United States Navy, one of the said ranks, or the rank of passed midshipman therein; or in default thereof, shall have seen at least six years of sea service in the navy and merchant service combined, and shall, before receiving his commission, successfully pass an examination before a Naval Examining Board, composed of captains or commanders to be designated by the Secretary of the Navy, touching his fitness for said appointment, in which case the officer so passed may be nominated and commissioned to a rank not higher than that of Lieutenant, *And, provided further,* that no officer shall be appointed, by authority of this act, who may at any time have committed any act of hostility against the Confederate States, or any one thereof.

SEC. 2. *And be it further enacted,* That in case any such officers of any State Navy or Navies, as are comprised in the first section of this act, should receive appointments in the Navy of the Confederate States, the President is authorized to affix to their commissions such dates as may be necessary to secure to them the same relative position that they held, or at the date of their said appointment would have held as aforesaid, in the Navy of the United States.

The bill was so referred.

There being no business on the public calendar, Congress resolved itself into secret session.[45]

Saturday, July 27, 1861[46]

Monday, July 29, 1861
(Richmond *Examiner*, July 30, 1861)
Congress met at 12 o'clock. Prayer was offered by Rev. J. A. DUNCAN.[47]

RE-ORGANIZATION OF THE COMMITTEES

The following are the standing committees of Congress as re-organized by President COBB consequence of the addition of the newly-elected delegates:

To Arrange for Government Buildings.—Messrs. SHORTER, CHILTON, MCRAE.

On Permanent Constitution.—Messrs. RHETT, CHESNUT, WALKER, SMITH, MORTON, OWENS, TOOMBS, COBB, T. R. R., DECLOUET, SPARROW, HARRIS.

On Flag and Seal of the Confederacy.—Messrs. MILES, SHORTER, MORTON, SPARROW, HARRISON.

To Organize the Executive Departments.—Messrs. STEPHENS, CONRAD, BOYCE, SHORTER, BROOKE.

On Foreign Affairs.—Messrs. RHETT, NISBET, PERKINS, WALKER, KEITT, WIGFALL, RIVES, MASON, VENABLE.

On Finance.—Messrs. TOOMBS, BARNWELL, KENNER, BARRY, MCRAE, HEMPHILL, HUNTER, MOREHEAD, SEDDON.

On Commercial Affairs.—Messrs. CRAWFORD, DECLOUET, MORTON, CURRY, MILES, WAUL, WATKINS, DAVIS of N.C., MACFARLAND.

On the Judiciary.—Messrs. HALE, COBB, T. R. R., HARRIS, OLDHAM, BROCKENBROUGH, SMITH of Alabama, SCOTT, CRAIGE, GARLAND.

On Naval Affairs.—Messrs. CONRAD, CHESNUT, SMITH of Alabama, WRIGHT, OWENS, OLDHAM, BOCOCK, PURYEAR, RUFFIN.

On Military Affairs.—Messrs. MILES, SPARROW, KENAN, GREGG, WARD, STAPLES, PRESTON, W. B., AVERY.

On Postal Affairs.—Messrs. CHILTON, BOYCE, HILL, HARRISON, CURRY, OCHILTREE, RUST, SMITH of N.C., JOHNSON of Va.

On Patents.—Messrs. BROOKE, JONES, HILL, KENNER, ORR of Miss., McDOWELL, RUSSELL.

On Territories.—Messrs. CHESNUT, CAMPBELL, MARSHALL, NISBET, OCHILTREE, DAVIS of Ala., OLDHAM, THOMASSON, PRESTON, WALTER.

On Public Lands.—Messrs. MARSHALL, HARRIS, WRIGHT, DAVIS of Ala., WARD, GARLAND, RUSSELL.

On Indian Affairs.—Messrs. MORTON, HALE, KEITT, SPARROW, WAUL, JONES, JOHNSON of Ark., DAVIDSON.

On Printing.—Messrs. T. R. R. COBB, HARRISON, MILES, CHILTON, PERKINS, PRYOR.

On Accounts.—Messrs. DECLOUET, CAMPBELL, SMITH, CRAWFORD, GREGG.

On Engrossments.—Messrs. SHORTER, KENAN, McRAE, ORR.

On Pay and Mileage.—Messrs. CAMPBELL, DAVIS of Alabama, OCHILTREE.

On Claims.—Messrs. GREGG, HILL, MARSHALL, ORR of Mississippi, WARD, JONES.

In pursuance of the rule adopted by the House, Congress resolved itself into secret session.

Tuesday, July 30, 1861[48]

Wednesday, July 31, 1861

(Richmond *Examiner*, August 1, 1861)

Congress met at 12 o'clock. Prayer was made Reverend Mr. READ.[49]

The House was called to order by Vice-President STEPHENS, who took the Chair.

THE CHURCH DONATIONS

The resolution heretofore referred to the Military Committee, to appropriate the church donations made on the last fast day (amounting to $5,278.88) as a fund for the use of the wounded at the late battle at Manassas, was reported back, with some slight amendments, and passed. The resolution, as passed, directs the disbursement and application of the fund to be made by the Secretary of the Treasury, with the concurrence of the Chairman of the Committee of the House.[50]

FIRST NORTH CAROLINA REGIMENT

The following resolution was introduced by Mr. AVERY, of North Carolina, and passed.

Resolved by the Congress of the Confederate States of America, That the President be and he is hereby authorized to receive and muster into the service of the Confederate States of America the First Regiment of North Carolina Volunteers, now stationed at Yorktown, for the term of six months from the time they were sworn in and mustered into the service of North Carolina, and to discharge them after the expiration of that period; said period to commence at the time the first company of said Regiment was mustered into the service of North Carolina.

Resolved, further, That the Cadets from the North Carolina Institute, at Charlotte, who may have been acting with said Regiment, be mustered into service in the same manner as the residue of the Regiment, and recognized as part thereof, with the pay of privates.

Congress went into secret session.

Thursday, August 1, 1861[51]

Friday, August 2, 1861

(Richmond *Examiner*, August 3, 1861)

Congress met at 12 o'clock. Prayer was made by Reverend Mr. HENDERSON.[52]

Vice-President STEPHENS took the Chair; and, under the general order, the House resolved itself into secret session.

Saturday, August 3, 1861

(Richmond *Examiner*, August 5, 1861)

Congress met at 12 o'clock. After the usual prayer, the body resolved itself into secret session.

Monday, August 5, 1861—Wednesday, August 28, 1861[53]

Thursday, August 29, 1861

(Richmond *Enquirer*, August 30, 1861)

Congress being in open session, Mr. CRAWFORD, of Ga., in the chair.

Mr. CHILTON, of Ala., rose and said that he desired to offer a resolution which he felt assured would meet with the cordial approval of each member of the body. The session, he said, was about drawing to a close, and before Congress will have assembled again, its President HOWELL COBB, will be in the tented field commanding a regiment of gallant volunteers, engaged in battling for the liberties of our infant republic.[54] The impartial and able manner in which he has discharged his duty and his courteous and dignified deportment towards his peers have not only contributed much to the unparalleled harmony and unanimity which had characterized the proceedings of Congress, but have secured for him our admiration as an officer and esteem as a friend. He was, Mr. President, the first to sign the great charter of our rights. He goes now to seal that charter with his blood.

Amid the fortunes of this fratricidal war which is being waged against us—a war the results of which none but the wickedly blind can fail to foresee, "bonds and afflictions" may await this apostle of our liberty. But whatever may be his condition, however trying the circumstances in which he may be placed, it will be a source of pleasure, as fixed as the events of the past, that he shares so unreservedly the confidence and esteem, not only of the members of this body, but of the whole country. Aye, sir, of a country as certainly destined to be free and independent as that Almighty God will vindicate the right.

He may borrow from the past a joyous light to illuminate the darkest future, and say:

> Come cold or hot, or rain or shine,
> The days that have been mine, are mine.
> Not e'en the Fates upon the past have power;
> What has been, has been; I have had my hour.

The members of this Congress have, as individuals, provided the amplest means for carrying into effect the resolutions which I now offer for adoption:

> *Resolved unanimously*, That the President of the Confederated States of America is hereby requested to cause to be prepared a stand of colours and sword, to be furnished and paid for out of the fund placed at the disposal of the President by the contribution of the members of this body, to be presented to Col. HOWELL COBB as a testimonial of the high esteem in which his patriotic services are held by the members of the Confederate Congress.

The resolution was unanimously adopted.

Friday, August 30, 1861

(Richmond *Examiner*, August 31, 1861)

President COBB made a brief speech in open session, returning his thanks to the members of the body for their complimentary notice of his intended departure for the seat of war, made in his absence the day before. He said:

> *Gentlemen of Congress*: Allow me to interrupt, for a single moment, the usual course of business. If, gentlemen, you could read the response which

my heart has already made to the resolution you were pleased to adopt during my absence from the chair on yesterday, I should remain silent this morning; for words cannot express the feelings which this renewed evidence of your kindness and confidence has excited.

Since the first hours of our meeting to the present moment, approaching the closing hours of this session, I have received from you such repeated marks of your friendly regard as no presiding officer ever received from his associates. Be assured, gentlemen, they will be borne in grateful remembrance; and in the new field to which I have been called—not by taste or ambition. but by the stern requirements of duty—they will greatly strengthen my heart, and, I trust, under the protecting guidance of a kind Providence, nerve my arm to the discharge of the humble part which I may be summoned to perform.

In the sincerity of my heart I believe that man was never engaged in a more just and holy cause than the one which has called our people to the defence of their homes, their families and their firesides, and that the Supreme Ruler of the earth will continue to manifest His favour towards us, hitherto so remarkable.

With this full conviction, I go forward to the discharge of a solemn and imperative duty.

Accept, gentlemen, my sincere thanks; and permit me to add, in behalf of the brave and true men under my command, in whose hands your banner will be placed, that I feel authorised to say, you will never have cause to regret the confidence you have shown in their valour and patriotism.

Saturday, August 31, 1861[55]

FOURTH SESSION

(RICHMOND, VIRGINIA, SEPTEMBER 3, 1861)

Tuesday, September 3, 1861

(Richmond *Enquirer*, September 3, 1861; Richmond *Examiner*, September 4, 1861)

PROCLAMATION BY THE PRESIDENT OF THE
CONFEDERATE STATES OF AMERICA

Whereas, through accident, a bill to authorize the President to continue the appointments made by him in the military and naval service during the recess of Congress or the present session, and to submit them to Congress at its next session, failed to be delivered to the President for his signature prior to the adjournment of Congress; and whereas the failure of said bill to become a law would cause serious inconvenience to the public service:

Now, therefore, I, JEFFERSON DAVIS, President of the Confederate States, do issue this my Proclamation, convoking the Congress of the Confederate States for the transaction of business, at the Capitol, in the city of Richmond, on the 3d day of September, at 12 o'clock noon, of that day, of which all who shall at that time be entitled to act as members of that body are hereby required to take notice.

Given under my hand and the seal of the Confederate States, at Richmond, this 2d day of September, Anno Domini, 1861.

By the President: JEFFERSON DAVIS
R. M. T. HUNTER, Secretary of State

Congress assembled yesterday at 12 M., in obedience to a proclamation of President Davis, issued September 3d, 1861, convening said body for the purpose of taking action on a bill empowering the President to make appointments in the Army and Navy, which had failed to be reported to him during the late session.

Hon. HOWELL COBB in the Chair.

The session was opened with prayer by Rev. Mr. FLYNN,[1] of Georgia.

The roll being called, the following named members were ascertained to be present:

From Alabama—Mr. SHORTER.

Arkansas—Mr. JOHNSON.
Florida—Messrs. MORETON and WARD.
Georgia—Messrs. HOWELL COBB and THOS. R. R. COBB.
Louisiana—Mr. DE CLOUT.
Mississippi—Mr. HARRIS.
North Carolina—Mr. CRAIG.
South Carolina—Mr. MILES.
Texas—Messrs. REAGAN, HEMPHILL, WAUL, OLDHAM and OCHILTREE.
Tennessee—Mr. HUGHES.
Virginia—Messrs. PRESTON, HUNTER, MACFARLAND and BROCKENBROUGH.

The PRESIDENT declared a quorum present.

On motion of Mr. MILES, a committee of three was appointed by the Chair to wait upon President DAVIS and inform him that Congress was ready to receive from him such communication as be might be pleased to make. The committee, returning, reported they had discharged their duties, and the President would send in a communication in writing.

The following message from the President was reported to Congress by Mr. JOSSELYN, his private secretary:

> Gentlemen of Congress—The bill important to the public service, being one to continue in office persons who had been appointed and nominated, and whose nominations had not been acted upon, was, I learned after your adjournment on the 31st ultimo, engrossed for my signature, but by some accident was not delivered to me, and thus failed to become a law; wherefore it has become necessary to convene you.
>
> You may either make the provisions contemplated, or, by acting upon the nominations, or otherwise, as in your judgment may seem best, relieve the Government of the embarrassment to which otherwise it must be subjected.

Mr. MILES introduced a bill to authorize the President to continue the appointments already made by him in the military and naval service during the recesses of Congress or at the last and the present sessions, and submit them to Congress at its next session.

The bill was read three several times, and passed unanimously.

Mr. REAGAN, on leave, introduced a bill supplemental and amendatory of a bill in relation to the pre-payment of postage, which was passed.[2]

The above bills being reported as signed by the President.

On motion of Mr. WAUL, Congress adjourned to meet on the third Monday in November, unless sooner called together.

FIFTH SESSION

(RICHMOND, VIRGINIA, NOVEMBER 18, 1861, TO FEBRUARY 17, 1862)

Monday, November 18, 1861

(Charleston *Mercury*, November 19, 1861)

The Congress of the Confederate States met to-day. There was barely a quorum present, and an adjournment took place without any business having been transacted. The President's Message will be sent in to-morrow.

Tuesday, November 19, 1861

(Charleston *Mercury*, November 20, 1861)

In Congress to-day, nothing of importance transpired, beyond the reception of the President's Message. That document is as follows:

PRESIDENT'S MESSAGE

To the Congress of the Confederate States:

The few weeks which have elapsed since your adjournment have brought us so near the close of the year that we are now able to sum up its general results. The retrospect is such as should fill the hearts of our people with gratitude to Providence for his kind interposition in their behalf. Abundant yields have rewarded the labor of the agriculturist, whilst the manufacturing industry of the Confederate States was never so prosperous as now. The necessities of the times have called into existence new branches of manufactures and given a fresh impulse to the activity of those heretofore in operation. The means of the Confederate States for manufacturing the necessaries and comforts of life within themselves increase as the conflict continues, and we are gradually becoming independent of the rest of the world for the supply of such military stores and munitions as are indispensable for war.

The operations of the Army, soon to be partially interrupted by the approaching winter, have afforded a protection to the country and shed a luster upon its arms through the trying vicissitudes of more than one arduous campaign which entitle our brave volunteers to our praise and our gratitude. From its commencement to the present period the war has been enlarging its proportions and expanding its boundaries so as to include new fields. The conflict now extends from the shores of the Chesapeake to the confines of Missouri and Arizona; yet sudden calls from the remotest points for military aid have been met with promptness enough not only to avert disaster in the face of superior numbers, but also to roll back the tide of invasion from the border.

When the war commenced the enemy were possessed of certain strategic points and strong places within the Confederate States. They greatly exceeded us in numbers, in available resources, and in the supplies necessary for war. Military establishments had been long organized and were complete; the Navy, and for the most part the Army, once common to both, were in their possession. To meet all this we had to create not only an Army in the face of war itself, but also the military establishments necessary to equip and place it in the field. It ought indeed to be a subject of gratulation that the spirit of the volunteers and the patriotism of the people have enabled us, under Providence, to grapple successfully with these difficulties. A succession of glorious victories at Bethel, Bull Run, Manassas, Springfield, Lexington, Leesburg, and Belmont has checked the wicked invasion which greed of gain and the unhallowed lust of power brought upon our soil, and has proved that numbers cease to avail when directed against a people fighting for the sacred right of self-government and the privileges of freemen. After more than seven months of war the enemy have not only failed to extend their occupancy of our soil, but new States and Territories have been added to our Confederacy, while, instead of their threatened march of unchecked conquest, they have been driven, at more than one point, to assume the defensive, and, upon a fair comparison between the two belligerents as to men, military means, and financial condition, the Confederate States are relatively much stronger now than when the struggle commenced.

Since your adjournment the people of Missouri have conducted the war in the face of almost unparalleled difficulties with a spirit and success alike worthy of themselves and of the great cause in which they are struggling. Since that time Kentucky, too, has become the theater of active hostilities. The Federal forces have not only refused to acknowledge her right to be neutral, and have insisted upon making her a party to the war, but have invaded her for the purpose of attacking the Confederate States. Outrages of the most despotic character have been perpetrated upon her people; some of her most eminent citizens have been seized and borne away to languish in foreign prisons, without knowing who were their accusers or the specific charges made against them, while others have been forced to abandon their homes, families, and property, and seek a refuge in distant lands.

Finding that the Confederate States were about to be invaded through Kentucky, and that her people, after being deceived into a mistaken security, were unarmed and in danger of being subjugated by the Federal forces, our armies were marched into that State to repel the enemy and prevent their occupation of certain strategic points which would have given them great advantages in the contest—a step which was justified not only by the necessities of self-defense on the part of the Confederate States, but also by a desire to aid the people of Kentucky. It was never intended by the Confederate Government to conquer or coerce the people of that State; but, on the contrary, it was declared by our generals that they would withdraw their troops if the Federal Government would do likewise. Proclamation was also made of the desire to respect the neutrality of Kentucky and the intention to abide by the wishes of her people as soon as they were free to express their opinions. These declarations were approved by me, and I should regard it as one of the best effects of the march of our troops into Kentucky if it should end in giving to her people liberty of choice and a free opportunity to decide their own destiny according to their own will.

The Army has been chiefly instrumental in prosecuting the great contest in which we are engaged, but the Navy has also been effective in full proportion to its means. The naval officers, deprived to a great extent of an opportunity to make their professional skill available at sea, have served with commendable zeal and gallantry on shore and upon inland waters, further detail of which will be found in the reports of the Secretaries of the Navy and War. In the transportation of the mails many difficulties have arisen, which will be found fully developed in the report of the Postmaster General. The absorption of the ordinary means of transportation for the movements of troops and military supplies; the insufficiency of the rolling stock of railroads for the accumulation of business resulting both from military operations and the obstruction of water communication by the presence of the enemy's fleet; the failure, and even refusal, of contractors to comply with the terms of their agreements; the difficulties inherent in inaugurating so vast and complicated a system as that which requires postal facilities for every town and village in a territory so extended as ours, have all combined to impede the best-directed efforts of the Postmaster General, whose zeal, industry, and ability have been taxed to the utmost extent.

Some of these difficulties can only be overcome by time and an improved condition of the country upon the restoration of peace, but others may be remedied by legislation, and your attention is invited to the recommendations contained in the report of the head of that Department.

The condition of the Treasury will doubtless be a subject of anxious inquiry on your part. I am happy to say that the financial system already adopted has worked well so far, and promises good results for the future. To the extent that Treasury notes may be issued the Government is enabled to borrow money without interest, and thus facilitate the conduct of the war. This extent is measured by the portion of the field of circulation which these notes can be made to occupy. The proportion of the field thus occupied depends again upon the amount of the debts for which they are receivable; and when dues, not only to the Confederate and State governments, but also to corporations and individuals, are payable in this medium, a large amount of it may be circulated at par. There is every reason to believe that the Confederate Treasury note is fast becoming such a medium. The provision that these notes shall be convertible into Confederate stock bearing 8 per cent interest, at the pleasure of the holder, insures them against a depreciation below the value of that stock, and no considerable fall in that value need be feared so long as the interest shall be punctually paid. The punctual payment of this interest has been secured by the act passed by you at the last session, imposing such a rate of taxation as must provide sufficient means for that purpose.

For the successful prosecution of this war it is indispensable that the means of transporting troops and military supplies be furnished, as far as possible, in such manner as not to interrupt the commercial intercourse between our people nor place a check on their productive energies. To this end the means of transportation from one section of our country to the other must be carefully guarded and improved. And this should be the object of anxious care on the part of State and Confederate governments, so far as they may have power over the subject.

We have already two main systems of through transportation from the north to the south—one from Richmond along the seaboard; the other through Western Virginia to New Orleans. A third might be secured by completing a link of about forty miles between Danville, in Virginia, and Greensboro, in North Carolina. The construction of this comparatively short line would give us a through route from north to south in the interior of the Confederate States and give us access to a population and to military resources from which we are now in great measure debarred. We should increase greatly the safety and capacity of our means for transporting men and military supplies. If the construction of this road should, in the judgment of Congress as it is in mine, be indispensable for the most successful prosecution of the war, the action of the Government will not be restrained by the constitutional objection which would attach to a work for commercial purposes, and attention is invited to the practicability of securing its early completion by giving the needful aid to the company organized for its construction and administration.

If we husband our means and make a judicious use of our resources, it would be difficult to fix a limit to the period during which we could conduct a war against the adversary whom we now encounter. The very efforts which he makes to isolate and invade us must exhaust his means, whilst they serve to complete the circle and diversify the productions of our industrial system. The reconstruction which he seeks to effect by arms becomes daily more and more palpably impossible. Not only do the causes which induced us to separate still exist in full force, but they have been strengthened, and whatever doubt may have lingered in the minds of any must have been completely dispelled by subsequent events. If instead of being a dissolution of a league it were indeed a rebellion in which we are engaged, we might find ample vindication for the course we have adopted in the scenes which are now being enacted in the United States. Our people now look with contemptuous astonishment on those with whom they had been so recently associated. They shrink with aversion from the bare idea of renewing such a connection. When they see a President making war without the assent of Congress; when they behold judges threatened because they maintain the writ of habeas corpus so sacred to freemen; when they see justice and law trampled under the armed heel of military authority, and upright men and innocent women dragged to distant dungeons upon the mere edict of a despot; when they find all this tolerated and applauded by a people who had been in the full enjoyment of freedom but a few months ago—they believe that there must be some radical incompatibility between such a people and themselves. With such a people we may be content to live at peace, but the separation is final, and for the independence we have asserted we will accept no alternative.

The nature of the hostilities which they have waged against us must be characterized as barbarous wherever it is understood. They have bombarded undefended villages without giving notice to women and children to enable them to escape, and in one instance selected the night as the period when they might surprise them most effectually whilst asleep and unsuspicious of danger. Arson and rapine, the destruction of private houses and property, and injuries of the most wanton character, even upon noncombatants, have marked their forays along our borders and upon our territory. Although we ought to have been admonished by these things that they were disposed to make war upon us in the most cruel and relentless spirit, yet we were not prepared to see them fit out a large naval expedition, with the confessed purpose not only to pillage, but to incite a servile insurrection in our midst. If they convert their soldiers into incendiaries and robbers, and involve us in a species of war which claims noncombatants, women, and children as its victims, they must expect to be treated as outlaws and enemies of mankind. There are certain rights of humanity which are entitled to respect even in war, and he who refuses to regard them forfeits his claims, if captured, to be considered as a prisoner of war, but must expect to be dealt with as an offender against all law, human and divine.

But not content with violating our rights under the law of nations at home, they have extended these injuries to us within other jurisdictions. The distinguished gentlemen whom, with your approval at the last session, I commissioned to represent the Confederacy at certain foreign courts, have been recently seized by the captain of a U.S. ship of war on board a British steamer on their voyage from the neutral Spanish port of Havana to England. The United States have thus claimed a general jurisdiction over the high seas, and entering a British ship, sailing under its country's flag, violated the rights of embassy, for the most part held sacred even amongst barbarians, by seizing our ministers whilst under the protection and within the dominions of a neutral nation. These gentlemen were as much under the jurisdiction of the British Government upon that ship and beneath its flag as if they had been on its soil, and a claim on the part of the United States to seize them in the streets of London would have been as well founded as that to apprehend them where they were taken. Had they been malefactors and citizens even of the United States they could not have been arrested on a British ship or on British soil, unless under the express provisions of a treaty and according to the forms therein provided for the extradition of criminals.

But rights the most sacred seem to have lost all respect in their eyes. When Mr. FAULKNER, a former minister of the United States to France, commissioned before the secession of Virginia, his native State, returned in good faith to Washington to settle his accounts and fulfill all the obligations into which he had entered, he was perfidiously arrested and imprisoned in New York, where he now is.[1] The unsuspecting confidence with which he reported to his Government was abused, and his desire to fulfill his trust to them was used to his injury. In conducting this war we have sought no aid and proposed no alliances offensive and defensive abroad. We have asked for a recognized place in the great family of nations, but in doing so we have demanded nothing for which we did not offer a fair equivalent. The advantages of intercourse are mutual amongst nations, and in seeking to establish diplomatic relations we were only endeavoring to place that intercourse under the regulation of public law. Perhaps we had the right, if we had chosen to exercise it, to ask to know whether the principle that "blockades to be binding must be effectual," so solemnly announced by the great powers of Europe at Paris, is to be generally enforced or applied only to particular parties.[2] When the Confederate States, at your last session, became a party to the declaration reaffirming this principle of international law, which has been recognized so long by publicists and governments, we certainly supposed that it was to be universally enforced. The customary law of nations is made up of their practice rather than their declarations; and if such declarations are only to be enforced in particular instances at the pleasure of those who make them, then the commerce of the world, so far from being placed under the regulation of a general law, will become subject to the caprice of those who execute or suspend it at will. If such is to be the course of nations in regard to this law, it is plain that it will thus become a rule for the weak and not for the strong.

Feeling that such views must be taken by the neutral nations of the earth, I have caused the evidence to be collected which proves completely the utter inefficiency of the proclaimed blockade of our coast, and shall direct it to be laid before such governments as shall afford us the means of being heard. But, although we should be benefited by the enforcement of this law so solemnly declared by the great powers of Europe, we are not dependent on that enforcement for the successful prosecution of the war. As long as hostilities continue the Confederate States will exhibit a steadily increasing capacity to furnish their troops with food, clothing, and arms. If they should be forced to forego many of the luxuries and some of the comforts of life, they will at least have the consolation of knowing that they are thus daily becoming more and more independent of the rest of the world. If in this process labor in the Confederate States should be gradually diverted from those great Southern staples which have given life to so much of the commerce of mankind into other channels, so as to make them rival producers instead of profitable customers, they will not be the only or even the chief losers by this change in the direction of their industry. Although it is true that the cotton supply from the Southern States could only be totally cut off by the subversion of our social system, yet it is plain that a long continuance of this blockade might, by a diversion of labor and an investment of capital in other employments, so diminish the supply as to bring ruin upon all those interests of foreign countries which are dependent on that staple. For every laborer who is diverted from the culture of cotton in the South, perhaps four times as many elsewhere, who have found subsistence in the various employments growing out of its use, will be forced also to change their occupation.

While the war which is waged to take from us the right of self-government can never attain that end, it remains to be seen how far it may work a revolution in the industrial system of the world, which may carry suffering to other lands as well as to our own.

In the meantime we shall continue this struggle in humble dependence upon Providence, from whose searching scrutiny we cannot conceal the secrets of our hearts, and to whose rule we confidently submit our destinies. For the rest we shall depend upon ourselves. Liberty is always won where there exists the unconquerable will to be free, and we have reason to know the strength that is given by a conscious sense not only of the magnitude but of the righteousness of our cause.

Jefferson Davis

Thursday, November 21, 1861

(Richmond *Daily Dispatch*, November 22, 1861)

Congress met, and, in the absence of its Chairman, Hon. HOWELL COBB, was called to order by Mr. MEMMINGER, member from South Carolina, who stated that Col. COBB had left the city to resume command of his regiment, and moved Mr. BOCOCK, member from Virginia, take the chair, which motion was carried, and Mr. BOCOCK took his seat as presiding officer.

Prayer was offered by Rev. Dr. HOGE, of Richmond.

The Clerk read the journal of Tuesday, and upon a call of the roll of States, it was found that three additional members answered to their names, viz: Messrs. ROBT. H. SMITH, WALKER, and JONES, of Alabama.

Congress then went into secret session.

Friday, November 22, 1861

(Charleston *Mercury*, November 23, 1861)

Congress met this morning, Vice-President STEPHENS in the Chair. After prayer, and the reading of the Journal, the body went into secret session.

Monday, November 25, 1861

(Augusta *Daily Constitutionalist*, November 26, 1861)

Congress was in secret session to-day. It is reported that several important resolutions were presented, and referred to the Committees on Finance, Commerce, and the Judiciary.

Tuesday, November 26, 1861—Wednesday, November 27, 1861[3]

Thursday, November 28, 1861

(Augusta *Daily Constitutionalist*, November 29, 1861)

The President, to-day, signed the bill admitting Missouri into the Southern Confederacy.

Congress has done nothing of importance so far as its business has transpired.

Friday, November 29, 1861

(Charleston *Mercury*, November 30, 1861)

The proceedings to-day were not important, so far as known.

Saturday, November 30, 1861[4]

Monday, December 2, 1861

(Charleston *Mercury*, December 3, 1861; Augusta *Chronicle*, December 4, 1861)

There was nothing in public in Congress to-day

Messrs. BELL, VEST and CONRAD, to-day to their seats as Members of Congress from Missouri. Other members from that State are *en route* hither.

Tuesday, December 3, 1861—Wednesday, December 4, 1861[5]

Thursday, December 5, 1861

(Charleston *Mercury*, December 6, 1861)

In Congress, to-day, Hon. HOWELL COBB, having returned, resumed his seat as President. WM. M. COOK and THOS. W. FREEMAN, members from Missouri, and A[LEXANDER]. B. BRADFORD, in place of Judge CLAYTON, of Mississippi, took their seats. The other business was in secret session.

Friday, December 6, 1861

(Charleston *Mercury*, December 7, 1861; Richmond *Daily Dispatch*, December 7, 1861)

In Congress to-day, Hon. THOS. H. HARRIS, from Missouri, appeared and took his seat. The President returned, with his approval, the resolution of thanks to Major-General POLK and Brigadier-Generals CHEATHAM and PILLOW, and to the troops under their command, for the victory gained at Belmont.[6] Messrs. CLARK and PRESTON, who were elected Senators by the Missouri Legislature, were admitted to seats on the floor, as delegates from the State at large.

> RESOLUTIONS OF THANKS TO MAJOR-GENERAL LEONIDAS POLK, BRIGADIER-GENERAL GIDEON J. PILLOW, BRIGADIER-GENERAL BENJAMIN F. CHEATHAM, AND THE OFFICERS AND SOLDIERS UNDER THEIR COMMAND, FOR GALLANT AND DISTINGUISHED SERVICES IN THE PRESENT WAR:
>
> *Whereas*, under the providence of God, the valour of the soldiers of the Confederate States has added another glorious victory, achieved at Belmont, in the State of Missouri, on the seventh day of November last, to those which had been so graciously vouchsafed to our arms, whereby the reduction of Columbus, in the State of Kentucky, has been prevented, and the contemplated descent of the enemy down the Mississippi river effectively stayed; Therefore,
>
> *Be it Resolved*, by the Congress of the Confederate States of America, That Maj.-Gen. LEONIDAS POLK, Brig.-Gen. GIDEON J. PILLOW, Brig.-Gen.

BENJAMIN F. CHEATHAM, and the officers and soldiers of their gallant commands, for the desperate courage they exhibited in sustaining for several hours, and under most disadvantageous circumstances, an attack by a force of the enemy greatly superior to their own, both in numbers and appointments; and for the skill and gallantry by which they converted what at first threatened so much disaster, into a triumphant victory.

Resolved further, That these resolutions are intended to express what is believed to be the grateful and admitting sentiment of the whole people of the Confederacy.

Resolved further, That they be communicated to the commands of Major General POLK, Brigadier General PILLOW, and Brigadier General CHEATHAM, by the proper Department of the Government.

Saturday, December 7, 1861—Wednesday, December 11, 1861[7]

Thursday, December 12, 1861

(Charleston *Mercury*, December 13, 1861)

Congress transacted no business in open session.

Friday, December 13, 1861

(Augusta *Chronicle*, December 14, 1861)

In Congress, to-day President DAVIS sent the following message to Congress:

To the Congress of the Confederate States:
The calamity which has laid to ashes a large portion of the city of Charleston,[8] calls for our sympathy, and seems to justify the offer of aid, in the manner hereinafter suggested. The State of South Carolina will, no doubt, desire to assist the people of Charleston, in their hour of need; but as her resources are now taxed to the utmost in resisting the invasion of her soil, the prompt intervention of this Government may not be deemed unsuitable to the occasion. The State of South Carolina, in common with the other States, has made liberal advances on account of the war, and this Government is, unquestionably largely her debtor. With the existing pressure upon her resources, it is probable that her desire to aid the suffering city of Charleston may be restrained by other demands upon her available means.

Under such circumstances, may we not exhibit our sympathy with her people by an offer to place at the control of the Legislature of that State, now in session, a portion of the sum we owe her? The magnitude of her calamities affords a reason for making an exception in her favor; and promptness of action will manifest in the most appropriate manner the sincerity of our regard for the people of that gallant State, and our entire sympathy in all that concerns them. I recommend, therefore, that Congress make an appropriation, of such an amount as may be deemed sufficient for the purpose proposed, to be placed at the control of the authorities of the State of South Carolina.

JEFFERSON DAVIS

In Congress, Mr. KENNER, of Louisiana, offered the following resolution, which was unanimously adopted:

A RESOLUTION TO MAKE AN ADVANCE TO THE STATE OF SOUTH CAROLINA, ON ACCOUNT OF HER CLAIMS AGAINST THE CONFEDERATE STATES:

Resolved, That the sum of $250,000 be, and is hereby appropriated as an advance on account of any claims of the State of South Carolina upon the Confederate States, and that the same be paid to such person as may be authorized by the Legislature of South Carolina to receive the same.

The following confirmations were made by Congress to-day:

Commissioners under the Sequestration Act—GEO. P. SCARBOROUGH, of Virginia, THOS. C. REYNOLDS, of Missouri, and WALTER BROOKE, of Mississippi

Confederate District Attorney—JOHN C. NICHOLL, for Georgia, and W. M. RANDOLPH for the Eastern District of Arkansas.

Saturday, December 14, 1861

(Augusta *Chronicle*, December 15, 1861)

Congress did nothing in public to-day.

Monday, December 16, 1861

(Richmond *Enquirer*, December 17, 1861; Charleston *Courier*, December 17, 1861)

Before Congress went into secret session . . . Mr. SEDDON, member from Virginia, announced the presence of Messrs. MONROE and BURNETT, delegates from the State of Kentucky.

The former is the venerable Judge MONROE, who was compelled to abandon his family and home in Kentucky and seek refuge where a man for opinion's sake is not proscribed.[9]

The President (*pro. tem.*) of Congress, J. W. BOCOCK, administered to the delegates the oath of fidelity to the Constitution of the Confederate States, and the delegates took their seats as duly qualified members of Congress.

We understand ten delegates in all have been sent to represent Kentucky in the Provisional Congress.

A large number of military appointments were confirmed and will be published in the Army register.

Tuesday, December 17, 1861—Tuesday, December 24, 1861[10]

Monday, December 30, 1861

(Richmond *Daily Dispatch*, December 31, 1861)

Congress reassembled [today] at twelve o'clock, and immediately went into secret session. Messrs. THOMAS and BURNETT, members from the state of Kentucky, appeared, were qualified, and took their seats.

Tuesday, December 31, 1861

(Charleston *Mercury*, January 1, 1862)

The proceedings of Congress to-day were secret.

Thursday, January 2, 1862

(Camden [SC] *Confederate*, January 10, 1862)

In Congress to-day, DANIEL P. WHITE, of Kentucky, qualified and took his seat. The proceedings otherwise unimportant. It is reported that the Committee of Congress will report measures and suggestions taken from the French army system.[11]

Friday, January 3, 1862—Saturday, January 4, 1862[12]

Monday, January 6, 1862

(Augusta *Daily Constitutionalist*, January 7, 1862; Richmond *Enquirer*, January 10, 1862)

In Congress, eulogies were pronounced over the death of Judge HEMPHILL, by OCHILTREE, of Texas, JOHNSON, of Arkansas, BOYCE, of South Carolina, and VENABLE, of North Carolina.[13]

Mr. OCHILTREE. As Senior Delegate from the State of Texas, the melancholy duty devolves on me to announce the death of our colleague, the Hon. JOHN HEMPHILL. Death, sir, is at all times a dread visitant, but when a warm, sincere and devoted friend is snatched away the great depths of the heart are stirred up.—Such is my feeling upon the present occasion.

I have known the deceased intimately for the period of twenty-two years; during this period it has been my lot to share with him duties of a great and extraordinary character, and I take this occasion to bear witness that a purer, better man, a nobler specimen of the hardy sense of duty, I have never known. About this time twenty years ago I took my seat by the side of the deceased upon the bench of the Supreme Court of the Republic of Texas. He was the successor of the lamented RUSK.

It is a fact not generally known out of the range of our earlier settlers, that General RUSK was the first Chief Justice of the Republic of Texas.[14] The triumph of San Jacinto having been secured, the President of Mexico having been held captive;[15] the gallant RUSK, with that sense of duty by which he was distinguished, sheathed his conquering sword to receive, at the hands of his countrymen, the Judicial ermine—he was elected by the first Congress Chief Justice of the Supreme Court of the Republic of Texas—which office he held for the term of two years. Of course during a period of so short, he had but little opportunity of fixing the marks of his ability upon the annals of jurisprudence of his country. Resigning his office, JOHN HEMPHILL was chosen as his successor. Never, Mr. President, did mantle fall on shoulders more worthy. Judge HEMPHILL had emigrated to Texas about three years anterior to his election; he brought with him a character for pure integrity and chivalry.—It has seemed to me, sir, that he was a special donation to our struggling Republic by a kind Providence. Up to the period of his election, Judicial precedence, he had none! He was emphatically the great Judicial pioneer of our Republic; he blazed out the road of Judicial decision, which, dim and intricate at first, is now recognized by all who travel it as the sign road to justice and right.

The system adopted by the Congress of 1837,[16] was very peculiar to Texas—while we did not distain the common law, we did not adopt civil law—it was left to Judge HEMPHILL under legislative enactment to shape our judicial system. Gloriously and faithfully has he performed this great work. The Rough Ashlar of the common law,[17] through his plastic influence has become so tempered by the amenities of the civil as to be become, in my estimate, the best judicial system extant.

Deeming our original land titles from the laws which had originated in Spain, passing through Mexico, as also our system of marital rights, previous to 1840, it required deep research into the laws as they "afore time" were to determine these rights. Well do I recollect that at the meeting of the Supreme Court in December 1842, cases involving these great principles came before the Supreme Court.—Not a man upon our bench at that period understood the Spanish language, while the main authorities adduced were all in that language. The cases were taken under advisement and by common consent were referred to the Chief Justice for consideration. As the evidence of his intense labor and application, I assert that at the next term of the Court, he had, as appeared from his report, mastered the Spanish language, and brought into Court opinions which formed the basis of decisions in our Courts, having been constantly approved as the ruler of decision in all the important class of cases to which they apply.[18]

The reputation of Judge HEMPHILL as a jurist was not confined to Texas, but the Centre College of Kentucky, deeply impressed with his real worth and high abilities as a lawyer, conferred upon him the honorable degree of L.L.D. It may be remarked that the same college simultaneously conferred the degree upon a distinguished citizen of her own State, now considered the most worthy members on this floor.[19]

When the great question arose in Texas, as to whether she should annex herself to the United States of America, Judge HEMPHILL was the decided advocate of annexation. I participated with him in the deliberations of the Convention of 1845, which formed the Constitution of the State of Texas, and determined the terms of annexation. Over that body, Gen. RUSK was, by common consent, called to preside. Recognizing the great ability and integrity of Judge HEMPHILL, he appointed him to the indispensable position of chairman of the Judiciary Committee. No man in that convention exercised a more potent and healthy influence upon their counsels. Upon the organization of the state government, Judge HEMPHILL was appointed by Governor HENDERSON,[20] chief justice of the Supreme Court. It is needless to add that he was unanimously confirmed by the Senate. The sixteen volumes of the reports of the Supreme Court of that State, which record his opinions, will prove a monument to his life more enduring than brass.

Mr. President, a strong characteristic of Judge HEMPHILL was his urbanity of manner—his love for his fellow man. He was the idol of the young men of the bar in his State. They all loved him, and his familiar patronymic of the "*padre*" showed the love they bore him. Mild and quiet as he most generally appeared, yet was he a lion in his wrath; and when Mexican raid or Indian foray visited the frontier of Texas in our earlier days, no man was more relied on to defend our bleeding frontier then Judge Hemphill. And, sir, I venture to say what many a manly tear will steal down the cheek of our old frontier citizens, when they read of the death of their old friend and protector.

Mr. President, I will conclude these remarks by saying that a man of firmer purpose, of more sterling purity of character, and of deeper and more intense love of country, than him who now lies before you wrapt in the cold ornaments of the dead, never lived. I have done.

Mr. JOHNSON, of Arkansas. I second the resolution just offered. It has been thought appropriate by those on whose judgment I rest, that my poor tribute should be offered here. It is in tribute of friendship. Our friend might have fallen at another day, and few might have felt it. But a narrow circle of brothers and sisters and neighbors would have gathered round his coffin, and the weeping wounded hearts and crushed affection would have offered a far more eloquent recital, as all silently they lifted him down to his grave. It would then have been the heart's loss.

But here, Mr. President, the mourners all are bearded men and fellow laborers, who actively mingle in doing the last sad rites around him. The heart is silenced in the march of mighty events about us—grief is distracted by a sense of duty and common danger. The Revolution moves onward; those who would weep here, must be brief. In the death of Judge HEMPHILL—so wise, so gentle, and so good—we witness the country's loss; and Congress, as the impersonation of the people, giving grace to his name by fitting tributes, bears honorable testimonial to his high public worth and many manly virtues.

I have known Judge HEMPHILL some years, and during all that time he has been in the enjoyment of the confidence of the people of Texas, and engaged in the fulfillment of the duties of the most honorable and exalted station, which it was in their power to confer. Of the manner in which he acquitted himself of his high duties, the unvarying testimony of his fellows, as well as the public records of the country, furnish the most satisfactory proofs.

I could not assert a claim to the enjoyment of any exclusive intimacy with Judge HEMPHILL. I felt happy in the belief, that I enjoyed his respect and friendly regard. I know not the strength of my own feelings for him until, by sheer accident, I found him extremely ill in his room, and no one with him. I sat down by him and learned that he was then under treatment of Dr. FAIRFAX,[21] a physician of standing and that, though suffering severely, his case was not one of danger in his judgment.

His disease at that time was an elongation of the palate, accompanied with considerable inflammation. I continued to visit him, and the next evening about 10 or 11 o'clock, I found him suffering under a high fever, but the condition of his throat improved. I felt uneasy; upon leaving his room I called the servant who attended him, and directed him to call me immediately upon the next arrival of the physician that I might see and converse with him of this fever, and of his condition, which was done. From that time he grew worse. A good nurse was procured and placed with him, and his nephew, ROBERT HEMPHILL, a young soldier of South Carolina,[22] who happened to be passing through the city, abandoned his trip and took post by the bedside of his uncle, where by day and by night he was steadily to be found until the hour of his death. About two days before his death the disease extended to both lungs, developing pneumonia, involving both sides, and on Friday night I was sent for and requested by Dr. FAIRFAX to make known to Judge HEMPHILL his true situation, that he might prepare for the end. It was the first time that a duty so painful had ever fallen to my lot. At about 12 o'clock at night I discharged it, with all the care and tenderness I could, his nephew standing by my side, restraining his deep grief, but with his eyes full of tears. He received my message apparently without emotion. He was entirely conscious and self-possessed. After a pause of some little time he asked me if his physician had authorized this communication; to which I replied that it was given by his request. He relapsed into silence, apparently unmoved; and I withdrew, as I thought most proper, reminding his nephew to arouse him, and ask him if he had no wishes to express. This was done, and he replied he was too weak to consider his affairs, but that he did not expect to die. He became drowsy then, his mind wandering occasionally, as had been usual for the last twenty-four hours, and sank gradually till about 10 o'clock, on Saturday morning, when he breathed his last.

I had retired about 8 o'clock, and requested to be called again, which was done before he expired. I saw him at his last breath. To speak of the sorrow I felt is idle, and would, perhaps, but feebly remind you of the shock occasioned at our last meeting, by the news of his unexpected death.

With the events of his life and the details of his career, for so many years connected with the public service of his State, I am too unfamiliar to speak. I can only speak of him as I knew him.

He was evidently a student; his habits were those of seclusion—his room filled with books of rare and curious interest, as well as those of a solid and valuable character; his time seemed given to a search after knowledge, and to calm reflection and philosophical thought. His was the most amiable character I ever knew; and for his high intellect and great knowledge, he was the most patient, and, perhaps, the most difficult man. I never knew him to lose his patience, and from his lips I never heard fall the first harsh or unkind expression of any human being during all our acquaintances. Of him, I would say in conclusion, living he had discharged faithfully all his duties to his country, and dying he had left no enemy behind hm. He was a brave, a gentle, a wise, and a good man. His countrymen will cherish and protect his memory, as an offering of the State of Texas, and as the first one of this revolutionary Congress who has fallen with his robes around him.

Mr. Venable, of North Carolina. I trust it will not be considered intrusive for me, comparatively a stranger to the deceased, to add a few remarks to those already made upon this sad occasion. The distinguished gentleman so recently removed by the hand of death, has had ample tribute paid to his merits by those whose intimacy and friendship with him authorized them to give those details of his life and virtues which always mitigate grief for a moment by their utterance. I knew him personally only since the meeting of this Congress in July. I have reason to know that a mutual regard was the result of that acquaintance, and now, as his bier passes before us, I offer incense due to the memory of one—brave, generous, enlightened and patriotic—whose loss we deplore, but whose name lives in the affections of that country to whose interest and honor he was so sincerely devoted. His illness was short, his death unexpected. I left him a few days since his usual health, and although boarding in the same house I only learned he was sick two days before his death. My first visit to him revealed to me his perilous situation, and on my next I saw him in the agonies of death. Sir, this is a solemn warning to us all of the truth, that we are merely soldiers in the battle of this world, surrounded by dangers not the less imminent because unseen, not the less certain because unheralded. Present time demands the performance of present duty; watchfulness and a Christian preparation for the hour of death is not only wise in itself, but enforced by considerations of our highest interest. Death, the mighty leveler, summons all of every condition in life, nor does he pass by and spare the Patriot or the Statesman; but with the humblest of our race, his summons is certain and inexorable, and from the coffin of our deceased colleagues, a voice continually falls upon our hearts and ears, "Be ye also ready: for at such an hour as ye know not, the son of man cometh."

Towards his family and friends our sympathies flow out spontaneously. The heart knows its own sorrows, and we trust that the consolation which a kind God and Father gives to his children may heal their grief and give them submission to his will. I miss his social intercourse, so delightfully adorned with the modest amenities, those ornaments of virtue itself, and so near akin to it that they are well nigh inseparable. His accurate knowledge and impartial knowledge of personal and contemporaneous history in a course of stirring and startling events in his own State, discovered his honesty of purpose, his freedom from guile, jealousy or envy; and his matured judgment of the value of facts and incidents made his association a source of continued pleasure. My friend from Arkansas has well said that Judge HEMPHILL was the first member of our body who has fallen into the embrace of death with his senatorial robes around him. We last July united our sorrows with bereaved friends over the fall of another who slept on the field of glory with his war cloak around him. Sir, the same courage, as well as the wise forecast, which characterized the "Roman Senator, when Rome had a Senate," is now as indispensable in the present glorious revolution in which we are engaged. It is now we need and now we miss the presence and the counsels of our friend, who leaves behind him the fragrance of a patriot's memory. His whole life, whether as a soldier in the early struggles of his State for independence, in the contest with Mexico at a late period, as a lawyer in the practice of his profession, as an enlightened and incorruptible judge, is but an accumulation of evidence that his loss is most deeply to be deplored, because occurring in the hour of his country's necessity.

Judge HEMPHILL was a brave man; quiet, modest and unobtrusive, but firm and unyielding, when convinced of the correctness of his conclusion. I conversed often with him on the affairs of the country. He looked calmly, cheerfully, hopefully upon our condition—Having confidence in the capacity and patriotism of those in whose hands the authority of the Confederacy was placed, he looked above and beyond small subjects of discontent, with the highest confidence in the glorious result of our struggle for independence and self-government.

Sir, let us emulate his high qualities, and be ever ready, like him as statesmen in the service of the Confederacy, to work to the last, to die, like the war horse in full harness. He walked from the council chamber to the tomb, filled with occupation in the business of his country. He, who was spared on the fields of Texas and Mexico; who, with the fierce courage of the soldier, knew nothing of cruelty; with the high authority of a Judge never soiled the ermine with tranny and corruption, but ornamented it by his purity and his learning; tempering, by his moderation, one revolution in his own State, whose jurisprudence he may be said to have modified and perfected, has not gone to the grave, amidst, our tears, leaving us the task of completing this second revolution which his heart approved and his efforts advanced until death closed his labors in the midst of his work. Soldier! Patriot! Jurist! Statesman! You rest from your labors. Honor to your memory!

Mr. BOYCE. Mr. President I trust it may not be considered inappropriate in me to add my feeble tribute of respect to the memory of our late colleague, as we are natives of the same State. Mr. HEMPHILL was born in Chester district, South Carolina, the adjoining district to that in which I live. He was descended from a highly respectable family. His father was a man of very marked character, a leading divine in the Seceder Church, a branch of the great Presbyterian denomination.[23] His ancestors were therefore from Scotland, and of a sect distinguished in Scottish history for their vehement devotion to duty, daring the anger of a bigoted king, and the dangers of the battle field, rather than compromise, even in matters of form, that religious belief which they held dearer than property, or life itself. It was to perpetuate the memories of these heroes and martyrs of the right of conscience, that the original of Old Mortality plied his chisel. It was from these Christian heroes that Mr. HEMPHILL drew his lineage. There is a great deal in blood, and the guarantee of individual virtue is often found in the inspiration of great recollections. It is thus that the past survives itself, and impresses itself upon the loving future.

After receiving a regular education, Mr. HEMPHILL commenced the practice of law in Sumter District, South Carolina and was rapidly rising to distinction, when he was attracted to the then Republic of Texas, by the heroic struggle she was making to relieve herself from Mexican tyranny. He bore an honorable part in that memorable struggle, and when it was successfully ended, resumed the practice of his profession in that State, which he had helped by his own arm to establish. He very soon rose to eminence in his profession, and was early called by the State of Texas to the head of her judicial system. The important part which he acted in fashioning the judicial system of the States of Texas had been very fully laid before you by the honorable gentleman who first addressed us. I shall therefore no longer dwell upon it, but simply add that as Solon is remembered in history for the laws which he gave to the Athenian Republic, so shall the name of HEMPHILL live in the annals of Texas for the part he performed in moulding her laws.

My personal acquaintance with Mr. HEMPHILL commenced after he became a member of the United States Senate. I naturally felt an interest in him, as that class of superior men which South Carolina with prodigal liberality, has given to her sister States. I soon discovered that he was a man of marked character, and of a very high order of intellect. I became intimately acquainted with him in the Congress at Montgomery, and witnessed his efficient services in laying the foundation of our great Confederacy. I was very much struck on a close acquaintance with him, with his extraordinary kindness of heart; indeed, I scarcely know any one to whom such was my opinion of his goodness of heart, I would sooner have gone for a favor. He was a man of the highest sense of duty, and the maxim upon which he seemed to act was that virtue was success. He was a man of unflinching firmness, and before he left his native State he had given the most signal evidence that he was of the heroic mould. I was prepared, therefore, to hear what has been stated to us to day by his colleague, that when a savage foe threatened Austin, he threw up arms, distinguished himself by his daring in driving them back.

As an intellectual man he was peculiarly distinguished for his good sense. He was preeminently a wise councilor. To lose such a man at this time from the councils of the country, is no common loss. It seems a pity, too, that he should have died in the midst of the great struggle in which we are now engaged. It would have been such a satisfaction to him to have lived long enough to see our success established on a sure foundation—to have witnessed our triumphant flag floating proudly over a peaceful land. But this has been denied him, he has fallen before our triumph has been achieved. But of a man who has lived as he has, and acted an important part so well, it cannot be said he has lived in vain. He died too soon for his country, but in the maturity of his fame. Peace and honor to his memory.

Appropriate resolutions were adopted, and a Committee of one from each States was appointed to arrange the funeral ceremonies for to-morrow, at eleven o'clock, a.m. No other business was transacted.

Members are returning daily from their recent enjoyments of the holidays.

Tuesday, January 7, 1862

(Augusta *Chronicle*, January 8, 1862)

Congress this morning attended Judge HEMPHILL's funeral. The afternoon session was unimportant.

Wednesday, January 8, 1862

(Augusta *Chronicle*, January 9, 1862)

Congress was in secret session to-day. No business of importance was transacted.

Thursday, January 9, 1862

(Charleston *Mercury*, January 10, 1862)

The proceedings of Congress to-day, so far as they are publicly known, were not of an important character.

Friday, January 10, 1862

(Augusta *Chronicle*, January 11, 1862)

Congress was in secret session to-day, nothing relative to its business has been publicly communicated.

Congress then resolved itself into secret session.

Saturday, January 11, 1862

(Richmond *Whig*, January 14, 1862)

Congress met . . . at the usual hour, and immediately went into secret session.

Monday, January 13, 1862—Wednesday, January 15, 1862[24]

Thursday, January 16, 1862

(Augusta *Daily Constitutionalist*, January 17, 1862)

Congress did nothing in public to-day.

Friday, January 17, 1862—Saturday, January 18, 1862[25]

Monday, January 20, 1862[26]

(Richmond *Whig*, January 21, January 24, 1862; Charleston *Mercury*, January 27, 1862; Richmond *Daily Dispatch*, January 21, 1862; Richmond *Examiner*, January 22, 1862)

Congress sat . . . with open doors, devoting their entire session to suitable tributes to the virtues and services of their late fellow-member, the venerable and lamented Ex-President TYLER.[27] All day long his honored remains lay in state, in the draped Hall of Congress, covered with the flag of his country, with a wreath of evergreens and white roses on his breast; and multitudes of both sexes visited the chamber to take a last look at his well known features, and testify by their presence their sense of the public loss. As the hour for the meeting of Congress drew near, the space allotted to spectators rapidly filled with ladies and gentlemen. At 12 o'clock, President COBB took the chair, and an earnest and touching prayer was by Rev. Mr. HOGE.

MR. MACFARLAND, of Virginia, rose and said:

> Mr. President—My colleagues have been pleased to assign to me the sad duty of preparing resolutions, to express the sense of Congress of the great bereavement it is summoned unexpectedly to mourn and lament. I wish it were in my power to perform the mournful duty in a manner satisfactory to the sensibilities of Congress and the country. Any announcement of the decease of the Hon. JOHN TYLER, is imperfect and inadequate, fails of giving utterance to the nation's lamentation, if it do not present him as a statesman and patriot, in whom his countrymen delighted to repose their confidence, and who failed not to derive fresh incentives to honor and revere him, from the faithfulness and ability with which he administered every trust.
>
> JOHN TYLER is an historical name. He was himself permitted to hear the judgment of his generation, and I might say, of posterity, upon the labors and motives of his life, pronouncing that they were alike elevated and successful. He was the venerable representative of the memories of a past age, with its renounced alliances and associations, and zealous and efficient in the reforms and progress, which have made the period of his latter days forever memorable. His fame is indissolubly blended with the history of his times, and shall survive the most enduring memorials of personal affection, or of public esteem. Live, he still does, and will, in his example, his deeds, the purity of his public and private life, in his matured counsels and inflexible devotion to Constitutional and Republican Government. However profoundly the blow smote upon our own feelings, "where else could he have been relieved of the yoke of his labors so well as in the field where he bore them?"

The time in which he lived was characterized by fierce political and party divisions; and Mr. TYLER was ever intrepid in avowing his opinions, and resolute in defending them. His career as Chief Magistrate of the United States, exposed him to painful collisions, and demanded of him the exercise of the highest fortitude and intrepidity. He met his trials then, as he did all others, as a good and brave man may, with patience and confidence, in the ultimate vindication of his motives. It was reserved for him, hero in his own State, and in her august Convention, to receive the unanimous vote of the entire body, on being proposed as a delegate to this Provisional Congress—an emphatic and deserved tribute to the fidelity of his eventful life, and to the weight of his character.

Mr. President, it is not alone for his Statesmanship, and the length and variety of his public services, that Mr. TYLER will be gratefully remembered, and that admiring memories will fondly revert to, and recall him. As in his successive elevation from one high trust to another, until he had compassed the entire round of political preferment, an increase of reputation, fame, homage, met him at every advance, so in private life it was his privilege to secure the respect, confidence and esteem of all who approached him. Of the most obliging courtesy, genial, generous and confiding; and withal, so engaging for his copious eloquence, his sympathy for his fellow men, and his profound views of the questions which engaged the public attention, all persons were instinctively attracted to him, nor did any go away without admiring him. You remember, sir, how the gentlemen of this House were accustomed to cluster around him, and how engaging and attractive he was always found. Nothing now remains for us, but the last sad office of mourning friends, to commemorate the afflicting dispensation.

I move the adoption of the following resolutions:

Resolved, That Congress has heard, with the deepest sensibility, of the death, in this city, on the morning of Saturday, the 18th inst., of the Hon. JOHN TYLER, a member of this Congress, from the State of Virginia.

Resolved, That as a testimonial of respect for the memory of this illustrious statesmen and honored patriot, the members of the Congress will wear the usual badge of mourning for thirty days and will attend the funeral of deceased at 12 o'clock to morrow.

Resolved, That a committee of one member from each State be appointed to superintend the funeral solemnities.

Resolved, That the proceedings of this body, in relation to the death of the Hon. JOHN TYLER, be communicated by the President of

Congress to the family of the deceased.

Resolved, That as a further mark of respect to the memory of the deceased, that Congress do now adjourn.

Mr. HUNTER, of Va., rose and said:

I rise to offer my tribute of respect to the memory of the deceased.

As has been well said, the name of JOHN TYLER, now passed into the possession of history, has an order of its own in that great sanctuary. Its sojourn is over.—Nothing can now dim its lustre as it passes down the tide of time.

It is said, sir, there is something in the story of the humblest life, which, if rightly told, will afford food for profitable study. With how much of interest, then, do we turn to the contemplation of the lives of those who have been martyrs of their kind, who have left examples for the imitation of posterity; of those whose voices have been the most persuasive and convincing in council, and whose shout, like that of the king, has been most potent in marshalling the hosts.

Amongst the public men of our day, JOHN TYLER has been one of the most marked and distinguished. With him disappears the last save one who now sits in this chamber, of those great men who adorned the Senate of the United States when I first entered upon public life with him.[28] We shall bury the last of the line, the illustrious line of Southern Presidents whose names have connected us with the highest honors of the Union from which we have just parted. Does not this deepen the sense of our separation as we see one by one pass away, not only the material links, but the ties of personal association which bound us to those whom we have lately left?

No man, Mr. President, has more fully completed the circle of honors which were opened to the aspirations of our public men than JOHN TYLER. Scarcely had he attained his majority when he was sent to the House of Delegates in Virginia. After a service of a few years there, he was successively elected a member of the Executive Council, a member of the House of Representatives of the United States, Governor of the State of Virginia, Senator of the United States, Vice-President of the United States, from which, by the death of General HARRISON, and through the operation of the Constitution, he was elevated to the Chief Magistracy of the land.—Nor, sir, did his career end even there. When secession began and presaged the storm which is now sweeping over the land, he was sent to the Convention of Virginia, and by that body to the Peace Congress, over the deliberations of which he presided; thence to this Congress, and afterwards was elected by his constituents to the House of Representatives of the Confederate Congress, soon to assemble in this place.

But full as was his life of honor, it was not more distinguished by them than by its achievements. From the commencement of his public career, he distinguished himself in whatever body he was serving, and by his eloquence and ability won an honorable place in the estimation of all with whom he associated. An advocate of the doctrines of the State Rights school of Virginia, he for the most part adhered to those doctrines with consistency through out a long and arduous career. Few men exerted themselves more to preserve the Constitution of the United States. He was among the first of our public men who, with the great CALHOUN, declared that "the Constitution and the union of the States was one and inseparable." From the period of the nullification controversy, from the time when he gave his solitary vote against the Force Bill in the Congress of the United States, to his last appearance in Washington at the Peace Conference, he declared the Union and the Constitution must live or perish together.

He exerted his utmost powers to preserve the Constitution and the administration of the executive affairs of the United States. Forced to choose between the desire to gratify the wishes of his personal friends, who had elevated him to the office, on the one hand, and a sense of constitutional obligation on the other, he determined finally to sacrifice the friends with whom he had been associated. From that time forward it was his lot to administer the affairs of the nation, over which he presided in the midst of the severest party struggles the country had ever known, without the cordial support of either great political division by which the people were then divided; and he had to discharge his high duties in the face of such difficulties as had never been encountered by any of his predecessors. But, in despite of that spirit, he called around him some of the ablest intellects of the land—WEBSTER, UPSHUR, LEGARE, CALHOUN—who aided him in one of the most successful administrations which appears in the annals of American affairs.

It was this administration that added Texas, an empire, to the Confederacy; and it was this administration that successfully accomplished the Ashburton treaty between Great Britain and the United States.[29] It was in this administration that Mr. CALHOUN, in his celebrated letter to Mr. KING, for the first time made a public demonstration in favor of the right of the slaveholding States to respect and protection;[30] and it was this administration which gave a final and fatal blow to the United States Bank. But prominent, sir, as was this administration, it was, perhaps, not so distinguished as his closing career. He had already reached the year of three score and ten, when he was called from his retirement to aid in making up that great issue of human destiny which is now being submitted to the arbitrament of trial, as it is said, between nearly a million of armed men. True to the life long professions of the past, his first effort was to preserve the Constitution, and, if possible, to save the Union with it; but when disappointed in that hope, none was more determined than he to cut loose his native State from its perilous connection with enemies in disguise—none more resolved to make common cause with the South and take whatever might be the consequences of the act.

We all know he threw himself into the cause with his whole soul. Gentlemen here present will testify to the truth of what I say when I affirm that to the last he devoted himself to it with a courage that did not quail, with a hope that did not falter, and with a purpose that held out to the last extremity and relaxed not to the end.

Mr. President, it may truly be said that with JOHN TYLER there has fallen a great man. I know, sir, that the death of any good man is the cause of grief to the friendly survivors; and yet I feel I do not err when I say that my deceased colleague was as fortunate in his death as in his life. As a soldier on the field of battle falls, he fell at the post of duty. A life, when it was full of years and honors, passed away. He left us before age had bowed his form or dimmed the lustre of his intellect; when the future course of his life was about to promise him more of pleasure than grief. To-morrow we shall deposit him beneath the sod of that soil which he loved so well—on the beautiful banks of the James, where his slumbers will be soothed by the sound of its falling waters. Day after day, in the years yet to come, the morning and evening shadows shall lend a silent and varied charm to the scene; and when her hour of struggle is over, Virginia, as she leans upon her bloody spear to contemplate the past, and beholding the rising glories of her day, will lift her gauntleted hand to brush away the tear for the loss of him who, in the decline of life, exhausted his dying energies in her behalf, and staked his life, his fortune, his reputation upon the result, which will bring her safety and honor. Sir, she will embalm his memory in her best affections, and hand it down to her generations yet to come; and their children's children will transmit his honored name as an inheritance of princely value—an heirloom which has already run through more than two generations of distinguished men.

But it is not my purpose, sir, to draw a portrait of this great man. His is a character which men will choose to study themselves; and they will seek it in the monuments of his own creation rather than in the testimonials of his friends; but perhaps, sir, it will not be deemed as usurping the historian's place, were I to say of him, he was kind and genial in all the relations of private lite, and that he used the gift of the eloquence with which he was so highly endowed, in the public service, and not for selfish purposes; that his faculties for usefulness seemed always to rise to the level of the demand upon them; that he was most able to discharge his duty under the most difficult circumstances, and that he served his native State with a love and fidelity which are beyond all praise.

Mr. President, is there no useful lesson which we ourselves may draw from this occasion? Is there nothing in it that will deepen our sense of the uncertainty of human life and the instability of human affairs! Within how short a period has Death sent its summons in our very midst? Does not this impress us with the utter worthlessness of the span of life, allotted to any one of us, deem we use it for the purpose of preparing for another, and better and more enduring state? Do not the scenes passing before us impress on us still more forcibly the sublime truth—"The duties of life are to be preferred to life itself."

Mr. RIVES, of Virginia, then spoke as follows:

I should be wanting, Mr. President, to my own feelings, if not to the memory of our departed friend, were I not to claim the privilege of an older and longer acquaintance with him, perhaps, than any other member on this floor possessed, to add a few words to what has been already so appropriately and eloquently said by my honorable colleagues. It is now somewhat more than half century since, a school-boy in the ancient city of Williamsburg, I first made the acquaintance of Mr. TYLER, then a law student of our common Alma Mater,[31] preparing to enter upon the career of active life. It was thus given me to observe the whole progress of his orb in the heavens from its first appearance above the horizon, through its meridian brightness and splendor, to its final and serene setting in the Western sky, which we are met this day to commemorate.

As a young man, when I first saw Mr. TYLER, he was distinguished by the same blandness and courtesy of manners, the prepossessing address, and the graceful and captivating elocution, which we have all seen displayed by him in this hall. These qualities, the sure passport in a government like ours, to popular favor and public distinction, bore him through a succession of public employments. As soon as he was of age, he was elected by his native county of Charles City to the House of Delegates of Virginia. His first session in that body was, if I mistake not, in the memorable year of 1811–'12, which witnessed the bold measure of the declaration of war made by the United States against Great Britain; and the young legislator became thus closely identified with that high-spirited generation of American statesmen, who, succeeding immediately to the great men of the Revolution—the conscript fathers of the Republic—continued, for thirty or forty years after them, to conduct the affairs of the Union with a patriotism, ability and success worthy of their noble sires.

In the different representative assemblies of which Mr. TYLER was successively a member, he was brought into contact with the highest intellects of the age. In the Legislature of Virginia, he was a member of the House of Delegates with LITTLETON WALLER TAZEWELL, BENJAMIN WATKINS LEIGH, CHARLES FENTON MERCER, ROBERT STANARD, PHILIP DODDRIDGE, General BLACKBURN, and many others of the most gifted spirits of this ancient Commonwealth. In the House of Representatives of the United States, he was contemporary with HENRY CLAY, WILLIAM LOWNDES, JOHN RANDOLPH, HENRY ST. GEORGE TUCKER, JOHN FORSYTH, LOUIS MCLANE, and a host of other distinguished men who then illustrated the national forum.—Being generally the youngest member of the body to which he belonged, and emulous of distinction, he was stimulated to the highest exertion of his powers by the living models of excellence with which he was surrounded, and his mind was thus kept in a perpetual progress of development and expansion.

Trained and formed under these auspices, he proved himself equal to all the various and arduous posts of public duty to which he was called by the favor and confidence of his countrymen. In the highest of them all, he gave an honorable proof of the elevation and magnanimity of his character bringing into the leading Executive Department the most towering talents of the country, to aid him in the administration of the Government. The selection of such men as WEBSTER, CALHOUN, LEGARE, UPSHUR and SPENCER proved how far he was above the operation of any unworthy sentiment of jealousy, or fear of being overshadowed in the public estimation by his official advisers; while his personal management of several of the most delicate questions of his administration—I refer more particularly to his broad and comprehensive treatment of the question of the annexation of Texas, and the firmness with which he upheld the cause of constitutional republican government in Rhode Island against the outbreak of an unlicensed democracy[32]—attested the large and matured statesmanship he had himself acquired in the schools of practical instruction in which he was bred.

But this is neither the time nor the place to enter upon a discussion of the merits of Mr. TYLER'S administration of the Federal Government, when, by a sudden and unexpected dispensation of Providence, be was placed at the head of it. No one would more earnestly have deprecated the revival of forgotten controversies than himself. Among the qualities which most eminently and honorably distinguished him was an habitual kindliness of disposition, and a generous appreciation of others, even of those who were his political enemies and opponents. It was about two years ago, in this city, on a public and memorable occasion, he did himself the highest honor by a warm, spontaneous and manly tribute to the character of a great man and deceased patriot, who had stood towards him in the attitude of a powerful and declared opponent.

In reviewing the eventful life of Mr. TYLER, we are led, almost irresistibly, to apply to him a descriptive epithet by which the Romans were accustomed to express a quality that ever inspired their confidence and admiration. By that epithet—*felix*—they did not mean to designate a person who was merely fortunate, but one who, by a happy combination of well-tempered attributes, know, in a measure, how to command or propitiate fortune. This sentiment was embodied by them in a maxim, tersely expressed by their great satirist—*nullum numen abest, si sit prudentia.*[33] Thus it was with Mr. TYLER. By a rare union of prudence, good sense and good temper, set off by the natural gifts of oratory and a persuasive address, he won the hearts of the people and commanded the favors of fortune; and success waited upon him in every stop of his public career.

Delegate in the Legislature of his State, Representative in Congress, Governor, Senator, Vice-President, President—he "sounded all the depths and shoals of honor" and in every trust he acquitted himself to the satisfaction of his constituents.[34] After having filled with honor the highest offices of the Government of the Union—which sank, at length, under the degeneracy and corruption of the times—he lived to take a leading part in the establishment of a new Confederacy for the South, which had all his affections and all his hopes; and as a member of this House, he gave his anxious labors to the great cause of securing and perpetuating the structure.

His duties as a member of this body engaged his deepest solicitude. Unwilling to withdraw himself from them for a single day without the proper and formal sanction of the House, he said to me the day before the fatal termination of his disease, that, if he should be compelled to go home to recruit his health, as he should probably find it necessary to do, he wished me to apply to the House for leave of absence for him. A far higher authority, the great Governor of the Universe, has granted him that leave of absence—not from this Hall merely, but from all sublunary concerns henceforward forever. He now rests from his labors; but he has bequeathed to us the rich inheritance of his patriotic example and of his counsels.

This second admonition of the transitory tenure of human existence, with which, after so short an interval, we have been visited in this Hall, reminds us most impressively that "the paths of glory lead but to the grave."[35] But still it is not permitted to us to repine. "One generation passeth away and another cometh; but the earth abideth forever."[36] Here, while we continue, we have our allotted work; and as those who have gone before us have labored and toiled, so assist we, in our turn, toil and labor, to carry forward the great schemes of Divine providence in the moral government of the world, and if we do so in humble submission to the will of Him who ruleth the destinies of men and nations, we, too, shall have our reward.

Mr. RHETT of South Carolina, said:

Mr. President:—I am, perhaps, the oldest political associate of the deceased on this floor, excepting citizens from Virginia; and South Carolina was peculiarly identified with him, in the leading acts of his administration, when President of the United States. For those reasons, it is perhaps not improper that I should say a few words upon the sad occasion which had brought us together.

My acquaintance with the deceased commenced when he was at the zenith of political power. He was President of the United States, by the death of General HARRISON. At first, those of us who belonged to the State Rights party of the South, stood aloof from him. He had been elected Vice-President upon the Whig ticket with General HARRISON. They were opposites in politics. The one was a consolidationist—the other a strict constructionist. Many of the State Rights party looked upon this conjunction with the sternest reprobation. Twenty years has passed since that time. The passions which agitated the day, have gone to rest, and we are now able to do justice to the motives and conduct of those who differed from us. All the great questions, with the parties they produced, which influenced or controlled the government of the United States are gone into history; and are never again to have any application to the living. The great statesmen who ruled them—CLAY, WEBSTER, CALHOUN, LEGARE, MARSHALL, LEIGH—were all equally patriotic. On the other side of the Potomac, the government of the United States has lapsed into a consolidated despotism. On this side of the Potomac, we have cast them out of the council, by the Constitution we have adopted for ourselves. Parties will doubtless arise on totally different bases than any which arose under the government of the United States. Considering, then, the events of 1840 as mere matters of history, was it wrong in the deceased to have consented that his name should have been united with that Gen. HARRISON in the Presidential election of that year?

That the Democratic party had become greatly demoralized by its long possession of power, is undoubted. It had brought the Union to the verge of dissolution by the tariff of 1828, in the subsequent contest of 1832 and '33. Those of us of the States Rights party who assented to support Mr. VAN BUREN against General HARRISON required a distinct declaration of principles as the condition of our support. Accordingly, the Hon. FRANCIS THOMAS, of Maryland, and myself, were appointed to prepare the Address put forth to the people of the United States by the

Democratic member of Congress, just previous to the Presidential election. Mr. TYLER, who had been prominent in the Senate in the contest of '32, thought less of the Democratic party than we did. He deemed it hopelessly corrupt; and that it was a work of patriotism to unite all the element of opposition to eject it from power. Accordingly, he joined the Whig part, to constitute a mere opposition power without any principles, or declaration of principles, to overthrow the Democratic party in the Presidential election. Was he wrong? Have not subsequent events proved that the Democratic party of the North was just as hostile to the rights of the South as their opponents? When they joined us, it was to subserve their sectional interests. Their co-action was only policy. In 1852 they wrested California from us. In the late Presidential election they joined the sectional effort for our subjugation; and now they swell the armies of the United States, our bitterest and most malignant foes. DALLAS, DICKENSON, WILKINS, MCCLERNAND, DIX, are foremost in urging on the work of slaughter and desolation over the South. The truth is, the South never had any real friends at the North. With the lights of the present day, can we condemn the course of any statesman of the South for any course of opposition to such invidious and deadly enemies?

President TYLER, on becoming President, soon found himself surrounded with the most embarrassing difficulties. Those who acted together as an opposition could not agree on any policy, so soon as they attained power. They had the possession of the Government, and must rule it by some policy. The Whigs, with Mr. CLAY at their head, insisted that that policy should be the policy of the Whigs, and that they should begin with re-establishing a United States Bank. Mr. TYLER protested against such an assumption. His State Rights principles were well known, and he was placed on the presidential ticket on account of them. He would not abandon them. The honorable gentleman over the way from Virginia (Mr. RIVES), also protested against such a course, and met Mr. CLAY in high and stern debate in the Senate, on the importance of a United States Bank.[37] I was present at that debate; and imposing and great as Mr. CLAY always was in the Senate, he was more than matched by the dauntless energy and ability displayed by my honorable friend; and Mr. CLAY seemed to be conscious of it. The truth was, the Senator from Virginia had the right, I think, on his side, and wielded its weapons with a courage and force, which won for him the admiration of all spectators. The Bank Bill, nevertheless, passed; and President TYLER vetoed it. Sir, I witnessed the tremendous denunciations of Mr. CLAY in the Senate, of President TYLER, for his act of simple consistency, with all the political principles of his life. It was the most fiery and magnificent display of eloquence I ever heard, excepting on one other occasion. Mr. CLAY, I doubt not, was as honest as he was earnest in these denunciations; but who now will condemn the deceased for his course? Mr. CLAY carried the party with him. Cut off thus from all parties, he determined, if possible, to enforce in the Government the principles he had professed; and, for this end, to throw himself upon the States Rights party. He offered Mr. CALHOUN the office of Secretary of State, with the power (common to the Premier of England), of forming the Cabinet.—Mr. CALHOUN consulted the honorable delegation from Virginia (Mr. HUNTER), and myself, whether he should accept of the office. Both of us earnestly advised him to accept it. After a night's consideration, however, he rejected it. The Whig party was broken by the veto, and by the succeeding elections was overthrown.

At a late period of his administration, Mr. CALHOUN entered his Cabinet, as Secretary of State, with a view of annexing Texas to the Union—the other great measure of Mr. TYLER's administration. It is not easy at the present day to understand the state of things existing at this time. They were felt, rather than seen. The determination of the North to rule the South could be understood, but could not be proved to exist. The annexation of Texas was opposed by them for no other reason than that it strengthened the South, and impeded their progress to national dominion. In all other respects, it was of vast advantage to them. At an early period of his administration, President TYLER had meditated annexing Texas to the Union. He accomplished it, and gained a vast territory for the South; but it helped on, by its agitators, to drive the sections asunder. From this time forth, every measure of importance in the Government assumed a sectional character, until at last, by the late Presidential election, the South was compelled to choose her destiny—of subjection in the Union, or independence out of it. Although long in retirement, President TYLER came forth to meet the emergency. His efforts to save the Union, consistent with the safety of the South, were in vain; and he took his stand for uniting Virginia to the Southern Confederacy. His labors for this purpose belong to his State, but their fruits to the Confederacy.

Mr. President, as age advances, the imagination usually declines. Burke and Milton were exceptions to this usual effect of time. Perhaps, however, this result is often more apparent than real. Indifference may produce the same effect as weakness. As age advances, the vanity of all things terrestrial is forced upon the mind. Interest flags, and without interest the power of the mind cannot be evolved. The effect of apathy is mistaken for decay. The distinguished dead before us, seemed to possess, to the last, all the energy and fire which an undimmed imagination and the strongest interest in public affairs produces. You all remember the speech he delivered at our last session, on the imposition of taxes. Virginia, and her contributions and sufferings—the Confederate States, and their high duties and obligations—our noble cause, and the lofty destiny which awaited us—were the themes of his graceful and striking oratory. The youngest of us could not have spoken with more fire and force. His faculties seemed undimmed to the last.

The deceased appeared to me to possess remarkable equanimity of temper. With the deepest interest in public affairs, he had but little of that acerbity which the conflicts of public life are but too apt to produce against political foes. He was an honest man, not merely in the vulgar sense of the term, confined to pecuniary relations, but in that higher meaning of the poet, when he says that "an honest man is the noblest work of God."[38] He gave every man his due. In their characteristics, in their services, in their moral worth. He had none of that narrow vindictiveness in the administration of public affairs, which makes them tributary to personal passions. He was faithful to himself, whilst faithful to the country. He lifted himself to the dignity of his positions, and filled the great offices entrusted to him with a single view to the objects for which they were created. He was a man of the kindliest benevolence; yet he could see, even in the sufferings and desolations of war, the hand of a beneficent Providence working out the grand result of an eternal separation from our foes. A truer and braver upholder of the independence of the Confederate States, did not exist throughout our wide borders.

Sir, in conversation held, just before I left here to attend the Convention of South Carolina, whilest pacing yonder portico, he mentioned to me the efforts he had made in the Peace Conference at Washington, to satisfy the Northern delegates of the inestimable value of the South to them. He urged, that any great nation in Europe would give countless millions for the advantages the Union afforded them; but he was unable apparently to produce the least impression, to arrest their obstinate persistence in a policy of non-concession. But as soon as we had cast off the union with them, they seemed to be suddenly awakened to the tremendous ruin they had dragged down upon themselves; "and now, sir," he added, "they propose, by murdering our people and desolating our country, to force us back into all association with them, that we might again minister to their aggrandizement and wealth; but as a just God lives, they must fail." Mr. President, even though dead, he speaketh. "As a just God lives, they must fail!" His venerable form will no longer be seen amongst us. His voice will no longer be heard to support the great cause in which we are engaged; but the pious conviction he uttered will be realized in history. May we not suppose his voice to be the voice of prophecy; and that that glorious reality be so in much desired to see, of a redeemed, free and happy people in the Confederate States, will have its righteous consummation—"as a just God lives, they must fail!"

Mr. President, South Carolina mingles her grief with Virginia over the loss of her Illustrious son.

Mr. WIGFALL of Texas, [and] Mr. VENABLE of North Carolina, [also] each delivered an eloquent eulogy upon the character and public career of the deceased; after which the resolutions were unanimously adopted.

The President laid before Congress a communication from the House of Delegates, signed by CHARLES F. COLLIER, Speaker *pro. tem.*, enclosing the resolutions adopted by the General Assembly on Saturday last, which were read by the Secretary; whereupon Mr. BOCOCK, of Virginia, offered the following, which was agreed to:

Resolved, That the communication just read be spread upon the journals of Congress, and that the Committee of Arrangements of this body be directed to invite the co-operation of the Committee of the General Assembly of the State of Virginia in arranging for the funeral of the deceased.

The President then appointed the following Committee of Arrangements:

Mr. BOCOCK, of Virginia
Mr. CURRY, of Alabama
Mr. JOHNSON, of Arkansas
Mr. WARD, of Florida
Mr. CRAWFORD, of Georgia
Mr. BURNETT, of Kentucky
Mr. CONRAD, of Louisiana
Mr. HARRIS, of Mississippi
Mr. BELL, of Missouri
Mr. SMITH, of North Carolina[39]
Mr. BOYCE, of South Carolina
Mr. ATKINS, of Tennessee
Mr. OLDHAM, of Texas

On motion, Congress adjourned.

Tuesday, January 21, 1862
(Richmond *Examiner*, January 22, 1862)

As the hour of noon approached yesterday, at which time was appointed the commencement of the funeral ceremonies of ex-President TYLER, the Capitol Grounds were thronged with carriages, and with crowds of pedestrians, many of them wearing badges of mourning. The spectacle was one of solemn animation. Crowds wended their way to St. Paul's Church to secure seats that they might hear the funeral discourse to be delivered there, while others lingered on the route of the procession to observe its order and movement.

Prayer in Congress Hall—Procession to the Church

The first exercise in Congress after the House was called to order, and before the body was removed to the church, was the offering of the following prayer, by Rev. Dr. HOGE, of the Presbyterian Church:

> Almighty and ever-blessed God! Thou hast established Thy throne in the Heavens, and Thy kingdom ruleth over all. The hearts of the children of men are in Thy hand; their lives are subject to Thy control; at Thy command their bodies return to the dust, and their spirits go to the God who gave them.
>
> We humbly beseech Thee to make us deeply sensible of our dependence on Thee, and to fill us with reverence and godly fear. And, now, that we are about to go to the House of God, there to hear the instruction of Thy Holy Oracles, and thence to the grave, there to behold the place appointed for all the living, we pray Thee "make us to know our end, and the measure of our days, what it is, that we may know how frail we are."[40] And may Thy Holy Spirit so accompany the solemn scenes and services of the day that we may thereby be better prepared for all that awaits us in future life, for the hour of death, and for the felicities and glories of Thine Everlasting Kingdom, through Jesus Christ, our Lord. Amen.

The order of procession was formed as indicated in the published programme of the committees of arrangements;[41] a slight exception being made, allowing a place to the officers and members of "the Maryland Society,"[42] after "the officers of the army and navy of the Confederate States." The coffin was lifted by a file of the State Guard, the military selected for duty on the occasion. The procession moved on foot to St. Paul's Church, the band playing a solemn dirge. Long before the procession reached the church, the galleries had been crowded by an interested audience, largely composed of ladies; the seats on the floor being mostly reserved for the members of the procession.—Notwithstanding the immense pressure of the crowd, the utmost order and decorum were maintained in the body of the church by the prompt and unwearying attentions of Mr. IRVIN, the well-known and popular sexton.[43] The remains having been deposited near the chancel, the procession filed into the seats allotted them, the front seats being occupied by the family of the deceased, the committees, and the President, and heads of departments.

The Funeral Discourse

After appropriate preliminary cervices, Dr. MINNIGHRODE officiating,[44] and the singing by the choir of the 189th hymn, Right Reverend Bishop JOHNS, of the

Episcopal Church,[45] delivered the funeral discourse from the text—*Romans, chapter xiii, 7th verse*: "Render, therefore, to all their dues; tribute to whom tribute is due; custom to whom custom; fear to whom fear; honour to whom honour."

The Right Reverend Bishop commenced his discourse by remarking that it was not required of him to pass in review the public character and public works of the venerated statesmen whose remains lay there in the drapery of death. Nor was it necessary for him to dwell upon topics to which others had done justice, and of which they were better calculated than himself to speak with accuracy and completeness The deceased had left behind him a rich and pure legacy, worthy to adorn the history of his country and to guide others by example.

JOHN TYLER was the worthy son of a patriotic sire, from whose lips he had learned those lessons of wisdom which he illustrated in his life, and public example, and private associations. When scarcely more than a stripling, he was sent to William and Mary Collage, then its palmiest days of renown and usefulness.—Those who knew him well would recollect with what fondness and warm enthusiasm he was wont to recur to the early reminiscences of those college days; and through all his life, his Alma Mater never lost her place in his heart; nor was that mother insensible to the honourable distinctions in life obtained by her son, and she herself added to his chaplet of fame every garland that was in her gift. He was for a long period, a prominent member of the Board of Visitors of the College, afterwards President, and was chosen to the office of Chancellorship—in which latter place he had no predecessor but the Father of his Country, GEORGE WASHINGTON, in respect to whose memory it continued vacant until JOHN TYLER was, by acclamation, appointed to it.

The Right Rev. Bishop continued in a general reference to the public life of the deceased. It could not be said even when he was elevated to the high office of the President of the United States that his career had culminated, for to the close of life he had never experienced a decline. In retirement he suffered no decay in his faculties, and in the hour of darkness and struggle that had fallen upon his country he had come forth with nursed and gathered strength, "rejoicing as a strong man to run his race."[46]

It was comforting to know that the great work of eternity had not been neglected by the deceased. His gifted mind held fast as a foundation of its faith and hope to the Oracle of GOD. He was long accustomed to meditate on the things of eternity; and when, a few years ago, he was prostrated by sickness and impressed with the idea of approaching dissolution, the testimony of the pastor, whose services he was so found of attending in the church he had so reverently joined, showed the brightness of faith in which he died.

The next ceremony of solemn service to be performed for the dead, was to convey the remains to their last resting piece and cover them in the grave. In bearing them to the cemetery, where they were to rest, memory would naturally recur to the burial in that ground of another President of the United States, whose body was brought to us here by those then bound up in relationship with us,[47] expressing common sympathy, and whose hands assisted in the solemn offices, but are now pressing upon our soil in ruthless invasion, and with purposes of violence and blood. But oh, when we repair to the scene that brings up these associations—when we stand by the grave, oh let us think of Him who heard the hosannahs of the crowd that thronged his path, and so shortly after the cry of "crucify him," "crucify him;" and as we stand by the grave let us remember too, and as far as in us lies, take into our hearts the words of the same blessed Saviour, "Father, forgive them, for they know not what they do."

The Procession to the Grave

After the services had concluded in the church, the coffin was borne out to the hearse, and the time of procession commenced, the State Guard presenting arms during the ceremony. Notwithstanding the indecency of the weather and a drizzling fall of rain, the streets in the neighborhood were filled with spectators, the piazzas of the Central Hotel being crowded with citizens and visitors, had every point of observation occupied by those eager to witness the progress of the procession.

A considerable time elapsed before the line of procession was completed. About one hundred and fifty carriages were in procession, extending over a distance of a quarter of a mile. The order was preserved as laid down in the programme. President DAVIS having the place next to the Committee of Arrangement, and being followed by the heads of departments, and they by the Governor of Virginia, the judiciary, members of Congress, members of the State Legislature, &c.

The whole line of procession was under the conduct of Captain ELLIS, chief marshal, and the following aids, distinguished by white scarfs trimmed with crape: Captain SELDON, Major TYLER, Captain HILL, Captain SMITH, and Messrs. BIGGER, EUBANK, THOMPSON, TAYLOR, ZIMMER, and SMITH.

The route of the procession was then taken up Grace street to Fifth, down Fifth to Main, up Main to Second, down Second to Cary, and up Cary to the road leading to the Cemetery.

On reaching the Cemetery, the procession extended from the top of the hill overlooking the river to a considerable distance beyond the gates of the enclosure. After reading the funeral service, the remains were deposited in the grave. The situation chosen for the last resting place of the mortal remains of JOHN TYLER is by the side of the tomb of MONROE. It is on a knoll which commands a broad and beautiful view, stretching over all the objects of the city, with water view and landscape intermingled and overhanging the islets and falls of the river, the sound of whose waters is heard as a constant and distinct music by day and by night.

Wednesday, January 22, 1862—Saturday, February 15, 1862[48]

Monday, February 17, 1862
(Richmond *Enquirer*, February 18, 1862)

Congress met to day at 10 o'clock, A.M. and was opened with prayer, by the Rev. Dr. HOGE.

Mr. BARNWELL announced the presence of JAMES L. ORR, a delegate from South Carolina who came forward, was duly qualified, and took his sent.

Congress then went into secret session, during which,

Gen'ls. W. W. LORING and GEORGE B. CRITTENDEN were confirmed as Major Generals. The injunction of secrecy was removed from said confirmations.

After sometime occupied in secret session, Congress resolved itself into open session. Mr. BOCOCK, of Virginia, offered the following resolution, which was unanimously adopted

> *Resolved*, That the thanks of this House are eminently due, and are hereby tendered to the Hon. HOWELL COBB, President of the Provisional Congress, for the dignity, ability and impartiality which have so highly distinguished his official conduct as the presiding officer of this body.

Mr. BOCOCK then moved that Congress do now adjourn.

The motion was agreed to, and President COBB addressed the Congress as follows:

> Gentlemen of the Confederate Congress,
>
> Not as a mere formality do I receive the unanimous adoption of the resolution just considered by the House; and before I discharge the last duty incumbent on me as your president in declaring this Congress adjourned "without a day"—permit me, in the sincerity of my heart, to return you my grateful thanks. With whatever success I may have discharged my duties, I can truly say that no presiding officer ever received such cordial cooperation or such generous support from the body whose chair he occupied. And though the hour has arrived for dissolving our connection at the expiration of our service, I trust the time will never come for severing the ties which have been formed during this connection.
>
> The occasion naturally bears our mind back to the time of our assembling—when the representatives of six sovereign States, in a distant capitol—in calm consultation, deliberated over their destiny and sought to perpetuate their free institutions upon the basis adopted by our Fathers. One after another of our sister States linked her fortunes with ours, until to day the significant thirteen of the old Government marks the number of our Confederates.
>
> Within that period the Constitution which you prepared and submitted to the country has received the almost unanimous approval of our constituents, while most of your legislation has been in like manner approved at the bar of public opinion. I am prepared to promise to

the country that when the veil of secrecy, which policy has induced us to throw over our deliberations, shall be removed, a like endorsement of the entire action of this body will be the verdict of an enlightened public.—For while it has been complimentary to you, it is but the meed of praise, due to the patriotism of this people to say, that a more generous confidence was never extended to rulers under more trying circumstances.

Several of our number have been taken by death from our midst. Pardon a more direct allusion to one who, with many other noble spirits, has sealed with his blood on the field of battle the policy and acts which his wisdom assisted to devise and prepare. The memories of the occasion would be incomplete without this passing tribute to the illustrious dead.

The scene of to day is something worthy to be remembered. At our assembling, we were clothed with almost unlimited power. The Provisional Constitution was a self-constituted limit to our powers—and, yet so scrupulously regarded and maintained as if it had been the charter of our right. The period of our existence was voluntarily affixed by ourselves, and to-day we cheerfully surrender our powers to those elected under a Government provided by ourselves. They are not our successors.—This Congress has no successor. They inaugurate a Government, which is the successor of the Provisional Government. To those facts, I refer not in the spirit of boasting—but to repel the unjust imputation so persistently cast upon us by our unscrupulous enemy—that this was a military despotism, sustained only by the power of our arms.

The new Government will be fully inaugurated on the 22d—an appropriate day for placing in operation a Constitution characterized by the conservatism which so eminently distinguished "the Father of his Country." In the Capital of the old Government on the same day, the cold, heartless and hypocritical ceremony will be performed by their rulers of listening to the precepts inculcated in his last legacy to his countrymen[49]—the persistent disregard of which by themselves has forced us to seek for safety and liberty under a new organization. The contrast is before the world—let them decide between us.

In truth, gentlemen, I must refer to one remarkable characteristic of this revolution which distinguishes it from all others recorded in history. It cannot be too prominently set forth, or too often considered—I mean its conservatism. Usually revolutions are the result of the excited passions of a people whose patience is exhausted, and hence their popular tendencies have too frequently degraded them into anarchy and discord. But here the people at the ballot box deliberately vote a revolution to escape from the very anarchy which they see impending and to preserve those conservative principles of the fathers of the Republican, which were fast being overwhelmed by popular fanaticism. Every step in the drama has been marked by the same tendency. The changes in the Federal Constitution were suggested and adopted with the same views, and every page of the history of this war will show that we, without the checks of Government, have imposed upon ourselves the most conservative principles, while our enemies, having the organized Government, have trampled under foot every constitutional limitation, and disregarded all public and private rights. That this springs from the people themselves and is not due alone to the wisdom of their rulers, is manifest from the fact, that in more than one of the States, the very occasion of revolution, has been used to reform their own Constitution; and to improve by impressing this same conservatism upon the fundamental law of the State.

Gentlemen, I have perhaps detained you too long. I cannot close without commending to those who follow us in government, one element of success to which I may perhaps attribute too much. I refer to the generous confidence which each department of the Provisional Government has exhibited towards all others. In our common danger there should be no divisions. The spirit of party has never shown itself for an instant in your deliberations, and I would that it should be the good fortune of each successive presiding officer, in the closing scene of every Congress to be able to bear the testimony I now publicly give to the honor of this body.

When I first took this chair, I ventured the opinion that our separation was "perfect, complete and perpetual." If any doubted then, the past year has dispelled that doubt, and no person can now be found who will say that the separation was too soon, or would be too perpetual. Relying on the harmony of our people; upon the justice of our cause; upon our own strong arms, and the smile of a kind and protecting Providence, from the incipiency of this revolution to this moment, I have never had one despondent hour.

These have been our reliance in the past and must be our hope for the future; for thus far we have successfully conducted our revolution, without even the benefit of that recognition which has never before been denied to a people who have shown the same capacity and determination to maintain their independence.

Renewing the expression of my heartfelt thanks, I proceed gentlemen, to discharge the last duty of the chair, and to pronounce this Congress adjourned "without a day."

APPENDIX I: DOCUMENTS

I. Edwin V. Sharpe to W. H. Pritchard, February 9, 1861[1]

Augusta, Ga., February 9, 1861

W. H. Pritchard,[2]
Montgomery, Ala.

Dear Sir: Herewith you will find devices for Seal and Flag for the Southern Confederacy, and description accompanying them. My desire is to have the same brought before the committee appointed for the purpose of getting up Seal and Flag, and earnestly request that you place them in the hands of some one who will give them due consideration. If Mr. Gardner is still in Montgomery he will appreciate my object,[3] and I know of no one with whom I would rather trust them.

Any favor performed in regard to the designs will be highly appreciated by me.

Your friend,
Edwin V. Sharp

P.S.—Design has got so dirty from handling that I am ashamed to send it. It has just returned to me.

Description of Devices

Seal.—An escutcheon composed of the following parts: A chief, occupying the whole length and one-third of its breadth, which represents Congress, bearing upon its blue area a number of stars (argent or white) equal to the States forming the Confederacy. Upon each side of the chief are three upright pales equal in width to each other, placed alternately, yellow (gold) and red, the red in the middle—*six original States*—the whole border done with oak and laurel. Just emanating from a dark cloud, which represents our late national troubles, relieved by the bosom of a cerulean sky, is a young moon, shining by *no borrowed* light, save that of our *own six suns*, denoting the infancy and purity of the new Republic. Over all, suspended in air, *for Independence*, floats a red scroll bearing the motto.

Flag.—To be twice as long as deep. The middle third to be blue, extending the whole length, and, placed upon it according to taste, a number of white stars equal to the States in the Confederacy; the upper and lower thirds to be divided into (each) three equal parts, each part having two yellow and one red stripe, the stripes horizontal. Colors used: White, purity; blue, perseverance; red, valor; yellow, wealth, prosperity.

II. JACOB B. PLATT TO ALEXANDER H. STEPHENS, FEBRUARY 12, 1861[4]

Augusta, Ga., February 12, 1801

Hon. A. H. STEPHENS,
Vice-President

DEAR SIR: Enclosed you will please find a description of my Flag, from my friend, Dr. H. F. CAMPBELL,[5] whom I have succeeded in interesting in my enterprise. The model itself will be delivered into your hands by the messenger of Adams' Express Company. I would prefer, when my model goes before the committee, that Dr. CAMPBELL's letter be read to them, as he has appeared to enter more fully into my ideas than any one else; and, also, if my Flag is accepted and a description published, I wish the letter used for that purpose. I am fully certain Dr. CAMPBELL will not object. I am sorry to give you so much trouble, but if your own State should furnish the National Emblem it will only be adding to her title to be called "Empire State."

Very respectfully, yours,
JACOB B. PLATT

P.S.—I must ask to have it remembered that the blue field, with my device of arrangement of stars, &c., may be changed to any part of my six-striped bunting, and yet the chief idea will still be mine, and, by all laws governing inventions and discovery, I will be entitled to the merit and honor of the award. My Flag has been described in print. I hope, my dear sir, that I will be protected from any surreptitious adoption of my really original idea to the injury of my just claims.

Very respectfully, yours,
J. B. PLATT

Augusta. Ga., February 11, 1861

J. B. PLATT, Esq.

DEAR SIR: I have carefully examined and considered the Flag shown me yesterday by you. It affords me pleasure to comply with the request that I furnish you with my opinion of the sketch as the model from which the National Flag of the Confederate States of North America may be made.

I must remark, however, you would have been more fortunate had you selected some one better versed in the science pertaining to the subject than myself. The model is made of silk, but contemplates the use of bunting as the material of the Flag itself. The Flag consists of six stripes of scarlet and white placed alternately; in the upper staff corner there is a blue field, on which is displayed the arrangement of stars, which constitutes not the only, but certainly the most significant, part of your device. These are the following: First, a very large six-pointed star placed in the centre of the field; and, secondly, at the intervals between the points of this large star, are six smaller stars, each composed of six points. You have told me that the position of the smaller stars in relation to the larger (whether opposite the points or at the intervals), as also the place on the entire Flag that the blue field with white stars should occupy, is a matter of indifference, so far as the main idea and significance of your device is concerned, and that you are also indifferent as to whether the series should begin or end with a white or a scarlet stripe.

I am much gratified to state that, at the first glance, your model struck me with its marked appropriateness and clear meaning, and the more carefully I have considered it, the more strongly have I been impressed with its plain and comprehensive significance. It possesses the rare and valuable quality of a most suggestive and fertile *complexity*, without either confusion, obscurity, or involvement of elements. Both in outline and in detail, whether viewed from a distance or more nearly, in its parts or as a whole, I am pleased to find that it possesses advantages over all other conceptions I have as yet heard of as models for the proposed National Emblem.

It is said that the superlative degree has been expressed by eastern nations in a *repetition* of the principal idea qualifying the object. Your device, though abounding in a multiplication of symbols, thus repeating and giving prominence to its fundamental idea, is yet not the less ready and easy of interpretation, thus: the six stripes on the bunting, the six points of the large central star, and also the six points of each of the six lesser stars, are designed to be permanent, commemorating, with a repeated and multiplied significance, by three distinct methods, *the six original States*, whose delegates in the first Congress of the Confederacy solemnly committed them to the founding of a great Southern Nation. This repetition of the important idea of the number of the original States coincides with the same point observed in the National Flag of the United States, of which we recently constituted a part. Your Flag, in this particular, presents the advantage over the United States Flag, as this commemoration is not only triple, but unchanging, whereas, in the old Flag it is at present indicated by only the thirteen stripes, the number of stars having been greatly increased and the points of the stars having never had any reference to the subject

The idea presented in the large central six-pointed star is very happy and appropriate, impressing the beholder, at a glance, with the image of a consolidated Republic of six component parts. The smaller stars, clustering around the great national orb after the manner of satellites, are, like all the other features of your device, of a multiplied significance. Firstly, they are the bright elements of a consolidated whole, so homogeneous and consistent that they together compose, when fused into one, a *magnificent counterpart* of each of its integral constituents; and, secondly, the difference in magnitude between the great star and those surrounding it unavoidably suggests the appropriate figure from the Physical Universe, viz., that of satellites revolving around and drawn towards the larger congenial mass as its centre of attraction.

An advantage which I further think well worthy of consideration is that any number of the smaller six-pointed stars may symmetrically cluster around the central one till all the Southern States are added to the Confederacy. At present each star, representing an integral State, is placed between the points of the central or "Confederate star," and all these places are already occupied; but, in like manner, suitable positions, *on the points* or elsewhere, may be selected till every Southern star adds its brilliancy to our national firmament.

I have thus, my dear sir, given you my impression of your truly ingenious device. To the apprehension of others cultivated in this particular art, in which I have no pretension, I have little doubt the close study of your Flag will prove even more fruitful and suggestive than it has to me.

I could add to what is expressed above other views which I forbear to dwell on. They are indicative rather of my own personal preference, and might fail to have the same weight with our national committee, to whose wisdom and judgment is confided the award, as they have with me; yet, perhaps not. I refer to the important feature that your Flag, though sufficiently peculiar to give *national individuality* to the emblem, still possesses the attribute of retaining all the hallowed associations which, both at home and abroad, have for years in every American breast clustered around "the stars and stripes" of a nation once the most glorious the world ever beheld; and of that nation we ourselves and all the world cannot fail to remember that the Southern States were but lately its *proudest element*, blest in its privileges, blest in its wide-spread fraternal love, and equal in the possession of all its common glories, past, present, and prospective.

I am, dear sir, very faithfully, yours,

HENRY T. CAMPBELL

III. F. W. McMaster to W. W. Boyce, February 11, 1861[6]

Columbia, S.C., February 11. 1861

Hon. W. W. Boyce,
Montgomery, Ala.

Dear Colonel: I send you by express a design of a Flag for the Southern Confederacy, gotten up in great haste this morning by Mr. R. B. Waddell,[7] which strikes me as being much more appropriate than the Southern Cross, proposed by a Charlestonian. The Flag made after Mr. Waddell's design will be very beautiful. It is the French tricolor, red, white, and blue; but in the French Flag the colors are parallel. I think it a very simple and tasteful Flag.

The *Cross* is a badge of *Papal* power, and will be repulsive to the taste of a *large* majority of the Southern people.

Please show the design to Mr. Memminger. In great haste for the express,

I remain, yours truly,

F. W. McMaster[8]

IV. Thomas H. Hobbs to R. W. Walker, February 11, 1861[9]

Chattanooga, Tenn., February 11, 1861

Hon. R. W. Walker,
Montgomery, Ala.

Enclosed I send you a design for the banner for the new Confederacy. If you think it has any merit, and the Congress chooses to adopt a new banner, you may lay this before them. Its merits are—

1. The stars represent States, and being arranged in a circle, the close union of those States. This arrangement (in a circle) will allow of indefinite increase of number, as other States come in, without destroying the original design.
2. We will still have a "Star Spangled Banner," which is dear to the people from old association, and we can afford to let the Yankees keep the stripes. We are entitled to a "Star Spangled Banner," because the best poetry in honor of it was composed by a Southern man, and the incident which occasioned its composition occurred on Southern soil and reflected honor on Southern soldiers.
3. The Flag to be of solid blue and the stars white.
4. The motto attributes the splendors of the stars to the honor and unbroken faith of the States.

Very respectfully, your friend and obedient servant,

Thomas H. Hobbs[10]

V. JOSEPH M. SHELLMAN TO [ROBERT TOOMBS], FEBRUARY 9, 1861[11]

Augusta, Ga., February 9, 1861

DEAR SIR: I send you a rude specimen of a Flag which I propose for adoption by the Southern Congress as the National Banner of the Southern Confederacy. It is, as you perceive, in form similar to the United States Flag, which is emblematic of our former Union; but the transposition of the colors, of our repudiation of that Union. The tricolor is the emblem of Liberty; the clustering stars, of Union; and their arrangement in the form of a crescent, of Progress. Hence, our motto may be: Liberty, Union, Progress. The artist has painted the faint outline of the new moon, which he intended merely to exhibit more clearly the arrangement of the stars in that form, and is not intended to form any feature in the Flag. I am a plain, unpretending man, who has now, for the first time, ventured to obtrude his views on any public body, and if they are not acceptable, I am content.

Yours, respectfully,

Jos. M. Shellman[12]

If you do not think it worthy of notice, please suppress it.

J. M. S.

VI. "RICHMOND COUNTY" TO ALEXANDER H. STEPHENS, FEBRUARY 10, 1861[13]

Augusta, Ga., February 10, 1861

Hon. A. H. STEPHENS,
Montgomery, Ala.

DEAR SIR: Enclosed herewith please find a design proposed for the Flag of "The Confederate States of North America."

I have used "checky"[14] in the shield, as it is "considered one of the most noble and ancient figures used in armory." As a chess-board, it represents the battle-field upon which we expect to contend for our independence.

Of the colors proposed it is unnecessary to say any thing as to their emblematic significance. The green, however, is unusual, and it may be well to state that it is intended to represent a large element in our population derived from the "Emerald Isle."

I also send you three plates of Flags now "afloat," by which you will see that the design is original.

Very respectfully, your obedient servant,

"Richmond County"

VII. A. BONAND TO F. S. BARTOW, FEBRUARY 12, 1861[15]

Savannah, Ga., February 12, 1861

Hon. F. S. BARTOW

DEAR SIR: I take the liberty of sending you two models for the Flag of the Southern Confederation, not that I think myself better posted than the honorable gentlemen composing your committee, but the desire to preserve the old Flag, if not in design, at least in color, has prompted me to submit to you the enclosed models. The main object in the composition of a Flag being, in my humble opinion, simplicity, solidity, and facility of making the same, the enclosed models have, in my opinion, that merit. The stars have six points, representing the six States who have first formed the present Confederacy.

Very respectfully,

A. Bonaud[16]

VIII. A. A. FREEMAN TO F. S. BARTOW, FEBRUARY 12, 1861[17]

Macon, Ga., February 12, 1861

Mr. F. S. BARTOW

Sir: Enclosed I send you a model of a Flag for the Southern Confederacy. The old Flag has thirteen stripes, representing the thirteen original colonies; this has only seven, representing the seven seceding States—seven stars on a blue field. The motto or emblem, I do not know which, should be under the seven stars.

Yours, &c.,

A. A. Freeman[18]

IX. W. J. LAVAL TO HOWELL COBB, FEBRUARY 9, 1861[19]

Charleston, S.C., February 9, 1861

Hon. HOWELL COBB,
President Southern Convention

DEAR SIR: I have the honor herewith to enclose to you several unpretending designs for the Flag of the Southern Confederacy, which you are most respectfully requested to submit for the consideration of the convention now assembled at Montgomery. The fair hands of a patriotic daughter of South Carolina have assisted in the preparation of the designs, and it is hoped therefore that some one out of the number submitted may commend itself to the approval and preference of the distinguished body over which you preside.

I have further to request that you would cause the package to be returned to me at the close of your deliberations, either by express or through any of the delegates from this State.

I have the honor to be, with great respect, your obedient servant,

W. J. Laval[20]

X. R. C. GILCHRIST TO C. G. MEMMINGER, FEBRUARY 4, 1861[21]

Charleston, S.C., *February* 4, 1861

Hon. C. G. MEMMINGER,
Montgomery, Ala.

DEAR SIR: I herewith send a design for the Flag of our Southern Confederation. I presume this subject will come before the convention, and am ambitious of being the author of the new Flag, which will float over every sea and protect the citizens of the proudest nation on the earth. May I not bespeak your influence? The description will be found on the back of the design. I have shown it to many persons of taste in this city, and it has been universally admired and commended.

Respectfully, yours,

R. C. GILCHRIST

Description

A new constellation has just taken its place among the galaxy of nations, and now the "Southern Cross" is the cynosure of all eyes. This Flag embodies this idea. At the same time it seeks to preserve the essential features of the beautiful Flag of the American Republic, to which we have as great a right as any other people on the earth.

The centre of the Flag is occupied by an azure "cross" bespangled with stars equal in number to the States composing the Southern Confederation—a star to be added as each State comes in.

Horizontally are alternate red and white stripes, equal in number to the States represented in this convention—the original seceding States.

There is no Flag in the world like it, and yet we have the "stars and stripes" still. The combination of its colors, although by no means gaudy, will make it conspicuous at the greatest distance on sea or land. As such it is respectfully presented to the consideration of the Southern Convention.

XI. MRS. E. G. CARPENTER TO "GENTLEMEN," FEBRUARY 20, 1861[22]

Cassville, Ga., February 20, 1861

GENTLEMEN: Having seen in the papers several designs for Banners, presented for the consideration of the Committee on Flags, I presume upon the privilege of sending one, designed and completed by myself, for the present use of the military of our village. I send you a model, though in rather a rude state. The centre star of six points represents the six States now in Congress; the eight surrounding stars, eight of the border slave-holding States, while the ninth is placed in the farther corner of the stripes, showing the right of single secession. The heart in the centre star means the heart of the people is in the Southern Confederacy; the dove and olive-branch, our wish for peaceable secession; but, if necessary, we must resort to the righteous defense of the sword. Under all circumstances, we must remember that the eye of God is upon us, and the cross that we must look to a higher power than the wisdom and arm of man. As the border States come into the Union they may be connected, first to the Congress star, by a chain, and the chain extended from star to star as the States may come in. If any, after a proper time, refuse to join the Southern Confederacy, strike them out; and if any of the non-slaveholding States see proper to unite with us, the circle may be enlarged by adding other stars. The motto should be painted on the satin, but, for want of room, I use a piece of paper. The stars might appear to better advantage on a ground of red.

Yours, with all respect,

MRS. E. G. CARPENTER

XII. H. AUG. POND TO S. F. HALE, FEBRUARY 18, 1861[23]

Greensborough, Ala., February 18, 1861

S. F. HALE, Esq.

DEAR SIR: Not having the pleasure of an intimate acquaintance with, still I can claim an introduction to you through Mr. C. E. BRAME,[24] of the academy at this place, two years since.

I have been for some time connected with Mr. BRAME, at the academy, in the artistical department of music, drawing, painting, &c., and, at his suggestion, have designed a Flag as a National Flag for our Southern Confederation.

If I mistake not, there is a committee appointed to consider the matter and report, and already, I suppose, many designs have been handed in. I do not wish to encroach upon your time to peruse a lengthy synopsis of my ideas, but if you will indulge me, I will briefly state my views: 1st, it is universally acknowledged that the American Flag is the handsomest of all the National Flags; 2d, that it is conceded by all mariners discernable at a greater distance than any other, and more readily distinguished; and 3d, that it is decidedly American in coloring and design.

Our Southern Confederacy, if I mistake not, design adopting as much of the Constitution as will answer their views and purposes. Why may we then not adopt as much of the old Flag as will answer our purposes, so celebrated in song and history?

We have seceded from the old Union and formed a new Union; let us do in like manner with the Flag, viz:—the blue square in the upper corner, containing the stars, representing the States of the Union, and termed the union part of the Flag—let us place that in the centre. Secede from the corner to the centre. We then have a square within a square, or, if preferred, make the centre piece an oval instead of a square; put in the number of stars corresponding to the number of States, adding thereto as they join our new Confederacy. We then preserve the American design, and the Flag will be at once recognized from the old Flag, and, in an artistical point of view, will be a much handsomer and better proportioned emblem. Also, the old Flag is sometimes burlesqued by exposing, upside down, or, as the old sailors say, union down: but, with the design I propose, we indicate that we have now formed a Union that cannot be put down; for turn the Flag which way you will the union part of it will be in the centre.

I have exhibited my design to several of our citizens, who approve and urge me to present it for consideration, and, presuming upon your indulgence in my intruding upon your already preoccupied moments, and soliciting the favor of your presenting the design to the committee on that subject for inspection and consideration, allow me to remain,

Very truly, yours,

H. Aug. Pond[25]

XIII. H. AUG. POND TO J. L. M. CURRY, FEBRUARY 18, 1861[26]

Greensborough Female Academy,
Greensborough, Ala., February 18, 1861

Hon. J. L. M. CURRY

DEAR SIR: I have taken the liberty of addressing you on the subject of a "National Flag" for our Southern Confederacy. I am induced to do so, having conferred with your brother, Mr. JACKSON CURRY, also Mr. JABEZ CURRY,[27] ELDER WALTHALL,[28] and others, who are pleased with my ideas, and have encouraged me to present it. If I am correctly informed, there is a committee appointed for the purpose of deciding upon a Flag, and hoping you will excuse a stranger for intruding upon your time, allow me to present to you, as well as to your associate from this district (himself also a stranger personally), Hon. S. F. HALE, of Eutaw, my ideas respecting a National Southern Confederacy Flag.

The old American Flag is particularly (in three points of view) entitled to consideration: 1st. That, by all nations, it is conceded to be the handsomest. 2d. That, by mariners, it is acknowledged to be more easily discerned at a distance. 3d. That it is most decidedly American in coloring and design.

It is designed, I believe, to adopt as much of the old Constitution in the Constitution of the new Southern Confederacy as will suit our purpose, and, in like manner, I propose to use the old Flag as far as suits our purpose, on the ground that it is so decidedly American, and, both in song and history, has a celebrity unequaled, founded upon the fame and heroism of men of the South as well as of the North. When we think of the "Star Spangled Banner," "Columbia, Gem of the Ocean," and other songs written by Southern men, can we not claim our Stars and Stripes?

Then, again, we have seceded from the old Union and formed a new Union; in a similar manner let us do with the Flag, viz: The blue square in the upper corner is termed the union part of the Flag, and contains the stars, representing the several States; let that be placed in the centre, and, as in olden times the stars were few in number, but surely and gradually increased, so in like manner our galaxy, though few, is bound to fill out and will secede from the corner to the centre; more than that, the old Flag is often burlesqued by being hoisted upside down, or, in nautical parlance, is termed union down, but by placing the union in the centre we indicate that we have formed a Union that cannot be put down; for turn the Flag endways, sideways, or whichever way you please, the union still remains in the centre.

The centre may be either square or oval, but by being placed in the centre is more in accordance with rules of design, is handsomer, is as readily distinguished, and is as fully American, and can be readily recognized from the old Federal Flag.

Thus I have endeavored to explain my ideas, as also in a similar letter to Mr. Hale. I trust you will pardon the liberty I have taken, and also that of soliciting, should you deem it worthy, your interest with the committee appointed to consider the subject.

Hoping, therefore, I may be excused for trespassing thus far upon your patience, allow me to remain,

Very truly, yours,

H. Aug. Pond

XIV. C. E. Brame to J. L. M. Curry, February 18, 1861[29]

Greensborough, Ala., February 18, 1861

Hon. J. L. M. Curry

Dear Sir: If the present Provisional Government intends adopting a National Flag, I beg leave, most respectfully, to submit the following: What is called the union in the old Flag to be placed in the centre; the seven stars, denoting the seceding States, to be grouped in the form of a sickle on a blue ground, and the stripes to be as they are on the old Flag. As a modification of that design, I would respectfully recommend that the union in which is placed the sickle be of an oval form, and surrounded by seven elliptic curves, alternately red, white, and blue.

My reasons for submitting the particular designs mentioned are found in the fact that the design is simple, beautiful, suggestive, and original. The idea of the sickle is taken from that figure in the constellation

"Leo," by which I would intimate our origin from Great Britain. It would also convey with it, as an agricultural implement, the peaceful tendencies of the Government established, whilst it might suggest the thought that the Divine Being would employ its power and overrule its grand destiny as a reaper in the great harvest of souls. Besides, from this constellation there emanated that most wonderful phenomena of shooting stars in 1833. This might suggest the idea that from our glorious Confederacy there might go out an influence filling the world with beauty, light, and admiration. The design is original, as no other nation has ever had a sickle for its ensign.

In regard to the rest of the Flag, it might be composed of red, white, and blue stripes, equaling the number of seceding States forming the Government, or there might be that many ellipses surrounding an oval blue one, which contain the sickle and stars.

If it is worth while, and you think the matter sufficiently worthy of consideration, you will much oblige one who entertains the warmest sentiments of esteem for yourself if you will bring my suggestions before any committee authorized to consider this matter.

I should feel very proud of having suggested the design which shall be adopted; but my anxiety to receive the honor would not preclude my devotion to any Flag which may be adopted by the Confederate States of America.

If you think it advisable, I can have a model of this Flag forwarded.

Respectfully,

C. E. Brame

XV. Alexander Walker to Charles Conrad, March 2, 1861[30]

New Orleans
2 March 1861

Dear Sir,

At the request of a number of persons interested in steamboat navigation, I beg to call your attention to the necessity of framing, as early as possible, an act for the Confederate States corresponding with the Act of the old Congress of Aug. 30, 1852 relating to steamboats.[31] It is thought that in the present state of affairs that two supervising inspectors will be needed, and it is suggested that the Alabama River is a good line of division between them. With the necessary change in the number and apportionment of the supervising districts, there is one other amendment which is greatly desired here and the reason for which will immediately occur to you. It is in the composition of the Board of Inspectors, which by Section 9 is required to be made up of one person of practical knowledge of ship carpentering and one other an engineer. It must be apparent to you that this Board, whose principal duty is the examination and license of Pilots and Engineers, ought to have upon it a person acquainted with the duties of a Pilot and a Pilot on our river is required to be acquainted with the power of steam and with the strength, sea worthiness, and other qualities of the hulls of steamers. It is [respectfully?] proposed to substitute "Pilot" for ship captain in the Rivers. There is but one opinion here on as regard to the advantage and necessity of the change. Our steamboats are as much dependent on the capacity of Pilots, as of any other officers, and under the Law of 1852 there is no one on the Board competent to examine Pilots.

You will confer a great favor upon your constituents by effecting this slight change in the law. The necessity of some early action on this subject must be obvious. At present the Board here feel very much embarrassed both as to their authority to perform any of their duties imposed upon them by the act of Congress. The Congress could relieve them by enabling the Law of 1852 with the changes suggested. I enclose the acts and a written note of the proposed changes. I am very resp[ectfully] yours

Alexander Walker[32]

XVI. BENJAMIN F. JONES TO A. R. WRIGHT, MARCH 11, 1861[33]

My Dear Sir

I take the liberty of offering some suggestions for your consideration on a subject of much importance to the new Confederacy & its friends here, to wit: The Tariff.

The duties imposed by the Confederate States upon goods imported within its limits is certainly one of great importance & to one in your position objections might not be so perceptible as to one engaged in merchandizing.

You cannot have failed to know that the duties have succeeded most completely in stopping all trade between the two sections which is no doubt the result aimed at. But if we take time to look a little further at the result, it will be found disastrous to the South. The South are without, goods cannot be supplied for the present from Southern importation or manufacturers.

You are obliged to have manufactured goods from the North until they can be manufactured South. You give no time for such a movement. If the act as pass[e]d was to have taken effect 3 or 6 months hence it would be quite a dif[feren]t matter. Many houses good & strong, tired & disgusted with the Northern sentiment would gladly go forth & for "weal or wo" abide the result but they have stocks on hand & the tariff amounts to a prohibition.

Your primary object no doubt was to raise revenue by the tariff to repay gov[ernmen]t expenses. Would it not have been better to have thrown your ports open free of duty to all nations for a limited time & let the taxes on the goods go toward defraying Gov[ernmen]t expenses.

In that way something would have been paid toward supporting revenue but now nothing absolutely nothing will be ship[pe]d from this section & commerce is so deranged that I imagine but few goods will be imported direct into Southern ports. Your planters won't have the test. They won't pay extra prices on brogans & such things & will begin to look around & conclude that secession is not so elegant after all & you will have dissatisfaction at home.

The Southern Confederated States don't want to cut the throats of *their friends* here. They have some been good & true—the true men of the land whose rights & interests should be respected so as to win them with you. *They want to go*. Therefore,

Open your ports, free of duty 6 mo[nth]s & capital & merchandise (taxable property) will flow in "like the rush of many waters." Give capitalists & manufacturers time to make their arrangements.

If they went now with stock on hand—your yeomanry "*vox populi*" should murmur & set up a yell that would echo throughout the land. You will soon find that the present tariff act gives much dissatisfaction at home & should be repealed & put upon a dif[feren]t base. In thus expressing the honest sentiments of myself & others here, I trust you will not regard it impertinent.

Yrs very truly B. F. Jones

XVII. Documents Related to the Washington Peace Conference Annexed to President Davis's Message, April 29, 1861[34]

The annexed proceedings transpired in secret session, but the secrecy was subsequently removed:

Gentlemen of the Congress

In the Message addressed to you on the 29th ult. I referred to the course of conduct of the Government of the United States towards the Commissioners of this Government, sent to Washington for the purpose of effecting, if possible, a peaceful adjustment of the pending difficulties between the two Governments. I also made allusion to "an intermediary, whose high position and character inspired the hope of success"; but I was not then at liberty to make my communication, on this subject as specific as was desirable for a full comprehension of the whole subject. It is now, however, in my power to place before you other papers, which I, herewith, address to you; from them you will perceive that the intermediary referred to was the Hon. John A. Campbell, a Judge of the Supreme Court of the United States, who made earnest effort to promote the successful issue of the mission entrusted to our Commissioners, and by whom I was kept advised, in confidential communications, of the measures taken by him to secure so desirable a result. It is due to you, to him, and to history, that a narration of the occurrences with which he was connected should be known, the more especially as it will be seen by the letters hereto appended, that the correctness and accuracy of the recital have not been questioned by the Secretary of State of the United States, to whom it was addressed.

I avail myself of this opportunity to correct an error in one of the statements made in my Message of the 29th April. It is there recited that I was prompted to call you together, in extraordinary session, by reason of the declarations contained in the Proclamation of President Lincoln of the 15th of April. My Proclamation convoking you, was issued on the 12th April, and was prompted by the declaration of hostile purposes, contained in the Message sent by President Lincoln to the Governor of South Carolina, on the 8th of April, as the Proclamation of President Lincoln, of the 16th April, repeated the same hostile intention in more specific terms and on a much more extensive scale, it created a stronger impression on my mind, and led to the error, above alluded to, and which, however unimportant, I desire to correct.

JEFFERSON DAVIS
MONTGOMERY, May 8, 1861

Washington City, April 13, 1861

SIR—On the 15th March ult., I left with Judge CRAWFORD,[35] one of the Commissioners of the Confederate States, a note in writing to the effect following:

"I feel entire confidence that Fort Sumter will be evacuated in the next five days. And this measure is felt as imposing great responsibility on the administration.

"I feel entire confidence that no measure changing the existing status, prejudicially to the Southern Confederate States, is at present contemplated.

"I feel an entire confidence that an immediate demand for an answer to the communication of the Commissioners will be productive of evil and not of good. I do not believe that it ought at this time to be pressed."

The substance of this statement I communicated to you the same evening by letter. Five days elapsed, and I called with a telegram from General BEAUREGARD to the effect that Sumter was not evacuated, but that Major ANDERSON was at work making repairs.

The next day, after conversing with you, I communicated to Judge CRAWFORD, in writing, that the failure to evacuate Sumter was not the result of bad faith, but was attributable to causes consistent with the intention to fulfill the engagement, and that as regarded Pickens, I should have notice of any design to alter the existing status there. Mr. Justice NELSON was present at these conversations,[36] three in number, and I submitted to him each of my written communications to Judge CRAWFORD, and informed Judge C[RAWFORD] that they had his (Judge NELSON's) sanction. I gave you, on the 22d of March, a substantial copy of the statement I had made on the 15th.

The 30th of March arrived, and at that time a telegram came from Gov. PICKENS,[37] inquiring concerning Col. LAMON,[38] whose visit to Charleston he supposed had a connection with the proposed evacuation of Fort Sumter.

I left that with you, and was to have an answer the following Monday, (1st of April). On the 1st of April I received from you the statement in writing: "(I am satisfied) the Government will not undertake to supply Fort Sumter without giving notice to Gov. P[ICKENS]." The words "I am satisfied" were for me to use as expressive of confidence in the remainder of the declaration.

The proposition as originally prepared was, "The President *may desire* to supply Sumter, but will not do so," &c., and your verbal explanation was that you did not believe any such attempt would be made, and that there was no design to reinforce Sumter.

There was a departure here from the pledges of the previous month, but, with the verbal explanation, I did not consider it a matter then to complain of. I simply stated to you that I had the assurance previously.

On the 7th of April I addressed you a letter on the subject of the alarm that the preparations by the Government had created, and asked you if the assurances I had given were well or ill-founded. In respect to Sumter your reply was, "Faith as to Sumter, fully kept—wait and see." In the morning's paper I read, "An authorized messenger from President LINCOLN informed Gov. PICKENS and Gen. BEAUREGARD that provisions will be sent to Fort Sumter—peaceably, or *otherwise by force*. This was the 8th of April, at Charleston, the day following your last assurance, and is the evidence of the full faith I was incited to wait for and see. In the same paper, I read that intercepted dispatches disclosed the fact that Mr. FOX, who had been allowed to visit Major ANDERSON, on the pledge that his purpose was pacific, employed his opportunity to devise a plan for supplying the Fort by force, and that this plan had been adopted by the Washington Government, and was in process of execution. My recollection of the date of Mr. FOX's visit carries it to a day in March.[39] I learn he is a near connection of a member of the Cabinet.[40] My connection with the Commissioners and yourself was superinduced by a conversation with Justice NELSON. He informed me of your strong dispositions in favor of peace, and that you were oppressed with a demand of the Commissioners of the Confederate States for a reply to their first letter, and that you desired to avoid it if possible at that time.

I told him I might perhaps be of some service in arranging the difficulty. I came to your office entirely at his request and without the knowledge of either of the Commissioners. Your depression was obvious to both Judge NELSON and myself. I was gratified at the character of the counsels you were desirous of pursuing and much impressed with your observation that a civil war might be prevented by the success of my mediation. You read a letter of Mr. WEED, to show how irksome and responsible the withdrawal of troops from Sumter was.[41] A portion of my communication to Judge CRAWFORD on the 15th March was founded upon these remarks, and the pledge to evacuate Sumter is less forcible than the words you employed. These words were: Before this letter reaches you (a proposed letter by me to President DAVIS) Sumter will have been evacuated.

The Commissioners who received those communications, conclude they have been abused and overreached. The Montgomery Government hold the same opinion. The Commissioners have supposed that my communications were with you, and upon the hypothesis were prepared to arraign you before the country in connection with the President. I placed a peremptory prohibition upon this as being contrary to the term of my communications with them. I pledged myself to them to communicate information upon what I considered as the best authority, and they were to confide in the ability of myself, aided by Judge NELSON, to determine upon the credibility of my informant.

I think no candid man who will read over what I have written, and considers for a moment what is going on at Sumter, but will agree that the equivocating conduct of the Administration, as measured and interpreted in connection with these promises, is the proximate cause of the great calamity.

I have a profound conviction that the telegrams of the 8th of April of General BEAUREGARD, and of the 10th of April of General WALKER, the Secretary of War, can be referred to nothing else than their belief that there has been systematic duplicity practiced on them through me. It is under an oppressive sense of the weight of this responsibility that I submit to you these things for your explanation.

Very respectfully,

[Signed] John A. Campbell,
Associate Justice of the Supreme Court U.S.

Hon. Wm. H. Seward, Secretary of State

Dispatches
To L. P. WALKER, Secretary of War:

An authorized message from President LINCOLN just informed Governor PICKENS and myself that provisions will be sent to Fort Sumter peaceably, or otherwise by force.

Gen. P. G. T. BEAUREGARD:

If you have no doubt as to the authorized character of the agent who communicated to you the intention of the Washington Government to supply Fort Sumter by force, you will at once demand its evacuation, and if this is refused proceed in such manner as you may determine to reduce it.

Washington City, April 20, 1861

SIR: I enclose you a letter, corresponding very nearly with one I addressed to you one week ago, (13th April,) to which I have not had any reply.—The letter is simply one of enquiry in reference to facts concerning which, I think, I am entitled to an explanation. I have not adopted any opinion in reference to them which may not be modified by explanation, nor have I affirmed in that letter; nor do I in this, any conclusion of my own unfavorable to your integrity in the whole transaction.

All that I have said and mean to say is, that an explanation is due from you to myself. I will not say what I shall do in case this request is not complied with, but I am justified in saying that I shall feel at liberty to place these letters before any person who is entitled to ask an explanation of myself.

Very respectfully,

John A. Campbell,
Associate Justice of the Supreme Court U. S.

Hon. WM. H. SEWARD, Secretary of State

No reply has been made to this letter.

April 24, 1861

Montgomery, Ala., May 7, 1861

SIR:—I submit to you two letters that were addressed by me to the Hon. W. H. SEWARD, Secretary of State of the U. S., that contain an explanation of the nature and result of an intervention by me in the intercourse of the Commissioners of the Confederate States with that officer. I considered that I could perform no duty in which the entire American people whether of the Federal Union or of the Confederate States, were more interested than that of promoting the counsels and the policy that had for their object the preservation of peace. This motive dictated my intervention. Besides the interview referred to in these letters I informed the assistant Secretary of State of the U.S.[42] (not being able to see the Secretary) on the 11th of April, ult., of the existence of a telegram of that date from Gen. BEAUREGARD to the Commissioners, in which he informed the Commissioners that he had demanded the evacuation of Sumter, and if refused, he would proceed to reduce it. On the same day, I had been told that President LINCOLN had said that none of the vessels sent to Charleston were war vessels, and that force was not to be used in the attempt to supply the Fort. I had no means of testing the accuracy of this information; but offered that if the information was accurate I would send a telegram to the authorities at Charleston, and it might prevent the disastrous consequences of a collision at that fort between the opposing force. It was the last effort that I would make to avert the calamities of war. The Assistant Secretary promised to give the matter attention, but I had no other intercourse with him or any other person on the subject, nor have I had any reply to the letters submitted to you.

Very respectfully,

JOHN A. CAMPBELL

Gen. Davis, President of the Confederate States

XVIII. A Bill to Be Entitled "An Act to Exempt from Duty Certain Cars Purchased by the New Orleans and Carrolton Rail Road Company & the New Orleans City Rail Road Company," May 17, 1861[43]

The Congress of the Confederate States do enact that four Rail Road passenger cars purchased by the New Orleans & Carrolton Rail Road Company from S. G. Lowe & Co., of St. Louis & also certain lounge cars ordered and contracted for by the New Orleans City Rail Road Company & which were not finished prior to the 10th day of Feby 1861 & could not be shipped before the 15th March 1861 be admitted into the port of New Orleans free from duty.

XIX. William Carey Crane to Howell Cobb, May 14, 1861

Hon. Howell Cobb,
President, of the Congress, C.S.A., Montgomery, Ala.

SIR: Herewith I beg leave to submit to you the report and resolutions adopted by the Southern Baptist Convention, on Monday, 13th instant.

I am instructed to request you to lay this document before the honorable body over which you preside.

Very respectfully, your obedient servant,

Wm. Carey Crane[44]

Senior Secretary of the Southern Baptist Convention

Report of Committee on the State of the Country

We hold this truth to be self-evident—that governments are established for the security, prosperity, and happiness of the people. When, therefore, any government is perverted from its proper design, becomes oppressive, and abuses its power, the people have a right to change it.

As to the States once combined upon this continent, it is now manifest that they can no longer live together in one confederacy. The Union constituted by our forefathers was one of coequal, sovereign States. The fanatical spirit of the North has long been seeking to deprive us of rights and franchises guaranteed by the Constitution, and after years of persistent aggression they have at last accomplished their purpose.

In vindication of their sacred rights and honor, in self-defense, and for the protection of all which is dear to man, the Southern States have practically asserted the right of seceding from a union so degenerated from that established by the Constitution, and they have formed for themselves a Government based upon the principles of the original compact, adopting a charter which secures to each State its sovereign rights and principles.

This new Government, in thus dissolving former political connections, seeks to cultivate relations of amity and good Will with its late confederates and with all the world; and they have thrice sent commissioners to Washington with overtures for peace and for a fair, amicable adjustment of all difficulties.

The Government at Washington has insultingly repelled these reasonable proposals and now insists upon devastating our land with fire and sword; upon letting loose hordes of armed soldiery to pillage and desolate the entire South, for the purpose of forcing the seceded States back into unnatural union or of subjugating them and holding them as conquered provinces.

While the two sections of the land are thus arrayed against each other, it might naturally have been hoped that at least the churches of the North would interpose and protest against this appeal to the sword, this invoking of civil war, this deluging the whole land in fratricidal blood; but with astonishment and grief we find churches and pastors at the North breathing out slaughter and clamoring for sanguinary hostilities with a fierceness which we would have supposed impossible among the disciples of the Prince of Peace.

In view of such premises this convention can not keep silence. Recognizing the necessity that the whole moral influence of the people, in whatever capacity or organization, should be enlisted in aid of the rulers who by their suffrages have been called to defend the endangered interests of person and property, of honor and of liberty, it is bound to utter its voice distinctly, decidedly, emphatically. And your committee recommend, therefore, the subjoined resolutions:

(1) *Resolved,* That impartial history can not charge upon the South the dissolution of the Union. She was foremost in advocating and cementing that Union. To that Union she clung through long years of calumny, injury, and insult. She has never ceased to raise her warning appeals against the fanaticism which has obstinately and incessantly warred against that Union.

(2) *Resolved,* That we most cordially approve of the formation of the Government of the "Confederate States of America," and admire and applaud the noble course of that Government up to the present time.

(3) *Resolved,* That we will assiduously invoke the Divine direction and favor in behalf of those who bear rule among us, that they may still exercise the same wise, prompt, elevated statesmanship which has hitherto characterized their measures; that their enterprises may be attended with success, and that they may attain a great reward, not only in seeing these Confederate States prosper under their administration, but in contributing to the progress of the transcendent kingdom of our Lord Jesus Christ.

(4) *Resolved,* That we most cordially tender to the President of the "Confederate States," to his Cabinet, and to the members of the Congress now convened at Montgomery the assurances of our sympathy and entire confidence. With them are our hearts and hearty cooperation.

(5) *Resolved,* That the lawless reign of terror at the North, the violence committed upon, unoffending citizens, above all the threats uttered to wage upon the South a warfare of savage barbarity, to devastate our homes and hearths with hosts of ruffians and felons burning with lust and rapine, ought to excite the horror of all civilized people. God forbid that we should so far forget the spirit of Jesus as to suffer malice and vindictiveness to insinuate themselves into our hearts, but every principle of religion, of patriotism, of humanity calls upon us to pledge our fortunes and lives in the good work of repelling an invasion designed to destroy whatever is dear in our heroic traditions, whatever is sweet in our domestic hopes and enjoyments, whatever is essential to our institutions and our very manhood, whatever is worth living or dying for.

(6) *Resolved,* That we do now engage in prayer for our friends, brothers, fathers, sons, and citizen soldiers who have left their homes to go forth for the defense of their families and firesides and all which is dearest to the human heart, and we recommend to the churches represented in this body that they constantly invoke a holy and merciful God to guard them from the temptations to which they are exposed, cover their heads in the day of battle, and give victory to their arms.

(7) *Resolved,* That we will pray for our enemies in the spirit, of that Divine

Master, who, when he was reviled, reviled not again, trusting that their pitiless purposes may be frustrated; that God will grant to them a more politic, a more considerate, and a More Christian mind; that the fratricidal strife which they have decided upon, notwithstanding all our commissions and pleas for peace, may be arrested by that Supreme Power who maketh the wrath of man to praise him, and that thus, through a divine blessing, the prosperity of these sovereign and once allied States may be restored under the two Governments to which they now and henceforth respectively belong.

(8) *Resolved*, And we do hereby recommend to the churches of the Baptist. denomination in the Southern States to observe the 1st day of June as a day of humiliation, fasting, and prayer to Almighty God that lie may avert any calamities due to our sins as a people and may look with mercy and favor upon us.

(9) *Resolved*, That whatever calamities may come upon us, our firm trust and hope are in God, through the atonement of his Son, and we earnestly beseech the churches represented in this body, a constituency of six or seven hundred thousand Christians, that they be fervent and importunate in prayer, not only for the country, but for the enterprises of the Gospel which have been committed to our care. In the war of the Revolution and in the war of 1812 the Baptists bated no jot of heart or hope for the Redeemer's cause. Their zeal and liberality abounded in their deepest afflications. Wc beseech the churches to cherish the spirit and imitate the example of tilts noble army of saints and heroes; to be followers of them who through faith and patience inherit the promises; to be steadfast, immovable, always abounding in the work of the Lord, forasmuch as they know that their labor is not in vain in-the Lord.

(10) *Resolved*, That these resolutions be communicated to the Congress of the "Confederate States" at Montgomery, with the signatures of the president and secretaries of the convention.

RICHARD FULLER, Maryland,
BASIL MANLY, Alabama,
JAMES B. TAYLOR, Virginia,
J. L. PRITCHARD, North Carolina,
E. T. WINKLER, South Carolina,
P. H. MELL, Georgia,
L. W. ALLEN, Kentucky,
R. B. C. HOWELL, Tennessee,
WM. CAREY CRANE, Louisiana,
JAMES E. BROOME, Florida,
G. H. MARTIN, Mississippi,

A true copy, as adopted May 13, 1861, at the city of Savannah, Ga.,

RICHARD FULLER, President
WM. CAREY CRANE,
GEO. B. TAYLOR,
Secretaries

XX. WILLIAM HENDERSON TO CHARLES CONRAD, MAY 8, 1861[45]

New Orleans, May 8, 1861

C. M. CONRAD, Esq.
My Dear Sir

I have taken the liberty of enclosing to you a bill of paving amounting to $5248 12/100 due to the contractor Mr. STEVENS by the New Orleans Custom House.

This paving was done in accordance with a contract entered into by Mr. STEVENS with the city of New Orleans, and had to be completed, on or before the present time.

The contracting and half of the expense to be paid by the city and half by the property owners. The city having paid their proportion, the Confederate States part remains unpaid, and I have sent it to you, with the request you will use your influence to assist Mr. STEVENS in getting his money, and I have no doubt in these pressing time for money, he would be quite willing to take Confederate bonds in payment.

My interest in this matter grows out of the fact that the street was improved through my exertions, and consequently I feel a deep interest in the contractor is getting his pay, as he is indeed not in a situation to remain long out of money.

Our city is quite excited by the glorious news from Arkansas and gallant Tennessee wheeling into line of the Confederate States, the news of which reached here yesterday. There remains only three more to complete our nation of "Southern Republic." They will not be long coming after they are prepared to resist aggression now threatened against them by northern vandalism.

Business dull, crops splendid, and city quiet and healthy.

Your friend

Wm Henderson[46]
100 Canal Street

XXI. SPECIAL REPORT: CONFEDERATE STATES OF AMERICA, TREASURY DEPARTMENT, RICHMOND, JULY 20TH, 1861[47]

Treasury Department,
Richmond, July 20th, 1861

Sir:

I herewith submit, for the information of Congress, a statement of the receipts and expenditures of the Government up to the date of the meeting of Congress, which will be found in Schedule A.

The subscriptions to the Confederate Loan, authorized by the act of Congress, approved February 28th, 1861, and the amount of Treasury notes issued in accordance with the act of Congress approved March 9th, 1861, are set forth in detail in Schedule B. To the subscriptions to the loan must be added the conditional subscription of $600,000 from South Carolina, making in the whole the sum of $9,667,950. I also report that I have reduced the official force at each of the Custom Houses from an expenditure of $443,930 04, to an expenditure of $113,218 04, as per Schedule C. herewith. This reduction is made to suit the present exigencies of the Government. Whenever trade shall be re-established, the proper addition can be made to the existing force.

I have further to report that since the States of Virginia and Tennessee have joined the Confederacy, I have discontinued the offices of the Collectors of the Customs at Norfolk, on the Mississippi, Holly Springs, Hernando, Eastport, Corinth, Athens, Stevenson, Atlanta, Chester and Florence. The internal trade has been so much interrupted since that time, that it has not been deemed necessary to have any other office open on the Northern frontier except Nashville.

In accordance with the resolution approved May 21st, 1861, making it the duty of the Secretary of the Treasury to furnish five hundred printed copies of the Tariff Act for the use of Congress, I herewith transmit the same. It will be found, by reference to said Act, that some difficulty will arise in its practical operation, from the fact that in several instances the same articles are placed in different schedules, thereby assessing a different rate of duty upon the same articles of merchandize. For instance, in Schedule C, upon all articles enumerated in said schedule, is assessed a duty of fifteen *per centum ad valorem*; on page 5 "carbonate of soda" is enumerated, on page 11 in Schedule D, which pays a duty of ten per centum "carbonates of soda" are enumerated. On page 8 in Schedule C, "*paving and roofing tiles and bricks and roofing slates and fire bricks*" are classed. In Schedule D, on page 10, "*clay burnt or unburnt, bricks, paving and roofing tiles*" is the language used. In Schedule D, on page 11, "lac sulphur" and "sulphur flour of" are enumerated. In Schedule G, which exempts all articles therein classed from duty, "gun powder and all the materials of which it is made" are enumerated. In Schedule D, on page 11, "terra, japonica, catechu" are subjected to the duty of that schedule. In Schedule E, paying a duty of five per centum *ad valorem* the article "cutch" is classed. Terra, japonica catechu and cutch, are commercial names designating one and the same article of merchandize. On page 7, in the designation of the various kinds of iron, there is none that will include sheet iron, and hence it must be classed among the non-enumerated articles, which class pay a duty of ten per centum *ad valorem*. Under the tariff of 1857, which is now in operation, with the exceptions made by the Congress of the Confederate States, after the word "slabs," is the expression, "or other form," which includes sheet iron. If it was the intention of Congress that the duty on the various kinds of iron should be uniform, it will be necessary to alter the late act in accordance therewith. The attention of Congress is called to these discrepancies that the proper remedy may be applied at an early day of their session, and before the act referred to shall go into operation. The same resolution makes it the duty of the Secretary of the Treasury to have five hundred copies of a comparative statement of the rates of duty, under the United States Tariff of 1857, the Confederate States Tariff just established, and the United States Tariff now of force, printed; I have to report that this statement is now in the hands of the printer and will be submitted to Congress at an early day.

Since the adjournment of Congress, measures have been taken to bring forward the remainder of the loan of fifteen millions, and also the loan of the proceeds of produce. Patriotic gentlemen have presented the subject to the people, and they have responded with a spirit indicating their determination to support the Government. The subscription lists not having yet come in, I am unable to report the aggregate amount; but presume that it will not fall short of fifty millions of dollars in value. This large amount may, therefore, he counted upon with certainty during the winter and spring, if sales of the produce can be effected.

The dimensions of the war have been so much enlarged since your adjournment that these additional means for carrying it on become essential. Sales of produce cannot, however, be made in time to make available the proceeds of crops as early as may be desirable, and the necessity arises for an increase of Treasury Notes. If the crop subscriptions were set apart as a security for such notes, they might be issued in advance of the sales, and the Government would derive the full benefit of the subscription even though the sales should be indefinitely delayed. The notes, too, would be circulated with confidence; for, besides the credit of the Government, they would rest upon a basis of real value which is second only to coin itself.

I would renew the suggestion made in a former report that to remove all danger to the currency, the larger notes be made to bear an interest of 2 cents per day on each hundred dollars. I think that in this way a large amount would be retired from the circulation leaving the field clear for the banks and for the circulation of smaller Treasury Notes.

The apprehension of danger to the currency does not appear to be well founded. Taking an average of six years, up to 1858 the circulation and deposits in the banks of the eight Confederate States where banks exist, was about eighty-five millions, with eighteen and a half millions of coin. It would be not unreasonable, therefore, to assume that at present a circulation could be sustained of one hundred millions. It also appears that there are at least two hundred millions of dollars of money now at interest in the Confederate States outside of the banks; the bank capital itself being a little short of eighty-five millions.

A very large portion of the interest-bearing Treasury Notes would eventually find its way as a substitute for this money at interest. The facility which it offers of being used as money while every day adds to its value, will tempt every one to prefer it to a bank note or a bond. It seems to me that it would not be rash to affirm that between these two modes of absorption one hundred and fifty millions of credit may be used with safety.

How large a proportion of this amount will be required, I am not able to say, inasmuch as the additional estimates of the War Department have not yet been prepared. But it is highly satisfactory to know that we are prepared with means to meet the worst contingency. It must be borne in mind, however, that an essential part of our financial scheme is the levying a direct tax. The Treasury Notes and bonds authorized by the laws already passed are based upon the declaration of Congress that such a tax would be raised. The increase of the proportions of other things call for a corresponding increase in this tax. In order to make proper provision on that subject, Congress directed me to lay before it certain information, which I have endeavored to obtain and which will more appropriately form the subject of another report.

All of which is respectfully submitted.

C. G. Memminger,
Secretary of the Treasury
Hon. Howell Cobb, President of Congress

XXII. RESOLUTION, MARIETTA, GEORGIA, JULY 17, 1861[48]

Resolved, That the Congress of the Confederate States take into consideration the propriety of throwing open our ports to the shipping and commerce of all neutral nations by granting to those who succeed in running or breaking the blockade a remission of all duties.

Resolved, That the seaboard cities take into consideration the importance of remitting port and city charges on all vessels which succeed in entering the same during the blockade.

Resolved, That the presence in the different manufacturing and shipping districts of Europe, of official representatives of the Confederate States, is a matter of immediate importance, and we hereby urge our Representatives in Congress to obtain from Government the execution, in this respect, of the Act of the Confederate Congress, passed in relation thereto.

Resolved, That Congress take into consideration the desirability of giving assurances to the owners of ocean steamers, suitable to war purposes, that upon the successful entry into our ports of such steamers with cargos, an impartial commission will examine and purchase the same for the Navy of the Confederate States, if found serviceable, at a fair valuation.

Resolved, That we hereby tender to the Government our unanimous support and united and undivided confidence.

Resolved, That these resolutions be transmitted to the Hon. B. H. Hill, member of Congress, representing this district.

XXIII. M. J. ZUNTS TO WALKER BROOKE, JULY 18, 1861[49]

New Orleans, July 18, 1861

Hon. Walker Brooke
Richmond
D[ea]r Sir

As a personal acquaintance, I take the liberty of addressing you upon a subject in which we are all interested. The commercial affairs of the Confederated States and how they can be alleviated by action of our Government. Unless some specific is applied we must experience severe distress for a large portion of our population. With heavy crops to produce now maturing upon which large sums of money have been advanced and are now due. How can those crops say sugar cotton & tobacco be made subservient as gold & silver to create a currency by which the liability of the country can be relived of its embarrassments? A healthy state of affairs ensure our crops retained in the country until our Independence is recognized or our ports open without molestation to imports as well as exports! And supplies furnished for the production of subsequent crops!

I would suggest that the government issue say $300,000,000 in Treasury notes payable on demand without interest and decreed a legal tender. Then appoint agents in each commercial city to loan to the Factors a specified amount when called for, upon each Bale of Cotton, Hhds [hogsheads] Sugar, and Tobacco on plantation or in warehouse, he, the Factor, pledging the same conjointly with the Planter or owner, with their note payable on demand bearing 8% interest, the terms of the pledge specifying that the number of Bales or Hhds of such mark to be received from such planter or owner. When sold the note given shall be at once redeemed including accruing interest subject to sworn penalty for non complying in each and every instance. The interest charged by the Government on such loans would more than compensate for the expenses. My reasons for suggesting that this loan should be made only through the Factor was, the application would be narrowed down to but free persons, business would flow on as usual thorough its accustomed channels, fewer agents, consequently lighter expense to the Government beside the possibility of fraud less likely to occur. It strikes me that when England & France ascertain that our government had executed a currency by which our financial embarrassments where completely relieved, the crop easily held back by Planters, a more speedy recognition and favorable treaties would be the sure result. Would not this course be preferable in some respects to the government purchasing the crop! As has been suggested by some! Or the issuing of Treasury Notes based upon special taxation by others? This latter appears objectionable as the Planter whose property is taxed has nothing by which he can realise sufficient to pay the tax (even his household expenses) until his Cotton or Sugar can be moved. The effect would be a circulation to be redeemed by taxing his property without any benefit resulting to him from it. The farmer has also a drawback. The numberless agents and expense with the difficulty of arriving at the quality and weights until ginned baled and ready for market besides foreign powers deeming it a monopoly by which government intended to speculate thereby retarding a more speedy expression of good will. This plan may appear extraordinary, but I think quite feasible. These are extraordinary time. Therefore require extraordinary measures. The question will naturally be advanced how is the government to be benefited by this? What relieves the country must necessarily relieve the government. The loan of Treasury notes upon the crop will liquidate off nearly the entire indebtedness of the country consequently there must be a large accumulated capitol which will be certain to seek investment. What presents a more favorable or safe security then Confederate bonds? These will be paid for in return by these same treasury notes which the government can reissue to its citizens in payment of all debts contracted. The redemption of these notes being perfectly secured on the produce of the country which when sold must bring either the coin or its equivalent.

I trust you will excuse my thus trespassing upon your valuable time, but as an humble [remainder of letter missing]

XXIV. AN APPEAL, JUNE 12, 1861[50]

To the Ministers of the different denominations throughout the Confederate States, in behalf of a Collection proposed to be taken up on the 13th of June, to assist in defraying the Expenses of the present War.

Fathers and Brethren: Behind an honored name we venture to address you.—The momentous hour has come! The death struggle for liberty has commenced! The foot of the invader presses the soil of Virginia, and even as we write, the blood of our sons and brothers is peradventure being poured our in defence of our altars and our homes—of all that we hold dear as men as patriots, and as Christians! Under such circumstances, all apology for thus addressing you is superfluous; it is enough that we feel the obligation of "helping every one his neighbor, and every one to his brother, 'be of good courage.'"

At the request of the Congress, our honored President has called us to a day of Fasting and Prayer: a request with which it is presumed, no one of us will fail to comply. But, besides this solemn, united and hearty appeal to the Supreme Power of the Universe for his merciful favor and protection, we beg to suggest, in all humility, whether it be not possible to make this coming occasion the opportunity of still farther aiding our country in this, the crisis of her destiny, by contributing of our substance for the support of our brethren in arms?—Need we be reminded that the expense of transporting large bodies of troops, is in itself a heavy item of the war; and that it is a matter of utmost moment that the treasury of the Confederate States should know no lack, at such a time as this? It is respectfully proposed, therefore, to all whom this plea may come, that collections may be taken up on the 13th day of June, wherever two or three are gathered together, and this whether in camp or church; and if not on that day, then upon the best opportunity—that these monies be immediately remitted to the Governors of the respective States, to be by them forwarded to the Hon. Mr. MEMMINGER, Secretary of the Treasury, who shall duly receipt for the same.

In the name, then, of the just and holy cause to which the exigencies of thee times have summoned us—in the name of the gallant States who are making a common stand against a blind and crushing despotism—a stand for Constitutional Liberty—a stand for the principles of '76—will you permit one who serves with you the Gospel, to entreat you to remember your country's need, on that day of Fasting and Prayer; and let you alms, and prayers, go up *together* as a memorial before God! Remember, beloved Christian men, that a million *to-day* may count more than millions *to-morrow*; and that which we do in this matter should not only be done with our might, but be done *quickly*.

We appeal, then to all who shall conduct devotional services upon that day, to allow an opportunity, at least for the free-will offering of every one "whose heart may be stirred up." We appeal, moreover, to our noble and patriotic Governors, in any way they may think proper, to give this plea a friendly welcome. We appeal to all editors to lend it the aid of their eloquent pens, for without their aide in this moment of time, we can do nothing. We finally appeal to all, whose hearts throb for liberty, to help—help now—and remember that our country calls TO-DAY.

"Let God arise—let his enemies be scattered. As smoke is driven away, so drive them away; as wax melteth before the fire so let the wicked perish at the presence of God."

Witherspoon.[51]

APPENDIX II: PROPOSED SEAL AND FLAGS

Figure I. Edwin V. Sharp, Confederate seal design, Thian, *Documentary History of the Flag*, Illustrations, pt. 2, plate XI

Figure II. Edwin V. Sharp, Confederate flag design, Thian, *Documentary History of the Flag*, Illustrations, pt. 2, plate XII

Figure III. Jacob B. Platt, Confederate flag design, Thian *Documentary History of the Flag*, Illustrations, pt. 2, plate XXV

Figure IV. Robert B. Waddell, Confederate flag design, Thian, *Documentary History of the Flag*, Illustrations, pt. 2, plate LXX

Figure V. Catherine Ladd, Confederate flag design, Thian, *Documentary History of the Flag*, Illustrations, pt. 2, plate XIII

Figure VI. Thomas H. Hobbs, Confederate flag design, *Documentary History of the Flag*, Illustrations, pt. 2, plate XVI

Figure VII. Joseph M. Shellman, Confederate flag design, Thian, *Documentary History of the Flag*, Illustrations, pt. 2, plate X

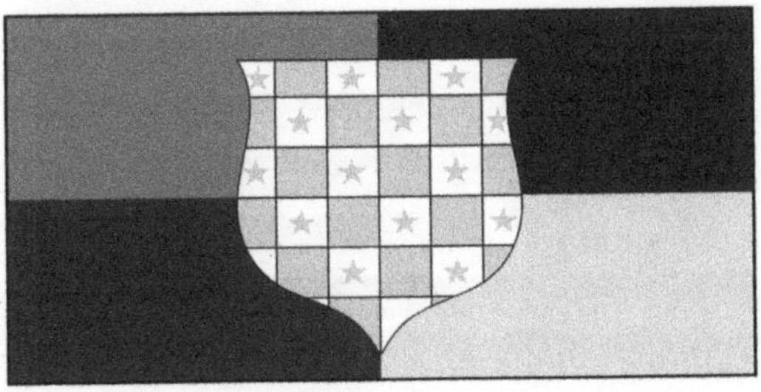

Figure VIII. "Richmond County," Confederate flag design, Thian, *Documentary History of the Flag*, Illustrations, pt. 2, plate XIV

Figure IX. Augustus Bonaud, Confederate flag design one, Thian, *Documentary History of the Flag*, Illustrations, pt. 2, plate XX

Figure X. Augustus Bonaud, Confederate flag design two, Thian, *Documentary History of the Flag*, Illustrations, pt. 2, plate XXI

Figure XI. R. C. Gilchrist, Confederate flag design, Thian, *Documentary History of the Flag*, Illustrations, pt. 2, plate IV

Figure XII. Mrs. E. G. Carpenter, Confederate flag design, Thian, *Documentary History of the Flag*, Illustrations, pt. 2, plate LXIX

Figure XIII. H. Aug. Pond, Confederate flag design one, Thian, *Documentary History of the Flag*, Illustrations, pt. 2, plate LVIII

Figure XIV. H. Aug. Pond, Confederate flag design two, Thian, *Documentary History of the Flag*, Illustrations, pt. 2, plate LIX

Figure XV. C. E. Brame, Confederate flag design one, Thian, *Documentary History of the Flag*, Illustrations, pt. 2, plate LXI

Figure XVI. C. E. Brame, Confederate flag design two, Thian, *Documentary History of the Flag*, Illustrations, pt. 2, plate LXII

Figure XII. W. P. Hilliard, Confederate flag design one, Thian, *Documentary History of the Flag*, Illustrations, pt. 2, plate CXXVII

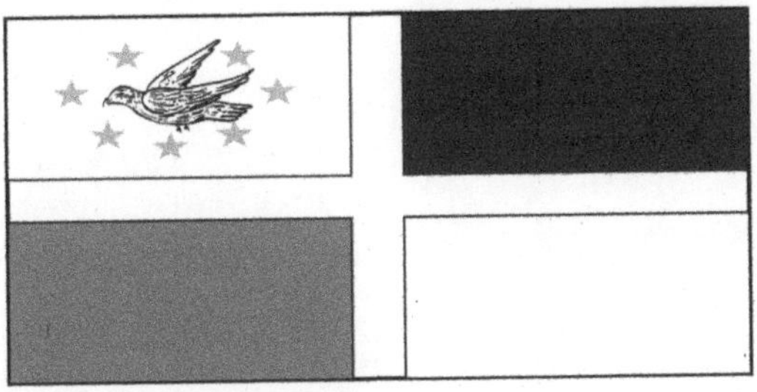

Figure XIII. W. P. Hilliard, Confederate flag design two, Thian, *Documentary History of the Flag*, Illustrations, pt. 2, plate CXXVIII

NOTES

Introduction

1. *Journal of the Congress of the Confederate States of America, 1861–1865*, 7 vols. (Washington, DC: Government Printing Office, 1904–5). Hereafter referred to as *JCCSA*.

2. Richmond *Times-Dispatch*, August 3, 1923; *Southern Historical Society Papers* (Richmond: Virginia Historical Society, 1876–1959), 44:4. Hereafter referred to as *SHSP* followed by volume and page number.

3. Richmond *Times-Dispatch*, August 3, 1923; *SHSP*, 44:4.

4. The seventh state, Texas, seceded on February 2, 1861. Its delegates began arriving February 15.

5. Charles Robert Lee Jr., *The Confederate Constitutions* (Chapel Hill: University of North Carolina Press, 1963), 55–57.

6. E. Merton Coulter, *The Confederate States of America*, 1861–1865: A History of the South, ed. Wendell Holmes Stephenson and E. Merton Coulter (Baton Rouge: Louisiana State University Press, 1950), 21; Richard E. Beringer, "A Profile of the Members of the Confederate Congress," *Journal of Southern History* 33, no. 4 (1967): 519; Wilfred Buck Yearns, *The Confederate Congress* (Athens: University of Georgia Press, 1960), 23–24; William C. Davis, *Look Away!: A History of the Confederate States of America* (New York: Free Press, 2002), 45–54. Stephens's quote is drawn from the report for February 5, 1861. Charleston *Mercury*, February 8, 1861.

7. The Provisional Congress of the Confederate States of America held two sessions in Montgomery, Alabama (first session: February 4 to March 16, 1861; second session: April 29 to May 21, 1861), and three sessions in Richmond, Virginia (third session: July 20 to August 31, 1861; fourth session: September 3, 1861; and fifth session: November 18, 1861, to February 17, 1862).

8. Wilfred B. Yearns, "North Carolina in the Confederate Congress," *North Carolina Historical Review* 29, no. 3 (1952): 362, 364.

9. While Edward Pollard, J. G. Ramsay, and Enoch Sikes published some of the earliest Confederate congressional histories, it was not until the 1950s that academic studies first began to appear. General histories may be found in Edward A. Pollard, "The Confederate Congress: A Chapter in the History of the Late War," *Galaxy* 6, no. 6 (1868): 749–58; J. G. Ramsay, "The Confederate Congress," *State Normal Magazine* 4, no. 3 (May 1900): 74–83; Coulter, *Confederate States of America*, ch. 6; Enoch Walter Sikes, *The Confederate States Congress* (Raleigh, NC: Edwards and Broughton, Printers, 1903); Yearns, *Confederate Congress*; Lee, *Confederate Constitutions*; William C. Davis, *"A Government of Our Own": The Making of the Confederacy* (New York: Free Press, 1994),and *Look Away!*, ch. 2–4.

Most Confederate congressmen have some form of individual biography in print. Collective congressional biographies may be found in Arthur R. Kirkpatrick, "Missouri's Delegation in the Confederate Congress," *Civil War History* 5, no. 2 (1959): 188–98; James M. Woods, "Devotees and Dissenters: Arkansans in the Confederate Congress, 1861–1865," *Arkansas Historical Quarterly* 38, no. 3 (1979): 227–47; Yearns, "North Carolina in the Confederate Congress," 359–78; Roger D. Hardaway, "Tennesseans at the Confederate Constitutional Convention," *Tennessee Historical Quarterly* 43, no. 1 (Spring 1984): 44–48; Beringer, "Profile of the Members," 518–41; and Ezra J. Warner and W. Buck Yearns, *Biographical Register of the Confederate Congress* (Baton Rouge: Louisiana State University Press, 1975).

For more specialized studies on voting patterns and the status of political parties in the Confederacy, see: Jeffery A. Jenkins, "Examining the Bonding Effects of Party: A Comparative Analysis of Roll-Call Voting in the U.S. and Confederate Houses," *American Journal of Political Science* 43, no. 4 (1999): 1144–65, and "Examining the Robustness of Ideological Voting: Evidence from the Confederate House of Representatives," *American Journal of Political Science* 44, no. 4 (2000): 811–22; Richard E. Beringer, "The Unconscious 'Spirit of Party' in the Confederate Congress," *Civil War History* 18, no. 4 (1972): 312–33; Adam Ramey, "National Survival and the Confederate Congress," *Historical Methods: A Journal of Quantitative and Interdisciplinary History* 46, no. 1 (January–March 2013): 31–40; Richard Bensel, "Southern Leviathan: The Development of Central States Authority in the Confederate States of America," *Studies in American Political Development* 2 (Spring 1987): 68–136; George C. Rable, *The Confederate Republic: A Revolution against Politics* (Chapel Hill: University of North Carolina Press, 1994); Thomas B. Alexander and Richard E. Beringer, *The Anatomy of the Confederate Congress: A Study of the Influences on Legislative Voting Behavior, 1861–1865* (Nashville: Vanderbilt University Press, 1972); and Kenneth C. Martis and Gyula Pauer, *The Historical Atlas of the Congresses of the Confederate States of America, 1861–1865* (New York: Simon and Schuster, 1994).

10. Lee, *Confederate Constitutions*, 58. Alexander and Beringer add executive functions to this list for the period prior to the inauguration of Jefferson Davis as provisional president on February 18, 1861. Alexander and Beringer, *Anatomy of the Confederate Congress*, 74.

11. Yael A. Sternhell, "The Afterlives of a Confederate Archive: Civil War Documents and the Making of Sectional Reconciliation," *Journal of American History* 104, no. 4 (March 2016): 1037–41; Caroline E. Janney, *Remembering the Civil War: Reunion and the Limits of Reconciliation* (Chapel Hill: University of North Carolina Press, 2013), 138–44.

12. Gaines M. Foster, *Ghosts of the Confederacy: Defeat, the Lost Cause, and the Emergence of the New South, 1865–1913* (New York: Oxford University Press, 1988), 50.

13. Foster, *Ghosts of the Confederacy*, 59–62, 91–92.

14. Foster, *Ghosts of the Confederacy*, 59–62.

15. Noah Andre Trudeau, "Start with the Basics," *Civil War Times* 51, no. 4 (August 2012): 52–57.

16. US Naval War Records Office, *Official Records of the Union and Confederate Navies in the War of the Rebellion* (Washington, DC: Government Printing Office, 1894–1922), hereafter referred to as *Officials Records*; US War Department, *The War of the Rebellion: A Compilation of the Official Records of the Union and Confederate Armies* (Washington, DC: Government Printing Office, 1880–1901) hereafter referred to as *Naval OR*; US War Department, *Atlas of the War of the Rebellion* (Washington, DC: Government Printing Office, 1892).

17. Richard D. Starnes, "Forever Faithful: The Southern Historical Society and Confederate Historical Memory," *Southern Cultures* 2, no. 2 (Winter 1996): 178–79; Sternhell, "Afterlives of a Confederate Archive," 1027.

18. Foster, *Ghosts of the Confederacy*, 51–54; David Blight, *Race and Reunion: The Civil War in American Memory* (Cambridge, MA: Belknap Press of Harvard University Press, 2001), 79.

19. There is some disagreement over the effectiveness of subscription-based histories of the

war. Blight suggests that such histories were widely purchased and read. Foster, on the other hand, claims that subscriptions to these periodicals were generally low and had little influence on public opinion. For Foster, the organizations that produced such journals had a far greater effect on the creation of the Lost Cause though their memorialization efforts than their publications. Blight, *Race and Reunion*, 151; Starnes, "Forever Faithful," 179, 189; Foster, *Ghosts of the Confederacy*, 57; Trudeau, "Start with the Basics," 52–57.

20. Foster, *Ghosts of the Confederacy*, 94–95.

21. *SHSP*, 45:4, 46:4, 47:4, 49:5, 52:15.

22. For information on the background to this project, see the introduction to Douglas Southall Freeman, *A Calendar of Confederate Papers* (Richmond: Confederate Museum, 1908).

23. William Harris Bragg, "'Our Joint Labor': W. J. De Renne, Douglas Southall Freeman, and Lee's Dispatches, 1910–1915," *Virginia Magazine of History and Biography* 97, no. 1 (January 1989): 3–32.

24. David E. Johnson, *Douglas Southall Freeman* (Gretna, LA: Pelican Publishing, 2002), 72–76, 82–83, 94–97, 104–5, 126. On Freeman and his relationship with the Lost Cause, historical research, and southern memory creation, see, Keith D. Dickson, *Sustaining Southern Identity: Douglas Southall Freeman and Memory in the Modern South* (Baton Rouge: Louisiana State University Press, 2011).

25. Foster, *Ghosts of the Confederacy*, 95

26. *SHSP*, 48:5.

27. In addition to tapping SHS accounts, Freeman sought financial support from John Stewart Bryan, publisher of the Richmond *News Leader*, and J. Ambler Johnston, a Richmond architect. Johnson, *Sustaining Southern Identity*, 206–7.

28. *SHSP*, vols. 44–47.

29. *SHSP*, 48:5; Richmond *Times-Dispatch*, January 1, 1942.

30. *SHSP*, 50:2, 52:v–vii.

31. *SHSP*, 52:15.

32. On journalism during the Civil War, see David W. Bulla and Gregory Borchard, *Journalism in the Civil War Era* (New York: Peter Lang, 2010); Patricia G. McNeely, Debra Reddin van Tuyll, and Henry H. Schulte, *Knights of the Quill: Confederate Correspondents and Their Civil War Reporting* (West Lafayette, IN: Purdue University Press, 2010); David B. Sachsman, S. Kittrell Rushing, and Roy Morris Jr., eds. *Words at War: The Civil War and American Journalism* (Ashland, OH: Purdue University Press, 2008); J. Cutler Andrews, *The South Reports the Civil War* (Princeton, NJ: Princeton University Press, 2000); David B. Sachsman and Gregory A. Borchard, eds., *The Antebellum Press: Setting the Stage for Civil War* (New York: Routledge, 2019).

33. The larger national story of secession is covered in David M. Potter's *The Impending Crisis: 1848–1861* (New York: Joanna Cotler Books, 1976) and William W. Freehling's *The Road to Disunion*, vol. 2: *Secessionists Triumphant, 1854–1861* (Oxford: Oxford University Press, 2007). A more nuanced consideration of state and sectional disunionism may be found in Elizabeth R. Varon's *Disunion!: The Coming of the American Civil War, 1789–1859* (Chapel Hill: University of North Carolina Press, 2010), while the secessionist histories of individual states are the subjects of William A. Link, *Roots of Secession: Slavery and Politics in Antebellum Virginia* (Chapel Hill: University of North Carolina Press, 2003); William W. Freehling and Craig M. Simpson, *Secession Debated: Georgia's Showdown in 1860* (Oxford: Oxford University Press, 1992); Michael P. Johnson, *Toward a Patriarchal Republic: The Secession of Georgia* (Baton Rouge: Louisiana State University Press, 1977); William L. Barney, *The Secessionist Impulse: Alabama and Mississippi in 1860* (Princeton, NJ: Princeton University Press, 1974); Eric

H. Walther, *William Lowndes Yancey and the Coming of the Civil War* (Chapel Hill: University of North Carolina Press, 2006); and Christopher J. Olsen, *Political Culture and Secession in Mississippi: Masculinity, Honor, and the Antiparty Tradition, 1830–1860* (Oxford: Oxford University Press, 2000).

34. Lee, *Confederate Constitutions*; Marshall L DeRosa, *The Confederate Constitution of 1861: An Inquiry into American Constitutionalism* (Columbia: University of Missouri Press, 1991); Charles Robert Lee Jr., *Federalism in the Southern Confederacy* (Washington, DC: Public Affairs Press, 1966); Don E. Fehrenbacher, *Constitutions and Constitutionalism in the Slaveholding South* (Athens: University of Georgia Press, 1989); Kermit L. Hall and James W. Ely, eds., *An Uncertain Tradition: Constitutionalism and the History of the South* (Athens: University of Georgia Press, 1989); Curtis Arthur Amlund, *Federalism in the Southern Confederacy* (Washington, Public Affairs Press, 1966); Rable, *Confederate Republic*; Alison LaCroix, "Continuity in Secession: The Case of the Confederate Constitution," *University of Chicago Public Law and Legal Theory*, working paper no. 512, 2015; Edward L. White, III, "The Constitution of the Confederate States of America: Innovation or Duplication?" *Southern Historian* 12 (1991): 5–28; David P. Currie, "Through the Looking-Glass: The Confederate Constitution in Congress, 1861–1865," *Virginia Law Review*, 2004, 1257–1399.

35. Christopher Phillips, *Missouri's Confederate: Claiborne Fox Jackson and the Creation of Southern Identity in the Border West* (Columbia: University of Missouri Press, 2000); Michael D. Robinson, *A Union Indivisible: Secession and the Politics of Slavery in the Border South* (Chapel Hill: University of North Carolina Press, 2017); Frank Towers, *The Urban South and the Coming of the Civil War* (Charlottesville: University of Virginia Press, 2004); Daniel W. Crofts, *Reluctant Confederates: Upper South Unionists in the Secession Crisis* (Chapel Hill: University of North Carolina Press, 1989); William W. Freehling, *The South vs. the South: How Anti-Confederate Southerners Shaped the Course of the Civil War* (Oxford: Oxford University Press, 2001); Dwight T. Pitcaithley, *Tennessee Secedes: A Documentary History* (Knoxville: The University of Tennessee Press, 2021); Gary Robert Matthews, *More American Than Southern: Kentucky, Slavery, and the War for an American Ideology, 1828–1861* (Knoxville: University of Tennessee Press, 2014); Berry Craig, *Kentucky's Rebel Press: Pro-Confederate Media and the Secession Crisis* (Lexington: University Press of Kentucky, 2018); James M. Woods, *Rebellion and Realignment: Arkansas's Road to Secession* (Fayetteville: University of Arkansas Press, 1987); Walter L. Buenger, *Secession and the Union in Texas* (Austin: University of Texas Press, 1984); Donald E. Reynolds, *Texas Terror: The Slave Insurrection Panic of 1860 and the Secession of the Lower South* (Baton Rouge: Louisiana State University Press, 2007).

36. W. Davis, *"Government of Our Own"*; William C. Davis, *The Union That Shaped the Confederacy: Robert Toombs and Alexander H. Stephens* (Lawrence: University Press of Kansas, 2001); Emory M. Thomas, *The Confederacy as a Revolutionary Experience* (Englewood Cliffs, NJ: Prentice Hall, 1971), and *The Confederate Nation, 1861–1865* (New York: Harper and Row, 1979).

37. For Confederate relations with European powers, see James Morton Callahan, *The Diplomatic History of the Southern Confederacy* (New York: Greenwood Press, 1968); Charles M. Hubbard, *The Burden of Confederate* Diplomacy (Knoxville: University of Tennessee Press, 1998); Frank Lawrence Owsley, *King Cotton Diplomacy: Foreign Relations of the Confederate States of America* (Chicago: University of Chicago Press, 1931); Howard Jones, *Blue and Gray Diplomacy: A History of Union and Confederate Foreign Relations* (Chapel Hill: University of North Carolina Press, 2010), and *Union in Peril: The Crisis over British Intervention in the Civil War* (Lincoln: University of Nebraska Press, 1997); and Stève Sainlaude, *France and the American Civil War: A Diplomatic History* (Chapel Hill: The University of North Carolina Press, 2019). On Confederate relations with Native Americans, see Joseph Connole,

The Civil War and the Subversion of American Indian Sovereignty (Jefferson, NC: McFarland, 2017); Laurence M. Hauptman, *Between Two Fires: American Indians in the Civil War* (New York: Free Press, 1995); Megan Kate Nelson, *The Three-Cornered War: The Union, the Confederacy, and Native Peoples in the Fight for the West* (New York: Scribner, 2020); Christine Schultz White and Benton R. White, *Now the Wolf Has Come: The Creek Nation in the Civil War* (College Station: Texas A&M University Press, 1996); Bradley R. Clampitt, *The Civil War and Reconstruction in Indian Territory* (Lincoln: University of Nebraska Press, 2015); Clarissa W. Confer, *The Cherokee Nation in the Civil War* (Norman: University of Oklahoma Press, 2007); Mary Jane Warde, *When the Wolf Came: The Civil War and the Indian Territory* (Fayetteville: University of Arkansas Press, 2013).

38. Drew Gilpin Faust, *The Creation of Confederate Nationalism: Ideology and Identity in the Civil War South* (Baton Rouge: Louisiana State University Press, 1988); Paul D. Escott, *After Secession: Jefferson Davis and the Failure of Confederate Nationalism* (Baton Rouge: Louisiana State University Press, 1978); Anne S. Rubin, *A Shattered Nation: The Rise and Fall of the Confederacy, 1861–1868* (Chapel Hill: University of North Carolina Press, 2005); John M. Coski, *The Confederate Battle Flag: America's Most Embattled Emblem* (Cambridge, MA: Harvard University Press, 2005); Ian Binnington, *Confederate Visions: Nationalism, Symbolism, and the Imagined South in the Civil War* (Charlottesville: University of Virginia Press, 2013); Paul Quigley, *Shifting Grounds: Nationalism and the American South, 1848–1865* (Oxford: Oxford University Press, 2012); Coleman Hutchison, *Apples and Ashes: Literature, Nationalism, and the Confederate States of America* (Athens: University of Georgia Press, 2012); Devereaux D. Cannon Jr., *The Flags of the Confederacy: An Illustrated History* (Memphis: St. Luke Press, 1988).

39. Yearns, *Confederate Congress*; Warner and Yearns, *Biographical Register*; Alexander and Beringer. *Anatomy of the Confederate Congress.*

40. Richard Cecil Todd, *Confederate Finance* (Athens: University of Georgia Press, 1954); John D. Majewski, *Modernizing a Slave Economy: The Economic Vision of the Confederate Nation* (Chapel Hill: University of North Carolina Press, 2009); Douglas B. Ball, *Financial Failure and Confederate Defeat* (Urbana: University of Illinois Press, 1991); Michael Brem Bonner, *Confederate Political Economy: Creating and Managing a Southern Corporatist Nation* (Baton Rouge: Louisiana State University Press, 2016); R. Douglas Hurt, *Agriculture and the Confederacy: Policy, Productivity, and Power in the Civil War South* (Chapel Hill: University of North Carolina Press, 2015); John Christopher Schwab, *The Confederate States of America, 1861–1865: A Financial and Industrial History of the South during the Civil War* (New Haven, CT: Yale University Press, 1913); John Martin Davis Jr. *Civil War Taxes: A Documentary History, 1861–1900* (Jefferson, NC: McFarland, 2019); James F. Morgan, *Graybacks and Gold: Confederate Monetary Policy* (Pensacola: Perdido Bay Press, 1985); John Munro Godfrey, *Monetary Expansion in the Confederacy* (New York: Arno Press, 1978).

41. Mark E. Neely Jr., *Southern Rights: Political Prisoners and the Myth of Confederate Constitutionalism* (Charlottesville: University Press of Virginia, 1999); William M. Robinson Jr., *Justice in Grey: A History of the Judicial System of the Confederate States of America* (Cambridge, MA: Harvard University Press, 1941); G. Edward White, "Recovering the Legal History of the Confederacy," *Washington and Lee Legal Review* 68 (2011): 467, 497; J. G. de Roulhac Hamilton, "The State Courts and the Confederate Constitution," *Journal of Southern History* 4 (1938): 425; Marc-William Palen, "The Civil War's Forgotten Transatlantic Tariff Debate and the Confederacy's Free Trade Diplomacy," *Journal of the Civil War Era* 3, no. 1 (2013): 35–61.

42. Questions of military organization faced by the Provisional Congress included all aspects of military recruitment, training, equipage, and deployment for both regular and provisional armies; a navy for coastal and riverine defense; artillery units; special service units

such as army intelligence, sappers, bombardiers, and zouaves, and the creation of ancillary departments such as commissaries, quartermasters, hospitals, topographical units, lighthouse bureaus, and intelligence agencies. The literature on Confederate military units, preparations, and actions is voluminous, but a sampling of key literature might include William A. Tidwell, James O. Hall, and David Winfred Gaddy, *Come Retribution: The Confederate Secret Service and the Assassination of Lincoln* (Jackson: University Press of Mississippi, 1988); Kenneth Radley, *Rebel Watchdog: The Confederate States Army Provost Guard* (Baton Rouge: Louisiana State University Press, 1989); Earl J. Hess, *Civil War Infantry Tactics: Training, Combat, and Small-Unit Effectiveness* (Baton Rouge: Louisiana State University Press, 2015); Andrew Haughton, *Training, Tactics, and Leadership in the Confederate Army of Tennessee: Seeds of Failure* (London: Frank Cass, 2000); Jerrold Northrop Moore, *Confederate Commissary General: Lucius Bellinger Northrop and the Subsistence Bureau of the Southern Army* (Shippensburg, PA: White Mane Publishing, 1996); Jane E. Schultz, *Women at the Front: Hospital Workers in Civil War America* (Chapel Hill: University of North Carolina Press, 2004); Libra Rose Hilde, *Worth a Dozen Men: Women and Nursing in the Civil War South* (Charlottesville: University of Virginia Press, 2012); George G. Kundahl, *Confederate Engineer: Training and Campaigning with John Morris Wampler* (Knoxville: University of Tennessee Press, 2000); Joseph H. Crute, *Confederate Staff Officers, 1861–1865* ([Virginia?]: J. H. Crute, Jr., 1982); David L. Cipra, "Confederate States Light House Bureau: A Portrait in Blue and Gray," *Keeper's Log* 8, no. 2 (Winter 1992): 6–13; Horace Herndon Cunningham, *Doctors in Gray: The Confederate Medical Service* (Baton Rouge: Louisiana State University Press, 1958); Guy R. Hasegawa and F. Terry Hambrecht, *Matchless Organization: The Confederate Army Medical Department* (Carbondale: Southern Illinois University Press, 2021); Carol Cranmer Green, *Chimborazo: The Confederacy's Largest Hospital* (Knoxville: University of Tennessee Press, 2004); Raimondo Luraghi and Paolo E. Coletta, *A History of the Confederate Navy* (Annapolis, MD: Naval Institute Press, 1996); Maxine T. Turner, *Navy Gray: A Story of the Confederate Navy on the Chattahoochee and Apalachicola Rivers* (Tuscaloosa: University of Alabama Press, 1988); Spencer Tucker, *Blue and Gray Navies: The Civil War Afloat* (Annapolis, MD: Naval Institute Press, 2006); F. Ray Sibley, *The Confederate Order of Battle* (Shippensburg, PA: White Mane Publishing, 1996); Dan C. Fullerton, *Armies in Gray: The Organizational History of the Confederate States Army in the Civil War, 1861–1865* (Baton Rouge: Louisiana State University Press, 2017); Harold S. Wilson, *Confederate Industry: Manufacturers and Quartermasters in the Civil War* (Jackson: University Press of Mississippi, 2002); Richard P. Weinert, *The Confederate Regular Army* (Shippensburg, PA: White Mane Publishing, 1991); and Robert P. Broadwater, *Civil War Special Forces: The Elite and Distinct Fighting Units of the Union and Confederate Armies* (Santa Barbara: Praeger, 2014).

43. Michael E. Lynch, *Confederate War Industry: The Niter and Mining Bureau*, master's thesis, Virginia Commonwealth University, 2001; Charles B. Dew, *Ironmaker to the Confederacy: Joseph R. Anderson and the Tredegar Iron Works* (Richmond: Virginia State Library, 1999); Frank E. Vandiver, *Ploughshares into Swords: Josiah Gorgas and Confederate Ordnance* (Austin: University of Texas Press, 1952).

44. Kenneth W. Noe, *Southwest Virginia's Railroad: Modernization and the Sectional Crisis* (Champaign: University of Illinois Press, 1994); John E. Clark Jr., *Railroads in the Civil War: The Impact of Management on Victory and Defeat* (Baton Rouge: Louisiana State University Press, 2001); Angus James Johnston II, *Virginia Railroads in the Civil War* (Chapel Hill: University of North Carolina Press, 1961); Robert C. Black III, *The Railroads of the Confederacy* (Chapel Hill: University of North Carolina Press, 1952); J. Moore, *Confederate Commissary General*; Joan E. Cashin, *War Stuff: The Struggle for Human and Environmental Resources in the American Civil War* (Cambridge: Cambridge University Press, 2018); Robert

A. Taylor, *Rebel Storehouse: Florida in the Confederate Economy* (Tuscaloosa: University of Alabama Press, 1995).

45. Davis, *"Government of Our Own,"* 218.

46. Articles published in some Northern newspapers were also checked although most were reprints of Southern reports. Databases used include Newspapers by Ancestry Historical Newspaper Archive, GenealogyBank, Chronicling America at the Library of Congress, and Georgia Historic Newspapers at the Georgia State Archives.

47. See James M. Matthews, ed. *The Statutes at Large of the Provisional Government of the Confederate States of America* (Richmond: R. M. Smith, 1864); and *Provisional and Permanent Constitutions Together with the Acts and Resolutions of the First Session of the Provisional Congress of the Confederate States* (Montgomery: Shorter and Reid, 1861).

First Session

1. Rev. Basil Manly Sr. (1798–1868) of the First Baptist Church served as the official chaplain of the Confederate government during its tenure in Montgomery. In 1844, Manly authored the Alabama Resolutions demanding that the national Baptist convention affirm the appointment of slaveholders as missionaries, the denial of which led to a schism in the Baptist church and the creation of the Southern Baptist Convention. See A. James Fuller, *Chaplain to the Confederacy: Basil Manly and Baptist Life in the Old South* (Baton Rouge: Louisiana State University Press, 2000), Mandy E. McMichael, "'We Must Go Out of This Union': The Two Secessions of Basil Manly Sr." *Baptist History and Heritage* 52 (Summer 2017): 8–19, and Robert Elder, *The Sacred Mirror: Evangelicalism, Honor, and Identity in the Deep South, 1790–1860* (Chapel Hill: University of North Carolina Press, 2016), 197. On the importance of religion in the Civil War, see Mark A. Noll, *The Civil War as a Theological Crisis* (Chapel Hill: University of North Carolina Press, 2006); Randall M. Miller, Harry S. Stout, and Charles Reagan Wilson, eds., *Religion and the American Civil War* (New York: Oxford University Press, 1998); and George C. Rable, *God's Almost Chosen Peoples: A Religious History of the American Civil War* (Chapel Hill: University of the North Carolina Press, 2010).

2. The correspondent for the Montgomery *Weekly Advertiser* reports a condensed version of this prayer with slight variations in terminology, admitting that "some of the words of the aged and pious Divine were scarcely audible to the reporter. Some slight inaccuracies in the language may, in consequence, have occurred." Montgomery *Weekly Advertiser*, February 6, 1861.

3. Several delegations to the Montgomery Convention and subsequent Congress were delayed due to torrential rains, flooded waterways, and damaged rail lines. Davis, *"Government of Our Own,"* passim.

4. Albert R. Lamar (1830–89) was a Georgia attorney and pre–Civil War editor of the Savannah *Georgian* and Columbus *Sun* newspapers. *Journal of the Public and Secret Proceedings of the Convention of the People of Georgia, Held in Milledgeville and Savannah in 1861* (Milledgeville: Boughton Nisbet and Barnes, 1861), 8; Columbus (GA) *Enquirer-Sun*, May 20, 1889. The *Journal of the Congress of the Confederate States* reports a slightly different order to the motions and events than those reported here. *JCCSA*, 1:11.

5. For biographical information on members of the Confederate Congress, see Warner and Yearns, *Biographical Register*.

6. The Savannah *Daily Morning News* reports that A. R. Wright was not in attendance having left for Montgomery on Friday, February 1, and being delayed "by some obstruction on the State road." Savannah *Daily Morning News*, February 6, 1861.

7. Johnson Jones "Jonce" Hooper (1815–62) was an attorney, humorist, and editor of the financially struggling Montgomery *Mail*. Hooper began lobbying Southern leaders in

mid-January for some position in any new Southern government, and no sooner had convention deputies arrived in Montgomery than they settled through unofficial discussions on his nomination and selection as convention secretary. Davis, *"Government of Our Own,"* 66. See also William Stanley Hoole, *Alias Simon Suggs: The Life and Times of Johnson Jones Hooper* (Tuscaloosa: University of Alabama Press, 1952); Paul Somers, *Johnson J. Hooper* (Boston: Twayne Publishers, 1984); and James H. Justus, "Johnson Jones Hooper" in *The Encyclopedia of American Humorists*, ed. Stephen H. Gale (New York: Routledge, 2016), 227–31.

8. The *Mercury* correspondent reports the creation of a committee of fifteen. He was mistaken. Both the Montgomery *Weekly Advertiser* and the Savannah *Daily Morning News*, as well as the subsequent creation of the committee itself, reflect a committee of five for the reporting of rules.

9. Born in Norway, Rev. John March Mitchell (1820–88) served as rector of the St. John's Episcopal Church in Montgomery from 1858 to 1868. Portland *Daily Press*, April 19, 1888; Edgar Legare Pennington, "The Organization of the Protestant Episcopal Church in the Confederate States of America," *Historical Magazine of the Protestant Episcopal Church* 17, no. 4 (December 1948): 320.

10. The secretary appointed Robert Emmett Dixon, assistant secretary, and Wiley N. Hutchins, journal clerk. *JCCSA*, 1:17.

11. Thomas Jefferson's *A Manual of Parliamentary Practice for the Use of the Senate of the United States*, first published in 1801.

12. Cf., Mr. Memminger. "I presume that, in the 20th rule, the words 'no resolution or measure' refer only to written matter." Montgomery *Weekly Advertiser*, February 13, 1861.

13. Cf., "From this, it will be seen, that four Delegates may constitute a quorum, as there might be but one Delegate in attendance from a majority of the states." Montgomery *Weekly Advertiser*, February 13, 1861.

14. The record of debate on the twenty-fourth rule is muddled. While the Charleston *Mercury* reports the debate driven by John Perkins of Louisiana, the official journal records Duncan Kenner of Louisiana as the prime mover. Further complicating the record is the Montgomery *Weekly Advertiser*'s report that the debate began with a question by Mississippi's William S. Wilson followed by a motion to amend by Louisiana's Charles Conrad:

> Mr. Wilson. With the explanation of the gentleman from Georgia, (Mr. Stephens,) I beg leave to call attention to the 24th. rule, which provides that "a majority of the members present" may second the call for the previous question. I would prefer that the vote be taken by States on this, as well as on all other questions.
>
> Mr. Stephens. It is immaterial which plan is the adopted. In this case I think the rule will work better as it is.
>
> Mr. Conrad. Under the instructions the Deputies from Louisiana have received, we feel compelled to vote, on all questions, as a unit. And as the call for the previous question may have an important bearing on the discussion of a subject, and on the result to be attained, we feel compelled to ask that the second to the call for the previous question shall be determined by States, and not by the votes of individual members.
>
> Mr. Stephens. I am willing that the rule shall be as the gentleman desires.

15. George H. Shorter and Samuel G. Reid were the editors of the Montgomery *Weekly Advertiser* and official printers for the state of Alabama. Montgomery *Weekly Advertiser*, September 21, 1859, and March 7, 1860.

16. The official congressional journal, the Montgomery *Weekly Advertiser*, and the

Savannah *Daily Morning News* all record Alexander H. Stephens as the mover. *JCCSA*, 1:19; Montgomery *Weekly Advertiser*, February 13, 1861, and Savannah *Daily Morning News*, February 7, 1861.

17. Cf., "The Congress went into secret session at quarter before one o'clock p.m." Montgomery *Weekly Advertiser*, February 13, 1861.

18. Isaac Taylor Tichenor (1825–1902) served as pastor of Montgomery's First Baptist Church from 1852 to 1867. See, Michael E. Williams, Sr., *Isaac Taylor Tichenor: The Creation of the Baptist New South* (Tuscaloosa: University of Alabama Press, 2005).

19. The Savannah *Daily Morning News* credits J. P. Anderson of Florida with introducing Jackson Morton. Savannah *Daily Morning News*, February 8, 1861.

20. The Crittenden resolutions, or Crittenden Compromise, were a series of proposed constitutional amendments offered by Kentucky senator John J. Crittenden in December 1860. The proposal sought to avoid war by permanently protecting slavery against federal interference in states and territories south of latitude 36'30° (the Missouri Compromise line), Washington, DC, and US military posts. It also offered compensation to the owners of fugitive slaves and barred state personal liberty laws that blocked cooperation with federal fugitive slave laws. Although Congress rejected the compromise, the state of Virginia resurrected an amended version to be brought before a peace conference to be held in Washington, DC, beginning February 4, 1861. Virginia's amended version included a stipulation that federal slave protections would be offered not only to existing states and territories but to all those acquired in the future. It also guaranteed right of passage with slave property through nonslaveholding states and territories. William W. Freehling, *The Road to Disunion*, vol. 1: *Secessionists at Bay, 1776–1854* (New York: Oxford University Press, 1991), 513–14; Potter, *Impending Crisis*, 531–32; *Official Records*, ser. IV, vol. 1, pt. 1:90–91.

21. The correspondent from the Savannah *Daily Morning News* noted that "I was only able to recognize among them Mr. Stephens, of Georgia, Memminger, of South Carolina, and Anderson, of Florida. The Committee, I presume, in accordance with Mr. Bartow's resolutions, composed of two from each State, which, with a Chairman appointed by the President, would make a Committee of thirteen." Savannah *Daily Morning News*, February 8, 1861.

22. Originally from South Carolina, Rev. George Hollinshead Whitefield Petrie served as pastor of the First Presbyterian Church in Montgomery, Alabama, from 1857 to 1885. Thomas McAdory Owen, *History of Alabama and Dictionary of Alabama Biography*, vol. 4 (Chicago: S. J. Clarke Publishing, 1921), 1350–51; Richard W. Griffin, "Student Days at Davidson College, 1838–1857, in Letters to the Reverend G. H. W. Petrie." *Journal of Presbyterian History* 40, no. 3 (1962): 181.

23. There are significant discrepancies in the chronology of this day's events between the official journal and the published newspaper accounts.

24. Born in Saint Augustine, Florida, Father Anthony Dominic Pellicer (1824–80) served as the pastor of St. Peter's Catholic Church from his ordination in Mobile in 1850 until his transfer back to the Mobile diocese in 1865. Richard H. Clarke, *Lives of the Deceased Bishops of the Catholic Church in the United States* (New York: R. H. Clarke, 1888), 404–11; "Historical Picture Gallery," *Records of the American Catholic Historical Society of Philadelphia* 11, no. 1 (1900): 117.

25. The Montgomery *Weekly Advertiser* incorrectly refers to the chief justice as A. J. Adams.

26. There is some confusion about who made the motion to enter secret session. The Charleston *Mercury* credits Rhett of South Carolina. The Montgomery *Weekly Advertiser* and Savannah *Daily Morning News* credit Memminger of South Carolina, while the official journal cites Barnwell of South Carolina.

27. The Montgomery *Weekly Advertiser* reports that Alabama Supreme Court chief justice

Abram J. Walker administered the oath, whereas the official journal reports Associate Justice Richard Wilde Walker, then representing Alabama in the Provisional Confederate Congress. *JCCSA*, 1:39.

28. Identities unknown.

29. The Southern Cross is a formation of four stars visible only from the Southern Hemisphere.

30. Memminger references Dante's *Purgatory*, canto I, lines 22–54: "To the right hand I turned, and fixed my mind / Upon the other pole, and saw four stars / Ne'er seen before save by the primal people." In the mid-nineteenth century, Dante's "four stars" were thought to be a reference to the Southern Cross, a Southern Hemispheric constellation he had never seen and which would not be "discovered" formally until a century after his death. Dante's reference thus was considered to be divinely inspired and the constellation equally imbued with divine meaning: the four cardinal virtues of "prudence, justice, fortitude, and temperance." Dante Alighieri, *The Divine Comedy of Dante Alighieri*, vol. 2, trans. Henry Wadsworth Longfellow (Boston: Houghton, Mifflin, 1867), 12; Dante Alighieri, *Dante's Divina Commedia,* (London: Tinsley Brothers, 1862), 248–49; Leigh Hunt, *Stories from the Italian Poets: with Live of the Writers*, vol. 1 (London: Chapman and Hall, 1896), 155.

Alexander von Humboldt (1769–1859) was a Prussian geographer, naturalist, and explorer who traveled extensively throughout North and South America between 1799 and 1804. The results of his studies were published in the highly influential five-volume *Cosmos: A Sketch of a Physical Description of the Universe.* Memminger is most likely drawing attention to volume two of *Cosmos* (1849) in which Humboldt gives a historical and scientific description of the constellation. Alexander von Humboldt, *Cosmos: Sketch of a Physical Description of the Universe*, trans. E. C. Otte, vol. 2 (London: Henry G. Bohn, 1849), 666–69.

31. The Montgomery *Weekly Advertiser* refers to this as the "Laburnum of Constantine." The correspondents are probably referring to a labarum, the military standard created by Roman emperor Constantine the Great. Constantine's labarum included the Christographic "Chi-Rho" symbol (☧) symbolizing the divine protection he claimed to fight under at the Battle of the Milvian Bridge (312 A.D.).

32. In this sign thou shalt conquer.

33. The identity of Lieutenant Hamilton has not been determined.

34. The Savannah *Daily Morning News* reports the secret session lasted fifteen to twenty minutes. Savannah *Daily Morning News*, February 11, 1861.

35. Written notifications to both Jefferson Davis and Alexander Stephens of their election may be found at *Official Records*, ser. 4, vol. 1, pt. 1, p. 101.

36. Rev. Archibald John Battle (1826–1907) was an educator and Baptist minister. Between 1847 and 1852, he tutored ancient languages at the University of Alabama. Upon entering the ministry in 1853, he led the Tuskegee Baptist Church and then returned to Tuscaloosa to assume the pastorate at the Tuscaloosa Baptist Church. He returned to teaching in 1856 as professor of Greek at the University of Alabama and founder of the Alabama Central Female College. Owen, *History of Alabama*, 3:115.

37. The Charleston *Mercury* is incorrect in its reporting. Howell Cobb's introduction of the flag patterns took place before Congress went into secret session. *JCCSA*, 1:43; Montgomery *Weekly Advertiser*, February 13, 1861.

38. Note that Conrad's motion to create this specific committee on February 11 was subsequent to and exclusive of Congress's authorization for Cobb to name standing committee members. Cobb thus was permitted to include Conrad in his deliberations over appointments to the Committee to Organize the Executive Departments.

39. Edwin V. Sharp (1835–88), was a portraitist and military illustrator based in Augusta,

Georgia. A lithograph of his painting "To the Macon Volunteers of Macon, Geo." was included in the February 1842 edition of Huddy and Duval's *U. S. Military Magazine*, a national journal that covered the nation's locally organized volunteer military organizations. On the eve of the Civil War, Sharp was painting military-styled banners for local fire companies in Augusta. He also provided candidate banners for local political contests. Montgomery *Weekly Advertiser*, February 20, 1861. Frederick P. Todd, "The Huddy & Duval Prints: An Adventure in Military Lithography," *Journal of the American Military Institute* 3, no. 3 (1939): 166–67, 176; Augusta *Weekly Constitutionalist*, July 7, 1858; Augusta *Chronicle*, May 10, 1855, and October 14, 1856.

40. The official journal records the Nisbet resolution preceding Mr. Harris's. *JCCSA*, 1:45.

41. The Charleston *Mercury* incorrectly refers to Platt as "F. B. Platt." Jacob B. Platt was an Augusta, Georgia, funeral director and inventor who obtained numerous design patents during and after the Civil War. *Scientific American* 14, no. 4 (November 6, 1858): 67; Montgomery *Weekly Advertiser*, February 20, 1861; Allen D. Candler and Clement A. Evans, eds., *Georgia: Comprising Sketches of Counties, Towns, Events, Institutions, and Persons, Arranged in Cyclopedic Form*, vol. 3 (Atlanta: State Historical Association, 1906), 108; William L. Platt and Jacob B. Platt, "Camp cots," Confederate States Patent 60, filing date unknown, issued January 7, 1862, Galileo, Georgia's Virtual Library, accessed May 7, 2020 (original located at Augusta-Richmond County [Georgia] Public Library System Collection); *Annual Report of the Commissioner of Patents for the Year 1869*, vol 1 (Washington, DC: Government Printing Office, 1871), 225; *Specifications and Drawings of Patents Issued from the United States Patent Office for March 1876* (Washington, DC: Government Printing Office, 1876), 200; *Miscellaneous Documents of the Senate of the United States for the First Session of the Fifty-Second Congress, 1891–1892*, vol. 4 (Washington, DC: Government Printing Office, 1892), 287.

42. There is not enough information to determine with certainty the identity of these correspondents.

43. Mark Anthony Cooper (1800–1885) was a lawyer, politician, and businessman who operated one of the leading industrial firms of Civil War Georgia. He was a veteran of the Second Seminole War, elected to the state legislature in 1833 and the US Congress in 1838 and 1842. With business partner Moses Stroup, he established the Etowah Manufacturing and Mining Company in 1842 to exploit northern Georgia's mineral wealth. See, Mark Cooper Pope III and J. Donald McKee, *Mark Anthony Cooper: The Iron Man of Georgia, A Biography* (Atlanta: Graphic, 2000); Robert S. Davis, "The First Golden Age of Georgia Industry, 1828–1860," *Georgia Historical Quarterly* 72, no. 4 (1988): 701–2, 704; G. Richard Wright and Kenneth H. Wheeler, "New Men in the Old South: Joseph E. Brown and His Associates in Georgia's Etowah Valley," *Georgia Historical Quarterly* 93, no. 4 (2009): 363–87.

44. Robert Toombs, of Georgia.

45. It is not known if or when Mr. Curry introduced these memorials. No record of them has been found to date.

46. In actual existence.

47. An 1845 graduate of New York University Medical School, Dr. Henry M. Jeter gained appointment as postmaster in 1858 under questionable circumstances. As the Augusta *Chronicle* reported, "We learn from a credible authority that Mr. Forsyth [the former postmaster] resigned for a valuable consideration, in favor of Dr. Jeter. . . . It really appears to us that if the office was a marketable commodity it ought to have been upon the market that all might have a chance at it." The details of Jeter's letter to Mr. Crawford are not known. *JCCSA*, 1:48; New York *Herald*, March 21, 1845; Augusta *Chronicle*, November 18 and 19, 1858.

48. The Montgomery *Weekly Advertiser* uses the term "nation" rather than "union." Montgomery *Weekly Advertiser*, February 20, 1861.

49. "To Anacreon in Heaven," also known as "The Anacreontic Song," was the official song of the Anacreontic Society, an eighteenth-century London gentlemen's club. Its tune forms the melodic core of the patriotic song (now American national anthem) "The Star-Spangled Banner." William Lichtenwanger, "The Music of 'The Star-Spangled Banner': Whence and Whither?" *College Music Symposium* 18, no. 2 (1978): 34–81.

50. Of no further official authority or legal effect.

51. The Montgomery *Advertiser* contains a slightly different account of this paragraph: "True sir; but I feel more pride in stating that the Palmetto Regiment was there and bathed its own State flag in the blood of many of its members and officers—and the warm heart of the gallant Colonel of the Regiment, the chivalrous Butler, beat its last pulsation there. [*Applause.*]" Former South Carolina governor Pierce Mason Butler (1798–1847), to whom Miles referred, commanded the Palmetto Regiment of South Carolina Volunteers in the Mexican War and was killed at the Battle of Churubusco in 1847. Russell D. James, "Pierce Mason Butler," in *The Encyclopedia of the Mexican-American War: A Political, Social, and Military History*, ed. Spencer Tucker (Santa Barbara: ABC-CLIO, 2013), 100; Montgomery *Weekly Advertiser*, February 20, 1861.

52. At length.

53. This is possibly a reference to Hannibal's invasion of Italy during the Second Punic War, one that Boyce hoped would draw parallels between Hannibal's failure to capture Rome and the expected failure of the United States to capture or reunite the seceded Southern states.

54. George Williamson Livermore Ladd (1802–64) was a portrait and miniature painter. Born in New Hampshire, Ladd is rumored to have studied painting under Samuel F. B. Morse before moving south as an itinerant artist in Virginia, the Carolinas, and Georgia. Patricia V. Veasey, "Correct Likenesses: George Ladd, Itinerant Miniature and Portrait Painter," *Journal of Early Southern Decorative Arts* 40 (2019).

55. Catherine Stratton Ladd (1809–1899) was an educator, author, and poet who served as creator and principal of the Winnsboro Female Institute. She published extensively on art and education in various southern journals including *Floral Wreath* and the *Southern Literary Messenger*. Ida Raymond, *Southland Writers: Biographical and Critical Sketches of the Living Female Writers of the South,* vol. 2 (Philadelphia: Claxton, Remsen, & Haffelfinger, 1870), 896–97; *Encyclopedia of Virginia Biography*, vol. 3 (New York: Lewis Historical Publishing Company, 1915), 196; *American National Biography*, vol. 13 (New York: Oxford University Press, 1999), 19–20.

Thian's *Documentary History of the Flag* includes a postscript to the letter that reads: "We shall need your services to deliver the Flag to the Boyce Guards in the course of ten days." Raphael P. Thian, comp., *Documentary History of the Flag and Seal of the Confederate States of America, 1861–1865* (Washington, DC: Government Printing Office, 1880), appendix, pt. 2, 6.

56. See Mr. Platt's original proposal made February 13, 1861.

57. The letter was from Elam Alexander (1796–1863), an architect and one of the founding fathers of Macon, Georgia. *JCCSA*, 1:51; Wilber W. Caldwell, *The Courthouse and the Depot: The Architecture of Hope in an Age of Despair: A Narrative Guide to Railroad Expansion and Its Impact on Public Architecture in Georgia, 1833–1910* (Macon, GA: Mercer University Press, 2001), 94–95.

58. From the firm of Sands and Edwards of New York City. J. A. Edwards worked as a New York–based agent and attorney for the British commercial shipping firm of T. B. Sands and Co. In 1860, Sands brought Edwards on as a full partner and renamed the company Sands and Edwards. By February 1861, the firm was in the process of dissolution. *JCCSA*, 1:54; *Boston Commercial Bulletin*, June 30, 1860, and March 23, 1861; *Smith v. Vertue* (1860) 30 LJCP 56.

59. See *Acts and Resolutions of the First Session of the Provisional Congress of the Confederate States, 1861* (Montgomery: Barnett, Wimbush, 1861), 3, 6.

60. Dr. John Braham Read obtained a US patent on a hard metal expanding artillery shell in 1857 that helped pave the way for rifled cannon. Robert Parrott, superintendent of the West Point Foundry, bought the rights to the shell design that same year. Union forces would use the renamed Parrott Shell to devasting effect against Confederate forces. Confederates used the design in the Brooke rifled cannon produced in Selma, Alabama. G. Ward Hubbs, *Tuscaloosa: 200 Years in the Making* (Tuscaloosa: University of Alabama Press, 2019), 43; John B. Read, "Projectile," US Patent No. 18,707, issued November 24, 1857. See related documents in John B. Read Papers, South Carolina Historical Society, Charleston, SC.

61. The Charleston *Mercury* says the letter was referred to the Committee on Military Affairs. Montgomery *Weekly Advertiser*, February 20, 1861.

62. Possibly T. J. Forsyth to Gen. C. J. McRae, February 10, 1861, in Thian, *Documentary History of the Flag*, appendix, pt. 2, p. 16.

63. The letter was from Judge Augustus H. Hansell (1817–1907) of Thomasville, Georgia. *JCCSA*, 1:56; Tifton (GA) *Gazette*, February 15, 1907.

64. Thian's *Documentary History of the Flag* records DeClouet making the presentation. The identity of the correspondent cannot be determined with certainty. *Documentary History of the Flag*, appendix, pt. 1, 3.

65. Not found.

66. See Read's earlier communication, February 15, 1861.

67. John M. Walden, railroad superintendent at Fort Valley, Georgia, received Confederate patent number 7 for his railroad switch design. Kenneth W. Dobyns, *The Patent Office Pony: A History of the Early Patent Office* (Boston: Docent Press, 2016), 274; 1860 US Census, Population Schedule.

68. A patent caveat is a provisional patent application or notice of intent to file a patent at a later date.

69. The communication was from Rufus Levi Dolbear Sr. (1814–88), a sketch artist and president of Dolbear Commercial College in New Orleans. By the time of the Civil War, Dolbear and his brothers had become well-known for their scientific methods of teaching penmanship, published originally in New York in 1836 as *Dolbear's Science of Practical Penmanship.* In all likelihood, Rufus Dolbear sought Confederate copyright protection for this book. *JCCSA*, 1:56; Robert C. Reinders, *End of an Era: New Orleans, 1850–1860* (New Orleans: Pelican Publishing, 1964), 143; John A. Mahé II and Rosanne McCaffery, eds., *Encyclopaedia of New Orleans Artists, 1718–1918* (New Orleans: Historic New Orleans Collection, 1987), 111; *The Science of Practical Penmanship: Or the Analysis of Taste and Freedom* (New York: Thomas P. Dolbear; Natchez: Levi Dolbear; New Orleans: Rufus Dolbear and J. W. Dolbear, 1850).

70. Rev. Jonathan (or James) Avery Shepherd (1816–98), founder of the Episcopal Female Seminary in Montgomery, was born in Vermont and entered the seminary in New York. He ministered in Montgomery throughout the Civil War before moving west to California. Montgomery *Daily Confederation*, October 6, 1858, and July 10, 1860; San Francisco *Call*, August 30, 1891, and March 31, 1898; Baltimore *Sun*, May 23, 1898; San Francisco *Chronicle*, March 31, 1898.

71. Rev. Richard Hooker Cobbs (1835–1920) was the son of Rev. N. H. Cobbs, first bishop of the Diocese of Alabama. He graduated from the University of Alabama in 1855 and entered the ministry in 1858, first in Huntsville and then at St. Paul's Episcopal Church in Greensboro, Alabama, where he continued to serve for fifty years. *Gospel Messenger and Church Record of Western New-York*, June 17, 1859; Montgomery *Advertiser*, Wednesday, September 27,

1911; Richard Hooker Cobbs and Walter C. Whitaker, "Statistics of the Protestant Episcopal Church in the Diocese of Alabama," *Transactions of the Alabama Historical Society, 1897–1898*, vol. 2, ed. Thomas McAdory Owen (Tuscaloosa: Alabama Historical Society, 1899), 83n1; "Death of Rev. R. H. Cobbs, D.D.," *Living Church* 63, no. 8 (June 19, 1920): 285.

72. See *JCCSA*, 1:67.

73. See *Acts and Resolutions of the First Session*, 4, 8–9.

74. See *JCCSA*, 1:66–67.

75. The Charleston *Courier* identifies the correspondent at Hon. John J. Ormond (1795–1866), former associate justice of the Alabama State Supreme Court (1837–47) and author of *The Code of Alabama*. Charleston *Courier*, February 22, 1861; *The Code of Alabama* (Montgomery: Brittan and De Wolf, State Printers, 1852); Owen, *History of Alabama*, 4:1303.

76. The Charleston *Mercury* incorrectly lists "Rev. Mr. Hind." Rev. Joshua T. Heard (1817–84) was a Methodist Episcopal minister who served several circuits and stations in the Mobile District of Alabama. Vicksburg *Herald*, January 3, 1885; *Minutes of the Annual Conferences of the Methodist Episcopal Church, South, for the Year 1858* (Nashville: Southern Methodist Publishing House, 1859), 69; *Minutes of the Mobile Conference of the Methodist Episcopal Church, South* (Mobile: Office of "The Army Argus and Crisis," 1864), 5, 8, 14, 16, 17, 20.

77. William Crosby Dawson (1798–1856) represented Georgia in the US House of Representatives (1836–41) and the US Senate (1849–55). US Congress, "William Crosby Dawson," Biographical Directory of the United States Congress, accessed May 12, 2020.

78. John Henry Lumpkin (1812–60) represented Georgia in the US House of Representatives (1843–49, 1855–57). He proposed the location of a national foundry in Cass County, Georgia, on December 19, 1845. Lumpkin's letter of referral to Rep. Archibald Yell of the House Committee on Military Affairs may be found in the Milledgeville *Federal Union*, March 10, 1846. US Congress, "John Henry Lumpkin," Biographical Directory of the United States Congress, accessed May 12, 2020.

79. Born in Germany, A. J. Brady opened a successful hardware mercantile in Atlanta in 1849. Pioneer Citizens' Society of Atlanta, *Pioneer Citizens' History of Atlanta, 1833–1902* (Atlanta: Byrd Printing, 1902), 355–56.

80. Slag separated from molten metal during smelting.

81. The correspondent is William P. Barker. No record of the documents has been found. *JCCSA*, 1:70.

82. For more information on the Union blockade of Confederate ports, see James M. McPherson, *War on the Waters: The Union and Confederate Navies, 1861–1865* (Chapel Hill: University of North Carolina Press, 2012); Kevin Dougherty, *Strangling the Confederacy: Coastal Operations of the American Civil War* (Philadelphia: Casemate, 2010); Paul W. Gates, *Agriculture and the Civil War* (New York: Knopf, 1965); Philip Leigh, *Trading with the Enemy: The Covert Economy during the American Civil War* (Yardley, PA: Westholme, 2014); David G. Surdam, *Northern Naval Superiority and the Economics of the American Civil War* (Columbia: University of South Carolina Press, 2001); Hamilton Cochran, *Blockade Runners of the Confederacy* (Indianapolis: Bobbs-Merrill, 1958); Stephen R. Wise, *Lifeline of the Confederacy: Blockade Running during the Civil War* (Columbia: University of South Carolina Press, 1988); Leslie S. Butler, *Pirates, Privateers, and Rebel Raiders of the Carolina Coast* (Chapel Hill: University of North Carolina Press, 2002); and George E. Buker, *Blockaders, Refugees, and Contrabands, Civil War on Florida's Gulf Coast, 1861–1865* (Tuscaloosa: University of Alabama Press, 1993).

83. Samuel P. L. Marshall was a judge in Kentucky before moving to northern Alabama. In 1852, he established one of the state's first furnaces, the Round Mountain Steam Hot-blast Charcoal Furnace, in Cherokee County. Marie B. Owen, comp., *Alabama Official and Statistical Register, 1919* (Montgomery: Brown Printing, 1920), 140; J. Peter Lesley, *The Iron*

Manufacturer's Guide to the Furnaces, Forges and Rolling Mills of the United States (New York: John Wiley, 1859), 79; *JCCSA*, 1:71.

84. See *Acts and Resolutions of the First Session*, 11–18.

85. The Charleston *Mercury* names Capt. W. W. Hall, although there is no evidence to substantiate this report. George Washington Lee enrolled over eighty plasterers, blacksmiths, painters, carpenters, mechanics, stone and brick masons, and general laborers into a volunteer company on March 8, 1861. Lee's Volunteers, as they were known, were accepted into Confederate service on March 25, 1861, as Company D, First Confederate Volunteer Infantry (also designated Co. D, Thirty-Sixth Regiment Georgia Infantry [Villepigue's]). Georgia Division of Confederate Pensions and Records, *Roster of the Confederate Soldiers of Georgia, 1861–1865*, ed. Lillian Henderson (Hapeville, GA: Longina and Porter, 1959), 1:35; Record and Pension Office in the War Department, Thirty-Sixth Georgia (Villepigue's) Infantry, *Compiled Service Records of Confederate Soldiers Who Served in Organizations from the State of Georgia*, National Archives RG 109, microfilm M266, roll 428, hereafter cited as CSR.

86. Environs.

87. The comparisons between French and British militaries in the Crimean War centered on their respective logistical successes and failures during the winter of 1854–55. To many, it appeared the French were better prepared than their British counterparts due, as the *Weekly National Intelligencer* pointed out in January 1855, to reforms growing out of French experiences in Algeria more than a decade earlier. "But the most important differences between the two armies," and arguably the most important reason for French superiority in the Crimea according to the *Intelligencer*, was that the

> French army is homogeneous; soldier and officer are one. The ideas, the confidence, the feelings which emanate from the highest find their way to the lowest. The English army, unfortunately, is divided into two classes, with a gulf between them, and no interchange of confidence exists. The result is, that with the English, if a commander be not fortunate, the soldier rails at him and thinks himself ill used; since an officer class which assumes such vast superiority over the soldiers in the ranks necessarily incurs the responsibility of showing and making good that superiority. The French soldier, on the contrary, expects nothing beyond what the average of human intellect and knowledge can accomplish from his officer; for that officer has never assumed such superiority.

Such comments were not limited to American observers. British war correspondents such as W. H. Russell, Thomas Chenery, and Lawrence Godkin noted similar comparisons as did British historian Henry Tyrrell. Citing the French newspaper *Patrie's* "truthful criticism," Tyrrell noted that the British officer

> is the proprietor of the men as much as the state; the country therefore is not all in all for the soldier. [However, in France] the army is eminently national; every citizen can and ought to be a soldier in his turn; he has a right to apply to himself the expression of one of his sovereigns, and to say with pride, "There is perhaps a marshal's baton in my knapsack." For him, if he possess merit and courage, if he be fortunate enough to render services to his country, there is no limit between the lowest and the highest grade in the military hierarchy.

Wright suggests that this image of the more egalitarian citizen-soldier, one which commands authority, unit cohesion, and battlefield success that arise from personal intimacy and talent rather than state or class authority, is better suited for the emerging Confederate army. Henry Tyrrell, *The History of the War with Russia*, vol. 2: *Giving Full Details of the Operations of the Allied Armies* (London: London Printing and Publishing, 1855), 27–28; *Weekly National Intelligencer*, February 17, 1855; Anthony Dawson, "The French Army and British Army Crimean War Reforms," *19: Interdisciplinary Studies in the Long Nineteenth Century* 20 (May 12, 2015).

88. Some reports erroneously list William P. Parker.

89. Memminger had been selected as the Confederate States's first secretary of the Treasury.

90. There is not enough information to identify Mrs. E. G. Carpenter.

91. Little, Brown and Company is an American publishing house founded in Boston in 1837 by Charles Coffin Little and James Brown.

92. The official journal and the Montgomery *Weekly Advertiser* list John C. Thornton, while the Charleston *Mercury* and the Savannah *Daily Morning News* incorrectly list John C. Parker. Thornton, a Macon, Georgia, carriage merchant, and Cox, his mechanic, had developed a new construction method for a "Light Brett" carriage that would allow easy conversion from four to six seats for passengers. However, according to the Confederate Citizen Papers for John C. Thornton, this application was related to either a new form or construction method for rifle butts. *JCCSA*, 1:80; Montgomery *Weekly Advertiser*, February 27, 1861; Savannah *Daily Morning News*, February 27, 1861; Augusta *Weekly Chronicle & Sentinel*, February 26, 1861; 1860 US Census, Population Schedule; John C. Thornton in Confederate Papers Relating to Citizens or Business Firms, National Archives RG 109: War Department Collection of Confederate Records, 1825–1927, M346, hereafter cited as Confederate Citizens Papers.

93. This is possibly Henry Winslow (born about 1817 in Georgia), who is listed as a merchant in Albuquerque, New Mexico, in the 1860 US Census, Population Schedule; *JCCSA*, 1:80; Montgomery *Weekly Advertiser*, February 27, 1861.

94. O. M. Roberts. *JCCSA*, 1:80.

95. Simpson Bobo (1804–85) founded the legal firm of Bobo and Edwards in the 1830s and became one of South Carolina's leading investors in industrial and railroad development. He was the largest stockholder in the South Carolina Manufacturing Company, which operated a furnace and iron rolling mill in Spartanburg county, South Carolina. Montgomery *Weekly Advertiser*, February 27, 1861; J. B. O. Landrum, *History of Spartanburg County* (Atlanta: Franklin Printing and Publishing, 1900), 156–57; Bruce W. Eelman, *Entrepreneurs in the Southern Upcountry: Commercial Culture in Spartanburg, South Carolina, 1845–1880* (Athens: University of Georgia Press, 2008), 18–19, 29, 41.

96. The official journal credits Mr. Hale, of Alabama, while the Montgomery *Weekly Advertiser* credits Mr. Smith, of Alabama. *JCCSA*, 1:86; Montgomery *Weekly Advertiser*, March 6, 1861.

97. The Macon Chamber of Commerce was formed on February 14, 1861, specifically to promote direct trade between Macon and Europe. *Weekly Georgia Telegraph*, February 21, 1861.

98. Between December 12 and 25, 1860, Macon simultaneously hosted its annual Cotton Planter's Fair and a Belgian Fair, the latter held to promote direct international trade between Belgium and the southern states. Richard W. Iobst, *Civil War Macon: The History of a Confederate City* (Macon, GA: Mercer University Press, 2009), 11; Thomasville (GA) *Southern Enterprise*, January 30, 1861; Augusta *Daily Chronicle & Sentinel*, September 23, 1860; Columbus (GA) *Daily Sun*, December 5, 1860

99. See *Acts and Resolutions of the First Session*, 28–31.

100. Rev. Thomas H. Capers (1811–66) of the Methodist Episcopal Church South served churches in both Alabama and Missouri before financial problems forced him to give up the

pulpit in 1846. He later studied medicine and served as president of the Southern Female College in Rocky Springs, Mississippi. In 1860, he resigned his presidency to return to Alabama where he became president of the Auburn Female College. He was officially readmitted to the Methodist Conference as a preacher in December 1862 and assigned to the Florida Conference in 1863. Columbus (GA) *Daily Sun*, September 7, 1861; Jackson *Weekly Mississippian*, July 25, 1860; Charleston *Courier*, August 25, 1858; Owen, *History of Alabama*, 3:296; John McClintock and James Strong, *Cyclopedia of Biblical, Theological, and Ecclesiastical Literature*, Supplement, vol. 1: A-CN (New York: Harper and Brothers, 1885), 785; *Minutes of the Annual Conferences of the Methodist Episcopal Church, South, for the Year 1862* (Nashville: Southern Methodist Publishing House, 1870), 397; *Minutes of the Annual Conferences of the Methodist Episcopal Church, South, for the Year 1866* (Nashville: Southern Methodist Publishing House, 1870), 31–32.

101. S. D. Gratiaa & Company was a New Orleans–based importer of fine European wines in partnership with the Bordeaux, France-based P. Longis & Co. New Orleans *Times-Picayune*, April 30, 1863.

102. William Glaze (1815–83) was the founder of the Palmetto Armory and Iron Works, manufacturer of South Carolina's state arms throughout the 1850s. Jack Allen Meyer, *William Glaze and the Palmetto Armory*, Museum Bulletin no. 6 (Columbia: South Carolina State Museum, 1982), chap. 2.

103. The Charleston *Mercury* makes two mistakes in its reporting. In addition to incorrectly citing a middle initial of "A" instead of "M", the paper mistakenly reports patent protection being sought on a "portable furnace." At the same time, the Montgomery *Weekly Advertiser* refers to the petitioner as "J. M. Fitch." Prior to the Civil War, Dr. John M. Pitts of Sumter County, South Carolina, had developed at least three inventions. In August 1860, he announced two: the first, a machine for crushing cotton seeds, the second, a splint "for binding up and replacing broken limbs." In October 1860, he received a patent for an ornamental portable fence for which he won awards at the 1860 North Carolina State Fair. The evidence suggests that Pitts was applying to the Confederate government for patent protection on his fence and splint. *JCCSA*, 1:90; Charleston *Courier*, August 21 and October 25, 1860; North Carolina *Standard*, October 24, 1860.

104. James E. Harrison (1815–75) was born in South Carolina but moved to west Texas in 1857. In early 1861, he served as a Texas state commissioner to negotiate alliances with Native American populations in the event of war with the United States. Ezra J. Warner, *Generals in Gray: Lives of the Confederate Commanders* (Baton Rouge: Louisiana State University Press, 1959), 127–28; Gregory Michno, *The Settlers' War: The Struggle for the Texas Frontier in the 1860s* (Lincoln: University of Nebraska Press, 2011), 70; Connole, *Civil War*, 40.

105. *Acts and Resolutions of the First Session,* 22–26.

106. The letter was written by J. E. Hutz. No further information on Hutz has been found. *JCCSA* 1:93.

107. The designer is listed as W. P. Hilliard, possibly William Preston Hilliard, a Montgomery, Alabama, attorney and son of former Alabama congressman Henry Washington Hilliard. Thian, *Documentary History of the Flag*, appendix, pt. 2, 60; 1860 US Census, Population Schedule; Mears and Turnbull, comp., *The Montgomery Directory for 1859–1860* (Montgomery: Advertiser Book and Job Printing Office, 1859), 47

108. Identity unknown.

109. The Charleston *Mercury* gives the name D. A. St. Clair. The Montgomery *Weekly Advertiser* lists T. K. St. Clair. Most likely, the reporters for these papers misheard the name reported in the official congressional journal: Lt. George T. Sinclair. Sinclair was a veteran of the US Exploring Expedition, also known as the Wilkes Expedition (1838–42), a surveying

expedition of the Pacific Ocean. During the secession crisis of 1860–61, he was assigned as a lieutenant of ordinance at the Norfolk navy yard and helped secure the powder magazines there for Confederate use. *JCCSA* 1:93; *American Newspaper Directory* (New York: Geo. P. Rowell, 1876), 227; Montgomery *Weekly Advertiser*, March 6, 1861; *Virginian-Pilot*, July 30, 1885; Baltimore *Sun*, August 3, 1885.

110. The Charleston *Mercury* incorrectly reports the name John D. Roberts, the Montgomery *Weekly Advertiser*, John C. Crawford. John C. Robertson (1824–95) was appointed chair of the Texas Committee of Safety and charged by the Texas Secession Convention with disarming and removing federal troops from the state. Montgomery *Weekly Advertiser*, March 6, 1861; *JCCSA* 1:93; Wentworth Manning, *Some History of Van Zandt County*, vol 2 (Madison, WI: Homestead Company, 1919), 193–94; *Texas Biographical Dictionary*, 3rd ed. (New York: Somerset, 1996), 183; Linda S. Hudson, "The Knights of the Golden Circle in Texas, 1858–1861: An Analysis of the First (Military) Degree Knights," in *The Seventh Star of the Confederacy: Texas during the Civil War*, ed. Kenneth Wayne Howell (Denton: University of North Texas Press, 2009), 56.

111. The letter was written by John M. Lapsley, a Selma, Alabama, merchant and president of the Alabama Manufacturing Company. Lapsley was also in correspondence with Congress regarding the use of the Selma Manufacturing Company as a Confederate armory. *Official Records*, ser. IV, vol. 1, pt. 1, pp. 107–8; *Alabama State Sentinel*, April 27, 1859; *JCCSA* 1:94; 1850 US Census, Population Schedule; Confederate Citizens Papers, John M. Lapsley.

112. For detailed information from the Committee on Postal Affairs on postal finances, see Mr. Chilton's report published in the Charleston *Mercury*, March 2, 1861.

113. See *Acts and Resolutions of the First Session*, 32–34.

114. Mr. Horace Ware (1812–90) was the owner of the Shelby Iron Works, one of Alabama's largest and most important ironworks. *JCCSA*, 1:97; Henry M. McKiven Jr., *Iron and Steel: Class, Race, and Community in Birmingham, Alabama, 1875–1920* (Chapel Hill: University of North Carolina Press, 1995), 9–10; James F. Doster, "The Shelby Iron Works Collection in the University of Alabama Library," *Bulletin of the Business Historical Society* 26, no. 4 (1952): 214–17.

115. On the Nullification Crisis in South Carolina see, Richard E. Ellis, *The Union at Risk: Jacksonian Democracy, States' Rights, and the Nullification Crisis* (New York and Oxford: Oxford University Press, 1989); William W. Freehling, *Prelude to Civil War: The Nullification Controversy in South Carolina 1816–1836* (New York and Oxford: Oxford University Press, 1992)

116. While the Confederacy sought formal recognition of its independence from numerous international partners, it coveted formal recognition by England and France most. Thus, it was crucial that the South gain the attention and support of Henry John Temple, Third Viscount Palmerston, prime minister of England (1858–59; 1859–65), and Napoleon III (Charles-Louis Napoléon Bonaparte), emperor of France (1852–70), possibly through free or low-tariff trading alliances. On Confederate diplomacy in general see Jones, *Blue and Gray Diplomacy*; Hubbard, *Burden of Confederate Diplomacy*; Owsley, *King Cotton Diplomacy*; Callahan, *Diplomatic History of the Southern Confederacy*; Jones, *Union in Peril*. On the role of tariffs in early Confederate diplomacy specifically, see Jones, *Blue and Gray Diplomacy*, 24–31; Sainlaude, *France and the American Civil War*, 84–85

117. Henry Penn Oden, James G. L. Huey, and Andrew W. Bowie were co-owners of H. P. Oden & Company, a marble quarry near Sylacauga, Alabama. *JCCSA*, 1:100; Ruth Beaumont Cook, *Magic in Stone: The Sylacauga Marble Story* (Montgomery: New South Books, 2019), 24–25, 31, 40.

118. Parian refers to a type of porcelain that imitates marble.

119. Chilton refers to public reporting of a contentious debate that had occurred in the Alabama Secession Convention. On January 9, 1861, Nicholas Davis, a delegate from Madison County in north Alabama, moved to submit the state's secession ordnance to a popular vote. William Lowndes Yancey of Montgomery responded with a rousing denunciation not only of Davis's motion but of those who opposed the act of secession. Anyone, he said

> who shall, after the passage of this Ordinance, dissolving the union of Alabama with the other States of this Confederacy, dare array themselves against the State, will then become the enemies of the State. There is a law of Treason, defining treason against the State; and, those who shall dare oppose the action of Alabama, when she assumes her independence of the Union, will become traitors—rebels against its authority, and will be dealt with as such.

Although Yancey denied a direct reference to the whole of north Alabama, Davis was not convinced.

> We are told, sir, . . . that resistance to the action of this Convention is treason, and those who undertake it, traitors and rebels . . . and not less odious, in my estimation, than the name of tory, is the doctrine which is claimed of the right to coerce an unwilling people. We must be dealt with as public enemies. But yesterday, sir, this Convention condemned this doctrine [the use of force by the US government]. With one voice, you declared against it, and expressed your determination to meet such an invasion of your rights as it ought to be met, with arms in your hands. It will be asserted as readily against a tyrant at home as abroad; as readily by the people of my section against usurpation and outrage here, as elsewhere.

Northern and Southern presses both leapt at the threats of coercion and armed response. Within a week, the Chicago *Daily Tribune* was reporting the confrontation. By the end of the month, papers from St. Louis, Missouri, to Burlington, Vermont, had picked it up. By the end of February, California newspapers carried the story, and the image of a divided Alabama showed no sign of abating in the east. Just three days prior to Chilton's speech, the *Daily National Intelligencer* in Washington, DC, reported that Gen. James Hickman of Huntsville warned that "North Alabama never will submit to be dragged out of the Union, and that the Union sentiment is predominating in that region." William R. Smith, *The History and Debates of the Convention of the People of Alabama* (Montgomery: White, Pfister, 1861), 55, 66–74, quote on page 69; Chicago *Daily Tribune*, January 18, 1861; *Weekly St. Louis Evening News*, January 21, 1861; Burlington *Weekly Free Press*, February 1, 1861; *Nevada* (CA) *Democrat*, February 23, 1861; Christine Dee, "Trying James Hickman: The Politics of Loyalty in a Civil War Community," *Alabama Review* 58 (April 2005): 83–112.

120. See Brooke's speech on February 13, 1861.

121. Gules is a heraldic red or a heraldic yellow.

122. Rebecca C. Ferguson (b. abt. 1844) was the daughter of Methodist minister Frederick "Frank" Guthrie Ferguson of Tuskegee, Alabama. 1860 US Census, Population Schedule; Owen, *History of Alabama*, 3:572.

123. Possibly Mary Ann E. Sinclair (b. abt 1842), daughter of Alfred E. Sinclair, a Tuskegee carpenter. 1850 US Census, Population Schedule; 1860 US Census, Population Schedule.

124. The Montgomery *Weekly Advertiser* reports Mr. Perkins of Louisiana. Montgomery *Weekly Advertiser*, March 6, 1861.

125. *JCCSA*, 1:106.

126. Miles referred to events from the French and Indian War (1755–63).

127. John Hampden (1595–1643), opponent of English monarch Charles I, whose attempted arrest sparked the First English Civil War. His family motto, *Vestigia nulla retrorsum*, translates as "Never surrender."

128. Dr. John Perkins Ralls (1822–1904), was a Gadsden, Alabama, doctor and Methodist minister who had been a member of the Alabama Secession Convention. Ben H. Severance, *A War All Over: Alabama Politics and the Confederate Cause* (Tuscaloosa: University of Alabama Press, 2020), 23.

129. For information on the domestic slave trade, see Michael Tadman, *Speculators and Slaves: Masters, Traders, and Slaves in the Old South* (Madison: University of Wisconsin Press, 1996); Walter Johnson, *Soul by Soul: Life Inside the Antebellum Slave Market* (Cambridge, MA: Harvard University Press, 1999); Robert H. Gudmestad, *A Troublesome Commerce: The Transformation of the Interstate Slave Trade* (Baton Rouge: Louisiana State University Press, 2003); Steven Deyle, *Carry Me Back: The Domestic Slave Trade in American Life* (New York: Oxford University Press, 2005).

130. The Swedish Iron Manufacturing Company was organized in 1850 by a group of Swedish and German immigrants to purchase the holdings of the defunct Nesbitt Manufacturing Company near Spartanburg, South Carolina. By 1853, the new concern was struggling financially and many of its investors were beginning to liquidate their stock. Although its owners did their best to promote its services, by late 1861 the state had levied Swedish Iron's property for back taxes. Ernest M. Lander, "The Iron Industry in Ante-Bellum South Carolina," *Journal of Southern History* 20, no. 3 (1954): 338, 348; Charleston *Courier*, March 12, 1851, and March 25, 1861; *Yorkville* (SC) *Enquirer*, September 12, 1861.

131. Possibly Baptist minister Sterling G. Jenkins of Talladega, Alabama.

132. The official journal gives the name of this gentleman as Wesley Miller. His exact identity cannot be determined; however, a Wesley Miller of Cambridge, New York, did obtain a patent in 1879 for an improved blasting powder. *JCCSA*, 1:115; Wesley Miller, "Improvement in Explosive Compounds," US Patent no. 212,726, application date May 31, 1878, patent date February 25, 1879.

133. Albert R. Lamar.

134. Possibly Henry Stebbs (b. abt. 1835) a Savannah miller. 1870 US Census, Population Schedule.

135. In late 1860, following the election of Abraham Lincoln, Anthony J. Guirot (c. 1802–70), assistant secretary of the US Treasury and treasurer at the New Orleans mint, had refused to transfer $350,000 in coin and bullion from the New Orleans mint to Philadelphia for safekeeping. He claimed not to have that amount on hand. However, on January 31, 1861, he oversaw the transfer of control of the mint to the Confederate government along with its deposits of almost $390,000. Edward S. Cooper, *Traitors: The Secession Period, November 1860-July 1861* (Madison, NJ: Fairleigh Dickinson University Press, 2008), 14, 20, 126–27; *New Orleans Republican*, December 13, 1870.

136. A. M. Dowling was the mayor of Macon, Mississippi. *JCCSA*, 1:123; 1860 US Census, Population Schedule.

137. See, *Laws Passed by the General Assembly of the Territory of New Mexico, 1859–1860* (Santa Fe: G. P. Hovey, 1860), 110–16.

138. *Congressional Globe*, 35th Cong., 2nd Sess. 753 (1859).

139. E. M. Apperson was a cotton merchant in Memphis, Tennessee.

140. Francis Terry Leak (1803–63) was a planter and businessman from Tippah County, Mississippi. For an extended record of the correspondence between Leak, Pettus, and Clayton, see Diary of Francis Terry Leak, typescript vol. 6 of vol. 5, pt. 1 (January 1859–May 6, 1861) in

Francis Terry Leak Papers #1095, Southern Historical Collection, Wilson Library, University of North Carolina, Chapel Hill.

141. See, Mr. Curry's resolution to ban the importation of slaves from the United States except for the purposes of immigration. *JCCSA*, 1:109.

142. Rev. Oliver Rufus Blue (1822–93), was the presiding elder of the Methodist Episcopal Church in the Montgomery district. Owen, *History of Alabama*, 3:167; *JCCSA*, 1:141.

143. John Sidney Sherman (1805–73), a veteran of the Battle of San Jacinto in the Texas Revolution, was named commandant of Galveston Island by the Texas Secession Convention. Ernest William Winkler, ed., *Journal of the Secession Convention of Texas, 1861* (Austin: Austin Printing Co., 1912), 393–94.

144. Johann Hartmann Auguste Gericke was a New Orleans–based engineer known for his Turbinate Force Pump, patented in 1865. Gericke moved to New York soon after the Civil War. *New Orleans Times*, August 23, 1865; *Flake's Bulletin*, May 1, 1866; Charles Gardner, comp., *Gardner's New Orleans Directory for 1866* (New Orleans: Charles Gardner, 1866), 194; *Commissioners of Patents' Journal* 1959 (October 11, 1872): 2233; *Commissioners of Patents' Journal* 1961 (October 18, 1872): 2303; *Commissioners of Patents' Journal* 1962 (October 22, 1872): 2332.

145. Benjamin F. Jones (born 1831) was the southern sales representative for B. M. & E. A. Whitlock & Company, a New York–based trading and importing firm whose owners were known southern sympathizers. "Maj. B. F. Jones" in *A Memorial and Biographical Record of Kansas City and Jackson County, Missouri* (Chicago: Lewis Publishing, 1896), 95–98; Andrew Johnson, *The Papers of Andrew Johnson*, vol. 3: *1858–1860*, ed. LeRoy P. Graf and Ralph W. Haskins (Knoxville: University of Tennessee Press, 1872), 447n4; Gobright and Pratt, *The Union Sketch-book* (New York: Pudney and Russell, 1860), 64–65.

146. See *JCCSA*, 1:145–46.

147. Gov. Sam Houston refused to swear loyalty to the Confederacy.

148. This mythical Roman warrior sacrificed himself to Hades in order the save the city of Rome.

149. Western portions of the original territory of Texas were ceded to the federal government as a part of the Compromise of 1850 to become the territories of Utah and New Mexico.

150. The Charleston *Mercury* cites "Comanches and other tribes, the most treacherous and cruel, who inhabit the whole frontier of her territory."

151. 1 Kings 12:1–16.

152. Quoted from a speech by Jefferson Davis on the Oregon question in 1846. *Congressional Globe*, 29th Cong., 1st Sess. 217 (1846).

153. George Gordon, Lord Byron, "Childe Harold's Pilgrimage," canto III, stanza II, in Ernest Hartley Coleridge, ed., *The Works of Lord Byron*, vol. 2: *Poetry* (London: John Murray; New York: Charles Scribner's Sons, 1922), 217.

154. Rev. Samuel Henderson (1817–90) was the editor of the *Southwestern Baptist*, Alabama's Baptist newspaper, and a delegate to the Alabama secession convention. Anson West, *A History of Methodism in Alabama* (Nashville: Publishing House Methodist Episcopal Church, South, 1893), 724–25; Wayne Flynt, *Alabama Baptists: Southern Baptists in the Heart of Dixie* (Tuscaloosa: University of Alabama Press, 1998), 70, 83, 87, 195; James Mallory, *"Fear God and Walk Humbly": The Agricultural Journal of James Mallory, 1843–1877* (Tuscaloosa: University of Alabama Press, 1997), 500n9.

Second Session

1. The firing on Fort Sumter, April 12–13, 1861.

2. Judge Alexander Baron Clitherall (1820–69) was a former clerk of the Alabama House

of Representatives. He resigned the position of assistant clerk of the Confederate Provisional Congress to become the registrar of the Confederate Treasury. Nelson F. Smith, *History of Pickens County, Ala.* (Carollton, AL: "Pickens Republican" Office, 1856), 69–74; *Vicksburg Whig*, March 20, 1861.

3. A native of Massachusetts, Robert Josselyn (1810–84) had been educated in Vermont and practiced law in Virginia before settling in Mississippi. He later served under Jefferson Davis in the Mexican War. On the outbreak of the Civil War, Josselyn resigned his position in the US Treasury Department to become Davis's personal wartime secretary. Davis later named Josselyn as the Confederacy's Secretary of the Arizona Territory. Following the war, Josselyn settled in Texas where he became a journalist and poet. Ernestine Clayton Deavours, *The Mississippi Poets* (Memphis, TN: E. H. Clarke and Brother, 1922), 101; Samuel Houston Dixon, *The Poets and Poetry of Texas* (Austin: Sam H. Dixon, 1885), 164–65.

4. Robert Emmett Dixon (1832–63), assistant secretary of the Provisional Congress, was a Columbus, Georgia, based lawyer. He was killed in 1863 by Confederate House of Representatives assistant clerk Robert E. Ford, of Kentucky, whom Dixon had fired for dereliction of duty. An account of the killing may be found in the April 30, 1863, edition of the Columbus (GA) *Daily Sun*. 1860 US Census, Population Schedule; Find a Grave.com, Robert Emmett Dixon (1832–24 Apr 1863), Find a Grave Memorial no. 62926473, citing Linwood Cemetery, Columbus, Muscogee County, Georgia, USA.

5. In response to the shelling for Fort Sumter by the South Carolina militia, President Lincoln issued a proclamation on April 15, 1861, calling out the militia of the loyal states to an aggregate number of seventy-five thousand troops for the purpose of suppressing "combinations [of rebellious states] too powerful to be suppressed by the ordinary course of judicial proceedings." "Proclamation Calling 75,000 Militia and Convening Congress in Extra Session," in Abraham Lincoln, *Complete Works, Comprising His Speeches, Letters, State Papers, and Miscellaneous Writings*, vol. 2, ed. John G. Nicolay and John Hay, (New York: Century Company, 1907), 34.

6. Martin J. Crawford of Georgia, John Forsyth of Alabama, and Andre B. Roman of Louisiana.

7. Associate justice of the US Supreme Court John A. Campbell.

8. The annexed documents, initially sealed by Congress, were not reported publicly until May 10, 1861.

9. *Official Records*, ser. IV, vol. 1, pt. 1, p. 247–54.

10. Brig. Gen. Pierre Gustave Toutant-Beauregard commanded the Confederate defenses at Charleston. Maj. Robert Anderson was in possession of Fort Sumter.

11. *Acts and Resolutions of the First Session*, 35–38.

12. James D. Richardson, *A Compilation of the Messages and Papers of the Confederacy Including the Diplomatic Correspondence 1861–1865* (Nashville: United States Publishing, 1905), 60–62.

13. "Proclamation of Blockade, April 19, 1861," in Lincoln, *Complete Works*, 35.

14. The Secretary of War's report may be found at *Official Records*, ser. IV, vol. 1, pt. 1, p. 247–54.

15. The appointees were William Lowndes Yancey of Alabama, Ambrose Dudley Mann of Virginia, and Pierre Adolphe Rost of Louisiana.

16. Davis nominated Carnot Posey as Confederate district attorney for southern Mississippi. Posey had resigned this position with the state's secession in 1861 and refused to accept renomination in favor of recruiting a local militia company which became Co. K, Sixteenth Mississippi Infantry. Henry E. McCulloch, Davis's nominee for Confederate marshal for Texas, also declined to retain his command of the First Texas Mounted Rifles. *JCCSA*,

1:185; John Fabian Chappo, "Carnot Posey" in *The Mississippi Encyclopedia*, Ted Ownby, ed. (Jackson: University Press of Mississippi, 2017), 1025; CSR, Carnot Posey (16th MS), Henry E. McCulloch (Officers); Confederate Citizens Papers, H. E. McCulloch.

17. *Official Records*, ser. IV, vol. 1, pt. 1, p. 247–54.

18. The CSS *Sumter* was the former USS *Habana*, a bark-rigged steamer built in Philadelphia in 1859 and purchased in New Orleans by the Confederate government in 1861. The "Machree" is the CSS *McRae* (mistakenly called the *Miramon* or *General Miramon* by the Union). She was the "former bark-rigged pirate ship" *Marques de la Habana* captured in March 1860 and purchased in New Orleans in 1861. James M. Merrill, "Confederate Shipbuilding at New Orleans," *Journal of Southern History* 28, no. 1 (1962): 88; "Sumter," Naval History and Heritage Command, April 2, 2014, and "McRae," Naval History and Heritage Command, April 2, 2014; *Naval OR*, ser. II, v. 2, p. 52.

19. The two companies were Leeds & Company and John Clark and Company, both of which produced field guns. Larry J. Daniel, *Cannoneers in Gray: The Field Artillery of the Army of the Tennessee* (Tuscaloosa: University of Alabama Press, 2005), 12–13.

20. A. Hatchett was a cotton factor and commercial merchant based in Memphis. *JCCSA*, 1:170; Memphis *Daily Eagle and Enquirer*, February 11, 1857; Andrew Morrison, *The Bluff City: Mistress of the Valley of the "Lower River"* (St. Louis: Geo. W. Engelhardt, 1892), 58.

21. Wright's inquiry is most likely in response to a letter of inquiry he had received from Lucius J. Gartrell, recently resigned US representative from Georgia, who sought to organize a volunteer company for Confederate service. See, *Official Records*, ser. IV, vol. 1, pt. 1, pp. 278–79.

22. For more information on Confederate chaplains, see Charles F. Pitts, *Chaplains in Gray: The Confederate Chaplains Story* (Nashville: Broadman Press, 1957); John Wesley Brinsfield Jr., *The Spirit Divided: Memoirs of Civil War Chaplains—The Confederacy* (Macon, GA: Mercer University Press, 2005).

23. Capt. Richard Phillip Crump (1824–69), was a veteran of the Army of the Republic of Texas who owned a grocery in Jefferson City, Marion County, Texas. "J. P. Nash" is most likely the misheard name of James V. Nash, a Marion County doctor. *JCCSA*, 1:170; Handbook of Texas Online, Aragorn Storm Miller and Brett J. Derbes, "Crump, Richard Phillip"; 1860 US Census, Population Schedule.

24. Nathanial Macon Crawford (1811–71), son of Georgia politician William H. Crawford, was the president of Mercer University throughout the Civil War. Jesse Harrison Campbell, *Georgia Baptists: Historical and Biographical* (Macon, GA: J. W. Burke, 1874), 482–92.

25. Richard Thomas Brownrigg (1831–63) was an Austin, Texas, attorney. He later served as a major on the staff of Gen. H. H. Sibley. John Howard Brown, ed., *Lamb's Biographical Dictionary of the United States*, vol. 1 (Boston: James H. Lamb, 1900), 457; CSR, Richard T. Brownrigg (Officers)

26. The official journal lists L. B. Collins. *JCCSA*, 1:175.

27. Anderson had been elected colonel of the First Florida Infantry on April 5, 1861. CSR, J. Patton Anderson (1st Florida Infantry).

28. For reporting on the meeting see, New Orleans *Daily True Delta*, April 27, 1861; New Orleans *Times-Picayune* April 25 and 28, 1861.

29. In March 1860, the Pensacola & Georgia (P&G) Railroad, then under construction in northern Florida, received a shipment of railroad iron imported from Cardiff, Wales, to St. Marks, Florida. Placed under a three-year bond, the iron was warehoused by collector of customs Alonzo B. Noyes until the import duty of $8,243.50 could be paid. In March 1861, Florida governor Madison S. Perry ordered Noyes to release the iron without payment of the duties, an order Noyes promptly and formally protested. Based upon the reporting in the

Montgomery *Weekly Advertiser* and Charleston *Mercury*, the memorial presented by Mr. Morton is presumably a request by P&G president Edward Houstoun for an endorsement of Governor Perry's order and a renegotiation of payment terms on the outstanding duties. Although the original petition has been lost, related documents can be found in Confederate Citizens Papers, Pensacola & Georgia Railroad.

30. Daniel Pike Hill (1824–1900) was a Georgia attorney, coauthor of the Georgia Ordinance of Secession, and Confederate commissioner dispatched to convince Arkansas to secede. Atlanta *Constitution*, August 4, 1900.

31. Pleasant Stovall (1798–1868) was a highly successful merchant in Augusta, Georgia, and father of Confederate brigadier general Marcellus A. Stovall. A. B. Caldwell, "Marcellus A. Stovall," in Northern, *Men of Mark in Georgia*, 47.

32. Judge John C. McGehee (1802–1882) was a Madison County, Florida, planter, signatory to the state's original 1838 constitution, and chair of the Florida Secession Convention. John Edward Johns, *Florida in the Civil War* (Gainesville: University of Florida Press, 1963), 16–7.

33. The press incorrectly reports the name as J. H. Gurley. The petitioner is most likely James W. Gurley, a clerk in the Confederate States District Court. Confederate Citizens Papers, James W. Gurley; New Orleans *Daily Crescent*, March 25, 1861

34. This could be either Payton S. Montgomery (b. abt. 1834), a Baptist minister from St. Clair County, Alabama, or William A. Montgomery (b. abt. 1832), a Methodist minister from Henry County, Alabama. 1860 US Census, Population Schedule.

35. *JCCSA*, 1:209; US Congress, Senate Executive Journal, 34th Cong., 1st sess., March 24, 1858; Confederate Citizen Files (Cade M. Godbold).

36. Identity is unknown.

37. Document has not been found.

38. Charleston *Mercury*, May 20, 1861; James M. Matthews, ed. *The Statutes at Large of the Provisional Government of the Confederate States of America* (Richmond: R. M. Smith, 1864), 136–49.

39. In 1857, South Carolina planter and former governor James Henry Hammond became intrigued by a variety of sugar cane known as Chinese sugar cane, sorghum sucre, or imphee, then being imported by a British entrepreneur named Leonard Wray from South Africa. Using seed distributed by the Agricultural Bureau of the US Patent Office and mechanical designs provided by Wray, Hammond planted 109 acres of imphee and constructed the necessary equipment to process the cane in the hopes of producing thirty thousand gallons of syrup. His experiment, which garnered press attention from New York to San Francisco, was deemed a failure as Hammond noted that "neither by his [Wray's] patented nor any other process could he [Hammond] make sugar from his Imphee." *North Carolina Standard*, November 25, 1857; New York *Tribune*, August 19, 1857; San Francisco *Weekly Bulletin*, October 3, 1857; "The Chinese Sugar Cane," *Country Gentleman* 9, no. 24 (June 11, 1857): 379; *Supplement to Encyclopedia Britannica*, "Agriculture," 9th ed., vol. 1 (New York: Henry G. Allen, 1888), 141; Drew Gilpin Faust, *James Henry Hammond and the Old South: A Design for Mastery* (Baton Rouge: Louisiana State University Press, 1982), 122–23.

40. Charleston *Mercury*, May 20, 1861; *Statutes at Large*, pp. 136–49.

41. This may be in reference to a long-standing claim by Jacob Barker against the US government to recoup the depreciated value of millions of dollars of negotiable papers accepted as collateral for a $5 million dollar loan to the US government to finance the War of 1812. *JCCSA*, 1:239; Jacob Barker, *Incidents in the Life of Jacob Barker of New Orleans, Louisiana* (Washington, DC, 1855), 280–83; R. R. Ward and others, Assignees of Jacob Barker, v. United States, House Doc. 258, 36th Cong., 2d sess. in *Reports of the Court of Claims Submitted to the*

House of Representatives during the Second Session of the Thirty-Sixth Congress, 1860-'61, vol. 1 (Washington, DC: Government Printing Office, 1861), np.

42. "Sec. 50. *And be it further enacted*, That in case the original inventor or discoverer of the art, machine or improvement for which a patent is solicited is a slave, the master of such slave may take an oath that the said slave was the original inventor; and on complying with the requisites of the law, shall receive a patent for said discovery or invention, and have all the rights to which a patentee is entitled by law." Matthews, *Statutes at Large*, 148.

43. For act as passed, see *Acts and Resolutions of the Second Session of the Provisional Congress of the Confederate States* (Richmond: Enquirer Book and Job Press, 1861), 63–83.

Third Session

1. Rev. Dr. Samuel Kennedy Talmadge (1798–1867) was a Presbyterian minister and president of Oglethorpe University in Midway, Georgia. *Princeton Standard*, June 21, 1867.

2. The southern tip of the lower peninsula of Virginia.

3. The *Savannah* was a converted pilot boat commissioned by the Confederacy as a privateer. On June 3, 1861, the *Savannah* was captured and its crew transported as prisoners to New York City. Jefferson Davis, *The Papers of Jefferson Davis*, vol. 7: *1861*, ed. Lynda Lasswell Crist (Baton Rouge: Louisiana State University Press, 1992), 221–23; *Official Records*, ser. II, vol. 3, p. 2

4. Previous to Davis's speech, Pres. Abraham Lincoln had issued two proclamations authorizing Winfield Scott, commanding general of the US Army, to suspend the writ of habeas corpus. The first, dated April 27, 1861, allowed suspension between Washington, DC, and Philadelphia, the second, dated July 2, 1861, between Washington, DC, and New York City. Lincoln, *Complete Works*, 39, 54.

5. Fort Zachary Taylor (Key West, Florida), Fort Jefferson (Dry Tortuga, Florida), Forts Monroe and Wool (Hampton Roads, Virginia) remained in Union hands. R. Scott Moore, *The Civil War on the Atlantic Coast, 1861–1865* (Washington, DC: Center of Military History, US Army, n.d.), 14.

6. Lt. Col. Thomas H. Taylor (1825–1901), First Regiment Kentucky Infantry. Davis, *Papers*, 7:221–23; CSR, Thomas H. Taylor (1st Kentucky Infantry); Arthur W. Bergeron, Jr., "Brig. Gen. Thomas Hart Taylor," in Allardice, *Kentuckians in Gray*, 258–63.

7. *Official Records*, ser. II, vol. 3, pp. 5–6.

8. Davis ordered South Carolina inspector general States Rights Gist to communicate with Capt. Samuel Mercer, captain of the USS *Wabash*. Davis, *Papers*, 7:221–23; *Official Records*, ser. II, vol. 3, p. 4.

9. See, for example, reports such as that in the New York *Commercial Advertiser*, which questioned why the captain of the *Savannah* had not been summarily executed for piracy. Instead, the paper conjectured, "officers and the crew of the *Savannah* will therefore almost certainly be sent ashore for trial, as in the case of officers and crew of slave traders, whose crime is also piracy." The crew were imprisoned at the New York House of Detention, otherwise known as The Tombs, to await indictment. New York *Weekly Day Book*, July 6, 1861; New York *Commercial Advertiser*, June 17, 1861.

10. "Proclamation of Blockade, April 19, 1861," in Lincoln, *Complete Works*, 35.

11. G. T. Beauregard to Brig. Gen. Irvin McDowell, July 7, 1861, in *Official Records*, ser. I, v. 2, p 738.

12. Brig. Gen. Milledge L. Bonham, First Brigade, Confederate Army of the Potomac.

13. Most likely, 2nd Lt. James Breckenridge, Thirtieth Virginia Volunteer Cavalry (Radford's Rangers), later designated the Second Virginia Cavalry. CSR, James Breckenridge (2nd Virginia Cavalry).

14. Colonel Andrew Porter, Sixteenth US Infantry. Andrew Porter, *States at War*, vol. 3: *A*

Reference Guide for Pennsylvania in the Civil War, ed. Richard F. Miller (Hanover, NH: University Press of New England, 2014), 371n263.

15. Evidence is circumstantial but strongly suggestive that Capt. Amiel Weeks Whipple and Lt. Haldimand S. Putnam of the US Army Topographical Engineers acted as escorts for Colonel Taylor as he passed through Union lines. Both Whipple and Putnam were attached to General McDowell in the days leading up to the First Battle of Bull Run, which occurred not long after and in the same area as Taylor's mission. *Official Records*, ser. I, v. 2, p 323, 738.

16. Col. Henry Bell Van Rensselaer, volunteer aide-de-camp to Gen. Winfield Scott, commanding general of the US Army. Edward P. Spillane, *Life and Letters of Henry Van Rensselaer, Priest of the Society of Jesus* (New York: Fordham University Press, 1908), 9.

17. Lt. Haldimand S. Putnam.

18. The press incorrectly reports his unit as the Second Kentucky Regiment.

19. Originally from New York, the Rev. Dr. John Lansing Burrows had served as the pastor of Richmond's First Baptist Church since 1856. Richmond *Whig*, May 17, 1870.

20. Joseph C. Mayo (1795–1872) served as Richmond's mayor from 1853–65 and 1866–69. William A. Blair, *Virginia's Private War: Feeding Body and Soul in the Confederacy* (Oxford: Oxford University Press, 1998), 139; Richmond *Whig*, August 13, 1872.

21. Rev. Moses Drury Hoge (1818–99) was the minister of Second Presbyterian Church, Richmond. Charles Kendall Adams, *Johnson's Universal Cyclopædia*, vol. 4 (New York: D. Appleton, 1899), 330. For more information see, Peyton Harrison Hoge, *Moses Drury Hoge: Life and Letters* (Richmond: Presbyterian Committee of Publication, 1899).

22. The Richmond *Examiner* cites Mr. Hunter making the motion. Richmond *Examiner*, July 24, 1861.

23. "The report was considered in secret session. It is understood that the report is mainly in answer to a resolution passed at the late session of Congress instructing the Secretary to prepare a statement touching the amount received from all sources and expended under direction of the Government and also tabular statistics of taxable property in the several States in the Confederacy. In round numbers, it is believed the expenditures have been about $10,000,000, up to 1st July, while receipts have been about $14,000,000. The former includes an item of $400,000 refunded to South Carolina, in part satisfaction of her outlay in way of preparation for defense, anterior to her adoption of the Constitution of the Confederate States.

"The secretary of the Treasury estimated the taxable property, real and personal, of the eleven states at $4.7 billion. Secretary Chase put that of the United States at $10 billion; but many of his values were fictious and ephemeral, while the estimates of the Confederate States were based on solid securities. The expenditure of the Confederate Government did, of course, include expenses incurred by the states prior to their connection with the Southern Confederacy, except the case alluded to of South Carolina. The balance of her outlay of $600,000 had been taken in Confederate bonds, no mention of which is made in the amount to the credit of the Government. The Secretary soon issued $20,000,000 Treasury notes, which the banks take on deposit and in liquidation of dues.

"No additional recommendation is understood to be made in this report touching the financial policy proper to be pursued by the Confederate States." *Richmond Examiner*, July 24, 1861.

24. The Charleston *Courier* reports "Lieut. Col. James Jones". Lt. Col. Samuel Jones (1819–87), chief of artillery and ordnance, Provisional Army of Virginia, mostly likely asked for past wages due as an assistant judge advocate of the US Army in Washington, DC. CSR, Samuel Jones (Officers); New York *Herald*, July 7, 1861; Samuel Jones, *The Siege of Charleston* (New York: Neale Publishing, 1911), 6; Charleston *Courier*, July 27, 1861.

25. Rev. George Washington Woodbridge (1804–78), graduate of West Point, was rector

of the Monumental Protestant Episcopal Church in Richmond. Fayetteville *Carolina Observer*, April 29, 1861; Richmond *Daily Dispatch*, February 15, 1878.

26. The complete text of the speeches by Cobb, Hill, Mason, and Chesnutt mourning the death of Bartow may be found in *Proceedings of Congress on the Announcement of the Death of Col. Francis S. Bartow* (Richmond: Enquirer Book and Job Press, 1861).

27. Francis Stebbins Bartow (1816–61) was a Georgia attorney and one of the largest slaveholders in the state. Prior to election to the Provisional Confederate Congress, he served as captain of the Oglethorpe Light Infantry and led the seizure of Fort Pulaski off the Savannah coasts in January 1861. After the firing on Fort Sumter, he returned to his command of the Oglethorpes and upon the unit's arrival in Virginia, he gained election as colonel of the Eighth Georgia Infantry Regiment. He died July 21, 1861, leading elements of the Eighth Georgia in an assault on a Union battery position at the First Battle of Manassas. He was the first high-ranking officer from Georgia to lose his life in the war. John J. Hennessy, *The First Battle of Manassas: An End to Innocence, July 18–21, 1861* (Mechanicsburg, VA: Stackpole Books, 2015), 106; W. T. Groce, "Francis S. Bartow (1816–1861)," New Georgia Encyclopedia.

28. The Richmond *Examiner* incorrectly names L. A. Ware. Rev. Thomas Alexander Ware (1830–87) was the minister of Richmond's Clay-Street Methodist Church. John J, Lafferty, *Sketches of the Virginia Conference, Methodist Episcopal Church, South* (Richmond: Christian Advocate Office, 1880), 61–62; Richmond *Whig*, July 26, 1861; Richmond *Examiner*, July 26, 1861; 1860 US Census, Population Schedule.

29. On Civil War confiscation, see Daniel W. Hamilton, *The Limits of Sovereignty: Property Confiscation in the Union and the Confederacy during the Civil War* (Chicago: University of Chicago Press, 2007).

30. This statement is premature and misleading. The US Senate had passed a version of the Confiscation Act of 1861 on July 22, 1861, three days earlier, but it had not made its way to the House of Representatives. Final congressional approval would come with Senate acceptance of House amendments on August 5, 1861.

31. On June 26, 1861, a convention of Virginia railroads agreed to a series of resolutions setting terms and costs for governmental use of trains for military and postal purposes. Charles W. Turner, "The Virginia Central Railroad at War, 1861–1865," *Journal of Southern History* 12, no. 4 (November 1946), 524–25.

32. Marcus J. Zunts (1826–95) was a partner in Rhorer & Zunts, Commission Merchants, in New Orleans. Leonard Victor Huber and Clarence August Wagner, *The Great Mail: A Postal History of New Orleans* (State College, PA: American Philatelic Society, 1949), 57; *New Orleans Price-Current and Commercial Intelligencer*, February 13, 1861; New Orleans *Times-Democrat*, September 7, 1895.

33. Everett W. Edgerton and Frederick Richards, partners in Edgerton, Richards & Company, were Charleston-based drapers and tailors, who served as the South Carolina agents for the sale of Wheeler & Wilson's Sewing Machines. Charleston *Courier*, October 15, 1860; Charleston *Mercury*, January 24, 1860; Confederate Citizens Papers, E. W. Edgerton and Frederick Richards.

34. The Richmond *Enquirer* incorrectly reports "Mr. Hale"; the Richmond *Whig*, Dr. P. Hale, of Petersburg, while the official journal records this as a "memorial of Henry Clay Pate, of Virginia, praying compensation for services rendered 'Wise Legion' as quartermaster and commissary." The compiled service record of Henry Clay Pate (Fifth Virginia Cavalry) does include an extract from the company book of Pate's Rangers, Wise's Legion, containing valuations for horses belonging to Pate in use by the Confederate military. CSR, Henry Clay Pate (5th Virginia Cavalry); *JCCSA*, 1:281; Richmond *Whig*, July 26, 1861. For information on

Pate's rangers at this time see, Michael B. Graham, *The Coal River Valley in the Civil War: West Virginia Mountains, 1861* (Charleston: History Press, 2014).

35. Matthews, *Statutes at Large,* 167.

36. See John Perkins Jr.'s comments on this same day.

37. A final amended version of this resolution would not pass until July 31, 1861.

38. Rev. Joshua Peterkin (1814–92) was rector of St. James Episcopal Church in Richmond. Romney (WV) *South Branch Intelligencer,* April 8, 1892.

39. Dr. Godwin Cotton Moore (1806–80) was a Hertford County, North Carolina, physician. Samuel A. Ashe, ed., *Biographical History of North Carolina* (Greensboro, NC: Charles L. Van Noppen, 1917), 8:354–58.

40. For full text, see *JCCSA*, 1:283.

41. The official journal cites "M. J. Rhodes and others, patentees from the state of Alabama." M. G. Rhodes and J. M. Skaggs, carriage makers from Talladega, Alabama, had obtained a patent in May 1860 for improvements to plough construction. *JCCSA*, 1:284; *Index to the Executive Documents, Printed by order of the Senate of the United States for the Second Session of the Thirty-Sixth Congress* (Washington, DC: George W. Bowman, 1861), 432–34; 1860 US Census, Population Schedule.

42. The official journal reports "Dr. P. M. Enders, of New Orleans, for services rendered as assistant treasurer of the United States Government at New Orleans." Dr. Peter Mortimer Enders (1818–68) was a Baton Rouge doctor and US Army veteran appointed an assistant surgeon at the Baton Rouge Arsenal in April 1861. *JCCSA*, 1:284; 1860 US Census, Population Schedule; CSR, P. M. Enders (Officers).

43. In May 1861, Dr. Alexander Yelverton Peyton Garnett (1820–88), son-in-law of Virginia governor Henry A. Wise and an outspoken supporter of the Confederacy, fled his home in Washington, DC, for safety in Richmond. In July 1861, he was named to the examining board of surgeons for the Confederate army and surgeon-in-charge at Richmond's General Hospital #3 and at Robertson Hospital. Prior to the war, Garnett had served as an assistant surgeon in the US Navy (1842–50) and a private surgeon (1851–61). Alexandria *Gazette,* April 24, 1861; CSR, Alex. Y. P. Garnett (Officers); Alex. Y. P. Garnett in Case Files of Applications from Former Confederates for Presidential Pardons ("Amnesty Papers") 1865–1867, National Archives RG 94: Records of the Adjutant General's Office, 1762–1984, M1003; "Memorial of Dr. A. Y. P. Garnett," *Transactions of the American Clinical and Climatological Association* 7 (1890), 323; Rebecca Barbour Calcutt, *Richmond's Wartime Hospitals* (Gretna, LA: Pelican Publishing Company, 2005), 172–74; James Grant Wilson and John Fiske, eds., *Appletons' Cyclopædia of American Biography,* vol. 2, (New York: D. Appleton, 1888), 607.

44. John Tyler would not appear and be qualified as a member of this session of Congress until August 1, 1861; thus, he was not eligible for franking privileges without a special grant. *JCCSA*, 1:303.

45. In secret session, Vice Pres. Alexander H. Stephens offered a resolution, which Congress passed, requiring the president of Congress to immediately convene in secret session following the reading of the previous day's journal. As a consequence, the Southern press provided, with some exceptions, limited coverage of congressional activities for the remainder of the Provisional Congress's existance.

46. This session went immediately into secret session or had no public session reported by the press.

47. Rev. James A. Duncan (1830–77) was minister at the Broad Street Methodist Church in Richmond. *Index to the Executive Documents of the House of Representatives for the Second Session of the Forty-Fifth Congress, 1877–1878,* vol. 9 (Washington, DC: Government Printing House, 1878), 261; New York *Herald,* September 25, 1877.

48. This session went immediately into secret session or had no public session reported by the press.

49. Identity unknown.

50. Matthews, *Statutes at Large,* 212.

51. This session went immediately into secret session or had no public session reported by the press.

52. Exact identity unknown.

53. These sessions went immediately into secret session or had no public sessions reported by the press.

54. Cobb was appointed colonel of the Sixteenth Georgia Infantry on July 15, 1861. CSR, Howell Cobb (16th GA Inf).

55. This session went immediately into secret session or had no public session reported by the press.

Fourth Session

1. Rev. William Flinn (1818–97) of the Presbyterian Church in Milledgeville, Georgia. Flinn was a close friend of Howell and Thomas R. R. Cobb, had provided the prayer to several sessions of the Georgia secession convention, and would serve as chaplain under Howell Cobb's command. *Journal of the Convention of Georgia,* 15, 55, 61, 89, 120; Lucian Lamar Knight, *A Standard History of Georgia and Georgians*, vol. 4: *Primary Source Edition* (Chicago: Lewis Publishing, 1917), 1987; Samuel Boykin, ed., *A Memorial Volume of the Hon. Howell Cobb of Georgia*, (Philadelphia: J. B. Lippencott, 1870), 148.

2. The bill modified the original act to require each newspaper or periodical sent through the mail or over the post roads to be endorsed by the postmaster of the office nearest the place from which they were sent, as prepaid, instead of as a "package." Matthews, *Statutes at Large,* 217; Richmond *Examiner*, September 4, 1861

Fifth Session

1. Charles James Faulkner (1806–84), US envoy to France, requested recall from his diplomatic post in May 1861 due to his pro-Confederate feelings. Upon his return to the United States, he was arrested by order of the War Department under suspicion of arranging arms transfers from France for the Confederacy. Sainlaude, *France and the American Civil War*, 81, 171; *Official Records*, ser. 1, vol. 2, pp. 463–79.

2. Declaration Respecting Maritime Law, Paris, April 16, 1856.

3. These sessions went immediately into secret session or had no public sessions reported by the press.

4. These sessions went immediately into secret session or had no public sessions reported by the press.

5. These sessions went immediately into secret session or had no public sessions reported by the press.

6. In the Battle of Belmont (November 7, 1861), Maj. Gen. Leonidas Polk defended a small Confederate outpost at Columbus, Kentucky, against Union brigadier general Ulysses S. Grant. Although Grant's forces initially seized the Confederate position, a reply by Polk supported by reinforcements under Pillow and Cheatham forced Grant to retreat.

7. These sessions went immediately into secret session or had no public sessions reported by the press.

8. At about 8:30 p.m., December 11, 1861, a fire broke out at William P. Russel's Sash and Blind Company and swept across Charleston toward the Ashley River. Carried by gusting winds, the fire burned 541 acres of the city (around 1,200 buildings valued at $5 million).

The cause was not conclusively determined with blame placed variously on carelessness, Union sympathizers, and rebellious slaves. Marie Ferrara, "Moses Henry Nathan and the Great Charleston Fire of 1861," *South Carolina Historical Magazine* 104, no. 4 (2003): 272–77; John F. Marszalek, "The Charleston Fire of 1861 as Described in the Emma E. Holmes Diary," *South Carolina Historical Magazine* 76, no. 2 (1975): 60–67; "Charleston's Great Fire of 1861," *Scientific American* 41, no. 22 (1879): 345.

9. In September 1861, US District Court judge Thomas Bell Monroe (1791–1865) resigned the bench and fled his Frankfort, Kentucky, plantation Montrose to become the first person to swear an oath of loyalty to the Confederate States of America. Monroe's renunciation of US citizenship and oath of Confederate citizenship may be found in the October 11, 1861, edition of the Richmond *Whig.* Lewis Collins, *Collins' Historical Sketches of Kentucky* vol. 1 (Covington, KY: Collins, 1878), 409; Samuel M. Wilson, *History of the United States Court for the Eastern District of Kentucky* (Lexington: n.p., 1935), 7–8; *Daily Nashville Patriot,* October 10, 1861; San Francisco *Bulletin,* October 25, 1861.

10. These sessions went immediately into secret session or had no public sessions reported by the press.

11. James Orr of South Carolina introduced in secret session "A bill supplementary to an act to organize the force of the Provisional Army of the Confederate States" dealing with the acceptance of volunteer troops into the Confederate army and the promotion and election of officers. *JCCSA,* 1:636.

12. These sessions went immediately into secret session or had no public sessions reported by the press.

13. Judge John T. Hemphill, delegate from Texas, died at the Exchange Hotel in Richmond, Virginia, on the morning of January 3 or 4, 1862. Hemphill's tombstone shows a death date of January 3, 1862, while newspaper reports place his death on January 4. Augusta *Chronicle,* January 6, 1862; Dallas *Weekly Herald,* January 22, 1862.

14. Thomas Jefferson Rusk (1803–57).

15. The Battle of San Jacinto (April 21, 1836) resulted in the capture of Mexican president General Antonio López de Santa Anna and the de facto recognition of Texas independence from Mexico.

16. The First Congress of the Republic of Texas was held in two sessions between October 3, 1836, and June 13, 1837.

17. Ashlar is a Masonic term that references man's moral and spiritual life. A Rough Ashlar is the imperfect form prior to enlightenment or refinement.

18. For discussion on Hemphill's role in the development of the Texas Supreme Court, his views on common and civil law, and early Texas appellate jurisprudence, see James L. Haley, *The Texas Supreme Court: A Narrative History, 1836–1986* (Austin: University of Texas Press, 2013), esp. chapters 2–3.

19. Hemphill received his honorary degree in 1851, as did Kentucky delegate Thomas Bell Monroe. "Centre College Board of Trustees Minutes (Vol. 2—1851)," Centre College Digital Archives, January 4, 2008.

20. James Pinckney Henderson (1808–58) served as the Republic of Texas's first governor.

21. Dr. Orlando Fairfax (1806–82) was an Alexandria, Virginia, physician who provided medical services to wounded Union and Confederate troops following the Battle of First Manassas. Offered a post as assistant surgeon in the Confederate army, he served for only a short time, resigning his commission to open a private practice in Richmond for the remainder of the war. W. Hurst, *Alexandria on the Potomac: The Portrait of an Antebellum Community* (Lanham, MD: University Press of America, 1991), 25; Amnesty Papers, Orlando Fairfax, National Archives, RG 94; *Philadelphia Inquirer,* January 13, 1882.

22. Most likely Robert Reid Hemphill (1840–1908), Co. B, Seventh South Carolina Infantry. Hemphill's unit was in winter quarters at Camp Reserve, four miles east of Richmond at this time. CSR, R. R. Hemphill & Unit Information (7th SC Inf.).

23. The Associate Presbyterian Church of North America.

24. These sessions went immediately into secret session or had no public sessions reported by the press.

25. These sessions went immediately into secret session or had no public sessions reported by the press.

26. For the complete proceedings including speeches not printed by the press, see *Proceedings of the Announcement of the Death of Hon. John Tyler, January 20, 1862* (Richmond: Enquirer Book and Job Press, 1862).

27. For information on the life and presidency of John Tyler, see: Norma Lois Peterson, *The Presidencies of William Henry Harrison and John Tyler* (Lawrence: University Press of Kansas, 1989); Edward P. Crapol, *John Tyler: The Accidental President* (Chapel Hill:University of North Carolina Press, 2006); Oliver Perry Chitwood, *John Tyler, Champion of the Old South* (New York: Russell and Russell, 1964); Gary May, *John Tyler*, ed. Arthur M. Schlesinger Jr. and Sean Willentz (New York: Times Books/Henry Holt, 2008); Dan Monroe, *The Republican Vision of John Tyler* (College Station: Texas A&M University Press, 2003).

28. The second is William Cabell Rives (1793–1868), who sat as senator from Virginia in the Twenty-Fifth Congress when Robert M. T. Hunter was a freshman US representative.

29. The Webster–Ashburton Treaty (August 9, 1842) settled boundary disputes between British Canada and the northeastern United States and defined Canadian-American usage rights for the Great Lakes.

30. "Mr. Calhoun's Letter to Mr. King," *Debow's Review* 9 no. 2 (August 1850): 184–91.

31. Tyler graduated from the College of William and Mary in 1807.

32. The Dorr Rebellion (1841–42) sought to broaden suffrage in Rhode Island by eliminating property requirements for voting carried over from the state's colonial charter. See, among others, Erik J. Chaput, *The People's Martyr: Thomas Wilson Dorr and His 1842 Rhode Island Rebellion* (Topeka: University Press of Kansas, 2013); George M. Dennison, *The Dorr War: Republicanism on Trial, 1831–1861* (Lexington: University Press of Kentucky, 1976); Marvin E. Gettleman, *The Dorr Rebellion: A Study in American Radicalism, 1833–1849* (New York: Random House, 1973)

33. This translates roughly as an admonition that those who act prudently have no need of luck. Juvenal, Satire X, verse 365 in Juvenal, *The Satires of Juvenal*, trans. Rolfe Humphries (Bloomington: Indiana University Press, 1958), 134.

34. Shakespeare *Henry VIII*, 3.2.

35. Thomas Gray, "An Elegy Written in a Country Church Yard" (London: R. Dodsley, 1751), 7.

36. Ecclesiastes 1:4.

37. In June 1841, Henry Clay introduced a bill to resurrect the then defunct Second Bank of the United State with authority to create state branches without the permission of states in which those branches would be located. It was a direct assault on a bill previously sponsored by the Tyler administration that would have required state approval to create state branches. While Whigs generally supported Clay's efforts, some Virginia Whigs such as William Cabell Rives backed Tyler's limitations on federal authority. David S. Heidler and Jeanne T. Heidler, *Henry Clay: The Essential American* (New York: Random House, 2010), 345; Michael F. Holt, *The Rise and Fall of the American Whig Party: Jacksonian Politics and the Onset of the Civil War* (Oxford: Oxford University Press, 1999), 133; New York *Evening Post*, July 3, 1841. The text of Mr. Rives's speech may be found at Richmond *Whig*, July 16, 1841.

38. Alexander Pope, "An Essay on Man," in *Epistles to a Friend*, Epistle IV (London: J. Wilford, 1734), 73.

39. The Richmond *Whig* lists Mr. Morehead. Richmond *Whig*, January 21, 1862.

40. Psalm 39:4.

41. See Richmond *Whig*, January 21, 1862.

42. Formed in Richmond in early December 1861, the Maryland Society was a charitable organization that provided resources and support for sick and wounded Maryland soldiers fighting for the Confederacy. Baltimore *Sun*, December 12, 1861.

43. The Richmond *Examiner* misspelled the name of William A. Irving who had been named sexton for St. Paul's Church in 1850. Elizabeth Wright Weddell, *St. Paul's Church, Richmond, Virginia: Its Historic Years and Memorials* (Richmond: William Byrd Press, 1931), 1:240; 2:589.

44. Charles Frederick Ernest Minnigerode (1814–94) was rector of St. Paul's Episcopal Church in Richmond. S. E. Woodworth, "Charles Minnigerode (1814–1894)," June 22, 2017, in Encyclopedia Virginia.

45. The Right Reverence John Johns (1796–1876) was the Episcopal bishop of Virginia and former president of the College of William and Mary. Walter Herbert Stowe, *The Episcopal Church: A Miniature History*, No. 15 (Philadelphia: Church Historical Society, 1944), 32.

46. Psalm 19:5.

47. Tyler was buried in Richmond's Hollywood Cemetery along with Pres. James Monroe.

48. These sessions went immediately into secret session or had no public sessions reported by the press.

49. February 22, 1862, marked the beginning of the now annual US Senate tradition of reading former president George Washington's 1796 Farewell Address into the record. The address urges Americans to set aside sectional jealousies and promote national interests. Richard A. Baker, *200 Notable Days: Senate Stories, 1787 to 2002* (Washington, DC: Government Printing Office, 2006), 71.

Appendix I: Documents

1. Thian, *Documentary History of the Flag*, appendix, pt. 2, 4–5.

2. William H. Pritchard, commercial editor of the Augusta *Constitutionalist*. 1860 US Census, Population Schedule.

3. James Gardner (1813–74), publisher and editor of the Augusta *Constitutionalist*. Russell K. Brown, "Augusta's Other Voice: James Gardner and the Constitutionalist," *Georgia Historical Quarterly* 85, no. 4 (2001): 592–607.

4. Thian, *Documentary History of the Flag*, appendix, pt. 2, 12–4, and illustrations, pt. 2, plate XXV.

5. Henry Fraser Campbell (1824–91) was professor of anatomy at the Georgia College of Medicine, coeditor of the *Southern Medical and Surgical Journal*, cofounder of Augusta's Jackson Street Hospital (which exclusively treated slaves), and medical researcher and inventor known for advancements in gynecological surgery. R. French Stone, ed., *Biography of Eminent American Physicians and Surgeons* (Indianapolis: Carlon and Hollenbeck, 1894), 73–74; Deirdre Cooper Owens, *Medical Bondage: Race, Gender, and the Origins of American Gynecology* (Athens: University of Georgia Press, 2017), 18–19.

6. Thian, *Documentary History of the Flag*, appendix, pt. 2, 9.

7. Robert B. Waddell was a partner in Burkaloo & Waddell, a stock and exchange brokerage and cotton factorage in Columbia, South Carolina. *Yorkville* (SC) *Enquirer*, April 2, 1857; 1850 US Census, Population Schedule.

8. Fitz William McMaster (1826–99) was a Columbia, South Carolina, attorney and former

librarian and treasurer at South Carolina College. Maximilian Laborde, *History of the South Carolina College* (Columbia, SC: Peter B. Glass, 1859), 438; 1860 US Census, Population Schedule.

9. Thian, *Documentary History of the Flag*, appendix, pt. 2, 8.

10. Thomas Hubbard Hobbs (1826–62) was a Limestone County, Alabama, planter and lawyer. *Northern Alabama: Historical and Biographical* (Birmingham: Smith and De Land, 1888), 85–86.

11. Thian, *Documentary History of the Flag*, appendix, pt. 2, 2, 4.

12. Joseph M. Shellman (b. abt 1806) was a language teacher at the Richmond Academy in Augusta, Georgia. 1860 US Census, Population Schedule; Augusta *Chronicle*, October 11, 1859.

13. Thian, *Documentary History of the Flag*, Appendix, pt. 2, 6–7.

14. A checkered pattern usually divided into equilateral rectangles of alternate colors.

15. Thian, *Documentary History of the Flag*, appendix, pt. 2, 10, and illustrations, pt. 2, plates XX and XXI.

16. French born Augustus Bonaud (b. abt. 1822) was a Savannah, Georgia, liquor merchant. Augusta *Chronicle*, May 25, 1855; Augusta *Daily Constitutionalist*, May 5, 1861; Augusta *Weekly Chronicle & Sentinel*, May 15, 1861; Savannah *Daily Republican*, April 18, 1857; *Bonaud v. Sorrel*, 21 GA 108.

17. Thian, *Documentary History of the Flag*, appendix, pt. 2, 11.

18. Albert A. Freeman (abt. 1842–85) was the son of Macon, Georgia, merchant Richard S. Freeman. 1860 US Census, Population Schedule; Macon *Weekly Telegraph and Messenger*, March 20, 1885.

19. Thian, *Documentary History of the Flag*, appendix, pt. 2, 5. See related correspondence to William Porcher Miles in Thian, *Documentary History of the Flag*, 7.

20. William Jacint Laval (1824–1907) was state treasurer for the lower division of South Carolina. *Census of Charleston, South Carolina for 1861* (Charleston: Evans and Cogswell, 1861), 26, 92, 105, 110; *Reports and Resolutions of South Carolina to the General Assembly* (Columbia: Charles P. Pelham, 1863), 11, 18, 39, 49, 106, 108, 169; *Journal of the Senate of South Carolina Being the Annual Session of 1853* (Columbia: R. W. Gibbes, 1853), 48; Lexington (SC) *Dispatch-News*, July 3, 1907.

21. Thian, *Documentary History of the Flag*, appendix, pt. 2, 2–3.

22. Thian, *Documentary History of the Flag*, appendix, pt. 2, 40, and illustrations, pt. 2, plate LXIX.

23. Thian, *Documentary History of the Flag*, appendix, pt. 2, 35–6.

24. Rev. Charles Edward Brame (c. 1823–92), a graduate of Princeton University and a veteran of the Mexican War, was the principal and professor of mathematics, natural sciences, and languages at the Greensboro (Alabama) Female Academy. By the end of 1861, Brame was serving as a special agent for the Confederate Government purchasing private rifles and muskets for the Confederate military. 1860 US Census, Population Schedule; *Alabama Beacon*, February 20, 1857, and August 3, 1860; Dunbar Rowland, *The Official and Statistical Register of the State of Mississippi, 1912* (Nashville: Press of Brandon Printing, 1912), 437; Confederate Citizens Papers (Charles Brame).

25. Hiram (or Henry) Augustus Pond (1820–89) was a composer and professor of music and painting at the Greensboro Female Academy. *Alabama Beacon*, August 3, 1860; (Washington, DC) *Evening Star*, July 27, 1889; *New-York Daily Tribune*, September 23, 1850; Philadelphia *Saturday Courier*, November 20, 1847; 1860 US Census, Population Schedule.

26. Thian, *Documentary History of the Flag*, appendix, pt. 2, 34–35.

27. Jackson C. Curry (c. 1824–64) and Jabez Curry (1797–1871), brother and uncle respectively of J. L. M. Curry. Edwin Anderson Alderman and Armistead Churchill Gordon,

J. L. M. Curry: A Biography (New York: Macmillan, 1911), 104; CSR, J. C. Curry (Officers); 1860 US Census, Population Schedule.

28. Possibly Judge Leonidas Nye Walthall (1822–93) of Perry County, Alabama.

29. *Documentary History of the Flag*, Appendix, pt. 2, p. 34–5.

30. Confederate Citizens Papers, Alexander Walker.

31. This act provided for the first federal licensure of river pilots. 10 Stat. 61 (1852); *Pacific Mail Steamship Company v. Joliffe*, 69 U.S. 450 (1864).

32. Alexander Walker (1818–93), former New Orleans city court judge and editor of the *Daily Delta* newspaper. *JCCSA*, 1:115; *Daily Delta*, February 14, 1863; New Orleans *Times-Picayune*, January 25, 1893.

33. Confederate Citizens Papers, Benjamin F. Jones.

34. Charleston *Mercury*, May 13, 1861.

35. Martin J. Crawford.

36. Samuel Nelson, Associate Justice of the Supreme Court of the United States

37. South Carolina governor Francis Wilkinson Pickens.

38. Ward Hill Lamon, US Marshal for the District of Columbia, commissioned by President Lincoln to visit Fort Sumter with Gov. Francis Pickens.

39. Gustavus Vasa Fox was commissioned by President Lincoln to command a resupply mission to Fort Sumter in April 1861. He arrived just as the bombardment of the fort by South Carolina began. Ari Hoogenboom, *Gustavus Vasa Fox of the Union Navy: A Biography* (Baltimore: Johns Hopkins University Press, 2008), ch. 6.

40. Fox was related by marriage to Montgomery Blair, Lincoln's postmaster general. Hoogenboom, *Gustavus Vasa Fox*, ix.

41. Thurlow Weed was the influential editor of the Albany (NY) *Evening Journal* and political adviser to William Seward, Lincoln's secretary of state. Both of these men supported an evacuation of Fort Sumter and were critical of Lincoln's decision to resupply and defend it.

42. Frederick William Seward.

43. Confederate Citizens Papers, New Orleans and Carrolton Rail Road Company.

44. William Carey Crane (1816–85) was a popular Baptist minister who had served congregations throughout the southeastern United States. At the beginning of the Civil War, in addition to serving as senior secretary to the Southern Baptist Association, he was president of Mount Lebanon University in Louisiana, coeditor of the *Louisiana Baptist*, and president of the Louisiana State Baptist Convention. Samuel Boykin, *History of the Baptist Denomination in Georgia*, vol. 2 (Atlanta: James P. Harrison, 1881), 149–51.

45. Confederate Citizens Papers, Nathan Stephens.

46. William Henderson was the proprietor of Henderson, Gaines & Company, a New Orleans crockery and glass merchantile. Charles Gardner, comp., *Gardner's New Orleans Directory of 1861*,(New Orleans: Charles Gardner, 1861).

47. *Special Report: Confederate States of America, Treasury Department, Richmond, July 20th, 1861* (Richmond: n.p., 1861).

48. Charleston *Courier*, July 23, 1861.

49. Confederate Citizens Papers, M. J. Zunts.

50. *Georgia Journal and Messenger*, June 12, 1861.

51. This pseudonym references Rev. John Witherspoon, Presbyterian minister, president of Princeton University, and Founding Father who helped draft the Articles of Confederation.

BIBLIOGRAPHY

Newspapers and Periodicals

Alabama Beacon
Alabama State Sentinel
Alexandria (VA) *Gazette*
Atlanta *Constitution*
Augusta *Chronicle*
Augusta *Daily Chronicle & Sentinel*
Augusta *Daily Constitutionalist*
Augusta *Weekly Chronicle & Sentinel*
Augusta *Weekly Constitutionalist*
Baltimore *Sun*
Boston Commercial Bulletin
Burlington *Weekly Free Press*
Camden (SC) *Confederate*
Charleston *Courier*
Charleston *Mercury*
Chicago *Daily Tribune*
Columbus (GA) *Daily Sun*
Columbus (GA) *Enquirer-Sun*
Commissioners of Patents' Journal
Congressional Globe
Daily Delta
Daily Nashville Patriot
Daily National Intelligence
Dallas *Weekly Herald*
Debow's Review
Fayetteville *Carolina Observer*
Flake's Bulletin
Georgia Journal and Messenger
Gospel Messenger and Church Record of Western New-York
Jackson *Weekly Mississippian*
Lexington (SC) *Dispatch-News*
Macon *Weekly Telegraph and Messenger*
Memphis *Daily Eagle and Enquirer*
Milledgeville *Federal Union*
Montgomery *Advertiser*
Montgomery *Daily Confederation*

Montgomery *Weekly Advertiser*
Nevada (CA) *Democrat*
New Orleans *Daily Crescent*
New Orleans *Daily True Delta*
New Orleans *Price-Current and Commercial Intelligencer*
New Orleans *Republican*
New Orleans *Times*
New Orleans *Times-Democrat*
New Orleans *Times-Picayune*
New York *Commercial Advertiser*
New-York Daily Tribune
New York *Evening Post*
New York *Herald*
New York *Tribune*
New York *Weekly Day Book*
North Carolina *Standard*
Philadelphia *Inquirer*
Philadelphia *Saturday Courier*
Portland *Daily Press*
Princeton *Standard*
Richmond *Daily Dispatch*
Richmond *Enquirer*
Richmond *Examiner*
Richmond *Times-Dispatch*
Richmond *Whig*
Romney (WV) *South Branch Intelligencer*
San Francisco *Bulletin*
San Francisco *Call*
San Francisco *Chronicle*
San Francisco *Weekly Bulletin*
Savannah *Daily Morning News*
Savannah *Daily Republican*
Savannah *Weekly Morning News*
Scientific American
Southern Historical Society Papers (*SHSP*)
Thomasville (GA) *Southern Enterprise*
Tifton (GA) *Gazette*
Vicksburg *Herald*
Vicksburg *Whig*
Virginian-Pilot
(Washington, DC) *Evening Star*
Weekly Georgia Telegraph
Weekly National Intelligencer
Weekly St. Louis Evening News
Yorkville (SC) *Enquirer*

Internet Archives and Resources

Augusta-Richmond County (GA) Public Library System Collection
Biographical Directory of the United States Congress

Centre College Digital Archives
Chronicling America
Encyclopedia Virginia
FamilySearch
Fold3
GenealogyBank
Georgia Historic Newspapers
Handbook of Texas Online
HathiTrust
Internet Archive
Naval History and Heritage Command
New Georgia Encyclopedia
Newspapers.com

Government Documents

1850 US Census
1860 US Census
1870 US Census

Acts and Resolutions of the First Session of the Provisional Congress of the Confederate States, 1861. Montgomery: Barnett, Wimbush, 1861.

Acts and Resolutions of the Second Session of the Provisional Congress of the Confederate States. Richmond: Enquirer Book and Job Press, 1861.

Annual Report of the Commissioner of Patents for the Year 1869. Vol. 1. Washington, DC: Government Printing Office, 1871.

Case Files of Applications from Former Confederates for Presidential Pardons ("Amnesty Papers") 1865–1867. National Archives Record Group 94: Records of the Adjutant General's Office, 1762–1984, M1003.

Census of Charleston, South Carolina for 1861. Charleston: Evans and Cogswell, 1861.

Code of Alabama. Montgomery: Brittan and De Wolf, State Printers, 1852.

Compiled Service Records of Confederate Soldiers. National Archives Record Group 109: War Department Collection of Confederate Records, 1825–1927.

Confederate Papers Relating to Citizens or Business Firms. National Archives Record Group 109: War Department Collection of Confederate Records, 1825–1927, M346.

Georgia Division of Confederate Pensions and Records. *Roster of the Confederate Soldiers of Georgia, 1861–1865.* Edited by Lillian Henderson. Hapeville, GA: Longina and Porter, 1959.

Index to the Executive Documents of the House of Representatives for the Second Session of the Forty-Fifth Congress, 1877–1878. Vol. 9. Washington, DC: Government Printing House, 1878.

Index to the Executive Documents, Printed by Order of the Senate of the United States for the Second Session of the Thirty-Sixth Congress. Washington, DC: George W. Bowman, 1861.

Journal of the Congress of the Confederate States of America, 1861–1865. 7 vols. Washington, DC: Government Printing Office, 1904–5.

Journal of the Public and Secret Proceedings of the Convention of the People of Georgia, Held in Milledgeville and Savannah in 1861. Milledgeville: Boughton Nisbet and Barnes, 1861.

Journal of the Senate of South Carolina Being the Annual Session of 1853. Columbia: R. W. Gibbes, 1853.

Laws Passed by the General Assembly of the Territory of New Mexico, 1859–1860. Santa Fe: G. P. Hovey, 1860.

Matthews, James M., ed. *The Statutes at Large of the Provisional Government of the Confederate States of America.* Richmond: R. M. Smith, 1864.

Miller, Wesley. "Improvement in Explosive Compounds." US Patent no. 212,726. Application date May 31, 1878. Patent date February 25, 1879.

Miscellaneous Documents of the Senate of the United States for the First Session of the Fifty-Second Congress, 1891–1892. Vol. 4. Washington, DC: Government Printing Office, 1892.

Owen, Marie B., comp. *Alabama Official and Statistical Register, 1919.* Montgomery: Brown Printing, 1920.

Proceedings of Congress on the Announcement of the Death of Col. Francis S. Bartow. Richmond: Enquirer Book and Job Press, 1861.

Proceedings of the Announcement of the Death of Hon. John Tyler, January 20, 1862. Richmond: Enquirer Book and Job Press, 1862.

Provisional and Permanent Constitutions Together with the Acts and Resolutions of the First Session of the Provisional Congress of the Confederate States. Montgomery: Shorter and Reid, 1861.

Read, John B. "Projectile." US Patent No. 18,707. Issued November 24, 1857.

Reports and Resolutions of South Carolina to the General Assembly. Columbia: Charles P. Pelham, 1863.

Reports of the Court of Claims Submitted to the House of Representatives during the Second Session of the Thirty-Sixth Congress, 1860-'61. Vol. 1. Washington, DC: Government Printing Office, 1861.

Rowland, Dunbar, *The Official and Statistical Register of the State of Mississippi, 1912.* Nashville: Press of Brandon Printing, 1912.

Special Report: Confederate States of America, Treasury Department, Richmond, July 20th, 1861. Richmond: n.p., 1861.

Specifications and Drawings of Patents Issued from the United States Patent Office for March 1876. Washington, DC: Government Printing Office, 1876.

Thian, Raphael P., comp. *Documentary History of the Flag and Seal of the Confederate States of America, 1861–1865.* Washington, DC: Government Printing Office, 1880.

US Congress. Senate Executive Journal. 34th Congress.

US Naval War Records Office. *Official Records of the Union and Confederate Navies in the War of the Rebellion.* Washington, DC: Government Printing Office, 1894–1922.

US War Department. *Atlas of the War of the Rebellion.* Washington, DC: Government Printing Office, 1892.

———. *The War of the Rebellion: A Compilation of the Official Records of the Union and Confederate Armies.* Washington, DC: Government Printing Office, 1880–1901.

Winkler, Ernest William, ed. *Journal of the Secession Convention of Texas, 1861.* Austin: Austin Printing, 1912.

International Treaties, Statute Law, and Judicial Proceedings

10 Stat. 61. 1852.

Bonaud v. Sorrel, 21 GA 108.

Declaration Respecting Maritime Law, Paris, April 16, 1856.

Pacific Mail Steamship Company v. Joliffe, 69 U.S. 450, 1864.

Smith v. Vertue, 30 LJCP 56, 1860.

Primary Sources

Alighieri, Dante. *Dante's Divina Commedia.* London: Tinsley Brothers, 1862.

———. *The Divine Comedy of Dante Alighieri*. Vol. 2. Translated by Henry Wadsworth Longfellow. Boston: Houghton, Mifflin, 1867.

Coleridge, Ernest Hartley, ed., *The Works of Lord Byron*. Vol. 2: *Poetry*. London: John Murray; New York: Charles Scribner's Sons, 1922.

Davis, Jefferson. *The Papers of Jefferson Davis*. Vol. 7: *1861*. Edited by Lynda Lasswell Crist. Baton Rouge: Louisiana State University Press, 1992.

Gardner, Charles, comp. *Gardner's New Orleans Directory of 1861*. New Orleans: Charles Gardner, 1861.

———, comp. *Gardner's New Orleans Directory for 1866*. New Orleans: Charles Gardner, 1866.

Gray, Thomas. "An Elegy Written in a Country Church Yard." London: R. Dodsley, 1751.

Juvenal. *The Satires of Juvenal*. Translated by Rolfe Humphries. Bloomington: Indiana University Press, 1958.

Johnson, Andrew. *The Papers of Andrew Johnson*. Vol. 3: *1858–1860*. Edited by LeRoy P. Graf and Ralph W. Haskins. Knoxville: University of Tennessee Press, 1972.

Leak, Francis Terry. Diary. Typescript. Francis Terry Leak Papers #1095, Southern Historical Collection, Wilson Library, University of North Carolina, Chapel Hill.

Lincoln, Abraham. *Abraham Lincoln, Complete Works, Comprising His Speeches, Letters, State Papers, and Miscellaneous Writings*. Vol. 2. Edited by John G. Nicolay and John Hay. New York: Century, 1907.

Mallory, James. *"Fear God and Walk Humbly": The Agricultural Journal of James Mallory, 1843–1877*. Tuscaloosa: University of Alabama Press, 1997.

Mears and Turnbull, comp. *The Montgomery Directory for 1859–1860*. Montgomery: Advertiser Book and Job Printing Office, 1859.

Minutes of the Annual Conferences of the Methodist Episcopal Church, South, for the Year 1858. Nashville: Southern Methodist Publishing House, 1859.

Minutes of the Annual Conferences of the Methodist Episcopal Church, South, for the Year 1862. Nashville: Southern Methodist Publishing House, 1870.

Minutes of the Annual Conferences of the Methodist Episcopal Church, South, for the Year 1866. Nashville: Southern Methodist Publishing House, 1870.

Minutes of the Mobile Conference of the Methodist Episcopal Church, South. Mobile: Office of "The Army Argus and Crisis," 1864.

Pope, Alexander. "An Essay on Man." In *Epistles to a Friend*, Epistle IV. London: J. Wilford, 1734.

Richardson, James D. *A Compilation of the Messages and Papers of the Confederacy Including the Diplomatic Correspondence 1861–1865*. Nashville: United States Publishing, 1905.

Smith, William R. *The History and Debates of the Convention of the People of Alabama*. Montgomery: White, Pfister, 1861.

Secondary Sources: Books

Adams, Charles Kendall. *Johnson's Universal Cyclopædia*. Vol. 4. New York: D. Appleton, 1899.

Alderman, Edwin Anderson, and Armistead Churchill Gordon. *J. L. M. Curry: A Biography*. New York: Macmillan, 1911.

Alexander, Thomas B., and Richard E. Beringer. *The Anatomy of the Confederate Congress: A Study of the Influences on Legislative Voting Behavior, 1861–1865*. Nashville: Vanderbilt University Press, 1972.

Allardice, Bruce S., ed. *Kentuckians in Gray: Confederate Generals and Field Officers of the Bluegrass State*. Lexington: University of Kentucky Press, 2008.

American National Biography. Vol. 13. New York: Oxford University Press, 1999.

American Newspaper Directory. New York: Geo. P. Rowell, 1876.

Amlund, Curtis Arthur. *Federalism in the Southern Confederacy*. Washington, DC: Public Affairs Press, 1966.

Andrews, J. Cutler. *The South Reports the Civil War*. Princeton, NJ: Princeton University Press, 2000.

Ashe, Samuel A., ed., *Biographical History of North Carolina*. Vol. 8. Greensboro, NC: Charles L. Van Noppen, 1917.

Baker, Richard A. *200 Notable Days: Senate Stories, 1787 to 2002*. Washington, DC: Government Printing Office, 2006.

Ball, Douglas B. *Financial Failure and Confederate Defeat*. Urbana: University of Illinois Press, 1991.

Barker, Jacob. *Incidents in the Life of Jacob Barker of New Orleans, Louisiana*. Washington, DC, 1855.

Barney, William L. *The Secessionist Impulse: Alabama and Mississippi in 1860*. Princeton, NJ: Princeton University Press, 1974.

Binnington, Ian. *Confederate Visions: Nationalism, Symbolism, and the Imagined South in the Civil War*. Charlottesville: University of Virginia Press, 2013.

Black, Robert C., III. *The Railroads of the Confederacy*. Chapel Hill: University of North Carolina Press, 1952.

Blair, William A. *Virginia's Private War: Feeding Body and Soul in the Confederacy*. Oxford: Oxford University Press, 1998.

Blight, David. *Race and Reunion: The Civil War in American Memory*. Cambridge, MA: Belknap Press of Harvard University Press, 2001.

Bonner, Michael Brem. *Confederate Political Economy: Creating and Managing a Southern Corporatist Nation*. Baton Rouge: Louisiana State University Press, 2016.

Boykin, Samuel. *History of the Baptist Denomination in Georgia*. Vol. 2. Atlanta: James P. Harrison 1881.

———, ed. *A Memorial Volume of the Hon. Howell Cobb of Georgia*. Philadelphia: J. B. Lippencott, 1870.

Brinsfield, John Wesley, Jr. *The Spirit Divided: Memoirs of Civil War Chaplains—The Confederacy*. Macon, GA: Mercer University Press, 2005.

Broadwater, Robert P. *Civil War Special Forces: The Elite and Distinct Fighting Units of the Union and Confederate Armies*. Santa Barbara: Praeger, 2014.

Brown, John Howard, ed. *Lamb's Biographical Dictionary of the United States*. Vol. 1. Boston: James H. Lamb, 1900.

Buenger, Walter L. *Secession and the Union in Texas*. Austin: University of Texas Press, 1984.

Buker, George E. *Blockaders, Refugees, and Contrabands, Civil War on Florida's Gulf Coast, 1861–1865*. Tuscaloosa: University of Alabama Press, 1993.

Bulla, David W., and Gregory Borchard. *Journalism in the Civil War Era*. New York: Peter Lang, 2010.

Butler, Leslie S. *Pirates, Privateers, and Rebel Raiders of the Carolina Coast*. Chapel Hill: University of North Carolina Press, 2002.

Calcutt, Rebecca Barbour. *Richmond's Wartime Hospitals*. Gretna, LA: Pelican Publishing, 2005.

Caldwell, Wilber W. *The Courthouse and the Depot: The Architecture of Hope in an Age of Despair: A Narrative Guide to Railroad Expansion and Its Impact on Public Architecture in Georgia, 1833–1910*. Macon, GA: Mercer University Press, 2001.

Callahan, James Morton. *The Diplomatic History of the Southern Confederacy*. New York: Greenwood Press, 1968.

Campbell, Jesse Harrison. *Georgia Baptists: Historical and Biographical.* Macon, GA: J. W. Burke, 1874.

Candler, Allen D., and Clement A. Evans, eds. *Georgia: Comprising Sketches of Counties, Towns, Events, Institutions, and Persons, Arranged in Cyclopedic Form.* Vol. 3. Atlanta: State Historical Association, 1906.

Cannon, Devereaux D., Jr. *The Flags of the Confederacy: An Illustrated History.* Memphis: St. Luke Press, 1988.

Cashin, Joan E. *War Stuff: The Struggle for Human and Environmental Resources in the American Civil War.* Cambridge: Cambridge University Press, 2018.

Chaput, Erik J. *The People's Martyr: Thomas Wilson Dorr and His 1842 Rhode Island Rebellion.* Topeka: University Press of Kansas, 2013.

Chitwood, Oliver Perry. *John Tyler, Champion of the Old South.* New York: Russell and Russell, 1964.

Clampitt, Bradley R. *The Civil War and Reconstruction in Indian Territory.* Lincoln: University of Nebraska Press, 2015.

Clark, John E., Jr. *Railroads in the Civil War: The Impact of Management on Victory and Defeat.* Baton Rouge: Louisiana State University Press, 2001.

Clarke, Richard H. *Lives of the Deceased Bishops of the Catholic Church in the United States.* New York: R. H. Clarke, 1888.

Cochran, Hamilton. *Blockade Runners of the Confederacy.* Indianapolis: Bobbs-Merrill, 1958.

Collins, Lewis. *Collins' Historical Sketches of Kentucky.* Vol. 1. Covington, KY: Collins, 1878.

Confer, Clarissa W. *The Cherokee Nation in the Civil War.* Norman: University of Oklahoma Press, 2007.

Connole, Joseph. *The Civil War and the Subversion of American Indian Sovereignty.* Jefferson, NC: McFarland, 2017.

Cook, Ruth Beaumont. *Magic in Stone: The Sylacauga Marble Story.* Montgomery: New South Books, 2019.

Cooper, Edward S. *Traitors: The Secession Period, November 1860–July 1861.* Madison, NJ: Fairleigh Dickinson University Press, 2008.

Coski, John M. *The Confederate Battle Flag: America's Most Embattled Emblem.* Cambridge, MA: Harvard University Press, 2005.

Coulter, E. Merton. *The Confederate States of America, 1861–1865: A History of the South.* Edited by Wendell Holmes Stephenson and E. Merton Coulter. Baton Rouge: Louisiana State University Press, 1950.

Craig, Berry. *Kentucky's Rebel Press: Pro-Confederate Media and the Secession Crisis.* Lexington: University Press of Kentucky, 2018.

Crapol, Edward P. *John Tyler: The Accidental President.* Chapel Hill: University of North Carolina Press, 2006.

Crofts, Daniel W. *Reluctant Confederates: Upper South Unionists in the Secession Crisis.* Chapel Hill: University of North Carolina Press, 1989.

Crute, Joseph H. *Confederate Staff Officers, 1861–1865.* [Virginia?]: J. H. Crute, Jr., 1982.

Cunningham, Horace Herndon. *Doctors in Gray: The Confederate Medical Service.* Baton Rouge: Louisiana State University Press, 1958.

Daniel, Larry J. *Cannoneers in Gray: The Field Artillery of the Army of the Tennessee.* Tuscaloosa: University of Alabama Press, 2005.

Davis, John Martin, Jr. *Civil War Taxes: A Documentary History, 1861–1900.* Jefferson, NC: McFarland, 2019.

Davis, William C. *"A Government of Our Own": The Making of the Confederacy.* New York: Free Press, 1994.

———. *Look Away!: A History of the Confederate States of America*. New York: Free Press, 2002.

———. *The Union That Shaped the Confederacy: Robert Toombs and Alexander H. Stephens*. Lawrence: University Press of Kansas, 2001.

Deavours, Ernestine Clayton. *The Mississippi Poets*. Memphis, TN: E. H. Clarke and Brother, 1922.

Dennison, George M. *The Dorr War: Republicanism on Trial, 1831–1861*. Lexington: University Press of Kentucky, 1976.

DeRosa, Marshall L. *The Confederate Constitution of 1861: An Inquiry into American Constitutionalism*. Columbia: University of Missouri Press, 1991.

Dew, Charles B. *Ironmaker to the Confederacy: Joseph R. Anderson and the Tredegar Iron Works*. Richmond: Virginia State Library, 1999.

Dickson, Keith D. *Sustaining Southern Identity: Douglas Southall Freeman and Memory in the Modern South*. Baton Rouge: Louisiana State University Press, 2011.

Dixon, Samuel Houston. *The Poets and Poetry of Texas*. Austin: Sam H. Dixon, 1885.

Dobyns, Kenneth W. *The Patent Office Pony: A History of the Early Patent Office*. Boston: Docent Press, 2016.

Dougherty, Kevin. *Strangling the Confederacy: Coastal Operations of the American Civil War*. Philadelphia: Casemate, 2010.

Eelman, Bruce W. *Entrepreneurs in the Southern Upcountry: Commercial Culture in Spartanburg, South Carolina, 1845–1880*. Athens: University of Georgia Press, 2008.

Elder, Robert. *The Sacred Mirror: Evangelicalism, Honor, and Identity in the Deep South, 1790–1860*. Chapel Hill: University of North Carolina Press, 2016.

Ellis, Richard E. *The Union at Risk: Jacksonian Democracy, States' Rights, and the Nullification Crisis*. New York: Oxford University Press, 1989.

Encyclopedia of Virginia Biography. Vol. 3. New York: Lewis Historical Publishing, 1915.

Escott, Paul D. *After Secession: Jefferson Davis and the Failure of Confederate Nationalism*. Baton Rouge: Louisiana State University Press, 1978.

Faust, Drew Gilpin. *The Creation of Confederate Nationalism: Ideology and Identity in the Civil War South*. Baton Rouge: Louisiana State University Press, 1988.

———. *James Henry Hammond and the Old South: A Design for Mastery*. Baton Rouge: Louisiana State University Press, 1982.

Fehrenbacher, Don E. *Constitutions and Constitutionalism in the Slaveholding South*. Athens: University of Georgia Press, 1989.

Flynt, Wayne. *Alabama Baptists: Southern Baptists in the Heart of Dixie*. Tuscaloosa: University of Alabama Press, 1998.

Foster, Gaines M. *Ghosts of the Confederacy: Defeat, the Lost Cause, and the Emergence of the New South, 1865–1913*. New York: Oxford University Press, 1988.

Freehling, William W. *Prelude to Civil War: The Nullification Controversy in South Carolina 1816–1836*. New York: Oxford University Press, 1992.

———. *The Road to Disunion. Vol. 1: Secessionists at Bay, 1776–1854*. New York: Oxford University Press, 1991.

———. *The Road to Disunion. Vol. 2: Secessionists Triumphant, 1854–1861*. Oxford: Oxford University Press, 2007.

———. *The South vs. the South: How Anti-Confederate Southerners Shaped the Course of the Civil War*. Oxford: Oxford University Press, 2001.

Freehling, William W., and Craig M. Simpson. *Secession Debated: Georgia's Showdown in 1860*. Oxford: Oxford University Press, 1992.

Freeman, Douglas Southall. *A Calendar of Confederate Papers*. Richmond: Confederate Museum, 1908.

Fuller, A. James. *Chaplain to the Confederacy: Basil Manly and Baptist Life in the Old South.* Baton Rouge: Louisiana State University Press, 2000.

Fullerton, Dan C. *Armies in Gray: The Organizational History of the Confederate States Army in the Civil War, 1861–1865.* Baton Rouge: Louisiana State University Press, 2017.

Gale, Stephen H., ed. *The Encyclopedia of American Humorists.* New York: Routledge, 2016.

Gates, Paul W. *Agriculture and the Civil War.* New York: Knopf, 1965.

Gettleman, Marvin E. *The Dorr Rebellion: A Study in American Radicalism, 1833–1849.* New York: Random House, 1973.

Gobright and Pratt. *The Union Sketch-book.* New York: Pudney and Russell, 1860.

Godfrey, John Munro. *Monetary Expansion in the Confederacy.* New York: Arno Press, 1978..

Graham, Michael B. *The Coal River Valley in the Civil War: West Virginia Mountains, 1861.* Charleston: History Press, 2014.

Green, Carol Cranmer. *Chimborazo: The Confederacy's Largest Hospital.* Knoxville: University of Tennessee Press, 2004.

Haley, James L. *The Texas Supreme Court: A Narrative History, 1836–1986.* Austin: University of Texas Press, 2013.

Hall, Kermit L., and James W. Ely, eds. *An Uncertain Tradition: Constitutionalism and the History of the South.* Athens: University of Georgia Press, 1989.

Hasegawa, Guy R., and F. Terry Hambrecht. *Matchless Organization: The Confederate Army Medical Department.* Carbondale: Southern Illinois University Press, 2021.

Haughton, Andrew. *Training, Tactics, and Leadership in the Confederate Army of Tennessee: Seeds of Failure.* London: Frank Cass, 2000.

Hauptman, Laurence M. *Between Two Fires: American Indians in the Civil War.* New York: Free Press, 1995.

Heidler, David S., and Jeanne T. Heidler. *Henry Clay: The Essential American.* New York: Random House, 2010.

Hennessy, John J. *The First Battle of Manassas: An End to Innocence, July 18–21, 1861.* Mechanicsburg, VA: Stackpole Books, 2015.

Hess, Earl J. *Civil War Infantry Tactics: Training, Combat, and Small-Unit Effectiveness.* Baton Rouge: Louisiana State University Press, 2015.

Hilde, Libra Rose. *Worth a Dozen Men: Women and Nursing in the Civil War South.* Charlottesville: University of Virginia Press, 2012.

Hoge, Peyton Harrison. *Moses Drury Hoge: Life and Letters.* Richmond: Presbyterian Committee of Publication, 1899.

Holt, Michael F. *The Rise and Fall of the American Whig Party: Jacksonian Politics and the Onset of the Civil War.* Oxford: Oxford University Press, 1999.

Hoogenboom, Ari. *Gustavus Vasa Fox of the Union Navy: A Biography.* Baltimore: Johns Hopkins University Press, 2008.

Hoole, William Stanley. *Alias Simon Suggs: The Life and Times of Johnson Jones Hooper.* Tuscaloosa: University of Alabama Press, 1952.

Hubbard, Charles M. *The Burden of Confederate Diplomacy.* Knoxville: University of Tennessee Press, 1998.

Hubbs, G. Ward. *Tuscaloosa: 200 Years in the Making.* Tuscaloosa: University of Alabama Press, 2019.

Huber, Leonard Victor, and Clarence August Wagner. *The Great Mail: A Postal History of New Orleans.* State College, PA: American Philatelic Society, 1949.

Hunt, Leigh. *Stories from the Italian Poets: with Live of the Writers.* Vol. 1. London: Chapman and Hall, 1896.

Hurst, W. *Alexandria on the Potomac: The Portrait of an Antebellum Community*. Lanham, MD: University Press of America, 1991.

Hurt, R. Douglas. *Agriculture and the Confederacy: Policy, Productivity, and Power in the Civil War South*. Chapel Hill: University of North Carolina Press, 2015.

Hutchison, Coleman. *Apples and Ashes: Literature, Nationalism, and the Confederate States of America*. Athens: University of Georgia Press, 2012.

Iobst, Richard W. *Civil War Macon: The History of a Confederate City*. Macon, GA: Mercer University Press, 2009.

Janney, Caroline E. *Remembering the Civil War: Reunion and the Limits of Reconciliation*. Chapel Hill: University of North Carolina Press, 2013.

Johns, John Edward. *Florida in the Civil War*. Gainesville: University of Florida Press, 1963.

Johnson, David E. *Douglas Southall Freeman*. Gretna, LA: Pelican Publishing, 2002.

Johnson, Michael P. *Toward a Patriarchal Republic: The Secession of Georgia*. Baton Rouge: Louisiana State University Press, 1977.

Johnston, Angus James, II. *Virginia Railroads in the Civil War*. Chapel Hill: University of North Carolina Press, 1961.

Jones, Howard. *Blue and Gray Diplomacy: A History of Union and Confederate Foreign Relations*. Chapel Hill: University of North Carolina Press, 2010.

———. *Union in Peril: The Crisis over British Intervention in the Civil War*. Lincoln: University of Nebraska Press, 1997.

Jones, Samuel. *The Siege of Charleston*. New York: Neale Publishing, 1911.

Knight, Lucian Lamar. *A Standard History of Georgia and Georgians*. Vol. 4: *Primary Source Edition*. Chicago: Lewis Publishing, 1917.

Kundahl, George G. *Confederate Engineer: Training and Campaigning with John Morris Wampler*. Knoxville: University of Tennessee Press, 2000.

Laborde, Maximilian. *History of the South Carolina College*. Columbia, SC: Peter B. Glass, 1859.

Lafferty, John J. *Sketches of the Virginia Conference, Methodist Episcopal Church, South*. Richmond: Christian Advocate Office, 1880.

Landrum, J. B. O. *History of Spartanburg County*. Atlanta: Franklin Printing and Publishing, 1900.

Lee, Charles Robert, Jr. *The Confederate Constitutions*. Chapel Hill: University of North Carolina Press, 1963.

———. *Federalism in the Southern Confederacy*. Washington, DC: Public Affairs Press, 1966.

Leigh, Philip. *Trading with the Enemy: The Covert Economy during the American Civil War*. Yardley, PA: Westholme, 2014.

Lesley, J. Peter. *The Iron Manufacturer's Guide to the Furnaces, Forges and Rolling Mills of the United States*. New York: John Wiley, 1859.

Link, William A. *Roots of Secession: Slavery and Politics in Antebellum Virginia*. Chapel Hill: University of North Carolina Press, 2003

Luraghi, Raimondo, and Paolo E. Coletta. *A History of the Confederate Navy*. Annapolis, MD: Naval Institute Press, 1996.

Lynch, Michael E. *Confederate War Industry: The Niter and Mining Bureau*. Master's thesis, Virginia Commonwealth University, 2001

Mahé, John A., II, and Rosanne McCaffery, eds. *Encyclopaedia of New Orleans Artists, 1718–1918*. New Orleans: Historic New Orleans Collection, 1987.

Majewski, John D. *Modernizing a Slave Economy: The Economic Vision of the Confederate Nation*. Chapel Hill: University of North Carolina Press, 2009.

Manning, Wentworth. *Some History of Van Zandt County*. Vol. 2. Madison, WI: Homestead, 1919.

Martis, Kenneth C., and Gyula Pauer. *The Historical Atlas of the Congresses of the Confederate States of America, 1861–1865*. New York: Simon and Schuster, 1994.

Matthews, Gary Robert. *More American Than Southern: Kentucky, Slavery, and the War for an American Ideology, 1828–1861*. Knoxville: University of Tennessee Press, 2014.

May, Gary. *John Tyler*. Edited by Arthur M. Schlesinger Jr. and Sean Willentz. New York: Times Books/Henry Holt, 2008.

McClintock, John, and James Strong. *Cyclopedia of Biblical, Theological, and Ecclesiastical Literature*. New York: Harper and Brothers, 1885.

McKiven Henry M., Jr. *Iron and Steel: Class, Race, and Community in Birmingham, Alabama, 1875–1920*. Chapel Hill: University of North Carolina Press, 1995.

McNeely, Patricia G., Debra Reddin van Tuyll, and Henry H. Schulte. *Knights of the Quill: Confederate Correspondents and Their Civil War Reporting*. West Lafayette, IN: Purdue University Press, 2010.

McPherson, James M. *War on the Waters: The Union and Confederate Navies, 1861–1865*. Chapel Hill: University of North Carolina Press, 2012.

Memorial and Biographical Record of Kansas City and Jackson County, Missouri, A. Chicago: Lewis Publishing, 1896.

Meyer, Jack Allen. *William Glaze and the Palmetto Armory*. Museum Bulletin no. 6. Columbia: South Carolina State Museum, 1982.

Michno, Gregory. *The Settlers' War: The Struggle for the Texas Frontier in the 1860s*. Lincoln: University of Nebraska Press, 2011.

Monroe, Dan. *The Republican Vision of John Tyler*. College Station: Texas A&M University Press, 2003.

Moore, Jerrold Northrop. *Confederate Commissary General: Lucius Bellinger Northrop and the Subsistence Bureau of the Southern Army*. Shippensburg, PA: White Mane Publishing, 1996.

Moore, R. Scott. *The Civil War on the Atlantic Coast, 1861–1865*. Washington, DC: Center of Military History, US Army, n.d.

Morgan, James F. *Graybacks and Gold: Confederate Monetary Policy*. Pensacola: Perdido Bay Press, 1985.

Morrison, Andrew. *The Bluff City: Mistress of the Valley of the "Lower River."* St. Louis: Geo. W. Engelhardt, 1892.

Neely, Mark E., Jr. *Southern Rights: Political Prisoners and the Myth of Confederate Constitutionalism*. Charlottesville: University Press of Virginia, 1999.

Nelson, Megan Kate. *The Three-Cornered War: The Union, the Confederacy, and Native Peoples in the Fight for the West*. New York: Scribner, 2020.

Noe, Kenneth W. *Southwest Virginia's Railroad: Modernization and the Sectional Crisis*. Champaign: University of Illinois Press, 1994.

Northen, William J., ed. *Men of Mark in Georgia*. Vol. 3. Atlanta: A. B. Caldwell, 1911.

Northern Alabama: Historical and Biographical. Birmingham: Smith and De Land, 1888.

Olsen, Christopher J. *Political Culture and Secession in Mississippi: Masculinity, Honor, and the Antiparty Tradition, 1830–1860*. Oxford: Oxford University Press, 2000.

Owen, Thomas McAdory. *History of Alabama and Dictionary of Alabama Biography*. Vol. 4. Chicago: S. J. Clarke Publishing, 1921.

Owens, Deirdre Cooper. *Medical Bondage: Race, Gender, and the Origins of American Gynecology*. Athens: University of Georgia Press, 2017.

Ownby, Ted, ed. *The Mississippi Encyclopedia*. Jackson: University Press of Mississippi, 2017.

Owsley, Frank Lawrence. *King Cotton Diplomacy: Foreign Relations of the Confederate States of America*. Chicago: University of Chicago Press, 1931.

Peterson, Norma Lois. *The Presidencies of William Henry Harrison and John Tyler*. Lawrence: University Press of Kansas, 1989.

Phillips, Christopher. *Missouri's Confederate: Claiborne Fox Jackson and the Creation of Southern Identity in the Border West*. Columbia: University of Missouri Press, 2000.

Pioneer Citizens' Society of Atlanta. *Pioneer Citizens' History of Atlanta, 1833–1902*. Atlanta: Byrd Printing, 1902.

Pitcaithley, Dwight T. *Tennessee Secedes: A Documentary History*. Knoxville: University of Tennessee Press, 2021.

Pitts, Charles F. *Chaplains in Gray: The Confederate Chaplains Story*. Nashville: Broadman Press, 1957.

Pope, Mark Cooper, III, and J. Donald McKee. *Mark Anthony Cooper: The Iron Man of Georgia, A Biography*. Atlanta: Graphic, 2000.

Porter, Andrew. *States at War. Vol. 3: A Reference Guide for Pennsylvania in the Civil War*. Edited by Richard F. Miller. Hanover, NH: University Press of New England, 2014.

Potter, David M. *The Impending Crisis: 1848–1861*. New York: Joanna Cotler Books, 1976.

Quigley, Paul. *Shifting Grounds: Nationalism and the American South, 1848–1865*. Oxford: Oxford University Press, 2012.

Rable, George C. *The Confederate Republic: A Revolution against Politics*. Chapel Hill: University of North Carolina Press, 1994.

Radley, Kenneth. *Rebel Watchdog: The Confederate States Army Provost Guard*. Baton Rouge: Louisiana State University Press, 1989.

Raymond, Ida. *Southland Writers: Biographical and Critical Sketches of the Living Female Writers of the South*. Vol. 2. Philadelphia: Claxton, Remsen, and Haffelfinger, 1870.

Reinders, Robert C. *End of an Era: New Orleans, 1850–1860*. New Orleans: Pelican Publishing, 1964.

Reynolds, Donald E. *Texas Terror: The Slave Insurrection Panic of 1860 and the Secession of the Lower South*. Baton Rouge: Louisiana State University Press, 2007.

Robinson, Michael D. *A Union Indivisible: Secession and the Politics of Slavery in the Border South*. Chapel Hill: University of North Carolina Press, 2017.

Robinson, William M., Jr. *Justice in Grey: A History of the Judicial System of the Confederate States of America*. Cambridge, MA: Harvard University Press, 1941.

Rubin, Anne S. *A Shattered Nation: The Rise and Fall of the Confederacy, 1861–1868*. Chapel Hill: University of North Carolina Press, 2005.

Sachsman, David B., and Gregory A. Borchard, eds. *The Antebellum Press: Setting the Stage for Civil War*. New York: Routledge, 2019.

Sachsman, David B., S. Kittrell Rushing, and Roy Morris Jr., eds. *Words at War: The Civil War and American Journalism*. Ashland, OH: Purdue University Press, 2008.

Sainlaude, Stève. *France and the American Civil War: A Diplomatic History*. Chapel Hill: University of North Carolina Press, 2019.

Schultz, Jane E. *Women at the Front: Hospital Workers in Civil War America*. Chapel Hill: University of North Carolina Press, 2004.

Schwab, John Christopher. *The Confederate States of America, 1861–1865: A Financial and Industrial History of the South during the Civil War*. New Haven, CT: Yale University Press, 1913.

The Science of Practical Penmanship: Or the Analysis of Taste and Freedom. New York: Thomas P. Dolbear; ; Natchez: Levi Dolbear; New Orleans: Rufus Dolbear and J. W. Dolbear 1850.

Severance, Ben H. *A War All Over: Alabama Politics and the Confederate Cause*. Tuscaloosa: University of Alabama Press, 2020.

Sibley, F. Ray. *The Confederate Order of Battle*. Shippensburg, PA: White Mane Publishing, 1996.

Sikes, Enoch Walter. *The Confederate States Congress*. Raleigh, NC: Edwards and Broughton, Printers, 1903.

Smith, Nelson F. *History of Pickens County, Ala.* Carollton, AL: "Pickens Republican" Office, 1856.

Somers, Paul. *Johnson J. Hooper*. Boston: Twayne Publishers, 1984.

Spillane, Edward P. *Life and Letters of Henry Van Rensselaer, Priest of the Society of Jesus*. New York: Fordham University Press, 1908.

Stone, R. French, ed. *Biography of Eminent American Physicians and Surgeons*. Indianapolis: Carlon and Hollenbeck, 1894.

Stowe, Walter Herbert. *The Episcopal Church: A Miniature History*. No. 15. Philadelphia: Church Historical Society, 1944.

Supplement to Encyclopedia Britannica. 9th ed. New York: Henry G. Allen, 1888.

Surdam, David G. *Northern Naval Superiority and the Economics of the American Civil War*. Columbia: University of South Carolina Press, 2001.

Taylor, Robert A. *Rebel Storehouse: Florida in the Confederate Economy*. Tuscaloosa: University of Alabama Press, 1995.

Texas Biographical Dictionary. 3rd ed. New York: Somerset, 1996.

Thomas, Emory M. *The Confederacy as a Revolutionary Experience*. Englewood Cliffs, NJ: Prentice Hall, 1971.

———. *The Confederate Nation, 1861–1865*. New York: Harper and Row, 1979.

Tidwell, William A., James O. Hall, and David Winfred Gaddy, *Come Retribution: The Confederate Secret Service and the Assassination of Lincoln*. Jackson: University Press of Mississippi, 1988.

Todd, Richard Cecil. *Confederate Finance*. Athens: University of Georgia Press, 1954.

Towers, Frank. *The Urban South and the Coming of the Civil War*. Charlottesville: University of Virginia Press, 2004.

Tucker, Spencer. *Blue and Gray Navies: The Civil War Afloat*. Annapolis, MD: Naval Institute Press, 2006.

Turner, Maxine T. *Navy Gray: A Story of the Confederate Navy on the Chattahoochee and Apalachicola Rivers*. Tuscaloosa: University of Alabama Press, 1988.

Tyrrell, Henry. *The History of the War with Russia*. Vol. 2: *Giving Full Details of the Operations of the Allied Armies*. London: London Printing and Publishing, 1855.

Vandiver, Frank E. *Ploughshares into Swords: Josiah Gorgas and Confederate Ordnance*. Austin: University of Texas Press, 1952.

Varon, Elizabeth R. *Disunion!: The Coming of the American Civil War, 1789–1859*. Chapel Hill: University of North Carolina Press, 2010.

von Humboldt, Alexander. *Cosmos: Sketch of a Physical Description of the Universe*. Vol. 2. Translated by E. C. Otte. London: Henry G. Bohn, 1849.

Walther, Eric H. *William Lowndes Yancey and the Coming of the Civil War*. Chapel Hill: University of North Carolina Press, 2006.

Warde, Mary Jane. *When the Wolf Came: The Civil War and the Indian Territory*. Fayetteville: University of Arkansas Press, 2013.

Warner, Ezra J. *Generals in Gray: Lives of the Confederate Commanders*. Baton Rouge: Louisiana State University Press, 1959.

Warner, Ezra J., and W. Buck Yearns. *Biographical Register of the Confederate Congress*. Baton Rouge: Louisiana State University Press, 1975.

Weddell, Elizabeth Wright. *St. Paul's Church, Richmond, Virginia: Its Historic Years and Memorials*. 2 vols. Richmond: William Byrd Press, 1931.

Weinert, Richard P. *The Confederate Regular Army*. Shippensburg, PA: White Mane Publishing, 1991.

West, Anson. *A History of Methodism in Alabama*. Nashville: Publishing House Methodist Episcopal Church, South, 1893.

White, Christine Schultz, and Benton R. White. *Now the Wolf Has Come: The Creek Nation in the Civil War*. College Station: Texas A&M University Press, 1996.

Williams, Michael E., Sr. *Isaac Taylor Tichenor: The Creation of the Baptist New South*. Tuscaloosa: University of Alabama Press, 2005.

Wilson, Harold S. *Confederate Industry: Manufacturers and Quartermasters in the Civil War*. Jackson: University Press of Mississippi, 2002.

Wilson, James Grant, and John Fiske, eds. *Appletons' Cyclopædia of American Biography*. Vol. 2. New York: D. Appleton, 1888.

Wilson, Samuel M. *History of the United States Court for the Eastern District of Kentucky*. Lexington: n.p., 1935.

Wise, Stephen R. *Lifeline of the Confederacy: Blockade Running during the Civil War*. Columbia: University of South Carolina Press, 1988.

Woods, James M. *Rebellion and Realignment: Arkansas's Road to Secession*. Fayetteville: University of Arkansas Press, 1987.

Yearns, W. Buck. *The Confederate Congress*. Athens: University of Georgia Press, 1960.

Secondary Sources: Articles and Chapters

Bensel, R. "Southern Leviathan: The Development of Central States Authority in the Confederate States of America." *Studies in American Political Development* 2 (Spring 1987): 68–136.

Bergeron, Arthur W. Jr. "Brig. Gen. Thomas Hart Taylor." In Allardice, *Kentuckians in Gray*, 258–63.

Beringer, Richard E. "A Profile of the Members of the Confederate Congress." *Journal of Southern History* 33, no. 4 (1967): 518–41.

———. "The Unconscious 'Spirit of Party' in the Confederate Congress." *Civil War History* 18, no. 4 (1972): 312–33.

Bragg, William Harris. "'Our Joint Labor': W. J. De Renne, Douglas Southall Freeman, and Lee's Dispatches, 1910–1915." *Virginia Magazine of History and Biography* 97, no. 1 (January 1989): 3–32.

Brown, Russell K. "Augusta's Other Voice: James Gardner and the Constitutionalist." *Georgia Historical Quarterly* 85, no. 4. (2001): 592–607.

Caldwell, A. B. "Marcellus A. Stovall." In Northern, *Men of Mark in Georgia*, 47.

"The Chinese Sugar Cane." *Country Gentleman* 9, no. 24 (June 11, 1857): 379.

Chappo, John Fabian. "Carnot Posey." In Ownby, *Mississippi Encyclopedia*, 1025.

Cipra, David L. "Confederate States Light House Bureau: A Portrait in Blue and Gray." *Keeper's Log* 8, no. 2 (Winter 1992): 6–13.

Cobbs, Richard Hooker, and Walter C. Whitaker. "Statistics of the Protestant Episcopal Church in the Diocese of Alabama." *Transactions of the Alabama Historical Society, 1897–1898*. Vol. 2. Edited by Thomas McAdory Owen. Tuscaloosa: Alabama Historical Society, 1899.

Currie, David P. "Through the Looking-Glass: The Confederate Constitution in Congress, 1861–1865," *Virginia Law Review*, 2004, 1257–1399.

Davis, Robert S. "The First Golden Age of Georgia Industry, 1828–1860." *Georgia Historical Quarterly* 72, no. 4 (1988): 699–710.

Dawson, Anthony. "The French Army and British Army Crimean War Reforms." *19: Interdisciplinary Studies in the Long Nineteenth Century* 20 (May 12, 2015).

"Death of Rev. R. H. Cobbs, D.D." *Living Church* 63, no. 8 (June 19, 1920): 285.

Dee, Christine. "Trying James Hickman: The Politics of Loyalty in a Civil War Community." *Alabama Review* 58 (April 2005): 83–112.

Doster, James F. "The Shelby Iron Works Collection in the University of Alabama Library." *Bulletin of the Business Historical Society* 26, no. 4 (1952): 214–17.

Ferrara, Marie. "Moses Henry Nathan and the Great Charleston Fire of 1861." *South Carolina Historical Magazine* 104, no. 4 (2003): 272–77.

Griffin, Richard W. "Student Days at Davidson College, 1838–1857, in Letters to the Reverend G. H. W. Petrie." *Journal of Presbyterian History* 40, no. 3 (1962): 181.

Hamilton, J. G. de Roulhac. "The State Courts and the Confederate Constitution." *Journal of Southern History* 4 (1938): 425.

Hardaway, Roger D. "Tennesseans at the Confederate Constitutional Convention." *Tennessee Historical Quarterly* 43, no. 1 (Spring 1984): 44–48.

"Historical Picture Gallery." *Records of the American Catholic Historical Society of Philadelphia* 11, no. 1 (1900): 113–28.

Hudson, Linda S. "The Knights of the Golden Circle in Texas, 1858–1861: An Analysis of the First (Military) Degree Knights." In *The Seventh Star of the Confederacy: Texas During the Civil War*, edited by Kenneth Wayne Howell, 52–67. Denton: University of North Texas Press, 2009.

James, Russell D. "Pierce Mason Butler." In *The Encyclopedia of the Mexican-American War: A Political, Social, and Military History*, edited by Spencer Tucker, 99–100. Santa Barbara, CA: ABC-CLIO, 2013.

Jenkins, Jeffery A. "Examining the Bonding Effects of Party: A Comparative Analysis of Roll-Call Voting in the U.S. and Confederate Houses." *American Journal of Political Science* 43, no. 4 (1999): 1144–65.

———. "Examining the Robustness of Ideological Voting: Evidence from the Confederate House of Representatives." *American Journal of Political Science* 44, no. 4 (2000): 811–22.

Kirkpatrick, Arthur R. "Missouri's Delegation in the Confederate Congress." *Civil War History* 5, no. 2 (1959): 188–98.

LaCroix, Alison. "Continuity in Secession: The Case of the Confederate Constitution." *University of Chicago Public Law and Legal Theory*, working paper no. 512, 2015.

Lander, Ernest M. "The Iron Industry in Ante-Bellum South Carolina." *Journal of Southern History* 20, no. 3 (1954): 337–55.

Lichtenwanger, William. "The Music of 'The Star-Spangled Banner': Whence and Whither?" *College Music Symposium* 18, no. 2. (1978): 34–81.

Marszalek, John F. "The Charleston Fire of 1861 as Described in the Emma E. Holmes Diary." *South Carolina Historical Magazine 76*, no. 2 (1975): 60–67.

McMichael, Mandy E. "'We Must Go Out of This Union': The Two Secessions of Basil Manly Sr." *Baptist History and Heritage* 52 (Summer 2017): 8–19.

"Memorial of Dr. A. Y. P. Garnett." *Transactions of the American Clinical and Climatological Association* 7 (1890): 323–25.

Merrill, James M. "Confederate Shipbuilding at New Orleans." *Journal of Southern History* 28, no. 1. (1962): 88.

Palen, Marc-William. "The Civil War's Forgotten Transatlantic Tariff Debate and the Confederacy's Free Trade Diplomacy." *Journal of the Civil War Era* 3, no. 1 (2013): 35–61.

Pennington, Edgar Legare. "The Organization of the Protestant Episcopal Church in the Confederate States of America." *Historical Magazine of the Protestant Episcopal Church* 17, no. 4 (December 1948): 308–38.

Pollard, Edward A. "The Confederate Congress: A Chapter in the History of the Late War." *Galaxy* 6, no. 6 (1868): 749–58.

Ramey, Adam. "National Survival and the Confederate Congress." *Historical Methods: A Journal of Quantitative and Interdisciplinary History* 46, no. 1 (January–March 2013): 31–40.

Ramsay, J. G. "The Confederate Congress." *State Normal Magazine* 4, no. 3 (May 1900): 74–83.

Starnes, Richard D. "Forever Faithful: The Southern Historical Society and Confederate Historical Memory." *Southern Cultures* 2, no. 2 (Winter 1996): 177–94.

Sternhell, Yael A. "The Afterlives of a Confederate Archive: Civil War Documents and the Making of Sectional Reconciliation." *Journal of American History* 104, no. 4 (March 2016): 1025–50.

Todd, Frederick P. "The Huddy and Duval Prints: An Adventure in Military Lithography." *Journal of the American Military Institute* 3, no. 3 (1939): 166–76.

Trudeau, Noah Andre. "Start with the Basics." *Civil War Times* 51, no. 4 (August 2012): 52–57.

Turner, Charles W. "The Virginia Central Railroad at War, 1861–1865." *Journal of Southern History* 12, no. 4 (November 1946): 510–33.

Veasey, Patricia V. "Correct Likenesses: George Ladd, Itinerant Miniature and Portrait Painter." *Journal of Early Southern Decorative Arts* 40 (2019).

White, G. Edward. "Recovering the Legal History of the Confederacy." *Washington and Lee Legal Review* 68 (2011): 467, 497.

White, Edward L., III. "The Constitution of the Confederate States of America: Innovation or Duplication?" *Southern Historian* 12 (1991): 5–28.

Woods, James M. "Devotees and Dissenters: Arkansans in the Confederate Congress, 1861–1865." *Arkansas Historical Quarterly* 38, no. 3 (1979): 227–47.

Wright, G. Richard, and Kenneth H. Wheeler. "New Men in the Old South: Joseph E. Brown and His Associates in Georgia's Etowah Valley." *Georgia Historical Quarterly* 93, no. 4 (2009): 363–87.

Yearns, Wilfred B. "North Carolina in the Confederate Congress." *North Carolina Historical Review* 29, no. 3 (1952): 359–78.

INDEX